International Development Policies

International Development Policies

Perspectives for Industrial Countries

———

Sidney Dell

Duke University Press　*Durham and London 1991*

Copyright 1991 Duke University Press
All rights reserved
Printed in the United States of America on acid-free
paper ∞
Library of Congress Cataloging-in-Publication Data
appear on the last page of this book.

For Ethel, an unfailing inspiration

Contents

Abbreviations

ABA	American Bankers Association		Organization/(UN)
AID	(U.S.) Agency for International Development	GAB	General Arrangements to Borrow
CFF	Compensatory Financing Facility	GATT	General Agreement on Tariffs and Trade
CICT	Commission on International Commodity Trade	GDP	Gross Domestic Product
		GNP	Gross National Product
DAC	Development Assistance Committee (OECD)	ICAO	International Civil Aviation Organization
EC	European Community	IDA	International Development Association
ECOSOC	Economic and Social Council	ILO	International Labor Organization
EEC	European Economic Community	IMF	International Monetary Fund
EFF	Extended Fund Facility	ITU	International Telecommunication Union
EFTA	European Free Trade Association		
EMS	European Monetary System	LAFTA	Latin American Free Trade Association
ERP	European Recovery Program	LIBOR	London Interbank Offered Rate
FAO	Food and Agriculture	MFA	Multifibre Arrangement

MFN   Most Favored Nation

NARS   (U.S.) National
        Archives and
        Records Service

NIC   Newly
        Industrializing
        Country

ODA   Official Development
        Assistance

OECD   Organization for
        Economic
        Cooperation and
        Development

OPEC   Organization of
        Petroleum Exporting
        Countries

PRO   Public Record Office

PSBR   Public-Sector
        Borrowing
        Requirement

RBP   Restrictive Business
        Practice

SAF   Structural
        Adjustment Facility

SAL   Structural
        Adjustment Loan

SDR   Special
        Drawing Right

STABEX (EEC scheme for)
        Stabilization of
        Export Earnings

SUNFED Special UN Fund for
        Economic
        Development

TNC   Transnational
        Corporation

TOT   Transfer of
        Technology

UN   United Nations

UNCTAD UN Conference on
        Trade and
        Development

UNDP   UN Development
        Programme

VER   Voluntary Export
        Restriction

International Development Policies

1
Introduction

These essays deal with some of the major problems of international economic and development policy that have confronted the international community in recent years. They are virtually all addressed primarily to readers in the industrial countries and aim at providing a rationale for what the author would regard as a more positive and constructive approach to the world development problem than prevails at the present time.

Some readers may feel that in order to be evenhanded the author should have addressed himself to the developing countries also, drawing their attention to shortcomings in their own performance. The fact that this has not been done certainly does not mean that the author is unaware of the need for better performance by the developing countries themselves. Such performance is, indeed, even more essential than the creation of a favorable international economic environment. A more favorable environment could enhance the effectiveness of the development efforts of the Third World but it could by no means substitute for those efforts. The mobilization of domestic savings, notably through equitable tax policies, the creation of a climate conducive to investment, both public and private, the adoption of fiscal and monetary policies that are supportive of growth without falling into the quagmire of inflation, the encouragement of exports, the stimulation of social change, notably through land reform, the promotion of human development, the satisfaction of basic needs—these and other conditions are indispensable for development. But to state the case for all these essential policies and measures would have required another book and another audience. This book is concerned with problems of international cooperation in achieving world development, in full recognition of the fact that such cooperation can be successful only if the developing countries themselves take the steps that are needed for their own advancement.

ALTRUISM AND SELF-INTEREST

In addressing the essays to readers in the industrial countries, the author does not rely simply upon the goodwill or altruism of the peoples of these countries. The essays suggest that hardheaded calculations of long-run self-interest should prompt the industrial countries to support the development of the Third World. In the nature of the case, development takes time and cannot generally yield measurable results from year to year. Nevertheless, it seems not unreasonable to expect the industrially advanced countries to be able to take a long view of their own interests. As the Pearson Commission pointed out, "The fullest possible utilization of all the world's resources, human and physical, which can be brought about only by international cooperation, helps not only those countries now economically weak but also those strong and wealthy. . . . But development will not normally create, nor should it be expected to create, economic windfalls for a donor country."[1] Willy Brandt's introduction to the report of the Brandt Commission recalls that in the presently industrialized countries, "A long and assiduous learning process was necessary until it was generally accepted that higher wages for workers increased purchasing power sufficiently to move the economy as a whole. Industrialized countries now need to be interested in the expansion of markets in the developing world. This will decisively affect job opportunities in the 1980s and 1990s and the prospect of employment."[2]

It is a curious phenomenon that outstanding political leaders such as Brandt and Pearson, as well as their colleagues in the commissions that they headed, were inspired to make far-reaching and forward-looking proposals for collective action by the international community, including the industrial countries, only when they were out of office. One wonders what it was that prevented them from taking the necessary steps toward world development when they held the reins of power.

No doubt part of the answer is to be found in the politician's inevitable sensitivity, when in office, to the articulated needs of his or her political constituency, to which the developing countries obviously do not belong. Budgetary constraints are also part of the explanation, though here again, it is constituency pressures that are decisive.

But one cannot help feeling that other factors are involved. Despite all the talk of "aid fatigue" in the industrial countries, one finds that parliamentary committees and commissions are frequently much more inclined to recognize an obligation to help in fostering world development than the governments of their respective countries. This is true even in the United States, where the blame for unwillingness to support multilateral and bilateral aid is usually placed on Congress. Congressional committees and subcommittees have repeatedly urged the U.S. government to adopt forward-looking policies on world development problems.[3]

REVIVING THE KENNEDY INITIATIVE

One factor that may have contributed to the reluctance of some of the leading countries to accept the kind of responsibilities for world development that President Kennedy had in mind in 1961 in launching the first United Nations Development Decade is the fact that proposals in this field have usually been mixed up with, or even subordinated to, a whole complex of political and military considerations connected with the cold war. Third World development projects requiring external funding are generally presented to industrial country legislatures and public opinion not as objectives for their own sake but as a means of ensuring the loyalty of this or that country in a confrontation with adversaries or as a base for troops, warships, or military aircraft. Very often the distribution of aid among beneficiary countries makes no sense at all in terms of any reasonable measure of their objective needs, and could be justified only in geopolitical terms. This inevitably gives rise to cynicism and suspicion regarding the true development content of programs purporting to be in the interests of development.

It might appear that current efforts toward ending the cold war would, if successful, make it possible to recreate the spirit of the Kennedy initiative. Not only would it become possible to separate the objective of world development from the dead weight of political and military confrontation, but the resources released by a substantial measure of disarmament would make it possible to increase the volume of aid far beyond any of the targets hitherto established by the United Nations. Aid even in large amounts cannot solve the problems of developing countries, but it could certainly help enormously in creating an environment within which some of the major constraints on development could be greatly reduced.

COUNTERING INFLATION AS THE PRIMARY GOAL

Most of the essays in this volume concern relationships between North and South in such areas as trade and aid policies and the problems of reconciling adjustment with growth in the context of Third World debt. Paradoxically, however, it may well be that the most important issue was one in which North-South relationships were involved only indirectly. This was the decision of the industrial countries to place the fight against inflation ahead of all other international objectives in the 1970s and 1980s. Although this decision was adopted mainly for domestic reasons—particularly with a view to overcoming the pressure of organized labor for higher wages—it had massive repercussions in the Third World. By curtailing the level of aggregate demand, it forced down the prices of commodity exports from developing countries to unprecedentedly low levels, and thereby severely depressed the level of export earnings used to finance debt service and the import of essential goods, including capital equipment and food. And by pushing up interest rates far beyond prudent expectations, the interest burden on borrowers was drastically increased. If it had not been for these developments, the economic difficulties facing the Third World in the 1980s would have been far less acute, and the adjustment process would have been much less disruptive. Only one of the essays in this volume is addressed solely to the macroeconomic policies of the industrial countries, but the importance of changing policies so as to create an environment favorable to world development is a recurring theme throughout the book.

FUNDAMENTAL POLICY CHANGES

The essays cover a period of extraordinary—perhaps fundamental—change in national and international policies for development. At the beginning of the period there was general agreement on two basic propositions. The first was that there was a collective responsibility of the international community as a whole for the development of the Third World. The second was that governments had a central role to play in the development process. These basic propositions were supported by certain ideas on international development strategy that included a recognition of the fact that while developing countries bear the responsibility for bringing about their own development, industrial countries have an obligation to support the efforts of the developing countries through the flow not only of private capital but also of official development assistance. It was also considered, especially after the establishment of the United Nations Conference on Trade and Development (UNCTAD) in 1964, that governments should create an international trading environment that would be conducive to the achievement of export-led growth in the Third World.

Underlying these views was a belief that market forces alone could not be relied upon to promote development, even if the policies of developing countries were optimal. It was, therefore, necessary for governments to intervene in cases of market failure so as to support the development process. It was recognized that a good deal of planning effort would be required at all levels, and that national plans in developed and developing countries alike would need to be adjusted to one another so as to permit the formulation of a consistent set of international economic policies supportive of the development of the Third World. This was the approach underlying the first United Nations Development Decade—the decade of the 1960s—and the subsequent adoption of an international development strategy for the second Development Decade.

Far different is the international economic environment at the beginning of the 1990s. While the governments of the industrial countries, East and West, still pay lip service to the development of the Third World, their commitment to development goals has been greatly diluted. And although per capita incomes in the industrial countries are far higher in real terms than they were at the beginning of the first United Nations Development Decade some of the leading countries maintain that they cannot afford to provide a net flow of capital to developing countries equivalent to 1 percent of their gross income, as recommended under long-standing resolutions of the General Assembly.

Earlier views of the role of government in economic decisionmaking have likewise undergone profound changes. The previous view that there were many cases of market failure warranting government intervention has been displaced by the conviction that the market almost invariably knows best, and that if only governments would refrain from interfering in the market, avoid imposing regulations on industry, and transfer state enterprise to private ownership and control, all would be well. Admittedly, the selfsame governments that claim to hold these views frequently act in direct contradiction of them, for example, by intervening in exchange markets whenever market-induced trends in exchange rates seem to them to diverge from long-run equilibrium; by imposing nontariff barriers on various kinds of import, especially from the Third World; by use of the threat of retaliation as a means of opening foreign markets; and by employing subsidies in support of industrial policies designed to promote certain industrial or research and development objectives.

THE FALLIBILITY OF MARKET FORCES

There is no doubt that market forces have an important role to play in world development. The truth of this proposition has been reemphasized only recently by the collapse of efforts in the USSR and a number of other centrally planned economies to plan their development in isolation from the world market and from the forces of competition. But the fact that Eastern Europe has suddenly been converted to a belief in market forces certainly does not mean that these forces can be relied upon to bring about spontaneous development either in that area or in the Third World.

Those who maintain that national and international goals, such as world development, can best be achieved through the response of private enterprise to market incentives that have not been distorted by government intervention are assuming that the stimulus of profit-making opportunities will suffice for the realization of these goals. But experience shows that this is simply not the case. A good example is the failure of market forces to prevent the degradation of the environment. Factories that pollute the atmosphere, or lakes, rivers, or oceans, or the soil do not have to bear the costs of the damage for which they are responsible. To them air and water are free goods, to be used—or used up—in any way they see fit. The market as presently constituted yields them a profit that is considerably in excess of what they would be able to realize if they had to pay for the rehabilitation of the environmental damage that they cause. That is why it is necessary for governments to protect the environment in various ways against the consequences of market failure. Just as there are unallocated costs that do not enter into the profit calculations of private enterprise, so that market signals are misleading, so also are there many cases in which there are benefits that cannot be fully captured by individual entrepreneurs so that the market does not provide the private sector with the incentives that are needed. An example of this is the building of infrastructure, such as roads and dams.

Similar considerations apply to world development. Left to themselves, market forces have developed the world unevenly—some countries growing rapidly, while others have grown slowly or not at all. The gap between income levels in the richest and poorest countries has widened tremendously during the two centuries since the Industrial Revolution. There is nothing about market forces that requires rates of development in various parts of the world to be comparable. It is nevertheless a major goal of the international community, set forth in unanimous resolutions of the United Nations, to speed up the development of the Third World and to narrow the huge intercountry differentials in living standards that now prevail. While every effort should be made to harness market forces to this goal, to the extent that this is feasible, it would be a mistake to suppose that the aims of private enterprise, national or international, always coincide with the development objectives of the Third World or of the international community.

Private enterprise will not undertake the investment in infrastructure that is needed in many developing countries, especially the low-income countries of Africa, involving the commitment of very large volumes of resources over long gestation periods. As far as industry is concerned, it has been shown repeatedly that even if countries do everything that orthodoxy requires by way of creating favorable conditions for private investment, domestic and foreign, private enterprise will not necessarily be prepared to take the risks involved in starting up new industries, especially in low-income countries. In most cases the establishment of state enterprise is intended to fill a vacuum, not to follow an ideological principle.

There is not a single industrially advanced country that relied exclusively on market forces for the attainment of its development goals. Every one of the industrial countries, at some stage of its history, employed government intervention in the form of tariffs and other restrictions on imports to protect infant industries against foreign competition. The industrial country that developed most rapidly of all—Japan—relied heavily in the past on an array of interventionist policies and measures, including the protection and/or subsidization of industry and industrial exports. Yet the governments of developing countries today are frequently criticized by the OECD countries and the Bretton Woods institutions for adopting government policies that seek to offset or compensate for the shortcomings of market forces.

Another frequent confusion is to assume that if governments refrain from interfering with market forces they will thereby bring into play all the benefits of competition. This is not the case, especially in developing countries, where the size of markets is often too small to support more than one or two manufacturing firms in particular sectors operating at the optimum scale of production. Moreover, market forces do not necessarily generate competition—they may, in fact, facilitate the creation of monopolies or oligopolies by the strongest firm or firms. The United States has had antitrust legislation on its books for a century with the aim of preventing the free play of the market from leading to monopoly. It is no accident that the obsession with the idea of giving maximum freedom to market forces coincided in the 1980s with a marked weakening of U.S. enforcement of antitrust legislation.

One effect of a free market of particularly doubtful benefit is the financial speculation and manipulation that have accompanied some of the most important industrial takeovers of recent years, especially in the United States. It is becoming increasingly clear that the large profit-making opportunities thus created place the short-term interests of shareholders and financiers far above the long-term interests of the firms involved, which are thereby prevented from undertaking the investments in new technologies and higher productivity needed to keep abreast of international competition. It is rare that takeovers of the manipulative kind are in the interests of the community as a whole, especially where they result in substantial layoffs of workers. Here, therefore, is a case where, in the absence of government regulation, market forces actually tend to obstruct development even in the most advanced countries.

The biggest market failure of all was, of course, the Great Depression. Overcome by market euphoria and the spectacle of economic collapse in the centrally planned economies many people seem to have forgotten that for more than a century the industrial world was plagued by persistent cycles of boom and depression that were due to the free play of market forces. These became increasingly severe as time went on and culminated in the worldwide collapse of business and trade in the 1930s from which no complete recovery took place until after World War II. In fact it was the market failure in Germany and the inability of the existing government to deal with the calamitous situation ensuing that led to the rise of Hitler and the most destructive war in history.

During and after World War II governments began to prepare for the task of intervening in the economy if necessary to prevent any resumption or recurrence of the Great Depression. Automatic stabilizers were built into the system to act as a cushion against economic fluctuations, and governments were ready to step in with more deliberate and powerful countercyclical weapons if the need arose. The pendulum of economic fashion and dogma has swung so far since then that one cannot help wondering whether governments faced with signs of a depression today might be inclined to take a laissez-faire position, apart from some tinkering with interest rates and perhaps a soupçon of competitive depreciation.

THE EFFECTS OF SUBNORMAL GROWTH

The first essay—entitled "The Case for World Economic Expansion"— was written in October 1982 at a time of widespread economic recession accompanied by the outbreak of the world debt crisis. The essay drew attention to the danger that subnormal growth rates would persist, largely because of the "widespread view among government officials in the industrial countries as well as among members of the international financial community, public and private, that the level of world demand may have to be held down by monetary and fiscal constraints for several more years."

There followed the forecast that "Such a prospect, if realized, would imply that the 1980s are to be a decade not of development but of retrogression."[4]

Unfortunately this forecast has proved to be only too accurate, at least as far as the Third World is concerned. This does not, of course, mean that every single country suffered a setback. For some of the countries of East Asia the decade witnessed a startling upsurge in income, productivity, and levels of living. But these were the exceptions, not the rule. Most countries in Africa and Latin America and several in Asia have been beset by a deep and protracted economic depression that has reached the point of undermining political stability. After allowing for the effect of sharp deterioration in the terms of trade, real per capita income in Africa (excluding South Africa) averaged 30 percent lower in 1989 than in 1980, and in Latin America 15 percent lower. Moreover, the capital stock of many of these countries has been so seriously run down that even if they began a process of recovery in the immediate future, which is unfortunately not in prospect, it would take them years to rebuild their productive capacity to previously attained levels.

Even more serious is the fact that the economic depression of the past decade in many countries of the Third World has created such disruptive social divisions and conflicts that it has become well-nigh impossible for governments to build the kind of social cohesion and morale that are indispensable for a flourishing society. This disintegration and demoralization of society are in many cases reflected in unprecedented inflationary pressures and the threat of hyperinflation as social groups struggle with one another to maintain or increase their shares of dwindling real national income. Some countries are, in fact, in danger of becoming—or have, in some cases, already become—ungovernable.

There is also no doubt of the severe retrogression in the countries of Eastern Europe, including the USSR. They have attested to it themselves with brutal frankness, and the rest of the world cannot but agree with the devastating criticisms of performance in this group of countries that have been made by their own leaders. Unfortunately, there is at present little sign in these countries that they have a clear sense of the direction in which they need to go to overcome their problems. In principle, their task ought to be much easier than that of countries in the Third World because of their greater productive capacity, skills, and infrastructure. But they are suffering from some of the same symptoms of social disintegration as many of the developing countries, and there may be serious dangers in a too abrupt swing of the pendulum toward laissez-faire policies that may be quite ineffective in coping with the deep structural problems resulting from past overemphasis on heavy industry and the neglect of food and consumer goods production.

The question whether the decade was one of progress or retrogression for the industrial countries is less easy to answer. No doubt statistical measures of output, income, and productivity would show some advance over the decade on the average, but in many of these countries, especially in Europe, growth was much too slow to prevent high levels of unemployment. In the United States as well as in European countries there was a rapid increase in poverty and in the numbers of homeless people, while the spread of drug addiction in the industrial countries was a startling symptom of social malaise.

THE DEFLATIONARY BIAS IN INDUSTRIAL COUNTRIES

The most important reason for the deflationary bias in the policies of industrial countries in the 1980s, which was so devastating in its impact on the export trade of the Third World, was the conviction that such policies are essential in avoiding inflation, and will continue to be indispensable in the 1990s. Unfortunately many academics who should know better have provided a pseudoscientific basis for this view by claiming that wage inflation has a predictable relationship to the level of unemployment, and that unemployment must therefore be held at a sufficiently high level to avoid any danger of wage advances in excess of productivity growth. I had the opportunity of discussing this matter with a well-known member of the MIT economics faculty some years ago, when the U.S. unemployment percentage was in the region of 7.5—having declined from levels that were previously between 9 and 10 percent. I was told emphatically on that occasion that virtually all U.S. economists were of the opinion that if ever the unemployment percentage were allowed to go as low as 6.5, this would trigger a sharp acceleration in wage inflation. This was regarded as a justification for strong government restraint on any spontaneous tendency of the economy to move ahead too rapidly. The fact that during earlier postwar years U.S. unemployment had been as low as 4 percent or even lower for lengthy periods without provoking inflation was considered irrelevant, on the grounds that a structural shift had meanwhile taken place in the relationship between unemployment and wage inflation in the United States. There was no evidence that such a shift had in fact occurred, but the explanation made it possible, apparently, to sustain the fiction that there was a reasonably stable relationship between unemployment and the rate of inflation. These views, which were shared by many U.S. academics and government officials, might well have been impossible to challenge empirically had it not been for the unintentionally Keynesian policies of President Reagan, which drove unemployment down to little more than 5 percent without triggering any acceleration of inflation. There were, in fact, grounds for thinking that the unemployment percentage could have gone significantly lower than 5 without undermining price stability.

In international trade the spirit of cooperation of earlier years for the achievement of common goals and the reduction of trade barriers has been markedly weakened, notably through the use by some of the major trading countries of bilateral pressure for the attainment of national trade objectives to reinforce the effectiveness, from their point of view, of multilateral negotiations through the General Agreement on Tariffs and Trade (GATT). Such bilateral pressure for trade concessions usually includes the threat of retaliation if the partner country's response is deemed unsatisfactory. The current atmosphere of trade conflict and even economic warfare owes much to the slow growth of world trade in recent years, leaving insufficient room for trade expansion for all. This slow growth is itself due to the macroeconomic constraints on the economy imposed by the leading industrial countries.

Thus the principal message of the first essay is at least as valid at the beginning of the 1990s as it was when it was written. The need for concerted policies of world economic expansion is perhaps even more pressing today than it was in 1982, if only because the debt overhang that is a barrier to the recovery of most of the Third World cannot be dealt with adequately except in the context of an expanding world economy.

BASIC NEEDS OR COMPREHENSIVE DEVELOPMENT?

The next essay deals with the choice between two alternative development strategies, one involving a "basic needs" approach while the other seeks to promote comprehensive development. Since 1979, when the essay was written, the basic needs approach has been widely discussed, and has been accepted by a large proportion, if not the majority, of the academics and practitioners concerned with questions of development strategy. Despite the extensive support of this approach by distinguished analysts with whose views in other areas I usually find myself in agreement, I have to confess that on this particular subject I remain unconvinced. Moreover, my distinct impression is that the developments of the past ten years lend more support to my views than to those of members of the basic needs school.

One point needs to be cleared away at once. There is no dispute between the basic needs strategists and those who favor comprehensive development policies with regard to the goal of social equity. I am not less concerned about the need for equity in the distribution of the gains from development than anyone else, and it is essential, in my view, for any comprehensive development strategy to include firm provision for satisfying the basic needs of the poorest members of the community within a reasonable time frame. I imagine also that members of the basic needs school would claim to be just as much concerned about the goal of comprehensiveness in development as I am. Where we part company, it seems to me, is in the absolutism of the basic needs approach. By absolutism, I mean the view of the basic needs school that there are certain levels of personal consumption and access to social services that should be adopted as minimum living standards for the very poor of every single country, and that the attainment of these standards should take priority over other development objectives. The essay points to the many difficulties in determining such universally applicable targets. But assuming that there were satisfactory ways of dealing with all these difficulties, the question would still arise at what rate the target levels should be approached, which would have a bearing on the extent to which the achievement of other goals should be deferred. Even the poorest countries might wish to do without certain essential items of consumption for a time if they felt that by so doing they could accelerate their rates of development. Nobody, and no international agency, has a right to tell such countries that there are absolute and overriding basic needs to which they must assign priority. Countries are entitled to define their development needs in terms relevant to their own goals and their own time horizons.

The basic needs strategists assign high priority to the provision of adequate employment opportunities for the unemployed and underemployed and the introduction of the "right kind of technology." There can be no dispute about the importance of raising employment levels, but there is a tendency to assume that achievement of this goal requires the use of labor-intensive technologies. This direct targeting of employment through labor-intensive technologies illustrates rather well the shortcomings in the basic needs strategy. At the outset of its development, a country such as Saudi Arabia could have elected to give preference to labor-intensive activities rather than to the development of the oil sector which could not, in itself, absorb a great deal of labor. This would have been a mistaken strategy since the enormous gains from petroleum development generated far more revenue—and hence employment-creating opportunities in the non-oil sectors of the economy—than could possibly have arisen from labor-intensive industries. It could be said, of course, that both types of activity could be carried on simultaneously, and if that were the case there would be no argument between the two schools of thought. If, however, there was a question of priorities, the case for petroleum development was overwhelming even from the standpoint of promoting rapid growth of employment.

When it comes to the question of the right or wrong technology, the experience of the 1980s seems conclusive. The extraordinary economic advance of South Korea, which forty years ago was among the poorest countries in the world, has involved the effective use of the most advanced technologies, whether capital-intensive or otherwise, first in consumer goods industries and subsequently in heavy goods industries as well.[5] Moreover, although the development strategy was clearly of the comprehensive kind and did not target the poor and unemployed directly, the rate of growth of the economy was sufficiently vigorous to permit the rapid expansion of employment and reduction of unemployment. Income distribution is probably at least as favorable to the poor in South Korea as in other developing countries and consumption standards of the poor are probably at least as high, if not higher than they would have been under any alternative strategy.

INTERNATIONAL TRADE ISSUES

Three essays are devoted to problems of international trade in goods and services. The first of these deals with two main problems—that of trade imbalance among the industrial countries and that of trade liberalization in developing countries. The reason for including a discussion of trade imbalance among the industrial countries in a volume of essays on international development policy is that the correct diagnosis and cure of the malady are likely to have profound repercussions in the Third World. The two factors most commonly cited to explain the persistent trade and balance-of-payments deficits of the United States are the budget deficit of that country and the unfair trade practices that are thought to be applied against it. The trouble is that a substantial reduction of the U.S. budget deficit might well trigger a worldwide recession, or at least a further collapse of the prices of commodities exported by developing countries, while U.S. countermeasures to allegedly unfair trade practices may have the effect of depressing Third World exports at a time when they are already encountering severe trade barriers.

The U.S. trade deficit is a problem of long standing—it was one of the factors that contributed to President Nixon's decision to break the link between the dollar and gold in 1971. But of the forty-four years from 1946 to 1989, thirty were years in which there were budget deficits. Only in seven of these thirty years were budget deficits accompanied by external deficits on goods and services. The essay gives reasons for believing that there are long-run structural factors that have caused the U.S. to lose ground in world trade during the past twenty-five years or more. The essay comes to the conclusion that as long as the United States and Western Europe maintain stop-go macroeconomic policies that deliberately hold down production, investment, innovation, and productivity, they must expect to lose ground in world trade, not only to Japan but also to other countries where production and productivity are growing rapidly.

TRADE LIBERALIZATION AND DEVELOPMENT

The discussion then moves on to a second major element in current international trade policy, namely the pressure by the industrial countries and the Bretton Woods institutions on developing countries to promote trade liberalization. Under conditions in which many developing countries are exposed to extreme pressure on the balance of payments, liberalization cannot increase the aggregate level of their imports very much, if at all, because the imports of developing countries are already constrained at a low level by the earning power of their exports, together with whatever limited capital inflows they are able to mobilize or attract. The policy is, therefore, largely self-defeating, since the effect of liberalization in such circumstances is chiefly to change the composition of imports without affecting their level very much. Such shifts in composition, determined mainly or entirely by market forces, may disregard social priorities such as essential food imports or even investment priorities.

Apart from these considerations, the methods used by the industrial countries to limit imports of certain manufactures from the developing countries are objectionable in and of themselves, and are highly prejudicial to international cooperation for development. It is true that these methods are also used to some extent by industrial countries against one another, but their impact is much more devastating when they are imposed on developing countries, many of which have a very limited range of exportable manufactures.

The greatest departure from the letter and spirit of multilateral cooperation is that brought about by the U.S. Trade Act of 1988, which provides for the listing of countries deemed by the United States to be engaged in unfair practices and for placing these countries on notice that failure to change these practices by a certain date would lead to tariff retaliation. This unilateral legislation is contrary to GATT principles, under which all rights in the field of trade are defined by and available to all GATT members, while provision is made for the settlement of disputes by multilateral procedures. Equally objectionable, however, are the measures adopted by both the European Community and the United States to induce other countries to impose so-called voluntary export restrictions (VERS) on certain goods under the threat that noncompliance would lead to even tighter restrictions by the importing countries themselves. Moreover, the Multifibre Arrangement (MFA), which restricts the textile exports principally of developing countries, although nominally agreed to by the parties, is in fact the most notorious of all the devices employed by industrial countries against Third World development and totally inconsistent with OECD country advocacy of the benefits of freely operating market forces. The alleged purpose of MFA is to ease the transition for labor and capital in declining textile industries of the industrial countries, but it is difficult to take this excuse seriously since restrictions on trade in textiles go back at least thirty years, with no sign that they will be brought to an end. Thus there has been ample time for the textile industries in the industrial countries to adjust to international competition, if this had been their aim. A more plausible interpretation of MFA is that it has become a means of providing long-run protection to textile industries in the industrial countries in disregard of the principles of GATT and the benefits of a more rational and mutually advantageous international division of labor.

One of the corollaries of free market theory is that "outward-looking" economic policies are far superior to "inward-looking" policies, a proposition that features prominently in the array of advice that the Bretton Woods institutions give to developing countries. While there is a germ of truth in this proposition, examination of the record shows that in many cases countries have adopted inward-looking policies at an early stage of their development as a means of protecting infant industries. Subsequently they have had no difficulty in shifting to outward-looking policies when their industries were ready to face international competition. Thus the dichotomy between inward-looking and outward-looking policies is to a considerable extent a false one.

REGIONAL INTEGRATION

A theme heard repeatedly in the discussion of international development policy is the need for small countries to integrate their economies so as to strengthen their bargaining position in a world of rapidly growing national and regional markets. There has, however, been very little success along these lines. The second essay in the trade policy group tries to find the reasons for this lack of success in the specific context of Latin America, which has been experimenting with integration schemes for several decades. It is at first sight puzzling that the Latin American region has been unable to match the European example. But the problems of integration in Europe and Latin America are quite different. While Western Europe was already highly industrialized, and could readily take advantage of the economies of specialization and exchange generated by the lowering of trade barriers, Latin America was faced with the need for a massive expansion of industry which could not be achieved simply by lowering the barriers to trade. Any such massive expansion was bound to raise questions of the geographic distribution of the new industries and hence the relative gains to be achieved by the integrating countries, large and small, relatively rich and relatively poor. The conclusion drawn is that regional integration among developing countries cannot be accomplished without a deliberate distribution of industry policy, accompanied by agreements on the means of carrying out that policy. None of the regional groups have thus far found it possible to negotiate policy agreements of this type.

TRADE IN SERVICES

A new issue in international trade negotiations is the question of including trade in services. This is an area where the structure of comparative advantage varies considerably from service sector to service sector. The question for developing countries is whether the liberalization that they are being called upon to undertake in certain of the service sectors, notably the high-technology sectors—thereby foregoing, as they fear, indigenous infant industry development in these sectors—would be sufficiently compensated for by their gains in other service sectors, such as construction, in which they may well have a comparative advantage.

There is also the question whether the industrial countries are entitled to demand concessions in the service sectors as a precondition for relaxing their restrictions on imports of textiles and other manufactures from developing countries—restrictions that are inconsistent with GATT and which the industrial countries should therefore be prepared to give up without demanding any reciprocal concessions from their trading partners. While a mutually beneficial deal could undoubtedly be struck in the area of services, the essay indicates some of the difficulties in achieving an equitable outcome for all parties concerned.

PROSPECTS FOR FOREIGN INVESTMENT

One area of international development policy in which there have been enormous changes in attitudes in recent years is that of foreign investment. In Eastern Europe and many developing countries foreign investment and foreign enterprise were, until relatively recently, viewed with many reservations—reservations very similar to those now manifesting themselves in North America and Western Europe in connection with the influx of foreign investment from Japan. The views of Eastern Europe and the Third World have changed to such an extent that many of these countries now see foreign investment as the key to economic revival and technological progress. Widespread hopes have been expressed by representatives of both the North and the South that private foreign investment can make good the shortfall in capital inflow into the Third World caused by the virtual cessation of voluntary lending by the commercial banks. There is unquestionably a useful role to be played by transnational corporations in reviving the economies of Eastern Europe and of all those countries in the Third World offering attractive profit-making opportunities to foreign enterprise. But the significance of the contribution of transnational corporations may well be much smaller than is commonly believed, and there are many illusions about prospects in this regard. It is unlikely that foreign investment can be a major factor in revitalizing the Third World, but it could contribute to that end in some of the developing countries.

THE UNSOLVED PROBLEM OF INTERNATIONAL DEBT

Several essays deal with the complex of questions associated with the world debt crisis and the consequential problems of adjustment. The two essays on the debt crisis deal with the origins of the crisis and the initial strategy adopted for dealing with it, together with the subsequent evolution of the problem and the alternative solutions that have been proposed.

It is suggested that the most serious shortcoming of crisis management was the failure to recognize that all the parties concerned had fundamental long-run interests in common that were much more important than the points on which their interests diverged. The creditor countries have nothing to gain from prostration of the debtors. On the contrary, the greater the disruption of debtor country economies brought about by programs of austerity, and the more acute the inner tensions resulting from efforts of various social groups in debtor countries to escape the effects of the austerity programs, the less likely it is that debt service obligations will be fulfilled on a steady, reliable, and continuing basis, and the more probable it is that political instability or upheaval followed by repudiation will be the ultimate outcome.

But the creditor countries have an even more direct and immediate interest in the economic recovery of the debtors. The preempting of an unusually large proportion of the export earnings of developing countries by debt service requirements has had a severe adverse reaction upon the demand of these countries for imports from the industrial countries, and hence upon production and employment in the manufacturing sectors of the latter countries. Creditor and debtor countries, therefore, have a common interest in easing the impact of debt service obligations on the import capacity of the latter countries. Despite this and other considerations, the steps that have been taken by the international community have been largely limited to avoiding any disruption of the international financial system and have done little to rehabilitate the economies of the debtor countries.

The approach has almost invariably been short term and ad hoc, has taken little or no account of the long-run dynamics of debt accumulation and management, and has been based on the presumption that responsibility for any difficulties associated with international lending lies mainly or wholly with the debtors. This is in spite of the fact that there is a long history of international debt crises exhibiting common features, in which the behavior of debtors interacted with external factors in the international environment such as recession or financial stringency in major markets, accompanied by insistence of creditors on unduly high rates of return and excessive reliance on short- and medium-term debt. These characteristics of the international environment continued in the 1980s and are broadly typical of the problems faced by all debtor countries, whether their debts originated mainly from commercial or from official sources.

Crisis management since 1982, as in earlier years, has consisted essentially of the postponement of debt amortization and the introduction of severe programs of austerity by the debtor countries. At the time of writing, more than seven years after the outbreak of the crisis in 1982, no long-run strategy has emerged that would permit the debtor countries to resume adequate rates of growth while meeting their debt service obligations. Such a long-run strategy could be developed only by agreement between the main actors—the debtors, the commercial banks, and the creditor country governments. The creditor countries, however, have been reluctant to entertain such a dialogue partly because of a fear that it might result in the formation of a debtors' cartel and partly because of unwillingness to accept any solution that might place burdens on the taxpayers of the creditor countries.

Initiatives by successive U.S. secretaries of the treasury—Baker and Brady—who developed the constructive ideas that the adjustment of debtor countries must take place in a context of growth and that the stock of debt must be reduced—failed to achieve their objectives for lack of adequate funding and because of the unwillingness of the creditor countries to compel the cooperation of the commercial banks. The second essay in this group considers the options for dealing with these various aspects of the problem.

THE ADJUSTMENT PROBLEM

There follows a group of essays dealing with the difficult problems of adjustment confronted by the debtor countries in their attempt to restore growth without defaulting on their debt service obligations. Problems of adjustment had, of course, a much longer history than that of the debt crisis. The "Grandmotherly" essay (chapter 8) reviews the evolution of International Monetary Fund (IMF) conditionality since the Bretton Woods Conference held in 1944. The problem of conditionality was closely linked to the adjustment process because the performance conditions required of a country seeking to borrow from the IMF were designed to ensure that the country concerned would take the steps necessary to remove the pressures on the balance of payments that had led to its need to borrow. The fundamental reason why the adjustment process involved considerable difficulties internationally had been summed up concisely by Keynes when he pointed out:

It is characteristic of a freely convertible international standard that it throws the main burden of adjustment on the country which is in the *debtor* position on the international balance of payments. . . . Thus it has been an inherent characteristic of the automatic international metallic currency (apart from special circumstances) to force adjustments in the direction most disruptive of social order, and to throw the burden on the countries least able to support it, making the poor poorer.[6]

This characteristic of the international financial system before Bretton Woods has persisted during the entire period since that time, and has been abundantly in evidence during the past decade. Although responsibility for the debt crisis must be shared between the debtor countries, the commercial banks, and the creditor country governments, it is the debtor countries that have had to bear the main burden of adjustment, which has taken the form of widespread declines not only in consumption but also, and most critically, in the investment needed for future growth.

A passive attitude to the distribution of the burden of adjustment is by no means the same as an impartial or objective attitude. To suggest that it is the deficit country that must invariably accept the full burden of adjustment, regardless of whether a disturbance is of domestic or foreign origin, is to settle the question of responsibility as decisively as if the matter had been addressed directly instead of indirectly. Such an attitude is tantamount to saying that those countries that have the power to shift the burden are entitled to do so. And it is precisely this approach that in the 1970s resulted in the imposition of a burden of adjustment on the poorest and weakest countries out of all proportion to their responsibility for the disequilibrium that had arisen.

INNOVATION AND RETROGRESSION IN IMF POLICIES

I have often been very critical of the IMF in regard to its dealings with developing countries, but in the Grandmotherly essay, which was published in October 1981, I expressed some optimism about the prospects for "a new departure" in Fund thinking and policies. Unfortunately this optimism proved to be ill-founded. The Managing Director had made a series of statements acknowledging the fact that structural changes of the type required to strengthen the balances of payments of developing countries might take longer than the one to three years normally set as the length of Fund programs. "Thus," he said, "while we continue to stress the importance of appropriate demand management, we now systematically emphasize the development of the productive base of the economy and we contemplate that countries may, therefore, need our financing for longer periods."[7] The 1981 loan to India (discussed in chapter 7 in the essay on Conceptions and Misconceptions of Adjustment) appeared at the time to be a very promising innovation in IMF programs because the restructuring of supply over a three-year period agreed upon between India and the Fund involved government investment in the energy and transport sectors within a general context of growth and at a high level of public and private savings and investment. This seemed to offer promise of a broader IMF approach to the balance-of-payments problems of developing countries than in the past, as well as a major expansion of the volume of finance to be provided in support of adjustment programs.[8]

It was, however, recognized in the Grandmotherly essay that, despite current indications in 1980–81 of a readiness on the part of the management to reexamine some of the basic assumptions of past IMF programs, the conditions required by the Fund in connection with balance-of-payments support had become much more stringent than they had been during a similar period of the mid-1970s. Regrettably, as it turned out, it was the latter tendency in IMF policies that prevailed over the former. The loan to India, which had been approved over U.S. objections, turned out to be a flash in the pan rather than a precedent. In the course of the 1980s the conditions imposed on borrowing countries were progressively tightened and even drawings on the IMF designed to cushion the effects of reversible declines in commodity export earnings were made subject to rigorous conditions, despite the fact that the Fund had traditionally not made major demands on countries that were able to show that their balance-of-payments deficits were due to reversible factors beyond their control.

The hardening of IMF policies coincided, of course, with the debt crisis of the second half of 1982 and its aftermath. It also reflected the decision of the major industrial countries to resist any liberalization of policies by the Fund management. Signs of such resistance had already developed at the annual meetings of the IMF and World Bank in September 1980, when the Minister of Finance of the Federal Republic of Germany asserted that the IMF had been created as the guardian of internal and external monetary stability and should resist all attempts that might call this mandate in question. "The conditionality of its lending," the minister said, "must be maintained." The principle of conditionality was not, of course, being challenged by anybody at the time. What the Managing

Director had in mind was the adaptation of conditionality to take into account the need for developing the productive base of the economy, with a corresponding lengthening of the period of financing and, where necessary, an expansion of the amount. The minister's statement, which undoubtedly reflected the views of other major Fund shareholders, was to be understood as opposing any such change in the *application* of conditionality as well as in the principle itself.

THE INTRUSIVENESS OF FUND AND BANK PROGRAMS

Yet there must be ways of safeguarding the legitimate interests of the IMF and the World Bank as creditor institutions without the kind of intrusive surveillance and monitoring that have become customary. The fact that such a high degree of intrusiveness is not essential can be seen from the experience of the Fund and Bank in the 1950s and 1960s when drawings even in the upper credit tranches of the Fund did not involve the kind of detailed supervision that would now be required in similar circumstances. The conditions attached to World Bank loans in the early years consisted of only the most general indications of a borrowing country's economic program and of the magnitude of its domestic efforts.

Under present policies the efforts of both of the Bretton Woods institutions in promoting structural adjustment in developing countries cannot avoid impinging on highly controversial and highly political issues of development strategy. Such issues concern

- the target rate of growth, and the balance to be struck between growth and price stability as national economic objectives;
- the overall role of the state and its contribution to production;
- the role of market forces in general and private enterprise in particular;
- the degree of openness of the economy, including the protection of infant industry and the treatment of foreign investors;
- social objectives, including the distribution of income.

In a democracy these issues are the subject of debate among political parties and the electorate has a chance to bring some influence to bear by choosing one party or another to govern. What the Bretton Woods institutions are now trying to do is to take these issues out of the realm of political controversy and public choice by imposing conditions for lending that imply that there are technical and noncontroversial answers to all these questions.

But there are no such answers. There is no technically correct or incorrect answer to the questions—how much growth should one sacrifice to the goal of price stability; how much state intervention in the economy is desirable; or how much inequality in the distribution of income is tolerable? These are questions of political judgment that cannot be settled by purely technical analysis. Nobody who has had any professional contact with the staffs of the Bank and Fund can doubt that they are, on the whole, highly qualified and skilled. But no national government relies exclusively on technocrats, however capable, in the determination of broad policy. The staffs of the Bretton Woods institutions report only to their governing bodies. Although these bodies are composed of the representatives of governments, it can hardly be said that there is a sensitive link between the activities of the Bretton Woods institutions and public opinion in their member countries, let alone a strict system of accountability. Moreover, the two institutions operate under conditions of tight security and their operations are not open to public scrutiny to the same extent as the activities of democratic national governments are. They do not even declassify their documents after a certain period as many democratic governments do.

Thus the Bretton Woods institutions are essentially technocratic in nature and the fact that the two technocracies are well motivated and of high professional caliber does not diminish the fact that there is no properly functioning democratic control. This does not mean that there are no outside political influences. Numerous cases could be cited in which external political factors weighed heavily in lending decisions, notably where a major industrial country wished to prevent a loan being granted to a country of which it disapproved on general political grounds. Moreover, as we have seen, broad policies have been greatly influenced by the ebb and flow of economic ideology in the leading industrial countries.

AN ALTERNATIVE APPROACH

The more I think about this whole subject the more impressed am I by the wisdom of Mason and Asher's conclusion that "There is a strong *a priori* case for tailoring Bank lending to an assessment of 'results' as measured by various development indicators, leaving it to the borrowing country to attain the results considered desirable by whatever mix of policy actions seems under the circumstances to be economically and politically feasible."[9]

Some years ago I had the privilege of participating in a group that was commissioned by the Group of Twenty-Four to review and make recommendations concerning IMF programs. The other members of the group were Carlos Diaz-Alejandro, Ricardo Ffrench-Davis, Toma Gudac, and

Cristián Ossa.[10] The central conclusion of our paper was that borrowing countries should be entitled to formulate their programs of domestic adjustment with maximum freedom in the use of various policy instruments and institutional arrangements. Moreover, the management of interactions between domestic and external variables should be left to the discretion of national authorities. In our view the only criterion for the effectiveness of a program that might be a matter for consideration by the international community was whether the program involved a measure of effort broadly consistent with the balance-of-payments target agreed upon.

Any government seeking to draw upon the Fund could legitimately be asked to set forth a comprehensive macroeconomic program together with policies required to implement it. The national authorities could be requested to propose some quantitative targets for policies included in the program that could in their view serve as intermediate performance criteria. It was likely, however, that consistency between the program proposed and the balance-of-payments target agreed upon would not be verifiable until the program was already under way. In the initial stages countries should be given the benefit of the doubt as to the consistency of the program with the balance-of-payments target. This consistency would, however, be monitored at appropriate intervals. If performance on external account proved to be satisfactory, the domestic variables and policies would no longer be required as performance criteria. If, however, the expected improvement in the balance of payments did not materialize, there would be a review of the program in the course of which agreement would be sought on an intensification of the domestic adjustment effort and/or the amendment of the balance-of-payments target, particularly in the light of any unforeseen development in the external environment.

It should be noted that we were not proposing any dilution of Fund conditionality. What we were saying, essentially, was that a reduction in the specificity of requirements regarding domestic policies might be accompanied by greater specificity regarding the external sector, notably through the formulation of subsidiary targets such as a minimum improvement in export performance.

Very similar conclusions were reached by the prestigious Commonwealth Study Group that, under the chairmanship of Professor G. K. Helleiner, submitted a report entitled, "Towards a New Bretton Woods" (Commonwealth Secretariat, 1983). The report contained the following paragraph:

Future disputes could be minimized and early resort to the Fund encouraged by a sensitive country-specific application of conditionality. There should be primary reliance on balance-of-payments targets rather than on monetary ones, and external prescriptions as to the precise character of domestic credit and fiscal management should be minimized. Formal performance targets, if retained, should be made more flexible through agreed margins of deviation, linked in a pre-agreed fashion to key exogenous variables, or be waived more readily as appropriate. Inadequate performance should trigger a review mission whose brief would be to form an overall view of progress and would not necessarily lead to curtailment of lending. (paragraph 10.37).

When it comes to Bank programs, including structural adjustment in the longer term, the policies and measures required are substantially more complex, and there is no single pattern of adjustment that could be agreed upon universally. Mention has already been made of some of the controversies that arise in determining an appropriate development strategy, and similar difficulties and controversies arise in many other areas in which government measures and policies may be thought necessary or desirable. It cannot be said that there is even agreement on the specific areas in which government intervention is required. On the one hand, the present approach of the Bretton Woods institutions is to say that since the market knows best, the best thing the government can do is to provide sound fiscal and monetary management and make sure that the pricing system is free to indicate the signals and inducements that private enterprise needs in determining its level and direction of business activity. On the other hand, there are those who would argue, as we did in our group, that the government needs to play a supportive role, not only in relation to the economy as a whole but also in dealing with sectoral maladjustments that do not yield easily or quickly to general aggregate incentives. Long-term planning is particularly necessary, we felt, in the energy and food sectors. In agriculture, particularly, price incentives alone do not usually yield the results required. Large landowners have frequently been lethargic in responding to price incentives and in the adoption of new techniques and increased prices for food may have an adverse effect on income distribution.

There is no doubt that the World Bank has had considerable experience on these and other questions of long-run development, and it is natural for the Bank to place its expertise at the disposal of its member governments. But this is not the same thing as saying that the Bank has at its disposal a generally agreed body of doctrine regarding long-run development that can be confidently applied in each and every case. For long-run structural adjustment as for short-term stabilization, it is the better part of valor for the Bank to refrain from insisting on particular domestic policies and measures. Here again the government should be asked to specify its long-run and intermediate goals and the manner in which it intends to mobilize domestic efforts to secure these goals, and the Bank should then make its decision as to whether the domestic efforts undertaken would justify Bank assistance.

By such means it should be possible for both of the Bretton Woods institutions to obtain all of the assurances that they need that the borrowing country will make a meaningful effort on its own behalf, and will be in a position to service its loans, without trying to substitute the judgment of the Fund or Bank for that of national authorities regarding the specific global and sectoral measures required.

More generally, a major international effort is needed to restore the Bretton Woods institutions to the role and importance envisaged for them by the founding fathers. It is an absurdity that they should have been allowed to degenerate into a mechanism for the supervision of Third World policies by the industrial countries, with resources that are totally inadequate for the tasks that confront them. If there is to be effective international cooperation in achieving and maintaining the kind of international monetary system that will facilitate the expansion of the world economy, and in helping actively to accelerate the development of the Third World, the Fund and Bank must fully assume the responsibilities that these goals entail, and must be given the resources to discharge those responsibilities.

THE FUTURE OF THE INTERNATIONAL MONETARY SYSTEM

The last group of essays in this volume are concerned with the future of the international monetary system. The reason why this is an important subject in the consideration of international development policy is that there is a need to create a system that will facilitate development rather than holding it back. It is not, of course, a primary function of the international monetary system to supply resources for development.[11] Such resources must be supplied primarily by savings of the developing countries themselves and, for the rest, through flows from the multilateral agencies established for this purpose as well as from bilateral development programs of governments and private capital flows, whether in the form of loan or equity capital.

What can be expected of the international monetary system is that it should create an international environment that is conducive to development, including the stability required to promote investment for the long run and provide encouragement for countries both developed and developing to manage their economies in a way that will enable them to come as close as possible to the realization of their full potential for growth. This in turn implies the need for a stable exchange rate system, an adequate supply of international liquidity and the availability of resources for balance-of-payments support to take care of problems of short-term balance-of-payments management, whether arising in industrial or in developing countries. In most of these respects the present system is entirely unsatisfactory. Exchange rates are subject to serious misalignment and short-term volatility, the arrangements for collective management of international liquidity introduced in 1969 have been reduced to a dead letter, and the provision of balance-of-payments support by the institution established for that purpose at Bretton Woods involves such a degree of surrender of national economic autonomy that the industrial countries no longer choose to make any use of it. Some suggestions are made for better ways of dealing with these and other deficiencies.

The last two essays deal with one specific proposal for reform whereby the creation of international liquidity would be linked to development finance. The flow of official development assistance from the Organization for Economic Cooperation and Development (OECD) countries to the Third World has for many years languished at a level that is less than one-half of the United Nations target.[12] Despite the major advance in the real per capita incomes of industrial countries from 1970 to 1990—in the case of the United States, for example, amounting to over 35 percent— the share of gross income allocated to official development assistance showed no increase from its 1970 level. Nevertheless, as the Pearson and Brandt commissions pointed out, a substantial expansion of aid to the Third World would be in the interests of the industrial countries themselves, and would in fact provide a means of reconciling the inconsistent trade objectives of these countries. All the industrial countries would like to be able to export more than they import—a collective goal that cannot be realized under conditions in which the Third World is itself compelled to achieve a surplus of exports over imports in order to service its foreign debt. It is obviously impossible for *all* countries to have positive trade balances at the same time. Everyone, moreover, agrees that the huge trade deficit of the United States is an anomaly that ought to be rectified as soon as possible, and yet it is quite clear that other industrial countries would strongly resist the declines in their own trade surpluses that would be required to accommodate a major upsurge of U.S. exports relative to its imports, at a time when the Third World is already importing as much as it can with its existing resources and could import more only if its purchasing power was augmented by additional aid.

THE SDR LINK TO DEVELOPMENT ASSISTANCE

The essays therefore explore the possibility of using the mechanism of Special Drawing Rights (SDRS) within the IMF to promote additional flows of aid. The conclusion is reached that "The creation of such a link should therefore be considered both as a means of bringing about the adjustment in United States payments needed in the near term and also in order to ensure consistency of the objectives of the industrial countries as a group in the long run." Although this was written in 1971 it is equally applicable to the 1990s, including the reference to the adjustment required in the U.S. balance of payments.

SHARING THE PEACE DIVIDEND

Mention was made earlier of the potential benefits for world development resulting from the end of the cold war. Unfortunately it is far from clear that the new détente will necessarily be to the advantage of the Third World, at any rate in the immediate future. The fact that East-West competition for influence in the Third World is tending to subside as détente gathers momentum means that in both groups of potential donors one of the arguments for aid to developing countries is losing force.

In addition, the Eastern European countries and China are now seeking to attract capital on a large scale from both multilateral and bilateral sources, public and private. It is widely assumed that this is bound to cause a reduction in the flow of capital to the Third World. It seems doubtful, however, whether capital is in general so short in the West that resources made available to the East would have to be at the expense of developing countries. Unutilized or underutilized capacity in the West is sufficiently large to support substantial flows of capital to the East as well as the South.

At the present time public and private capital flows to developing countries amount, on average, to considerably less than 1 percent of the gross income of the OECD countries. Even if one assumed that this proportion might be doubled or trebled in order to permit larger flows to both East and South to take place, there is no doubt that increases of these magnitudes could be accommodated within the productive capacity of the West without undue strain. What it would mean, in effect, is that the OECD countries would have to increase their production from present levels by, say, 1 to 2 percent. During the early postwar years, under various programs of aid for European recovery, the United States was exporting capital to the extent of 3 to 4 percent of its gross national product at a time when unemployment amounted to less than 4 percent of the labor force, compared with over 5 percent in 1989. There is no reason from a purely economic standpoint why the United States, Japan, and other leading OECD countries could not match or even exceed the effort of the Marshall Plan, especially having regard to the enormous increases in per capita incomes that have taken place in these countries during the past four decades.

An effort on this scale would be in the long-run interests of the industrial countries themselves even if there were no disarmament, but obviously the available resources would be all the greater if defense expenditures were reduced. If, for example, the OECD countries as a group reduced their current defense expenditures by one-quarter, and were prepared to allocate one-quarter of that quarter to Third World development this would make it possible to double the present level of official development assistance to developing countries. Such a willingness of the industrial countries to use part of the peace dividend in support of world development goals could be made conditional on a comparable percentage reduction in the defense expenditures of the developing countries themselves.

It is true that the Marshall Plan had important political objectives, particularly the strengthening of Western Europe's ability to resist the spread of communism. But there are equally or even more important political objectives to be attained at the present time in helping Eastern Europe and the developing countries to build viable economies and reverse the declines in per capita incomes of recent years that were due in the one case to the failures of central planning and in the other to the accumulation of massive indebtedness. To argue that the one area is more important to the interests of the countries of the West than the other—that the rehabilitation of Eastern Europe is more important than the recovery of Africa and Latin America—implies a mistaken sense of priorities. It is no accident that all the wars since World War II originated in the problems of one or more countries of the Third World. Equally, recent developments in Eastern Europe have brought to the center of public concern the dangers to peace that could arise from ethnic rivalries and disputes over boundaries. Help to both groups of countries is not only a moral imperative, it goes to the heart of the problem of maintaining peace and security in the three-quarters of the globe where in recent years standards of living have been stagnating at low levels or declining.

Another argument frequently encountered is that there is no case for going to the help of the foreign poor so long as there are large numbers of domestic poor who have not been provided for adequately. Here, once again, the argument is usually confused by the general lack of awareness that the proportion of national income devoted to capital flows to the Third World falls far short of 1 percent. Even if the 1 percent capital flow target of the United Nations General Assembly were achieved, that would still leave 99 percent of the national income available for domestic purposes in the capital exporting countries. There is plenty of room within that 99 percent for a redistribution of income that would lift all the domestic poor of the industrial countries above the poverty line. So long as national resources are wasted on excessive defense expenditure, and so long as the distribution of income is as unequal as it is at the present time in most of the industrial countries, so long will it be unreasonable to argue that the only way of improving the lot of the domestic poor is at the expense of the foreign poor. Foreign aid is an expression of international solidarity, a recognition of the fact that concern about poverty cannot end at national frontiers and an acknowledgment of the fact that poverty *anywhere* is a threat to prosperity *everywhere*. Many are the manufacturers in the industrial countries, as well as their employees, who have had firsthand experience of the shrinking of their export markets following the loss of purchasing power in developing countries that was a result of the need to use scarce foreign exchange to meet debt service commitments.

No doubt there are those who would claim that increasing the production of OECD countries from present levels by 1 or 2 percent would rekindle the fires of inflation—the same argument that is being used to defend the deflationary bias in the economic policies of these countries. We shall discuss this point further below, but here we can simply say that concerns about inflation are greatly exaggerated, and are colored by fears of the effects of high levels of employment on the militancy of the labor force. If governments were willing to address themselves more directly to the need for cooperation between social groups in the interests of the community as a whole, there would be no need to rely on the threat of unemployment as a means of ensuring social cohesion.

Whether the sense of international solidarity is strong enough to persuade the OECD countries that they should make a major contribution to the building of a new world in which the East and the South would prosper, as well as the West, is another matter. Although there is plenty of rhetoric about interdependence, this has not prevented the emergence of serious tensions in international economic relations, expressed most clearly in conflicts over trade policy. It is arguable that the end of the cold war may be accompanied by an actual intensification of such conflicts since there will be less concern about any potential weakening of the common front of NATO or Warsaw Pact powers.

But there cannot be any doubt that in the longer run the end of the cold war will create immense opportunities for mankind to devote itself to the solution of a multitude of problems that have been set aside for too long and allowed to fester. The East and the South will not be able to make the contribution to world advancement of which they are capable until they have pulled themselves out of the economic depression that is now afflicting them. It is, therefore, in the long-run interests of the West to do whatever it can to accelerate that recovery process. The efforts of the West do not need to be in the form of unrequited gifts except to African and other exceptionally impoverished countries. The West can expect a high rate of return on its efforts, not only in the form of interest and dividends but much more importantly in the widening and deepening of the international economic community itself.

2

The International Economic Environment

The Case for World Economic Expansion

Many parallels have been drawn between the world economic situation in 1982 and that of the 1930s, though clearly the present economic setback has not reached the proportions of the 1930s. But there is one difference between the two periods that overshadows all others. In the 1930s the Depression was an unwelcome shock to all. Governments were overwhelmed by it and had no strategy, individual or collective, for dealing with it, at any rate at the outset. Today the methods of raising or lowering the level of economic activity are fairly well known and understood. Yet the increasing unemployment of today is, in a sense, the direct result of policy decisions by governments. This does not, of course, mean that governments reached a deliberate decision to raise the general level of unemployment. What happened was that the particular methods adopted by governments to control inflation and, in some cases, to correct balance-of-payments disequilibrium, led inevitably to higher unemployment. Governments were convinced that unless deflationary measures were taken to eliminate internal and external imbalance, severe unemployment would be unavoidable in any case. This being the assumption, a long period of "wringing inflation out of the system" was, as governments saw it—and still see it—the only way of rebuilding a sound and growing economy and hence of restoring a high level of employment. There is a widespread view among government officials in the industrial countries as well as among members of the international financial community, public and private, that the level of world demand may have to be held down by monetary and fiscal constraints for several more years. It has even been suggested that it will be necessary to wait until the latter part of the 1980s for a substantially better performance of the world economy.[1]

Originally published in the *Journal of Development Planning* 14 (United Nations, 1984). The issues raised remain of central importance for the 1990s.

Such a prospect, if realized, would imply that the 1980s are to be a decade not of development but of retrogression. The question is whether those who contemplate such an outlook with apparent equanimity have fully calculated the costs. Quite apart from the political and social risks of current policies, their economic costs are unacceptably high. The most important of these costs are, of course, those that result from the loss of employment and output in industrial and developing countries alike, and particularly from the slackening of development momentum in the developing world, where the countries most severely affected are precisely those that can least afford an economic setback of the current magnitude. In addition, however, the persistence of stagnation and recession is endangering the international trading system and is generating acute instability in the international financial system.

The following discussion deals first with the threats to international trade and finance and then proceeds to contest the view that a major recovery of the world economy must be postponed for some considerable period of time. In conclusion, some elements of an immediate recovery program are presented.

THE THREAT TO THE WORLD TRADING SYSTEM

While the differences between the 1930s and the 1980s are, as we have seen, of great importance, there are a number of striking parallels. None is more disquieting than the progressive disruption of world trade. Addressing the Council of the Organization for Economic Cooperation and Development (OECD), on May 11, 1982, the Director-General of the General Agreement on Tariffs and Trade (GATT), Arthur Dunkel, said:

Recent months have been marked by further proliferation of sectoral and bilateral difficulties in trade relations, giving rise to serious tensions, and to an increasing number of disputes, in the agricultural as well as industrial sectors, brought for settlement to GATT. A large and still growing segment of trade is being restricted and distorted, often through measures unsanctioned by the GATT rules. Attempts to resolve a number of these differences through the GATT dispute settlement procedures have been blocked because governments disagree on the scope and aims of the rules at issue. This is exceedingly serious. Large economic and political interests are directly at stake. Worse, prospects for future trade growth are being clouded because the validity of the GATT rules on which trade is based is being called into question.

Both the United States and the European Community are seeking a bilateral balancing of trade with Japan. Yet in the past those selfsame countries had often denounced policies in a number of developing countries that were deemed to have the very same objective, namely, to regulate the two-way flow of trade with individual trading partners. Nor do the industrial countries have the same kind of logical justification for bilateralism in trade policies that developing countries have had at times of severe pressure on the balance of payments, when the most strenuous efforts to conserve foreign exchange were unavoidable.

It has been estimated that no less than 25 to 30 percent of total world trade is now accounted for by "counter-trade"—a variety of different forms of barter not seen on this scale since the years of the Depression and the Second World War. There are an increasing number of agreements involving major companies in OECD member countries, by which exports from one industrial country to another are linked to a corresponding flow of exports in the opposite direction. Moreover, commercial banks have entered the counter-trade business as middlemen, bringing buyers and sellers together for a fee.[2]

Counter-trade has considerable advantages for developing countries because new investment opportunities are more likely to come to fruition and to find the requisite finance if industrial country suppliers are willing to undertake to buy part of the output of the factories they are helping to equip. This is also a procedure favored by socialist countries. But in transactions among industrial countries, which have in the past been committed to a more open system, counter-trade is clear evidence of efforts to preempt shrinking markets.

The tensions in world trade are by no means limited to those resulting from the proliferation of barter arrangements. Charges and counter-charges of unfair trade practices are being exchanged increasingly against one another by the industrial countries, as are threats of retaliation. This, again, is a symptom of depressed world markets. The one thing that unites the industrial countries in the trade field is resistance to imports of manufactures from the developing countries. This is particularly obvious in the Multifibre Arrangement (MFA) providing for the stringent curtailment of textile exports from developing countries to industrial countries—a process that began, as a "temporary" measure, in 1962. Although the MFA was negotiated within GATT, it is fundamentally incompatible with the spirit of GATT. The discrimination against low-income countries that it embodies is not only contrary to the basic thrust of GATT toward nondiscrimination, but is contrary to the principle of specialization on the basis of comparative advantage that the industrial countries have repeatedly commended to the developing countries as the key to a sound international trade policy. Moreover, the MFA's sanctioning of quantitative restrictions on textile trade on what appears to be a virtually permanent basis is in conflict with the basic principles of GATT.

Apart from textiles, the sectors now subject to protectionist arrangements (including so-called orderly marketing agreements) include agriculture, automobiles, shipbuilding, steel, and synthetic fibers. As Dunkel has pointed out, "these sectoral deals differ from the MFA in being essentially bilateral and wholly outside the rule of law. So far they have involved mainly the industrialized countries, though some developing countries of Asia are being drawn into them."[3]

There cannot be much doubt that the sharp intensification of conflict in the world trade arena reflects the efforts of individual countries to protect their own levels of employment at the expense of other countries, a process in which the weakest countries are the ones that suffer the most. As in the 1930s, trade policies are increasingly of the "beggar-my-neighbor" variety and are likely to become more and more disruptive of the world economy and of the fabric of international cooperation if deflationary pressures are intensified.[4]

DESTROYING THE CAPACITY TO REPAY: THE DEFLATIONARY ROUTE TO FINANCIAL CRISIS

Owing to the progressive erosion of the resources of the International Monetary Fund (IMF) as a proportion of world trade since Bretton Woods, the capacity of the Fund to provide balance-of-payments support fell far short of requirements during the 1970s. In these circumstances the commercial banks of the industrial countries, which had received massive inflows of funds from the capital-surplus oil exporting countries, were able to step in and take over the major part of the role of the IMF by channeling these funds to deficit countries they considered creditworthy, including both industrial and the more advanced developing countries. Providing balance-of-payments support was a task of which the private banks had had little or no experience but, under the conditions of excess liquidity in which they found themselves, they pressed their loans upon the deficit countries.

For some years the borrowers and intermediaries both prospered. The banks earned a satisfactory spread between their borrowing and lending rates while the entities to which they were lending frequently found themselves paying interest rates that were less than the rate of inflation of their export prices.[5] The situation was, however, completely transformed by the intense monetary deflation that ensued in the industrial countries. Negative real interest rates on commercial bank lending were replaced by the highest positive real interest rates ever recorded and those rates had, of course, to be paid, not merely on new loans but on the accumulated old loans that had been contracted at variable rates.

What was frequently overlooked was that the ability to service debt without disruption of the borrowing country's economy depends on two conditions: uninterrupted world economic expansion, and access to the markets of the creditor countries. The only source from which debt can be serviced internationally is the proceeds of exports of goods and services by the borrowing countries. No matter how responsible the borrowing country is in regard to its fiscal and monetary policies, no matter how wisely the borrowed funds are used, and no matter how productive the new investment made possible by borrowing may be, the capacity to repay will ultimately depend on the willingness of creditor countries to accept larger imports of goods and services from the borrowers.

Thus the deflationary policies of the industrial countries simultaneously increase the debt-service burden of the borrowing countries—through the high interest rates brought about by excessive reliance on monetary restrictions as a means of fighting inflation—and place obstacles in the way of the borrowers' efforts to shoulder that burden by reducing the demand for imports from the borrowing countries in line with the deteriorating domestic economy.

Particularly ominous is the collapse of the prices of primary commodities exported by non-oil developing countries to their lowest level, in real terms, in thirty years—a collapse brought about by the industrial countries through their curbs on business activity. The difficulties resulting from commodity price declines are compounded by the protectionist barriers erected against imports from the debtor countries.

Efforts by the debtor countries to overcome these obstacles through devaluation, export subsidies, more aggressive marketing, and so forth frequently aggravate the problem insofar as they prompt retaliation by other countries, leading, when demand elasticities are low, to an actual reduction in export earnings.

Thus the deflationary policies of industrial countries are not merely disruptive of world trade and development, but they sharply intensify the dangers of international financial crisis.

The same basic forces are at work in the domestic financial markets of the industrial countries. There too the capacity of borrowers to meet their debt service obligations has been seriously weakened by deflationary pressures and falling profits. In fact the general experience of commercial banks has been that performance on their domestic loan portfolios has been substantially worse than on their foreign loans.[6]

Declining bank liquidity coupled with substantial increases in the volume of nonperforming loans had resulted, by March 1982, in the downgrading by Moody's of the bonds of nine out of ten leading U.S. banks from the triple A to the double A rating. Since confidence in the banking system is one of the most crucial elements of financial stability, national and international, this downgrading of the major U.S. banks must be regarded as a particularly serious warning.

THE INCOHERENCE OF THE ADJUSTMENT PROCESS

The incoherence of international economic policy at the present time is nowhere more evident than in the adjustment process. Although the term "adjustment" is often used narrowly to denote the process by which disequilibrium in the balance of payments is removed, there is a broader sense in which countries are required to adjust to many different kinds of shifts in their economic relationships with one another, including shifts in comparative advantage, in relative rates of growth, in trade policies, and so forth. Adjustment both in the broader and in the narrower senses should, of course, be continuous because change is continuous and because national economies cannot function effectively unless they adapt themselves to change and, indeed, initiate changes of their own.

Adjustment could in principle take various forms; it is not, per se, incompatible with growth. On the contrary, adjustment is likely to be smoother and more effective if it takes place under conditions of vigorous growth, especially since in many cases adjustment calls for new investment, and the inducements to new investment are strongest at a time of growth. Thus the correction of a balance-of-payments deficit does not have to involve a reduction of aggregate demand. It may take place in a context of rising demand and rising output, provided that the share of output allocated to exports is increased or the import content of output is decreased.

Under present conditions, however, the term adjustment has virtually become a euphemism for deflation. Moreover—and this is where the incoherence originates—deflation is regarded as the universal remedy in all countries both for balance-of-payments deficits and for inflationary pressures. In other words, deflationary measures are applied in surplus and deficit countries alike—in both groups as a means of resisting inflation and in the deficit group as a means of reducing external imbalance.

But if contraction of demand is the universally applied nostrum, two consequences follow. In the first place, efforts by the deficit countries to restore external balance by increasing exports are continually frustrated by the simultaneous decline in import demand of the surplus countries. Secondly, the downward pressures on world demand from the various groups of countries begin to reinforce one another and the dangers of a cumulative downward spiral throughout the world are intensified. These dangers are further aggravated by the illiquidity in the system and by the slowing down of financial flows from commercial banks and international financial institutions.

Thus the continuous emphasis on adjustment through deflation as the indispensable path for all countries is an unsatisfactory basis for an international economic policy. As at present conceived, it creates more problems than it solves because it aggravates the existing international imbalance. Even the slowdown in inflationary pressures that it helps to bring about is achieved largely through excessive reductions in primary commodity prices, which are themselves responsible for much of the growing international disequilibrium.

Adjustment in the sense of adaptation of the structure of production in industrial and developing countries to relative shifts in productive capacities and skills is, if anything, slowing down under cover of new measures for the protection of declining industries in the developed countries. As noted earlier, such measures are a response, in part, to the worldwide slackening of demand and contribute to the perpetuation of disequilibrium.

THE CASE AGAINST REACTIVATION OF THE WORLD ECONOMY: SOME FALLACIES

Mention has already been made of the view that several years of monetary and fiscal constraint are needed, marking a transitional period during which inflation would be reduced and economic efficiency improved. Only after such a period of stringency would the stage be set for a better performance of the world economy in the late 1980s.

In the annual report of the IMF for 1982, it is argued that, under present conditions, "a shift to expansionary fiscal and monetary policies might be expected to have only limited and temporary positive effects on output and employment and would run a grave risk of aggravating inflationary expectations and pressures that, all too soon, could lead to an even worse condition of stagflation."[7] Meanwhile, the hard-won gains of the past few years in the fight against inflation would have been dissipated and the restoration of noninflationary economic growth would be put off for an indefinite period.

The hard-won gains brought about by deflationary policies may, however, be more apparent than real. Much has been made of the slowing down in rates of increase in prices in 1982. In fact, however, much of this was due, as noted earlier, to the collapse of primary commodity prices, which would inevitably be reversed in the event of a general economic recovery. As the Bank of England has pointed out, the situation has deteriorated to such a degree that some commodity producers are now being forced to sell at prices below their costs of production. The Bank concludes that "the reduction of inflation to some extent represents a drawing on the future."[8] Moreover, low prices have also led to reductions in productive capacity for certain commodities. The Bank points out that, if continued, such curtailment of capacity could lead to upward price reactions later.[9]

On the other hand, the slowing down of inflation owed little to any deceleration of the rise in money incomes through 1981.[10] And while there was some evidence of moderating wage increases toward the end of 1981 and in 1982, the factors underlying these developments may not outlast the recession itself, for reasons that will be discussed later.

The view that the level of demand must continue to be held down well below high employment levels for several years is based on certain definite assumptions. Although these assumptions have rarely, if ever, been spelled out by those who hold that view, it appears that the following are some of the more important of them:

- Inflation is the most serious danger to the world economy at the present time;
- There cannot be any question of balancing the need for reducing or eliminating inflation against other economic objectives of the international community because reduced inflation is a precondition for the attainment of all other objectives, and must, therefore, take priority over them;
- The predominant cause of price increases at the present time is excessive demand in both industrial and developing countries; in this context, mention is made of fiscal deficits and expansion in the money supply;
- There is, therefore, no effective way of countering price increases except by restrictive demand management, both fiscal and monetary;
- A period of prolonged demand stringency will reduce the danger of resumed inflation.

All of these assumptions are open to question. There is no dispute that inflation is indeed a serious obstacle to sound economic growth and tends to divert resources into undesirable and unproductive channels. But while the path of noninflationary growth is clearly to be preferred, experience shows that it is simply not true that inflation is, per se, an obstacle to growth or that inflation, even at double-digit rates, necessarily tends to become explosive. If this had been the case it would not have been possible for Brazil, in the space of only twenty years, to emerge from its relatively backward state in the early 1960s into a position that marks it as one of the potential industrial giants of the future. During that twenty-year period, Brazilian consumer prices increased more than one-thousandfold—a rate of inflation that was obviously excessive by any standards and one that went far beyond the rates that are considered so intolerable in the industrial countries at the present time that all policy goals other than countering inflation are relegated to a subordinate position. But Brazil would have had no success at all if it had given first priority to the elimination of inflation by contraction of demand. It would never have been able to embark on a program of rapid industrial investment and growth, and whether there would have been an appreciable gain in terms of slowing down inflation is debatable.

It is not suggested that Brazil can or should be a model for the rest of the world. But one can agree that every effort should be made to resist the forces of inflation without accepting the much more dubious proposition that inflation is now, in October 1982, the greatest menace to the world economy. Current levels of unemployment are a much more serious threat, and the prospect of raising these levels still further through the continuation of deflationary measures is unconscionable. Criticizing the view that inflation is the chief economic problem, the chairman of the Bank of America, Leland Prussia, in a press interview, reported by Reuters, Toronto, on September 7, 1982, stated that "we have a tendency in the United States to fight yesterday's battles." He went on to say that what the United States needed was rapid growth to combat unemployment.

To suggest that measures should be taken to revitalize the world economy is certainly not to imply that nothing should be done to counter inflation. What it does mean is that the steps taken to prevent inflation should not be of the type that lead to additional unemployment. This is discussed further below.

DIAGNOSING AND COUNTERING INFLATION

The third assumption—that demand is still excessive—is particularly ill-founded. It results from the mistake commonly made by monetarists of lumping all kinds of inflation together as being induced by a single factor—an increase in the money supply. They thereby fail to distinguish between demand inflation and cost inflation.

Of course it is nothing new that there are those who contest the validity of such a distinction and yet one would have thought that the existence of large-scale unemployment and idle capacity side by side with rising prices would have prompted them to reexamine their approach to this matter. Large-scale unemployment and idle capacity indicate a deficiency of real demand, not an excess.

Demand inflation occurs when planned expenditure exceeds supply. Particularly critical in this context are investment, export surplus, and budget deficit. These three elements of national expenditure have the common property that they all add to private incomes without simultaneously adding to the currently produced supplies of goods for consumption. Consequently, if there is to be a balance between the demand for and supply of consumption goods at current prices, an amount must be saved out of private income that is equal to the sum of investment, export surplus, and budget deficit. If private savings fall short of this amount, planned demand for consumption goods will exceed the supply, leading to a rise in prices. This rise will continue to the point at which the shift from wages to profits is sufficient to bring about the requisite increase in private savings.

Thus demand inflation is characterized by a high level of activity and of employment, by high profits, and by shortages of goods. This is certainly not the kind of situation that prevails at the present time, when activity, employment, and profits are low, and goods are in surplus supply.

It may be noted parenthetically that a budget deficit, per se, is not necessarily inflationary, as is often claimed. What counts is whether the planned savings of the private sector are sufficient to finance the combined sum of investment, export surplus, and budget deficit. The magnitude of any one of these three components, taken by itself, is not decisive.

If wage earners accept the reduction in real wages brought about by the initial rise in prices, the upward pressure on prices is eased and price stability is reestablished. But wage earners may offer what Sir John Hicks has called "real wage resistance."[11] In other words they may attempt to recoup their losses by demanding higher money wages. This may lead to a wage-price spiral and, if supplies of consumption goods are not increased, the spiral can continue indefinitely without any recovery in average real wages. The original demand inflation is thus transformed into a cost inflation, which may persist regardless of the amount of unemployment.

But not all cost inflations are preceded by periods of excess pressure of aggregate demand. The most obvious example is a country operating at a low level of activity and demand that experiences a rise in import prices. The increase in import prices can set off a domestic cost-price spiral despite the absence of demand inflation. A similar situation can arise as a result of a crop failure, leading to a rise in food prices.

It is the height of folly to try to deal with cost inflation by applying restrictions on demand through monetary or fiscal contraction. Such restrictions depend for their success not on their direct impact on the causes of the inflation but on their indirect effects—by depressing output and raising the level of unemployment. Depending on the circumstances, the country may have to incur heavy costs in the form of additional and unnecessary losses of real income over and above the losses resulting from deterioration in the terms of trade, crop failure, or other factors. The country may also have to forgo substantial investment essential for the economic health of the economy, including the need to keep abreast of the latest technological advances. One major reason for the failure of the United States and the United Kingdom to keep pace with technical progress in the Federal Republic of Germany and Japan is the stop-go policies of alternately expanding and contracting demand that has deprived business enterprise of the assurance of steadily growing markets that are the best stimulus to new investment. The resulting slower growth of productivity in the United States and the United Kingdom contributed significantly to the differential movements in wage costs per unit of output in favor of their competitors.

If deflationary policies were the only way of dealing with cost inflation, the costs involved might be justified, though it would always be necessary to weigh up the costs and benefits in a rational manner, free of dogma. But alternative methods of dealing with cost inflation are available that do not involve so large a reduction in real income and, in some cases, no reduction at all. What is required is the mobilization of the social consensus needed to slow down and ultimately halt the struggle between social groups to safeguard their respective shares of national real income. When a cut in living standards is unavoidable—for example, because of a rise in the cost of essential imports—price stability in a democratic society depends on general agreement on the way in which the burden should be shared, not on deflationary measures that will add to the economic losses, intensify the frictions between social groups, and thereby ultimately risk an acceleration of the spiral of prices and costs.

These ideas, though still rejected by most governments, are beginning to gain greater support—some of it in unexpected quarters. Felix Rohatyn, the well-known New York investment banker, gave a perceptive account of them in the course of an address at Middlebury College on May 23, 1982:

> Modern democracy's biggest weakness is its inability to allocate sacrifice fairly. A growing economy allows even an arthritic political system to apportion some of that growth to all elements of society; this cannot happen in a stagnating economy. We have seen, in 1981, that legislation of sacrifice puts the burden on those least able to afford it and that moderating inflation can only come through the bitter medicine of steep recession. Those solutions are neither fair nor are they likely, ultimately, to be effective. At a time of stress, when on the part of all sacrifice is clearly needed, sacrifice has to be negotiated and not legislated. That requires a government willing and eager to take its place at the negotiating table, and it requires business and labor as the other participants.[12]

FISCAL FACTS AND FANTASIES

Those who argue that the level of demand is excessive seek justification for their point of view in the fact that budget deficits have been increasing. The current wave of fiscal radicalism that holds that budgets must be balanced under any and all circumstances is nothing new. President Roosevelt, who is generally remembered for his efforts to stimulate economic recovery in the United States through increased public expenditure, held quite different views at the outset of his administration. In his first budget message, in March 1933, he asked for legislation to balance the budget by cutting military pensions and the numbers and salaries of civil servants, being unaware of the depressing effect this would have on the economy. Already at that time, however, there were those who recognized that budget-balancing is the way to intensify and prolong a depression, not to overcome it. Professor Jacob Viner, one of the most orthodox and conservative economists of his generation, delivered an address at the University of Georgia in May 1933 in which he took issue with Roosevelt. "It is a mouldy fallacy," said Viner, "that, regardless of circumstances, the government must balance its budget in each year. Why not in each month, or each week, or hour?" Incidentally, it is remarkable that Viner entitled his address, "Inflation as a Possible Remedy for the Depression."[13] To be abreast of fashionable economics today, one would have to turn Viner's thesis upside down and call it, "Depression as an Indispensable Remedy for Inflation."

President Eisenhower is not usually considered to have favored fiscal irresponsibility: on the contrary, he and his administration were strongly committed to the principle of balanced budgets. Yet he informed Congress in January 1954, in commenting on the expected growth in the public debt at a time of recession, that "the Administration recognizes that a federal budget should be a stabilizing factor in the economy."[14]

In its *World Economic Outlook* of April 1982, IMF suggested that "in the past two or three years, fiscal deficits have been a source of problems in many [industrial] countries," and contended that it would be difficult to reduce those deficits substantially "because they are largely the result of long-run pervasive trends rather than short-run factors."[15] No mention was made—at any rate in the context of the above statements—of the relationship between fiscal deficits and the level of economic activity in the industrial countries concerned. As is well known, a decline in business activity has the effect of reducing tax payments to the government and of increasing government payments to the unemployed. These developments may force a government into an unintended budget deficit. Moreover, efforts to remove the deficit may be counterproductive in the sense that they will cause a secondary decline in activity and thus a reappearance of the budget deficit.

OECD appears to take a markedly different view of current fiscal policy in the industrial countries from that cited above. In the *Economic Outlook* of July 1982, on the basis of data adjusted for the level of employment, OECD reported that the budget balance of the seven major OECD countries, taken as a group, moved toward surplus in 1980 and 1981 by 0.8 percent of potential gross national product (GNP) and that the employment-adjusted balance was expected to be virtually unchanged in 1982 and 1983, despite the deterioration in actual deficits.[16]

So much for the idea of a "long-run pervasive trend" to budget deficits. But IMF goes further, arguing that budget deficits may lead to a "crowding out" of private investment through high real interest rates as the government and the private sector compete for available funds. While this may not reduce economic growth in the short run, it will do so in the longer run, according to the Fund, because it hinders capital formation and productivity growth in the private sector, thereby making the control of inflation even more difficult.[17]

Here again the reasoning is faulty. It is based on the assumption that the total volume of private savings is a given and fixed amount and that in order to accommodate government borrowing to cover the budget deficit, "real interest rates must rise enough to squeeze out private borrowing."[18] But the idea that total private savings are invariant with respect to the budget balance is clearly incorrect. In a situation of less than full employment, a budget deficit raises the national income above the level that would otherwise have prevailed. Savings increase at least in proportion to income, but probably even faster than income because the share of profits tends to recover as activity rises. Thus a budget deficit makes more resources available for investment by the private sector, not less, and there is no crowding out effect in these circumstances.

FISCAL PROBLEMS IN DEVELOPING COUNTRIES

The fashionable criticisms of fiscal imbalance in the developing countries are likewise frequently ill-founded. It is not suggested here that justifiable criticisms may not be made of some of the developing countries in this regard, but rather that the criticisms that are made are usually too simplistic and are not supported by convincing analysis.

IMF takes the non-oil developing countries to task for what it calls "the absence of adequate restraint" as reflected in rising budget deficits. The weighted average of fiscal deficits in these countries (excluding China) is said to have risen from 3.25 percent of gross domestic product (GDP) in 1979 to 4 percent in 1981 and is expected to remain at the latter level in 1982.[19]

These figures, however, would require much deeper analysis before one could reach the judgment that they reveal "the absence of adequate restraint." As in the case of the industrial countries, one is bound to ask to what extent the rise in fiscal deficits was due to an increase in items of public expenditure that reflect deliberate expansionary policies as against, say, various forms of payment that are only a passive response to deteriorating business conditions or the effect of soaring interest rates payable on the public debt. Even more important, what happened to government revenue? What proportion of the rise in deficits was due to declining taxable capacity resulting from the collapse of commodity prices in 1982 to their lowest level in real terms since the 1950s? IMF recognizes that such tightening occurred in a number of countries but considers that well over half of the countries in the group were still following expansionary or insufficiently restrictive policies. But this has yet to be demonstrated convincingly on the basis of data adjusted for the effects of the world recession on government receipts and expenditures.

BREAKING INFLATIONARY EXPECTATIONS

We now come to the last of the five assumptions on which current views favoring deflation are based—the assumption that a period of prolonged demand stringency and unemployment will reduce the danger of resumed inflation.

This assumption is based on the belief that people have become adjusted to the idea that prices are going to continue rising for an indefinitely long period ahead and that this "inflationary psychology" prompts them to act in ways that are incompatible with the restoration of price stability. For example, workers demand higher wages as a means of offsetting expected increases in the cost of living and these wage advances, insofar as they exceed the rates of growth of productivity, help to keep the inflation going.

A deflationary policy seeks to deal with wage inflation by confronting workers with the choice between reducing their wage demands and accepting a rise in unemployment. Some successes for this policy are already being claimed, since the threat of unemployment appears to have been a factor in the moderation of wage demands in the United States and certain European countries in 1981–82. One does not have to be a monetarist to accept the proposition that the threat of unemployment is a formidable one. This threat, it is felt, will have to be maintained for a number of years—perhaps indefinitely—if noninflationary growth is to be restored. It is for this reason that conventional wisdom now envisages a protracted period of subnormal business activity and rising unemployment in the industrial countries.

The difficulty with this approach to the problem of inflation is that while it risks severe social and political disruption, sooner or later, in the industrial countries themselves as well as in all countries affected by the associated retrenchment of world production and demand, long-term success for the strategy is not certain. Quite the contrary: the social divisiveness of the policies involved and the demoralization engendered thereby make it more than likely that whenever normal growth is ultimately resumed those who have been forced to accept cuts in real income will seek to recover all the ground lost and more.

Any expectations there may be that a weakening of trade union militancy will create a better climate for noninflationary growth are based on an illusion. Trade union organization developed in the past against much greater opposition and intimidation than prevails today in the industrial countries and it would be unwise to assume that the events of 1981–82 on the wage front portend a willingness of the labor force to surrender past gains indefinitely.

Thus the idea that prolonged unemployment will discipline the labor force is based on surmise and little else. It is at least arguable that it would have exactly the opposite effect of creating, in the end, an explosive situation with incalculable consequences. In any case, the judgment involved is a political one and cannot derive any support, either way, from economic theory or empirical economic analysis.

THE NEED FOR COORDINATED EXPANSION

World recovery will necessitate concerted action by industrial and developing countries to promote an expansion of world production and trade. Governments would need to program levels of public expenditure and revenue consistent with steady and reasonably expeditious progress toward full employment. In most cases this would involve increases in budget deficits over and above those resulting from present levels of unemployment.

If, however, there are cases in which the fiscal thrust of the budget deficit, adjusted for the level of employment, is already substantial, considerable caution may be needed to avoid the intensification of inflationary pressure. Such was certainly not the case in any of the major industrial countries as of mid-1982. Projected budget deficits in the United States were expected, according to some estimates, to generate a fiscal thrust of more than 3 percent from 1982 to 1985, but this was still not sufficient to provide much immediate stimulus to the economy, and investment in fixed capital was showing signs of serious weakness. The predominant explanation given for this phenomenon was the exceptionally high level of real interest rates. But there was reason to doubt whether a reduction in interest rates would suffice to promote a recovery of fixed investment because of current low levels of capacity utilization. Thus in the immediate future additional fiscal stimulus may well be needed even in the United States, though once recovery is soundly established the stimulus may have to be reduced.

Tax reduction is not necessarily the best way of obtaining the degree of stimulus to the economy that is required. Since part of the proceeds of any tax reduction is saved, a larger budget deficit is needed to exert a given rate of stimulation if tax revenues are reduced than if public expenditures are increased. In view of the widespread fear of budget deficits, there is something to be said for holding deficits to the minimum level consistent with recovery.

An additional consideration in favor of raising government expenditure is that in many countries public capital expenditure in the form of new construction and upkeep of roads, ports and harbors, bridges, railways, airports, schools, colleges, libraries, hospitals, sewage works, and many other facilities has been severely cut back as a result of budgetary retrenchment, often over a substantial period of years. It is a fallacy that public and private expenditure are invariably substitutes for one another—the relationship between them is frequently of a complementary rather than of a competitive character.

The very same factors that lead to budget deficits at times of recession will begin to reduce such deficits as economic recovery gathers speed. In other words, increases in incomes will result in higher flows of tax revenue to governments, while reductions in unemployment will be accompanied by corresponding declines in unemployment compensation. The objective should be that budgets are balanced once again at a high level of employment, and any adjustments in public revenue and expenditure policies necessary to this end should be introduced accordingly as soon as the economic uptrend is firmly based.

A second prerequisite for economic expansion is a sharp reduction of interest rates as quickly as possible through a relaxation of monetary restrictions. This is a necessary though not a sufficient condition for a major recovery in fixed investment, which is itself an indispensable element in bringing about a sustained recovery as well as in restoring more normal rates of productivity growth. Most of the slackening of productivity growth of the past several years has probably resulted from the slowdown in the growth of output and will disappear as output itself begins to accelerate. But a great deal of new investment is needed to make good the arrears that have accumulated during a long period of stagnation as well as to carry forward the rapid advances in technology that scientific research has made possible. It is likely that, in addition to stepping up public investment, governments will have to provide strong incentives to stimulate a recovery in private investment on the scale required and to overcome the depressing effect on investment of widespread excess capacity.

As already noted, economic expansion accompanied by declining interest rates is likely to bring about considerable swings in the balances of payments and exchange rates of particular countries unless effective coordination of economic policies is achieved. This is more easily said than done. There have been many occasions during the past thirty years when efforts at economic policy coordination have foundered on the rocks of inconsistent balance-of-payments objectives among the major industrial powers. The most common form of inconsistency is a general desire for export-led growth, without a corresponding willingness to provide larger import markets for the goods exported by other countries. There is, therefore, a continuing need for confrontation of balance-of-payments objectives, and a determination to reach a consistent pattern of such objectives.

There is, of course, no reason why all those industrial countries that so desire should not run surpluses in their balances of payments, provided that they are prepared to finance them on a long-term basis. In fact, in a rational world the industrial countries would do exactly that—they would run large individual and collective surpluses with developing countries as a means of stepping up rates of growth in both groups of countries. This would provide an opportunity for restoring aid programs, multilateral and bilateral. An alternative approach would be to create Special Drawing Rights (SDRS) in the requisite amounts in the hands of the potential deficit countries. In any event, balance-of-payments targets need to be reconciled and made broadly consistent with one another.

Would a resumption of business expansion lead to a rise in prices? The immediate effect would certainly be a marked recovery in commodity prices, which are abnormally low at the present time. Such a recovery in commodity prices is a normal feature of any business upturn and is essential if the benefits of economic recovery are to be equitably distributed among countries. But there is ample reserve capacity for the production of primary commodities and there is no reason why that reserve capacity should not be successfully exploited, given the right kind of economic and financial environment.

Within manufacturing the natural tendency is for unit costs and prices to fall as output rises because of economies of scale, including the effects of distributing fixed overhead costs over a larger output. This natural tendency can, however, be offset, or more than offset, as a result of the wage-bargaining process, depending on the relationship between the agreed rate of wage increases and the rate of growth of productivity.

Consequently, there is a considerable responsibility on the shoulders of the authorities to promote the kind of atmosphere and consensus in which the recovery process will be regarded as a cooperative venture among all members of society and not as a free-for-all in which each social group seeks to maximize its share of the national income. There is a particular danger of this because of the cuts in real income that important sectors of the labor force have had to accept in recent years. It is important that the recovery of lost ground should proceed at a rate consistent with the noninflationary growth of the economy as a whole. This does not necessarily imply that wage earners will not be able to recover their share of total real income, where that share has declined. What is needed, however, is a social consensus on the progression of incomes and income shares.

INTERNATIONAL ASPECTS OF THE RECOVERY PROCESS

Recovery in the major industrial countries would be likely, in itself, to bring some relief at the international level. The resumption of more normal growth, accompanied by a rebuilding of inventories of primary products, would lead to an upturn in world import demand and, as already noted, to a strengthening of commodity prices.

It is not sufficient, however, to rely on the trickle-down effects of rising activity in the industrial countries. There are at least three reasons why a time lag between recovery in the industrial and in the developing countries should be regarded by both groups as unacceptable. The first is that it was the developing countries that suffered most from the stagnation of the past ten years—particularly the least developed and other structurally disadvantaged countries.

The second reason is that a rapid recovery in the developing countries could contribute significantly to the revival of economic activity in the industrial countries. During the mid-1970s the availability of balance-of-payments support through the Euro-currency market made it possible for a number of developing countries to maintain relatively high rates of growth, despite a sharp deterioration in their terms of trade and a recession in the industrial countries. It has been shown that the resulting increase in the import demand of these countries made a significant contribution to employment in the industrial countries at that time.[20]

A third point is that the present state of uncertainty regarding the ability of debtor countries to service their debt should be removed as quickly as possible. In the longer run the recovery of the export earnings of these countries will restore their debt-servicing capabilities, but a more immediate reinforcement of their financial strength is needed.

REBUILDING THE LIQUIDITY POSITION
OF DEVELOPING COUNTRIES

All these considerations argue in favor of prompt action to strengthen the international liquidity positions of developing countries. By the end of 1981 reserve levels of some thirty developing countries had been reduced to the equivalent of one month's imports or less. The most efficient and expeditious means of dealing with this situation would be to resume the creation of SDRs, which was discontinued as a result of opposition by the industrial countries to even a token distribution.

The grounds for this opposition are that under present conditions it is felt that SDR creation, even at a modest level, would be inflationary. This concern appears to overlook the fact that national reserve currency creation has not been subject to discipline for many years, and led to a liquidity explosion during the 1970s, as a result of which world reserves, excluding monetary gold, rose from SDR 56 billion at the end of 1970 to SDR 324 billion at the end of 1980. Since, under the Articles of Agreement of IMF, members have undertaken to make the SDR the principal international reserve asset, it would clearly be improper to regard the SDR creation as simply residual and subject to the amount of national reserve currency creation deemed appropriate by the issuers. This would be tantamount to placing the decision whether to create SDRs in the hands of the reserve currency countries instead of in the hands of the IMF membership as a whole, as provided in the Articles of Agreement.

Early in 1981 the IMF management presented a series of options for SDR allocations during the five-year period beginning in January 1982. Options for the annual rate of allocations ranged from SDR 4 billion to SDR 19 billion. All of those rates of SDR creation were considered to be noninflationary. It was pointed out, for example, that on the basis of past experience regarding the use of SDRs by non-oil developing countries (the countries most likely to spend their SDR allocations) a total distribution of SDR 10 billion would lead to an increase in the imports of those countries by approximately one-hundredth of 1 percent of the prospective 1982 GNP of IMF member countries.

Since the above calculations were made, world demand has slackened considerably. If a distribution of SDR 19 billion could be considered noninflationary in 1981, a corresponding figure for 1983 might well be of the order of SDR 25 billion to SDR 30 billion, or even higher.

If SDRs were allocated according to the usual IMF rules, most of the allocation—the more than two-thirds that goes to the industrial countries—would contribute little or nothing to world liquidity. This is because the reserves of industrial countries are "demand-determined": they can be raised to whatever level the countries desire by borrowing. Consequently, the addition of SDRs to the reserves of industrial countries would probably not have much net effect on their reserve levels.

There is, therefore, a good deal to be said for confining the new allocations of SDRs to the developing countries, most of which are not in a position to add to their reserves by borrowing, especially at current interest rates. Since it would take time to effect the amendments to the IMF's Articles of Agreement required to modify the present rules of distribution, the objective of a limited distribution could be attained if the industrial countries would agree to forgo the allocations to which they are entitled. This procedure would make it possible to determine the maximum amount that could be considered noninflationary for the world economy as a whole and to allocate that amount to developing countries alone. It could be argued that distribution to developing countries alone would increase the potentially inflationary impact of any given volume of SDR creation, owing to the greater propensity of developing countries to draw on their reserves. It should, however, be borne in mind that SDR use now involves interest costs at market-related rates.

RESTORING THE FLOW OF CAPITAL

Apart from substantial SDR creation to rebuild the liquidity positions of developing countries, it is vital that steps be taken to restore the flow of capital, both concessional and nonconcessional, to developing countries. At a time when the international economic situation calls for an expansion of such flows, the slowing down of net lending from both public and private sources is aggravating the difficulties of borrowing countries and is forcing upon them an unnecessarily severe degree of retrenchment. This in turn reacts upon the creditor countries in the form of a reduction in demand for their exports, thereby compounding the effects of the recession.

Recent sharp declines in net new lending by the commercial banks has not been accompanied by any growth in IMF lending. On the contrary, in the first eight months of 1982 gross commitments by IMF declined steeply from the level reached in the corresponding period of 1981, despite the fact that countercyclical considerations clearly pointed to the need for a major increase in such commitments. Thus, while it was a deliberate policy of the Fund in 1974–75 to encourage, through the low conditional oil facilities, "policies that would sustain appropriate levels of economic activity and employment, while minimizing inflation," in 1982 there is no such objective, and attention is concentrated instead upon adjustment which, in the circumstances, is generally construed to mean curbing the level of demand and hence of economic activity.[21]

It is important to provide IMF with the resources it needs to regain its position as the world's major source of balance-of-payments support. It is also necessary to restore the balance between high conditional and low conditional resources of the Fund which has been completely distorted by the failure to increase IMF quotas in line with world trade. The method of expanding access to the Fund employed in recent years has had the effect of forcing member countries into upper credit tranche conditionality much sooner than would have occurred if quotas had been adjusted appropriately.[22] The quota resources of the IMF should be at least doubled. Even a doubling would not go very far toward restoring the ratio of Fund quotas to world imports to the level at which it had stood in the early 1960s, namely, about 12 percent (as against 4 percent in 1980).

At the same time the resources of the World Bank, concessional and nonconcessional, will need to be considerably augmented. Moreover, the proportion of such enlarged resources available for program lending should also be increased substantially so as to yield quick-disbursing funds that can exert much greater upward leverage at a time of recession than project funds, since essential imports of raw materials and other current inputs have a higher priority under such conditions than the import requirements of new projects.

In order to ensure that the total net flow of capital to developing countries, multilateral and bilateral, public and private, reaches the order of magnitude required for a vigorous recovery program, it would be desirable to initiate intergovernmental consultations on the basis of a realistic confrontation of data on projected resources and needs. If the separate decisions of a multitude of agencies are to add up to a total effort commensurate with the requirements of the situation, some such effort at coordination seems called for.

CONCLUDING REMARKS

Clearly the foregoing discussion has not set out all the requirements of a recovery program, either at the national or at the international level. Great efforts will be needed at both levels to restore the tattered fabric of intra-national as well as international cooperation. The 1970s and early 1980s have been a period of growing tensions within and between countries. Not since the Second World War has the world been so divided against itself, with so little sense of common purpose. To be successful, a world recovery program will need to begin with the rebuilding of that sense of common purpose—the sense of collective interest in the greatest possible measure of national and world development. This is not the place to restate all the elements of that collective interest, but they are bound, nonetheless, to be an indispensable feature of any worthwhile cooperative effort.

3
Development Objectives

Basic Needs or Comprehensive Development?

Strong political, intellectual, and moral forces have been mobilized in favor of a basic needs strategy of development, and the strategy received powerful endorsement by the World Employment Conference and by the General Assembly of the United Nations in 1976. The present essay seeks to question not at all the goal of more equitable development policies but the general framework within which such policies have been presented for the consideration of the international community. The essay also indicates some of the pitfalls for international development agencies in limiting themselves to a particular development strategy, including the basic needs strategy, to guide their operations.

One of the difficulties in getting to grips with this elusive subject is that the idea of a basic needs strategy means different things to different people. For some it is a basically humanitarian issue, a categorical imperative that transcends all other considerations. To others it represents a fundamental reordering of development priorities, often assigning a leading role to rural development. Some members of the latter school completely reject the development path traced by the industrially advanced countries of today, while others take a less radical position. A curious feature of the strategy is that it finds supporters in all parts of the political spectrum from left to right, and in all schools of economic thought from dirigiste to laissez-faire and from neoclassical to neo-Marxist. In the discussion that follows, mention will be made of several of the above schools, and it is inevitable that points made in relation to one school may be less applicable, or even inapplicable, to another.

Originally published in *World Development* 7, no. 3 (Oxford: Pergamon, 1979): 291–308. The author gratefully acknowledges valuable comments received from Shahen Abrahamian, Michael Dell, Gerald Helleiner, Paul Streeten, and Laurence Whitehead. He has benefited particularly from reading certain unpublished papers by Paul Streeten. The author alone is responsible for any errors or shortcomings that remain.

THE NATURE OF A BASIC NEEDS STRATEGY

Perhaps the best known exposition of a basic needs strategy is that contained in a report submitted in March 1976 by the Director-General of the International Labor Organization (ILO) to the World Employment Conference. It was proposed to the conference in that report that "development planning should include, as an explicit goal, the satisfaction of an absolute level of basic needs."[1] In this context, basic needs are considered to include two elements: "First, they include certain minimum requirements of a family for private consumption: adequate food, shelter and clothing, as well as certain household equipment and furniture. Second, they include essential services provided by and for the community at large, such as safe drinking water, sanitation, public transport and health, educational and cultural facilities."[2]

These goals should be achieved, in the view of the ILO staff, within one generation or by the year 2000. To this end there was a need for measures aimed at changing the pattern of growth and use of productive resources by the various income groups—including, in a number of cases, "an initial redistribution of resources, in particular land."[3] Additional elements would be the provision of adequate employment opportunities for the unemployed and underemployed, the introduction of the "right kind of technology" and "quite high levels of investment, without which there would be neither growth nor meaningful redistribution."[4]

The literature on poverty-oriented development contrasts these approaches with those of the past. It is suggested that past strategies sought maximum growth at any price and that questions of social equity were ignored. These strategies were, it is believed, based on the assumption that the benefits of high rates of growth would somehow trickle down to the low-income groups. It was also assumed, according to the critics, that GNP was a satisfactory measure of development and that if real GNP grew at an adequate rate, this in itself implied that development was proceeding satisfactorily. All this, said the critics, was quite wrong. The growth process had often bypassed the poorer members of the community: the latter would benefit from growth only if distributional goals were made a deliberate and explicit element of policy. It was said to be necessary to dethrone "King GNP" and enthrone "basic needs" in its place.

There are certainly countries where it was considered essential to establish the growth process on a secure and self-sustaining basis before proceeding to any redistribution of income. In Brazil, for example, the argument was advanced that the release of resources for investment in growth required the enforcement of strict austerity, and that any effort to improve present welfare through a premature redistribution of income, or through wage "prodigality," was incompatible with the maximization of future welfare.[5]

THE INTERNATIONAL DEVELOPMENT STRATEGY

But it would be a mistake to suppose that growth-at-any-price, or the trickle-down approach, were either explicit or implicit in the United Nations International Development Strategy.

The Strategy adopted by the General Assembly for the 1970s has the following major statement in the preamble: "Governments designate the 1970s as the Second United Nations Development Decade and pledge themselves, individually and collectively, to pursue policies designed to create a more just and rational world economic and social order in which equality of opportunities should be as much a prerogative of nations as of individuals within a nation."[6]

In defining the content of the above declaration so far as "individuals within a nation" are concerned, the Strategy places in the forefront of national objectives, along with the promotion of higher growth rates, a more equitable distribution of income and wealth. Moreover, "qualitative and structural changes in the society must go hand in hand with rapid economic growth, and existing disparities—regional, sectoral and social—should be substantially reduced." To this end, the Strategy calls for measures to reduce unemployment and underemployment; to improve the quality of education; to raise general levels of health and sanitation; to improve levels of nutrition, placing special emphasis on the needs of vulnerable groups; to expand and improve housing facilities especially for low-income groups; to foster the well-being of children and participation of youth; and to integrate women fully in the development effort.[7]

The General Assembly Strategy was drafted with the assistance of the Committee for Development Planning at sessions held in 1969–70, under the chairmanship of Professor Jan Tinbergen. The report of the sixth session stated that "It cannot be over-emphasized that what development implies for the developing countries is not simple increase in productive capacity but major transformation in their social and economic structures."[8] It was therefore necessary to eliminate the dualism between the traditional economy and the modern sector. A separate section of the report was devoted to methods of improving the distribution of income and providing for the needs of the people in the fields of employment, education, health, and housing. "The glaring inequalities in the distribution of income and wealth prevailing in the developing countries will have to be eliminated. . . . It is a fallacy that more rapid growth and reduction of inequalities of income and wealth are necessarily competing elements."[9] National measures to this end should include "activation of broad masses of the population and assurances of satisfaction of their primary needs and aspirations."[10] As for "King GNP," Tinbergen and his colleagues had this to say: "Although the rate of growth of gross product per head is by no means an adequate indicator of economic and social progress—since it does not reflect such major conditions of development as income redistribution or structural change—it is the one aggregate indicator which comes closest to providing some quantitative impression of the underlying change."[11]

THE REAL ISSUES

The real issues between the basic needs strategists and those who favor comprehensive development policies lie not in the goal of social equity, which is common ground between them, but in the means for achieving that goal.

There are three main issues. The first relates to the need for higher or accelerated rates of growth: some of the basic needs strategists agree that such objectives are important, but others seem not to do so. A second issue, closely related to the first, is whether the preempting of resources for the attainment of a minimum absolute level of consumption in the nearest possible future would entail a lower rate of growth than would otherwise be possible as well as socially acceptable, and hence a lower level of provision for the basic needs of future generations. Are there not societies that, if they could control their own destinies, would certainly seek the reduction of inequality, but would also prefer to tighten their belts a little more now in the interests of more adequate provision for the future?

The third issue arises out of the view held by many of the basic needs strategists, as noted earlier, that the road to development adopted by the present high-income countries is inappropriate for the developing countries of today; and that the current maldistribution of income is due largely to the development of modern industrial sectors, employing capital-intensive techniques, accompanied by neglect of rural areas. Some of those who take this view play down large-scale industrial growth and focus their attention on rural development. Others recognize the need for rapid industrial advance, but consider that its direction needs to be changed in a labor-intensive direction.

Basic Needs: The Meaning of Absolutism

Before embarking on an examination of these issues, it is important to note some of the difficulties in the use of "basic needs" as an operational tool for planning. There are difficulties of concept, of measurement, and of implementation.

As to the concept, the Director-General of ILO suggested to the World Employment Conference that there are certain minimum levels of personal consumption and access to social services that should be adopted "as minimum targets for raising the living standards of the very poor for the entire international community." [12] It is, however, difficult to envisage how such universally applicable targets would be defined. Differences in climate alone result in different minimum requirements for calorie intake and clothing. Would not additional differences arise owing, if not to intercountry differences in levels of income, then at least to differences in social and cultural traditions and circumstances? In fact the World Employment Conference rejected the idea of a worldwide standard and invited each country to set its own standard.

But how is such a minimum standard to be established, even for a single country? No doubt the idea of a minimum standard of nutrition is acceptable—although even here one runs into difficulty, as we shall see. But as soon as one includes such items as shelter and clothing, and even household equipment and furniture, as the World Employment Conference did, the line to be drawn between basic and nonbasic needs is bound to be arbitrary. If "absolute" norms are set for such nonfood items, does this mean that attainment of the norms must constitute a prior claim on resources, to be preempted for that purpose regardless of all other needs, however pressing?

Equally arbitrary is the setting of absolute standards for the essential services that appear on the ILO list of basic needs. In the case of educational and cultural facilities, for example, it would be odd to define standards in the abstract without taking into account the alternative goods or services that would have to be foregone—even by the poorest 20 percent of the population—in order to attain such standards.

Even if certain norms for basic needs had been generally agreed upon in a particular country, the question would still arise as to how rapidly the minimum standards should be achieved. Should all resources be allocated for the quickest possible achievement of the chosen goals, or would it be permissible to use resources for other valid development programs? As regards nutrition, for example, should all food exports be discontinued irrespective of the degree of essentiality of the counterpart imports? And should the entire proceeds of nonfood exports be used for the purchase of food—up to the point at which every man, woman, and child was adequately fed? If not, what degree of provision for the food needs of the poor could be regarded as "adequate" in the immediate future, and how soon should the norms be attained?

There are other conceptual difficulties in interpreting the "absolutism" of basic needs. Does it mean that no one should be allowed a level of consumption in excess of basic needs until every member of the community has reached that level? If not, what degree of "excess consumption" should be permitted, and where does one draw the line between tolerable and intolerable degrees of inequality? If "excess consumption" can be allowed, is it also acceptable to provide for "excess investment" in the sense of investment not required to meet basic needs? If so, how much excess investment is tolerable? And in what respect is a basic needs strategy that permits excess consumption and investment to be preferred over a comprehensive strategy that seeks to deploy available resources for the attainment of all socially acceptable ends, including basic needs?

A further difficulty arises for the many countries at the low end of the resource and income scale. How are they to determine the particular bundle or combination of basic needs, the satisfaction of which should constitute their overall minimum target? What are the relative priorities to be assigned to such items as public health and sanitation, potable water supplies, public transport, housing, and household equipment? What should be the trade-offs between these items at the margin, and what resources should be invested in each?

Answers to these extremely difficult questions of judgment are not made any easier by the assertion that absolute standards must prevail. The use of the term "absolute" has no meaning without a time dimension and once it is acknowledged that the fixing of the time dimension involves decisions on overall development requirements and not merely on basic needs, it will be apparent that a basic needs strategy must form part of a comprehensive development strategy. As such, basic needs are no longer absolute but relative, and there is no valid difference between the Development Decade strategies and basic needs strategies except possibly in emphasis.

Setting the Standards

Problems of measurement of basic needs, though not fundamental, are far from trivial for what is intended as an operational approach to planning. One might think that at least in the case of food consumption, quantitative targets would be readily available. Surely there is some minimum intake of food below which people can be said to be undernourished, and it should clearly be a primary and overriding objective to ensure that even the poorest of the poor do not suffer from malnutrition.

On closer examination, however, it appears that the setting of absolute standards even for food consumption raises unexpected problems. According to a report published in February 1977 by the staff of the Select Committee on Nutrition and Human Needs of the U.S. Senate, "there is only limited knowledge of human requirements for most nutrients." An appendix to the report prepared by the Nutrition Institute of the U.S. Department of Agriculture describes the state of knowledge even on total human energy requirements as "fragmentary" except for school-age and adolescent children and for young adults.[13] If the gaps in knowledge of nutritional requirements are so great in the United States, the state of knowledge on this matter in developing countries may be even more inadequate, since requirements in one country are not applicable elsewhere because of differences in climate and other factors.

It turns out, moreover, that the record of institutions responsible for reaching conclusions in this field has been one of continual, and generally downward, revision. The changes in assessments made have, in fact, been surprisingly large, suggesting that the scientific basis of the assessments is still quite shaky. As Thomas T. Poleman has pointed out, "The energy allowances for the U.S. 'reference man'—in his twenties, moderately active, weighing 70 kg—now stand at 2,700 calories daily, 500 calories less than the 1953 recommendation"—in other words a 15 percent reduction in the twenty-one years to 1974. Poleman goes on to point out that in 1974 the FAO estimated that perhaps 25 percent of the population of the developing world (excluding China) were inadequately fed, while the corresponding estimate in 1963 had been at least 60 percent. Poleman shows further that "depending on your assumptions you can prove beyond a statistical doubt that 43 percent of Ceylonese suffer protein-calorie malnutrition or none do."[14]

This does not, of course, mean that the problem of malnutrition is not extremely grave and preoccupying. What the foregoing discussion does show, however, is that the scientific, statistical, and analytical foundations for a basic needs strategy are extraordinarily weak even in the sector where they should presumably be strongest—namely, the food consumption sector–while in other sectors they are nonexistent. Let us imagine that the basic needs strategists had won their battle against the GNP-at-any-cost school (sic) in 1963 instead of thirteen years later in 1976. The planners in developing countries in 1963 would have been told to preempt the resources required to eliminate malnutrition among 60 percent of the population, whereas the true dimensions of malnutrition must have been very much smaller.[15] No doubt this would have been beneficial to the extent that malnutrition, where it existed, might have been reduced more quickly, and that elsewhere food consumption might have advanced beyond minimum levels. But the more important point in the present context is that choices would have been made and strategies devised on the basis of data that were quite wrong, and wrong by a very large margin.

Implementing a Basic Needs Strategy

The problem of ensuring that basic needs are met even among the poorest members of the community is complex, especially since the requisite systems and channels of distribution would have to be provided or created. What would the respective roles of governments and private sector be? Distribution of foodstuffs might be undertaken directly by governmental entities, and provision for educational, health, and housing requirements might also be a governmental responsibility. But in most if not all countries governments are not likely to be involved in the distribution of other essential goods and services such as household furniture and equipment and clothing. To this extent income supplements or subsidies might have to be provided to those lacking employment and to those for whom employment does not provide sufficient money income. Some countries might prefer to use income supplements or subsidies to cover food needs also.

Of course, the fact that a minimum ration of goods and services is distributed, or that income supplements or subsidies are provided, does not mean that the recipients will necessarily enjoy the corresponding benefits. If they are extremely poor and, as is often the case in such circumstances, heavily indebted, they may sell part or all of the income in kind in order to service their debts and use money income for the same purpose.

Thus the basic needs of the poorest will be satisfied only if broader conditions are conducive to that end, and this in turn implies fundamental social and structural change, and a rate of growth of the economy sufficient to absorb the unemployed and underemployed progressively into remunerative employment. In other words, it emerges here also that the satisfaction of basic needs can be secured only in the context of a broader process of comprehensive change and development, and that efforts to give an "absolute" priority to basic needs are unlikely to be productive.

Growth and Development

Thus far, reasons have been given for doubting whether the satisfaction of basic needs for the consumption of particular goods and services can be regarded as an overriding priority, even in a society with egalitarian development objectives. We may now revert to the three issues raised earlier concerning a basic needs strategy, beginning with the problem of growth and development.

It is often difficult to determine what exactly the stand of the basic needs strategists on this problem is. They deplore "growth-at-any-price," as any sensible person would, but their own overall prescription for growth is usually obscure. This obscurity is a matter of concern in itself since no strategy for overcoming poverty is worthy of the name if it does not indicate the means whereby the requisite rate of growth is to be attained. It is striking that the ILO report's summary of the six "main ingredients of the proposed new approach to development" does not even mention either growth or industry.[16]

The Director-General's introduction to the report suggests that measures to implement a basic needs strategy "need not imply a slower growth of output. They place greater emphasis on patterns of growth leading to a more equitable distribution of the gains from growth, and they may well lead to increasing growth rates as well."[17] The report itself, on the other hand, argues that "a rapid rate of economic growth is an essential part of a basic needs strategy."[18] On the basis of certain econometric exercises, the conclusion is reached that "All these calculations, tentative though they be, strongly suggest that in many countries minimum incomes and standards of living for the poor cannot be achieved, even by the year 2000, without some acceleration of present average rates of growth, accompanied by a number of measures aiming at changing the pattern of growth and use of productive resources by the various income groups."[19] The ILO report is, moreover, "forced reluctantly to conclude, from this model, that the growth target of the Second Development Decade (6 percent per annum) is not consistent with the proposed objective of fulfilling basic needs within one generation."[20]

The "reluctance" of the ILO in reaching the above conclusion is noteworthy. The context suggests that it would have been preferable if basic needs could have been satisfied through income redistribution, but in the light of available evidence the ILO judges that "the extent of redistribution that would be required would be such that social changes of this magnitude are unlikely to occur." The alternative, therefore, is to step up growth rates so that basic needs can be satisfied out of the additional resources thereby generated.

But even if basic needs *could* be met entirely through redistribution of income, would not higher growth rates be desirable as well, so as to shorten the transition period and attain the targets by, say, 1990 instead of by 2000? Can it be that the Development Decade strategists knew what they were about in pressing for higher growth rates, even from the standpoint of effecting the redistribution of income required under the preamble and paragraph 18 of the Strategy? They pointed to the widespread experience that at low rates of growth, a large part of the increasing labor force fails to find productive employment, and obstacles to economic and social mobility persist. Thus the absorption of underemployed labor, the redistribution of income, and the acceleration of growth are interdependent goals.

Already in 1970, when the Second Development Decade had barely begun, Raúl Prebisch was pointing out that the targets of the Decade were much too low to make any impact on the growing problem of unemployment and underemployment or on the maldistribution of income. Prebisch considered in the case of Latin America that a growth rate of 8 percent would need to be attained by the end of the 1970s if the region was to proceed on a viable development path and if the benefits of development were to be widely shared.[21]

The Choice Between Present and Future Consumption

Reference has already been made to the problems involved in determining the rate at which any particular level of basic consumption should be approached.

Of course, the lower the level of consumption of basic essentials in any country, the more difficult will it be for the people to release resources for investment. But if the basic needs strategy were to be pressed to the point at which the attainment of minimum levels of nutrition, health, sanitation, and education—to say nothing of household equipment and furniture—had to take priority over all other goals, some of the poorest societies might be condemned to an indefinite period of stagnation at the subsistence level, since virtually all resources might have to be preempted for consumption, little or nothing being set aside for investment in future growth and development. Even at the lowest levels of per capita income, countries in which social morale and sense of unity and purpose are high will deliberately forego even essential items of consumption, including food, if they feel that by so doing they can improve the prospects for their children. No international agency has a right to tell such countries that there are absolute and overriding basic needs to which they must assign priority. These countries are entitled to define their development needs in terms relevant to their own goals and their own time horizons.

Does the above imply acceptance of the view, cited earlier, that inequality of income distribution must be accepted in the short and medium run as part of the price to be paid for a high rate of growth and effective redistribution of income in the long run? Not at all. On the contrary, the greater the degree of austerity required in the interests of setting aside resources for the future, the more important is it to ensure that the burden is divided fairly, and in some reasonable relationship to the capacity to bear it. The argument that inequality is indispensable in achieving an adequate level of savings because the rich save a larger proportion of their incomes than the poor is unconvincing. Societies with a strong sense of common purpose are quite capable of imposing the most stringent limits on consumption, on an egalitarian basis, as has been shown in time of war. Inequality, on the other hand, can be highly divisive and whatever may be gained in terms of savings ratios may be more than lost through lower labor productivity and even social strife. In many developing countries, moreover, the richer classes scarcely offer a model of thrift, but tend rather to squander large proportions of their incomes on luxury consumption.

Thus the fact that a country prefers to postpone the attainment of basic needs targets in order to permit a more rapid rate of growth and structural transformation does not in the least imply that it thereby gives up ideas of social equity.

Perhaps the basic needs doctrine can be adjusted to take all these broader considerations into account, so that, as suggested earlier, the goals are defined in the wider context of comprehensive development strategies for the society as a whole. Whether we speak of the equitable distribution of the benefits of total growth (as per the Development Decade resolution) or of the attainment of adequate levels of consumption in the context of overall development needs (as per the basic needs strategy suitably amended) is a matter of small moment. It is to be hoped that a reconciliation of approaches and strategies can be achieved in some such terms as these.

The Pattern of Development

The third and most complex of the issues raised by the basic needs school is that of the pattern of development. Is the inequitable distribution of the benefits from growth in many countries due to their having followed the example set by the industrially advanced countries, concentrating on the development of a modern sector, to the detriment of rural areas, where the majority of the population is to be found?

According to the Twenty-Fourth Pugwash Symposium, "a development strategy imitative of highly industrialized countries does not appear to be possible, necessary or even desirable for the majority of the developing countries."[22] According to the report "it is unlikely to be possible because the quantum of natural resources—both renewable and non-renewable—as well as of the resources of capital, technology and markets to which the developing world would need to have access in order to traverse successfully such an imitative road, is infinitely greater than the prevailing international political and economic order, dominated as it is by the demands (not needs) of the highly industrialized countries, will make available."[23] It is not quite clear what is meant by the words "will make available" but what the above passage seems to be saying is that, in the first place, the natural resources of the world are insufficient to make it possible for developing countries to consume the same volume of material goods per capita as is presently consumed in the industrial countries. The insufficiency may be due simply to such factors as the exhaustion of available supplies of minerals, or perhaps the wording of the statement is to be understood as implying that those in control of the limited supplies available will not release them to meet the needs of the poor countries. Either way the thesis would appear to come close to saying that the developing countries had better content themselves with the natural resources, capital, and technology that are left over after the demands of the industrial countries have been satisfied.

If the foregoing interpretation is correct, the Pugwash Symposium was in effect giving a neo-Malthusian twist to the basic needs strategy. For the implication appears to be that in order to avoid the pressure of population on resources, the developing countries should adopt a development strategy that satisfies basic needs without seeking the high levels of material consumption characteristic of the industrial world. It is not possible to discuss the neo-Malthusian theories in the present context, but they have been thoroughly refuted—most recently by Professor Wassily Leontief's study for the United Nations entitled *The Future of the World Economy*.[24] Leontief's study shows that resource constraints would not prevent the income gap between developed and developing countries from being reduced by half by the end of the present century and eliminated by the middle of the twenty-first century.

A low level of material consumption per capita may or may not be desirable for other reasons, but the case for it certainly cannot be based on a presumption that supplies of food or natural resources would be inadequate. It is even less credible that shortages of capital or technology would impose such limitations on consumption.

Even if a development strategy imitative of the industrial countries were possible, it would not, according to the Pugwash group, be desirable. This is

because of the acute concern in the highly industrialized countries themselves that the kind of natural resource, energy and technology-intensive development strategy which they had adopted is not leading to genuine development—it is leading instead to growing personal and group alienation, to disruption of the human and social environment in a variety of ways ranging from organized crime to acute pollution and urban claustrophobia, and more recently, monetary and economic crises.[25]

It is, of course, quite true that the industrial societies of today are plagued by enormous problems and tensions, but whether this is the result of modern technology is something that has to be demonstrated, not taken for granted. It is at least arguable that any effort to put the clock back by suppressing modern technology would compound the problems and tensions of the world instead of easing them. There are remedies for pollution and crime that do not involve throwing the baby out with the bath water.

Rural and urban development. It is not necessary to accept the back-to-nature implications of the Pugwash reasoning in order to agree with the basic needs strategists in their emphasis on the importance of rural development. Much of the hard-core poverty in developing countries is concentrated among the peasantry in rural areas and greater attention to their needs is imperative, not only in itself but as a means of raising their productivity. Moreover, the inadequate absorption of labor by urban industry makes it necessary to create additional employment opportunities in rural areas, not only on the land but in rural industry, rural public works, and rural services.

Thus far no controversy arises. Sometimes, however, the basic needs strategists seem to be suggesting that rural development can supply a wholly new approach that can replace the traditional strategy of industrialization. While urban industry led the development process in the past, the leading sector of the future will, it seems, be the rural sector, a viable and comprehensive economy in its own right.

Thus Ponna Wignaraja writes of "the village becoming the focal point of development." It is there that the creative energies of the people can best be mobilized to bring about "a social transformation of enormous magnitude," indispensable in satisfying their needs. "The capital fetishism of the past must give way to the fullest utilization of labor power and creativity" as well as of local resources and appropriate technology.[26]

But neither Wignaraja nor other writers in this field have indicated how exactly the village is to lead the development process, and, in particular, what is to happen to the agricultural workers released by rising labor productivity on the land.

The problem is a formidable one. In the least developed countries it takes as much as 80 to 90 percent of the economically active population, or even more, to supply the barest food subsistence requirements of the community. On the other hand, at the levels of agricultural productivity obtaining in the United States, the food needs of the entire population can be supplied by approximately 3 percent of the work force. Long-term development planning must therefore provide for the ultimate absorption of at least 80 percent of the working population of the lowest-income countries into nonagricultural employment. Does the new approach to development imply that the rural sector of the future will generate alternative employment for all or most of the people released from agriculture? In a world rushing headlong toward urban chaos, it is easy to see the attraction of such an idea and the scope for studies of its feasibility. But it would be a mistake to act as if the feasibility of such an approach, in political, economic, and social terms, had already been demonstrated.

In China, rural industry presently occupies approximately 3 percent of the working population, while another 2 percent are engaged in a network of extension services covering agriculture, public health, and industry. Rural industry is certainly not regarded as an alternative to medium- and large-scale enterprises, but only as a complementary element in the industrialization process.[27] Thus if rural development were to provide the leading edge of the development strategy of the future, it would have to be conceived on a scale far beyond anything currently contemplated in China.

There are, of course, powerful reasons for the concentration of industries and associated services in urban centers that go well beyond the economies of large-scale operations. As Professor Kaldor has pointed out, the advantages of geographic concentration lie in the opportunities for greater specialization between enterprises and the consequent subdivision of industrial processes, in the availability of labor with the whole range of specialized skills, in the accessibility of engineering and marketing know-how, and so forth.[28]

Unless something occurred to remove or offset the advantages of geographic concentration, it seems doubtful whether the rural sector would, in the foreseeable future, be capable of taking over from urban industry the leadership of the development process. The fact that most of the population is to be found in the countryside does not mean today—any more than it meant in eighteenth-century Britain or nineteenth-century Germany and the United States—that the primary stimulus to development will come from the rural sector. This is not to say that the urban concentrations of the past and present provide a satisfactory model for the future. An immense effort of imaginative planning will be required to overcome the defects of contemporary urban society. But there is no evidence that there will be any less need in the next twenty years than there has been since the Industrial Revolution for the concentration of interdependent manufacturing and service facilities in towns, although it may prove desirable to place limits on the growth of any single urban center.[29]

Great as is the preoccupation of the basic needs strategists with rural development, one of the key issues in this regard is often overlooked. Most of the concern is, quite rightly, addressed to improving the economic prospects of the small family farm through a variety of convergent measures. The fruits of rising productivity on the small farm are, however, likely to be consumed by the occupants themselves, so that relatively little contribution may be made to the marketable surplus of production over consumption. There is abundant evidence that the growth of employment-generating activities outside agriculture has been constrained far more by the size of the food surplus available for sale to the nonagricultural sector than by any other single factor. On the one hand, efforts to expand nonagricultural employment faster than the marketable surplus of food have foundered on the inflationary spiral that resulted. On the other hand, the size of the agricultural surplus, which determines the purchasing power of the farm sector for industrial products, has helped to limit the growth of industrial employment. Although no program for rural development can therefore be complete without a prescription for increasing the marketable supply of food, an adequate treatment of the subject can rarely be found.[30]

Some members of the basic needs school show a certain reticence about structural change in the rural sector. Respects are paid to the need for agrarian reform but, as the ILO report puts it, "agrarian reform is practicable only if political forces with more strength than those of the landlords can be mobilized."[31] An alternative view would be that the entire fabric of rural development programs that feature so prominently in the basic needs strategy would be of doubtful value in a considerable number of countries in the absence of land reform.

The role of industry and the modern sector. Among those who think about these matters in the industrial countries it has become distinctly unfashionable—or worse—to hold the view that industrial transformation is the key to the development of low-income countries.[32] Yet there is nothing very new or shocking about the idea, which still commands general support in the developing world. It is over 200 years since Adam Smith pointed to the increasing returns generated by manufacturing activities and explained them in terms of the division of labor, or specialization, which itself depended on the extent of the market.

Paul Streeten has shown that "To rise above poverty, industrialization is necessary, for industrialization means the application of power to production and transport. Output and consumption per head can rise towards the desired modern levels only with the help of mechanical aids. In this sense, development, including rural development, *is* industrialization."[33] And he goes on to point out that there is no evidence of an inevitable conflict between high rates of industrial growth and the achievement of other development objectives such as rural development and the equitable distribution of income; if anything, as he says, there is evidence to the contrary. In many, though not in all cases, the achievement of social objectives has been consistent with high rates of industrial growth and, indeed, has depended on them.

Despite the disappointing rate of absorption of labor by industry in developing countries in recent years, there cannot be any doubt that faster growth means a more rapid rate of increase in employment. Employment does not rise as quickly as industrial output because of increases in productivity, which are due to economies of scale, technological progress, and the process of "learning by doing." However, analysis of rates of growth of output, employment, and productivity by Professors Verdoorn, Kaldor, and others has led to the conclusion that each percentage addition to the growth of industrial output requires, in general orders of magnitude, a 0.5 percent increase in man-hours of employment and a 0.5 percent increase in productivity.[34]

Basic needs strategists are as reticent about the role of the modern sector in poverty-oriented development as they are about the growth requirements of the economy in general. It is, however, usually left to be inferred that since modern industry has not been able to absorb as much of the labor force as had been hoped or expected, it has little or no role to play in a basic needs strategy and that a fundamental shift toward a labor-intensive pattern of industry is indispensable for the future. Such a shift would, it is thought, be facilitated if a concept of the international division of labor were adopted whereby industrially advanced countries specialized in capital-intensive and developing countries in labor-intensive industries, and exchanged their output to mutual advantage.

The comments of Charles Paolillo, staff consultant to the U.S. House of Representatives Committee on International Relations, who attended the World Employment Conference, are of particular interest in this context. He suggests, "many countries may well want to take steps toward a basic needs strategy while at the same time expanding the modern sector, increasing the use of advanced technology, and strengthening the heavy industrial base." He goes on to say that their reasons for acting in this way "may include politics, prestige, psychology, security and self-reliance."[35]

Paolillo appears to be implying that "expanding the modern sector" would not normally be regarded as part of a basic needs strategy. Indeed, such an idea would have to be justified, in his view, on one or more of several grounds among which he places politics and prestige in the forefront, and none of which includes rational economic calculation (except perhaps to the extent that this is involved in self-reliance). In his view, then, modern industrial installations in developing countries can be explained only in noneconomic terms.

The labor-intensive strategy. Yet there are strong reasons for doubting whether the pattern of industrial specialization in developing countries can be determined even in the short run by the simple criterion of the amount of labor employed per unit of capital. It is often taken for granted that labor-intensive techniques are capital saving, but in many instances they certainly are not. In fact the capital cost of labor-intensive techniques is often quite high. For example, the ILO Employment Mission to Colombia was informed that the capital-output ratio in the traditional sector of Colombian industry averaged about twice as high as in the modern sector. Some insight into possible reasons for this kind of unexpected result is provided by studies of cotton textile production in India. These have shown that cottage industry employs substantially more capital per unit of output than factory production, principally because the much longer time period required for manual operations involves the tying up of far greater amounts of working capital per unit of output.

Thus capital-intensive techniques are not necessarily associated with higher capital costs per unit of output than labor-intensive techniques: on the contrary, there is reason to believe that over a wide range of industry capital-output ratios are actually lower for capital-intensive than for labor-intensive techniques.

In general, labor-intensive techniques are clearly advantageous to developing countries only if they permit the same volume of output to be produced at no greater capital cost. The available evidence suggests that in many core industrial processes techniques requiring a large volume of investment per worker generate a far higher level of output, as well as of output per worker, while capital outlays per unit of output are no greater than for less capital-intensive techniques.

The principal qualification to be made in respect of this conclusion is that in some cases the choice of a capital-intensive technique may be precluded by the fact that the domestic market is too small to permit the advantages of the technique to be realized. At the same time there may be difficulties in breaking into export markets.

There are a number of ancillary activities, notably construction and materials handling, as well as services, in which the use of labor-intensive methods may yield economies in the use of capital per unit of output. However, the successful application of labor-intensive methods in large-scale road and dam construction has been found to depend on a high degree of managerial efficiency in the deployment of labor as well as on tight labor discipline. Failing this, capital-intensive methods may be preferable even here.

The point is often made that capital-intensive techniques have in effect been subsidized in developing countries through low interest rates and the remission of duties on imported equipment embodying advanced technology, coupled with high levels of protection on the finished products manufactured with such equipment. Examples can be cited in which the value added by heavily protected modern industry in certain developing countries was actually negative at world market prices: motor vehicle production in some of the Latin American countries is a case in point.

It is doubtful whether subsidization of such magnitude, especially of luxury consumer durables, can be justified. Equally, however, it would be inadvisable to introduce distortions of precisely the opposite character, namely distortions that would result from indiscriminate incentives or subsidies to labor-intensive technologies. There are instances in which the subsidization of capital-intensive as well as of labor-intensive techniques can be justified: both may find their place in a purposeful development strategy so long as decisions are based on rational calculation rather than on general doctrine.

Notwithstanding the above considerations, it appears to be implied in some of the employment-maximizing strategies that labor-intensive techniques should be adopted even though they do not yield a higher aggregate output, and even though total capital requirements may be greater. This, however, is a self-defeating strategy under almost any conditions. It amounts to saddling industry with the additional costs of a public works program. This inevitably makes it more difficult to gain export markets, and may even necessitate high levels of protection against cheaper imports from abroad. In such cases it would obviously be preferable to adopt capital-intensive techniques in the industries concerned, and use the savings in capital costs to help in financing employment-creating public works programs of value to the community.

"Appropriate" technology. It is, nevertheless, true that most of the technology employed in developing countries was originally designed for use in the quite different conditions of industrial countries, and has usually undergone only minimal adaptation to the requirements of a new environment. Much greater efforts are therefore needed, as the basic needs strategists emphasize, to design or adapt technologies that would be more "appropriate" to the conditions prevailing in developing countries.

Whether a program to promote appropriate technology would bring about a significant change in the strategic options available to developing countries is far from clear. In the first place the mobilization of an adequate scale of R&D for this purpose will take more time than is generally realized, and the production of usable prototypes may take even longer. Moreover, account will have to be taken of the fact that differences in factor prices and in other relevant conditions among developing countries are greater than average differences between developing and developed countries. Consequently there is no technology that is equally appropriate for all developing countries, and adaptations will themselves have to be graduated accordingly. Secondly, it will be necessary to accommodate the effects of changes in factor price ratios over the lifetime of durable equipment: for example, at a rate of growth of 7 percent per annum real wages double in 10 years. Thus the problems involved in elaborating appropriate technology over a significant range of industry are immensely complex, and for many of the most important industrial processes solutions cannot even be envisaged at this stage, let alone anticipated. Meanwhile, life must go on and choices will have to be made from the options presently available.

The application of up-to-date scientific and engineering know-how could undoubtedly help to improve the performance of traditional techniques. Whether the improvement could ever be sufficient to outweigh the productivity advantages of capital-intensive techniques in a major part of industry is open to doubt. In many, and perhaps most cases, traditional techniques do not lend themselves to development beyond a certain point, because of such factors as their inability to accommodate high rates of power utilization. It would have been useless, for example, to try and harness a steam engine to a stagecoach. In fact, no matter how much scientific and technological ingenuity had been invested in trying to bring pre-railway methods of transport up-to-date, it is scarcely conceivable that any system competitive with the railway could have been invented at the time, under any configuration of factor price ratios.

All of this in no way diminishes the need for an effort of adaptation, and indeed of innovation, to be begun, and on a massive scale. In fact, this is a case where the minimum critical mass of resources required is exceedingly large. This is not only because of the immense variety and complexity of industrial technology and the enormous differences among developing countries, and hence in the degree of adaptation required in particular cases, but because small amounts of R&D devoted to appropriate technology are likely to produce their results too slowly ever to be put into practice, since the dynamics of technological progress will have rendered them obsolete before they are applied. One can only hope that the strong support of the industrial countries for a basic needs strategy of development will be accompanied by a recognition of the need for this kind of massive effort.

Even if adequate resources are allocated, and a successful R&D effort is mounted, there is no presumption that the new and appropriate technologies would be more labor intensive than the technologies presently imported without adaptation—at any rate in the core processes of the principal branches of industry. Their appropriateness may lie rather in the capacity to achieve maximum cost effectiveness at a lower level of output than existing technologies require.

The issue of appropriateness must, however, be seen in terms of the products themselves, as well as in terms of the technologies required to produce them. As Frances Stewart puts it: "When techniques designed for use in rich countries are transferred to much poorer countries, the products produced by those techniques are transferred too. The two—the techniques and the products—are inseparable aspects of the technology. Thus products designed for consumption in much richer societies are transferred to economies where, on average, incomes are much lower." [36] In the case of durable consumer goods there may be the further adverse consequence that the creation and maintenance of an adequate market may require a high degree of inequality in the distribution of income—over and above the kind of socially uneconomic protection referred to earlier.

There are, of course, various ways of preventing the diversion of resources into luxury consumption, including the creation of strong disincentives to domestic manufacture, the levying of high duties on imports, and the redistribution of income through taxation and public expenditure. It is, in fact, a surprising feature of the basic needs approach that far less attention is usually devoted to direct and practical measures of income redistribution than to a reorientation of development strategy that may well turn out to be as nebulous as it is ambitious, and which can, in any event, hardly be relied on to yield the desired result. We have already noted that the treatment of land reform is likewise often more tentative than one might have expected from a school that is profoundly concerned about rural poverty. In both these instances there appears to be an implicit hope or expectation that a basic needs strategy, by encouraging poverty-oriented development projects, might be able to sidestep the issue of direct redistribution of land and income. Perhaps the political and social strains of such a strategy would be less severe than of a program of land reform and tax reform; but the costs in terms of slowing down the rate of modernization of the economy may be high, while the benefits may prove quite elusive.

The international division of labor. The idea of an international division of labor between developed and developing countries based on labor and capital intensities is not viable for at least two reasons. In the first place, just as it does not necessarily follow that labor surplus countries should adopt labor-intensive technologies across the board, so also there is no presumption that the comparative advantage of such countries in world trade lies exclusively in the export of labor-intensive products.

Any such principle for the international division of labor is in any case ruled out because the developed countries are not less opposed to it than the developing countries are. Imports of labor-intensive products hit the most vulnerable industries of the developed countries—industries that often employ the poorest workers and members of minority groups. While a few developing countries have been able to establish strong positions in world textile markets, further export growth is under severe and discriminatory constraints, and there is no possibility at all that developing countries generally could look to textile markets as potential sources of substantial expansion in export earnings. The first international agreement on restricting textile imports from developing countries was adopted in 1962 as a temporary measure to be applied "during the next few years." The restrictions have, however, been renewed periodically ever since, and the rate of expansion of imports has been curtailed to the point at which there appears to be an intention to avoid the need for adjustment by preventing any significant further encroachment on domestic markets. Similar considerations apply to other restrictions on trade in manufactures with developing countries, whether imposed by importing countries or by exporting countries under duress.

Thus the idea we have been considering is not only poor economics. It is also quite impracticable in a world of growing protectionism, in which it is the labor-intensive industries that are the weakest in the developed countries.

The Chinese example. The point that never emerges either from the ILO report or from other versions of the basic needs strategy is that there is no necessary incompatibility between rapid development of the modern sector and promotion of new employment opportunities by more traditional methods in other sectors. If the Chinese model, which the basic needs strategists frequently quote with approval, proves anything, it surely proves that.

Chinese experience is often cited in support of the labor-intensive, small project approach to industry combined with the concentration of major resources and intensive efforts upon rural development. But the parallel drawn is often founded on a misunderstanding of that experience. The Chinese strategy is to walk on two legs, not on one, which is not a bad idea if the pedestrian is to remain upright. China encourages the simultaneous development of industry and agriculture, making use of the most modern capital-intensive technologies as well as of traditional methods of labor-intensive production. Provision is made for a minimum level of consumption accessible to all, while at the same time heavy industry is the key industry that is given the highest priority in the allocation of resources.[37] Thus the Chinese model is based on a strategy of comprehensive development quite different from what is usually understood as the basic needs approach, even though China clearly does have a definite policy on providing for a minimum level of living for all.

SHOULD THE UNDP HAVE A DEVELOPMENT STRATEGY?

The preceding discussion brings us to the second main issue of this essay—namely, should the aid donors in general, and the UNDP in particular, use their resources to further a poverty-oriented or basic needs strategy of development?

Except in the Netherlands and the Scandinavian countries, the constituency for aid programs in the developed countries is at the best of times relatively weak. Evidence that the distribution of income is becoming less rather than more equitable in some of the developing countries has been grist to the mill of the opponents of aid, who make the persuasive point that it is irrational to transfer income from poor taxpayers in developed countries to the well-to-do of the developing world.[38]

Thus acceptance by the developing countries of a commitment to a poverty-oriented development strategy has come to be regarded in the industrial countries as indispensable if aid programs are to be sustained. In fact the case for such a strategy emerged in the developed countries long before the World Employment Conference. Charles Paolillo notes that "The basic needs strategy bears a striking resemblance to the 'participation' strategy of development that underlies the 'new directions' in development assistance which the U.S. Agency for International Development (AID) has been pursuing over the past several years, in accordance with legislation put forth initially by the House International Relations Committee and enacted into law in 1973 and 1975."[39] Similarly, in a Blue Book issued in October 1975, the British government stated, "we and other aid donors are now adapting our aid policies to give more help to the poorest countries and the poorest people within these countries."[40]

Why, then, are developing countries reluctant to enter into a compact whereby development assistance would be linked to programs in aid of the poor? In the first place, they resent what they regard as an unwarranted assumption by the developed countries that it is only they who are concerned about the poor, and that the developing countries have to be offered the bait of foreign aid to induce them to show equal concern. The British Blue Book recognizes that these are "highly sensitive matters at the heart of the political process in all countries both developed and developing" and that efforts to exert pressure in this field might well be resisted even by countries otherwise favorably inclined toward poverty-oriented development.[41] The chairman of the OECD's Development Assistance Committee writes, "Experience with the African Club de Sahel indicates that no nation in this century would be likely to accept a minimal standard of life as an objective of policy for more than a temporary emergency period. More serious is that attempts to reach agreement on minimal poverty lines are certain to be deeply resented by developing country leaders and people as overly technocratic and paternalistic on the part of the affluent North."[42]

Moreover, the developed countries carry little conviction in this field at a time when unemployment and deprivation among disadvantaged and minority groups within these countries have risen to levels not seen since the Great Depression.

It is not as though the campaign for poverty-oriented programs of development is accompanied by offers of a substantially larger volume of aid in support of such programs. On the contrary, there is deep concern among developing countries that narrowing the scope of the international community's development objectives so as to concentrate upon poverty in a restricted sense of that term may be intended to provide a rationale for eroding the trade and aid commitments of the industrial countries. According to the World Bank, official development assistance declined as a percentage of the total GNP of developed countries from 0.52 in 1960 to about 0.33 in the mid-1970s, and there is no prospect in the near term that there will be a really significant move toward the General Assembly's target of 0.7 percent of GNP.[43] At the same time the trade objectives of the United Nations International Development Strategy seem further than ever from realization as the commodity problem remains unresolved, and the new protectionism of the industrial countries is particularly severe in its treatment of manufactured imports from developing countries, as noted earlier. There is, therefore, a profound uneasiness among developing countries that the poverty slogan and the basic needs approach are being used to undermine the International Development Strategy and to divert attention from the failure to meet the international obligations set forth in that Strategy.

In addition, the developing countries consider that concentration of aid efforts on the poorest 40 percent of the populations of the poorest countries ignores the fact that in most countries the majority of the remaining 60 percent are, by any reasonable standards of basic needs, themselves extremely poor and deprived. It is, in this view, a dubious procedure to separate out the poorest 40 percent in, say, Tanzania when four-fifths of the population are probably living at levels below the $100 line per capita.[44]

It is not necessarily in the poorest countries that the greatest inequities in income distribution are to be found. Even if it were regarded as desirable and efficacious to use aid programs to exert leverage on the developing countries in favor of the poor, which is itself open to question for the reason given in the British Blue Book, that leverage should presumably be directed toward the countries where inequities are greatest, rather than toward countries where the overwhelming majority are so poor that poverty-oriented development is virtually the same thing as development for all. But it is obvious that aid cannot be used as a means of pressure upon a country that receives no aid, and it is the countries that have been excluded from programs of concessional assistance because of their relatively high incomes that could do the most for their poorest citizens.

Thus there is more than a possibility that the pressure will be applied most strongly at precisely the point where it is least needed, and will not be felt at all in the cases where resources are indeed available for making significant progress toward the eradication of poverty, if the will were there.

The Transfer of Development Strategies: The Basic Needs Approach

Earlier we saw that while there is unquestionably a need for more equitable distribution of the gains from development, the strategy devised by the basic needs school to achieve this goal is at best highly controversial and at worst likely to slow down the process of development and with it any real hope for improving the living standards of the poor.

But even if the above analysis were too pessimistic, and even if it could be shown that rural development and small-scale, labor-intensive industry held the key to development with social justice, it still would not follow that the international agencies have any comparative advantage in planning, designing, and implementing projects in these particular fields. The simplistic assumption is often made that the best way for the international community to improve the lot of the rural or urban poor is to go to them directly, and involve them in internationally supported projects, multilateral or bilateral. Such projects frequently neglect the most basic preconditions for success.

Rural Development

In her important book, *The Design of Rural Development*, Uma Lele stresses the crucial importance of appropriate policies and commitment of resources by governments, without which rural development programs cannot succeed.

In the field of broad policy, for example, if the system of land tenure precludes participation of the lowest income groups in rural development programs, land reform may be an indispensable precondition for the success of such programs. Likewise pricing policies of the government or of marketing boards may have to be adjusted to permit low-income groups to benefit from increases in productivity.[45]

Popular participation in and support for rural development programs are also essential, and the general ineffectiveness of past attempts to secure such support is noteworthy. As Uma Lele points out, most programs have "suffered from poor knowledge of the socio-cultural and institutional environment in which they were to be implemented," combined with "extreme scarcity of trained local manpower."[46] These considerations prompt the conclusion that "without a very major commitment of resources by national governments to rural development and, equally important, to suitable training of the manpower necessary for expansion of these services, intensity of most of these programs cannot be replicated on a large enough scale to reach a mass of the rural population in the foreseeable future."[47]

It can hardly be said that of the entire spectrum of development support that international agencies are capable of providing, rural development is the sector in which their comparative advantage is greatest. Even if it were true that rural development should have the highest claim on the total resources available for development (which is itself far from certain), it still would not follow that it should also rank first in claims for external resources which, it should be remembered, represent only a small proportion of the total—less than 10 percent on the average.

It stands to reason that no outsiders, however well meaning, can be expected to have the intimate knowledge of the sociocultural and institutional environment that Uma Lele points to as crucial in any such program. Indeed, in the overwhelming majority of cases, the outsider will not even have the minimum understanding of the local language that is indispensable if close contact with the people is to be achieved and maintained.

Consider two countries, A and B, with similar per capita income levels and similar sectors of extreme poverty. Let us suppose that A has a laissez-faire government that does not believe in direct domestic aid for the poor but prefers to rely on market forces to put things right. B, on the other hand, has an active program of employment generation for both rural and urban poor; and a system of taxes and subsidies that effectively narrows the internal per capita income differentials, and puts a floor under the real income of the poorest.

UNDP proposes, and country A accepts, a program of integrated rural development. Efforts are made to raise the productivity of the small producer. Gradually it is noticed, however, that the fruits of the productivity increase are not retained by the producers but are passed on by them, involuntarily, to the industrial population in the form of lower food prices. The suggestion is made by the UNDP team leader that the government should consider supporting producer prices, but the government replies that Nobel prizewinner Milton Friedman is against such interference with the market.

Country B's officials do not want an externally financed rural development program at all—they feel that they understand the rural development problems of their country better than any external agency, and do not need any external inputs in solving them. UNDP's comparative advantage, they feel, lies in helping them to obtain and master advanced technology. They have some mineral resources already being exploited, and would like UNDP to help in establishing facilities for semi-manufacture. The program will not generate much employment and it certainly will not go directly to the poorest sectors. But, says the government, it *will* accelerate the rate of growth of the economy as a whole, and benefits will be redistributed by the government so that the poor obtain a more than proportional share.

Which of these two programs is more effective as a means of dealing with poverty? Views may differ, but certainly the second approach is not obviously inferior to the first.

It is, no doubt, considerations of this kind that prompted the British government to take an extremely cautious approach to poverty-oriented development in its Blue Book cited above. The Blue Book suggests that a poverty-focused aid policy "has to proceed by means of detailed programmes related carefully to the circumstances and wishes of each country, and not by way of general guidelines to be applied regardless of all countries." The Blue Book argues against direct methods whereby the donor would "specify in advance the economic or social sectors, types of projects, geographic areas, or particular beneficiary groups within a country to which it wishes to confine, or preclude the use of, its aid." [48]

Programs of poverty-oriented development have nevertheless gone ahead with the best of intentions, and the expected difficulties have materialized. In a certain Asian country, for example, a large-scale development project encountered severe problems resulting at least in part from the lack of familiarity of the international agency concerned with the cultural and political crosscurrents of the host of small communities that were involved. More surprising, the agency did not foresee the consequences of upgrading provision for water, sewage, and other improvements in isolation from more comprehensive development measures (that would, of course, have required a large multiple of the already substantial resources made available for the project). As the improvements raised the value of land and housing in the area concerned, the impoverished occupants felt compelled to sell out to richer people and move to slums on the outskirts of the country's capital city.

Again, at a recent intergovernmental meeting to discuss the basic needs strategy, a representative of one of the poorest African countries described how a certain international agency had created "a state within a state" in his country. The motives underlying the project in question were no doubt of the highest and best—the agency was determined that the experiment should succeed, that a significant impact should be made on the poor of the area concerned, and that nothing should be allowed to interfere with the progress achieved. But in order to achieve this result the agency felt compelled to assert a degree of control over the project, and a degree of protection from outside influences, that isolated it from the rest of the country. Moreover, conditions were created in the project area that made it quite impossible for the country concerned to repeat the experiment elsewhere. Thus a purely artificial entity had been established with no spread effects to the economy as a whole, and posing a serious problem for the government once the international agency concerned leaves the scene.

External support for a basic needs approach does not have to consist of basic needs projects. International agencies have acquired a high degree of competence in a number of areas, and it is in those areas that their efforts can be most productive, whatever the overall development strategy of the country concerned.

CONCLUSION

The basic needs school has made a contribution to the development dialogue by emphasizing the importance of equitable distribution of the benefits of development. But it claims too much—there is no such thing, thus far, as a basic needs strategy that clearly defines the direction to be taken by the economy as a whole.

While apparently radical in intent, the basic needs approach is, in fact, to a considerable extent backward looking. This is particularly evident in the absence of unambiguous provision for the structural changes that are indispensable in releasing the potential for development, and in the playing down of the role of modern industry and modern technology. Even in the rural sector, proposals for structural change seem hesitant and half-hearted.

It does not follow that, because a country has egalitarian development goals, it will necessarily wish to give overriding priority to the attainment of certain absolute targets for consumption. It may prefer to hold down present and near-term consumption in order to permit a more rapid rate of growth and structural transformation. The success of such a strategy may well depend on the fairness with which the associated burden of deprivation is distributed within the society as a whole.

Just as experience has shown that the success of efforts to limit the growth of population depends on placing such efforts squarely within the context of general economic and social development, so also will programs to assist the poor succeed only if established as part of a broader development strategy. The goals of growth and equity are not only compatible but interdependent, and their achievement certainly does not call for weakening or slowing down the growth of the modern sector, or for one-sided reliance on labor-intensive technologies.

Finally, however important it may be for countries to make more deliberate provision for the needs of their poorest citizens, it does not follow that international agencies have any special competence or expertise to offer in dealing with poverty problems through projects addressed directly to the poor. On the contrary, lack of familiarity with the complex political, economic, social, and cultural problems of assisting the rural and urban poor should prompt the agencies to offer their resources and services in the areas where they know from past experience that they can perform well. They do, however, have a responsibility to advise governments on the goals that the latter have freely accepted in international forums, and on the means of achieving those goals within the framework of each nationally determined strategy.

But the agencies should not aspire to be leaders in development theory or the principal authorities on the development process; and they have no mandate to impose particular development strategies on member countries. Development is a long-run task requiring from the international agencies steadiness and persistence, as well as a certain humility and restraint; a sense of proportion about their own capacities and about the importance of what they do; and the strict avoidance of both complacency and evangelism, and the ups and downs of development fashion.

4
International Trade Policies for Development

Trends and Issues in World Trade*

The subjects covered briefly in this discussion paper are the following: the macroeconomic environment for world trade; trade imbalance in the North; the new protectionism; trade successes and constraints in the South; and trade liberalization in developing countries.

THE MACROECONOMIC ENVIRONMENT FOR WORLD TRADE

The economic environment within which world trade flourished during the 1950s and 1960s differed greatly from that prevailing at the end of the 1980s. The earlier years were characterized by reasonably steady growth in world output and income, by a stable international monetary system, and by substantial transfers of resources to developing countries through official bilateral and multilateral channels.

In recent years, by contrast, the economic environment for world trade has deteriorated considerably, the international monetary system is much less stable, and the net flow of resources has been sharply reversed so that many developing countries are being compelled to run trade surpluses long before their stage of development would, under normal conditions, warrant such surpluses. The normal situation for developing countries is to be net borrowers from abroad, and hence to be net importers of the goods required for building up the economy.

One of the assumptions underlying the strategy for solving the debt problem adopted from 1982 onward was that the major OECD countries would grow at a rate of not less than 3 percent per annum and thereby generate an adequate growth of demand for imports from the debtors and stabilize their terms of trade. For several years the 3 percent goal was

*Paper presented to a seminar at the Economic Development Institute of the World Bank, April 17, 1989.

not achieved, especially in Europe, and even the 3 percent growth objective was not high enough to provide the degree of stimulus required, especially for stabilizing (let alone improving) the terms of trade of the debtor countries. In fact, the terms of trade of developing countries deteriorated throughout most of the 1980s, thereby greatly increasing the real burden of servicing the foreign debt.

The slowing down of world economic growth in the 1980s compared with the 1950s and 1960s was inevitably accompanied by much slower rates of expansion in world trade. Thus the average rate of growth in the volume of world trade from 1950 to 1970 was about 7 percent per annum, while from 1980 to 1987 the growth rate of trade was less than half of this. Here we have the most important single explanation of the growing frictions and tensions in world trade and the increasing frequency with which industrial countries threaten one another with economic warfare. When world trade is expanding rapidly it is possible for some countries to increase their shares of the world market, while even those experiencing a decline in market share may continue to experience increases in exports in absolute terms. But when world trade is stagnating or growing slowly, gains for one group of countries mean inevitable losses for others, not only in terms of market share but in absolute terms as well. The same goes for the penetration of domestic markets by imports. If the economy is expanding sufficiently a larger volume of imports can be absorbed without detriment to the sales of domestic producers. But if the economy is faltering, more imports mean fewer sales by domestic enterprise and rising unemployment. In short, it makes a tremendous difference whether world trade is a positive sum game as it was in the 1950s and 1960s or close to a zero sum game as it has been during most of the 1980s.

The year 1988 was an exception. World GDP growth increased to about 4 percent and the volume of world trade advanced more than 9 percent. But this modest upturn has already prompted some head shaking among the central bankers, who seem determined to put the brakes on, on the grounds that there has been some slight acceleration in price increases. The fact that slower growth creates problems in world trade and that higher interest rates aggravate the world debt crisis and choke off domestic investment does not seem to worry the central bankers very much.

There is no dispute about the need to avoid inflation, but it would be a mistake to suppose that we are faced with the same kind of pressures that led to double digit inflation ten years ago. It is important to strike a sensible balance between fighting inflation and other international objectives such as raising the rate of world economic expansion, thereby supporting recovery in the Third World, and creating elbow room for shifts in world trade. The fact is that unemployment remains high in Europe, and even in the United States the recorded figures of unemployment do not allow for substantial hidden unemployment or underemployment. The latter is particularly evident in the service sectors where large numbers of skilled workers have been compelled to accept unskilled jobs. The unemployment figures also do not reflect workers who are involuntarily employed part-time and those who have given up looking for work because they believe that prospects for them are hopeless. Nor does the rate of utilization of capacity in manufacturing indicate any immediate grounds for alarm.

It would also be a serious mistake to be overly concerned about recent increases in commodity prices. Considering that commodity prices in the last several years have been at their lowest levels since World War II it is little short of absurd to be seeking to slow down the world economy to the point at which commodity prices would be prevented from increasing. There has been no economic upturn in the past century and more that was not accompanied by some increase in commodity prices, and if we are going to set ourselves the target of holding down commodity prices at all costs, we will be condemning the world to perpetual stagnation, and growing conflict between the major trading countries will become unavoidable.

Nor should the industrial countries risk a recession by overreacting to moderate upward pressures on costs such as are unavoidable from time to time. Certainly there is nothing that would dim the prospects for world trade and the Uruguay Round as much as a recession or threat of recession.

TRADE IMBALANCE IN THE NORTH

Few phenomena in world trade are as well known or as much misunderstood as the trade deficit of the United States.

In the view of most non-Americans, and indeed of many Americans as well, the U.S. trade deficit is the inevitable result of the budget deficit, and the trade deficit will never disappear as long as the budget deficit persists. In addition there is a strong impression in the United States that the trade deficit is due to unfair trade practices abroad—agricultural protectionism in Europe, illegitimate protection of both agriculture and industry in Japan, and unfair dumping and export subsidization by foreign countries in the U.S. market as well as in third markets.

There may be some substance in these views, but much less than is usually supposed. In the first place budget deficits do not invariably generate trade deficits. Out of the forty-four years from 1946 to 1989, thirty were years in which the U.S. government had budget deficits, but only in seven of these thirty years—from 1983 to 1989—were the budget deficits accompanied by trade deficits. The United Kingdom is a leading example of a country in which, at the present time, a trade deficit is accompanied by a huge budget surplus. It would, therefore, seem to follow that a reduction in the U.S. budget deficit is neither a necessary nor a sufficient condition for a reduction of the trade deficit.

Nor is it clear that unfair trade practices are a major cause of the trade deficit. There is, of course, no denying that unfair trade practices exist, but the question to be answered is whether such practices are more common in countries other than the United States than in the United States itself. It is not very easy to compare the fairness or unfairness of the trade practices of various countries, but U.S. scholars who have looked into the matter are not in agreement on whether the United States has a better record than other countries in this respect. For example, William Cline of the Institute for International Economics in Washington, D.C., has expressed doubts that U.S. markets are more open than foreign markets. He noted that the United States had imposed major nontariff barriers on one-third of the U.S. market—a figure comparable to that in some of the European countries and higher than in other industrial countries.[1] And Gary Saxonhouse, of the University of Michigan, did a study that reached the conclusion that the removal of all Japanese import barriers would have only a small effect on the total level of Japanese imports.[2]

A dissenting view has been expressed by Robert Lawrence, who undertook a statistical analysis relating import shares to production for twenty-two countries and thirteen industries. His conclusion was that Japan's manufactured imports were about 40 percent lower than would be expected from an open economy—that is, an economy without import restrictions.[3] This research has been cited by the U.S. government's Advisory Committee for Trade Policy and Negotiations as a basis for recommending that trade policy solutions "lie somewhere between free trade and managed trade"—a remarkable conclusion to have been put forward by leading businessmen of the leading world economic power. Interestingly enough, Lawrence objects to this use of his results, and points out that this solution would require the cartelization of trade, which is precisely what is objectionable about Japan's import trade, as he sees it. Jagdish Bhagwati believes that "Most professional opinion . . . remains skeptical of claims that Japan is unfairly and asymmetrically denying access to its markets in manufactures."[4]

Even if Lawrence is correct in concluding that Japanese imports are low in relation to Japan's national income and production, it still would not follow that the low level was due entirely or even mainly to unfair trade practices. It might be due to such factors as tastes, language, and, particularly, geographic location. Lawrence himself recognizes that there are a number of factors other than unfair trade practices that could account for the Japanese import ratio.

If the U.S. trade deficit is not due to the budget deficit, and if it is not certain how far, if at all, it can be attributed to unfair trade practices, what *is* it due to?

The study by Saxonhouse just mentioned blamed exchange rate misalignment, and there is no doubt that at certain times overvaluation of the dollar has contributed to the problem. The trouble is that excessive reliance on changes in interest rates for the management of the economy brings with it an unwanted side effect, namely fluctuations in the exchange rate. If, for example, U.S. interest rates rise more than those of other countries, it pays investors to shift liquid funds into short or medium-term dollar assets, and this sets up additional demand for dollars and hence a rise in the dollar exchange rate. This in turn makes it more difficult for U.S. exporters to compete in world markets and increases the price advantage of imports from other countries in the domestic market of the United States. For example, the IMF estimated that in the second quarter of 1985 the real effective exchange rate of the U.S. dollar was more than 50 percent above the level implied by purchasing power parity.

While exchange rate misalignment certainly plays a role from time to time in aggravating the U.S. trade deficit, it cannot be the main factor underlying the deficit. The United States has been losing ground in world trade for at least twenty-five years, and while there were some years in which the dollar was overvalued, equally there were others in which it was undervalued, and still the trend continued. One of the main reasons why President Nixon severed the link between the dollar and gold in 1971 was because the U.S. trade balance had been deteriorating in the latter half of the 1960s and the U.S. administration believed that the fixed link to gold was depriving it of the ability to devalue the dollar as a means of regaining the ground that had been lost. Then too, as now, the main surplus countries were the Federal Republic of Germany and Japan, and then too Germany and Japan argued that the United States was responsible for its own trade problems because it was overinflating its economy. In the 1980s likewise the United States has tended to maintain a higher level of business activity and a lower level of unemployment than Europe, and this has meant that the demand for imports has been stronger in the United States than in Europe. But Japan does not fit into this explanation because Japan also has maintained a high level of growth, business activity, and investment, and has, nevertheless, managed to run a huge trade surplus.

It seems, therefore, that there are long-run structural factors that have caused the United States to lose ground in world trade. First, the United States had built up a position of exceptional strength in world trade immediately after World War II because of the low level of supply capability in Europe and Japan at that time. That was the period of so-called dollar shortage. It was inevitable that sooner or later traditional suppliers would regain their capacity to compete with the United States. A second structural factor was that in the process of rebuilding their export capacity the Federal Republic of Germany and Japan devoted considerable attention to quality control and technological superiority. If, for example, one asks oneself why Japan has made such inroads into the U.S. market for automobiles, a good deal of the answer has to be found in the high quality and reliability of Japanese cars. Year after year the well-known Japanese cars are rated at the top of the list compiled by Consumer Reports for frequency of repair. In this field as in the field of consumer electronics it is nonprice competition that has contributed at least as much to Japanese success as price competition, and the same goes for German products.

Both the price and nonprice competitiveness of Japan are due in turn to the fact that the momentum of production and productivity growth generated in Japan during the earlier postwar years has continued. Since productivity increases are known to be in part a function of the rate of growth of the economy as a whole, the fact that Japan continues to grow faster than the other industrial economies including the United States means that year in and year out productivity in Japan is continually increasing relatively to productivity in the United States and Europe. Moreover, as Ryuzo Sato has shown in a paper for the National Bureau of Economic Research, while about 60 percent of U.S. spending on research and development has been in the defense and aerospace industries, in Japan the same percentage has been allocated to chemicals, electronics, communications, and automobiles—industries that produce for export.

Another paper for the National Bureau by Melvyn Fuss and Leonard Waverman has estimated that the costs of the U.S. motor vehicle industry were 34 percent higher than those of Japanese carmakers in 1980. This cost advantage of the Japanese industry must have increased rapidly with the appreciation of the dollar up to 1985. Consequently the Voluntary Restraint Agreement limiting U.S. imports of cars from Japan cannot be justified by allegations of Japanese dumping. The subsequent sharp decline in the dollar must have narrowed the Japanese cost advantage, and the prices of Japanese cars have increased considerably in the United States. But these price increases were probably due more to the relative scarcity of Japanese cars as a result of the quantitative controls on imports than to cost increases in terms of dollars. This is because much of the effect of dollar depreciation will have been offset by the continuing rapid advance of Japanese productivity.

To sum up, the Japanese bilateral trade surplus with the United States, and, indeed, its overall surplus with the rest of the world, probably result much more from the steady trend of higher production and productivity growth in Japan than from unfair trade practices. As long as the United States and Western Europe maintain stop-go macroeconomic policies that deliberately hold down production, investment, and productivity, so long must they expect to lose ground in world trade, not only to Japan but also to other countries where productivity is growing rapidly.

The attempt to resist this trend by managed trade is shortsighted because it does not strike at the root of the matter, namely the productivity lag resulting from stop-go policies. In fact managed trade will, if anything, aggravate the problem. The Nippon Electric Company announced some time ago that it had won the race to build supercomputers. Whether the claim was well grounded is not yet clear. But supposing it was, will the United States forego the technological gains offered by the Nippon Electric supercomputer by placing restraints on imports? If it does, U.S. industry will, to that extent, be left even further behind. The industrial countries frequently warn the developing countries that it is counterproductive for them to deny themselves the benefits of imported technology and services, but in this area what is good for the goose is likely to be good for the gander also.

THE NEW PROTECTIONISM

GATT allows protection in certain cases, for example to deal with dumping or in cases where countries experience severe balance-of-payments difficulties. These escape clauses are governed by rules to prevent abuse.

Since the latter part of the 1970s a new development in the world trading system has been the proliferation of trade restrictions that contravene specific provisions of GATT. These restrictions include particularly so-called voluntary export restraints and orderly marketing arrangements. Thus in 1977 the United States negotiated orderly marketing agreements limiting exports of footwear from the Republic of Korea and Taiwan and similar arrangements were made for color television sets exported from these countries and Japan. A number of European countries also acted to restrict such imports by imposing quotas. Other sectors covered by quotas and other restrictive arrangements were textiles and apparel, steel, shipbuilding, and automobiles. The simultaneity of restrictive action in several industrial countries reflected not only the weaknesses of the respective domestic industries but also a ricochet effect whereby as soon as one industrial country imposes import restrictions other industrial countries follow suit because they are afraid that supplies excluded from the first country will be diverted to their own markets.

A further evolution of the new protectionism includes the development of a new style of aggressive reciprocity whereby countries, especially the United States, use threats of retaliation to counter what they regard as unfair trade practices by their trading partners. In addition, as the use of discriminatory trade practices embodied in orderly marketing arrangements and voluntary export restraints expands into more and more sectors of world trade, the principle of unconditional most favored nation (MFN) treatment that is basic in GATT is increasingly displaced by conditional MFN treatment—that is to say MFN treatment tends to be limited to those countries whose trade policies are deemed to be, in some sense, fair. The world of conditional MFN treatment and aggressive reciprocity is, of course, a world for the strong and not for the weak, but even the strong cannot in the end count on benefiting from such policies since the ultimate result is likely to be that all countries, strong as well as weak, will suffer losses. It is the world of "beggar-my-neighbor," which was tried before in the 1930s and failed miserably even in the strong countries. It is no more likely to succeed today. That is why all countries, strong as well as weak, rich as well as poor, have an enormous stake in the success of the Uruguay Round, provided, of course, that the Uruguay Round itself does not become a vehicle for discrimination and aggressive reciprocity.

TRADE SUCCESSES AND CONSTRAINTS IN THE SOUTH

A new feature of world trade during the past twenty years has been the marked diversity of experience of developing countries. In the days when all or most developing countries relied mainly on primary products for their export earnings, there was a tendency for trade experience to be quite similar among countries and regions. During cyclical upswings in the industrial countries the demand for primary products would increase, and most developing countries would experience substantial gains in their commodity export earnings from increases in the prices as well as volumes. The reverse would take place in times of cyclical downswings.

More recently, differences in the degree of success of various countries in diversifying their production and export structures have sharply affected their trade experience. A number of countries in Asia have had remarkable successes in penetrating the markets for manufactures in the industrial countries, enabling them to service their external debts without undue difficulty. African countries have faced the greatest problems because of their continuing dependence on the vulnerable primary commodity sector coupled with their heavy indebtedness to official lenders. In Latin America a number of countries have had considerable success in diversifying their production structures, and in this respect their experience is quite similar to that of the East Asian countries. But their scale of indebtedness has been so large that their debt service obligations have encroached severely on essential requirements for investment and consumption. Thus African and Latin American countries have been experiencing acute economic depression while some of the Asian countries have been maintaining their development momentum.

There are some who believe that the reasons for this diversity in experience can be set out in fairly simple terms, and that if only the underachievers would emulate the policies of the overachievers all would be well. It seems likely, however, that the issues are much more complex than is generally recognized, and that serious mistakes are being made both in the identification of the reasons for the successes and failures of various countries and in the setting down of policy prescriptions for the less successful countries. It is particularly important to clarify the extent to which success can be identified with "outward-looking strategies" and failure with "inward-looking strategies": this is, perhaps, the most popular of the current misconceptions in this field.

TRADE LIBERALIZATION IN DEVELOPING COUNTRIES

There is a substantial body of academic research that claims that the developing countries that have experienced the greatest balance-of-payments difficulties are those that have followed what are referred to as "inward-looking" development strategies, which essentially involve erecting high import barriers around the economy and building up various types of industries under the protection of those barriers. This, it is believed, has had several adverse effects. In the first place, the domestic markets of many developing countries are too small to realize the economies of scale available in many industrial sectors, so that industries catering to domestic demand alone tend to be inefficient. In addition, the high cost of imported inputs into the domestic production process is a handicap to industries that could have developed a strong export potential if they had had access to raw materials, machinery, and components at world market prices. Moreover, the economies employing "inward-looking" strategies have tended to maintain overvalued exchange rates, thus further handicapping the export sector.

Since the economies of developing countries are typically constrained by shortages of foreign exchange, the failure to develop adequate export capabilities has proved to be a major obstacle to their overall development. The success of the Republic of Korea, Taiwan, and other Asian countries with high rates of growth is attributed to their "outward-looking" strategies and their strong emphasis on export promotion of all kinds.

The point of view just described is a highly controversial one in the professional literature, and virtually every point that has been made, both theoretical and practical, has been challenged. In the first place, the theory thus expounded is essentially static and fails to take account of the dynamics of industrial development. Every one of the advanced industrial countries has employed strong protection at one time or another in its industrial history and has traversed a series of stages, beginning with protected import-substituting production for the local market followed eventually by the development of export capabilities in the very same industries. In other words, industries that begin by being "inward-looking" often end up, after completion of the learning process, as "outward-looking."

Japan began with a highly protectionist regime, and is still considered by many to be regulating its imports with the aid of strong direct or indirect controls. Moreover, for a considerable number of years after the end of World War II, the yen was substantially overvalued and foreign exchange was tightly rationed, with Japanese exporters compelled to surrender their foreign exchange earnings to the government within ten days. Obviously it would not make much sense to say that Japan was "inward-looking" even at that time, because the economic strategy of the country was clearly oriented toward developing in due course a strong export capability and exploiting that capability for all it was worth. Exactly the same thing can be said of the Republic of Korea during the early postwar years. No country could have been more "inward-looking" than Korea was in those years, employing as it did the standard array of devices for protecting the domestic market and controlling foreign exchange. Yet even at that time the government in alliance with industry was taking steps that led ultimately to the development of a remarkable export capacity. Prior to 1964 Brazil was frequently criticized for being "inward-looking" but in recent years it has come to be recognized that the protected growth of Brazilian industry during that period laid the foundation for the subsequent export successes of the 1970s and 1980s, especially in the manufacturing sector.

If Brazil, Japan, and Korea had liberalized prematurely, they would have inhibited and probably prevented the creation of an export potential in sectors where the learning process was still going on and output prices were still well above world levels. Very few people, if any, outside Korea believed that that country could possibly succeed in the highly competitive world market for motor cars, and if the liberalizers had had their way in Korea they would certainly have advised against the building up of a protected automobile industry.

This is not to imply that the liberalizers are always wrong; not at all. There have been many cases in which countries have sought to develop industries in which they had no long-run prospects, with the result that resources were wasted and heavy losses were incurred. Nor is it easy to determine in advance when a country will succeed in a particular industry and when it will not. But the liberalizers did not know the answers either, and to promote liberalization as a matter of doctrine or blind faith is to jeopardize opportunities for development.

It is particularly regrettable that the Bretton Woods institutions have been promoting trade liberalization as an integral part of the policy conditions required for their lending programs in recent years. For example, in a report to the Joint Development Committee of the Bank and Fund in March 1984, the World Bank staff stated that in the course of policy dialogue with its members on macroeconomic issues "The Bank has stressed that trade liberalization in member countries, even without better access, will improve resource allocation and *assure a higher growth path*" (emphasis added). The confidence with which this statement was made and the assurance given to governments of "a higher growth path," even without better access, is astonishing in the light of the intense disagreements among professional economists on this subject. There are at least three grounds for concern on this score.

The first and most important point has already been mentioned, namely that liberalization across the board may destroy domestic industries having excellent prospects along with those that have no such prospects. The second consideration arises out of the extreme balance-of-payments pressure to which many developing countries are now exposed. For them, liberalization cannot increase the aggregate level of imports very much, if at all, because the level of their imports is determined by the earning power of their exports together with whatever limited capital inflows they are able to mobilize or attract. Thus the effect of liberalization, by and large, is to change the composition of imports without affecting their level very much. Such shifts in composition, determined mainly or entirely by market forces, may disregard social priorities such as essential food imports, or even investment priorities.

In those countries, such as Mexico, where liberalization has led to an increase in imports, this has had the effect of adding to the pressures on the balance of payments, and this is no doubt part of the reason why it has become so urgent for Mexico to seek massive debt relief. It is a case of jumping from the frying pan into the fire.

The third reason for concern about the trade liberalization campaign of the Bretton Woods institutions is that what they are asking, in effect, is that the developing countries should dispose of some of their bargaining chips outside the framework of the Uruguay Round trade negotiations. It is true that there is well-meaning talk about taking such unilateral liberalization by the developing countries into account in the course of the Uruguay Round negotiations. But it is difficult to avoid a certain skepticism as to how much compensation of this kind the developing countries will really be able to collect.

When Jacques de Larosière was IMF Managing Director he floated the idea that developed countries should eliminate some of the voluntary export restraints in the case of developing countries that undertake trade liberalization under Fund programs. The idea was not accepted for the good and sufficient reason that voluntary export restraints are illegal under GATT and it would therefore be impossible for GATT to sanction a bargain of the kind proposed. This principle was adopted unanimously in the Ministerial Declaration at Punta del Este which stated that there should be no GATT concessions requested for the elimination of trade restrictions that are inconsistent with GATT. It is the illegal types of trade restriction, rather than tariffs, that are the most damaging to the export trade of developing countries. Many of these countries also do not wish to bind the unilateral trade concessions they may have made under Fund or Bank programs, especially in view of the uncertainty as to whether they would gain anything thereby. Without such binding, they are not eligible for reciprocal concessions. Mexico has repeatedly indicated during the Uruguay Round negotiations that it expects to receive compensating benefits in consideration of its sweeping unilateral liberalization, but it is not at all clear whether this will in fact happen.

Problems of development and trade expansion cannot be solved by slogans. Nor can the trade policies of a country be adequately evaluated by trying to fit them into such categories as "inward-looking" and "outward-looking." Indeed no static classification can yield much enlightenment because the development of export capabilities is a dynamic process that has to go through a series of stages. History shows that in the early stages of development the protection of infant industries is indispensable. Protection should, however, be gradually phased out as the protected industries gain strength and experience, and it is important to avoid a situation where protection becomes a permanent subsidy to inefficiency. But it is important to recognize also that policies loosely described as inward-looking may have an important role to play in the early stages of development.

The Viability of Small Countries: Problems of Economic Integration*

In a world of superpowers it has become fashionable to regard the merging of small countries as an end in itself, and nationalism as a luxury fit to be enjoyed only by those able to measure their military strength in nuclear megatons, or those able to acquire such strength. On this reasoning the United States and the USSR are viable, as also are the Western European groupings, China, and India. But what other countries are viable? Of 112 developing countries throughout the world, 91 have populations of under 15 million and 65 have less than 5 million. In a congregation of giants, surely the 65 must be regarded as nonviable?

Yet the small countries are entitled to say—here we are and here we stay. It is true that 65 of us have populations of less than 5 million. But the population of England in the time of Queen Elizabeth I was also 5 million or less. No one has thought of suggesting that the country that defeated the Spanish Armada was not viable. Our right to freedom and independence cannot be denied simply by looking at the shape of the economist's cost curves. Our soil is sustaining a very rapidly growing population—more rapidly growing, in fact, than ever before. Is that not

*Originally published in *International Development 1965*, ed. Stefan H. Robock and Leo M. Solomon (New York: Oceana, 1966). Although certain points in this essay are illustrated by references to regional groupings that subsequently became defunct, notably those in Central and South America and East Africa, the conclusions drawn from the experience cited remain valid.

in itself an indication of viability that even Darwin would have readily accepted?

Viability is, however, a *relative* term. Granted that scores of small developing countries can sustain rapidly growing populations, will they be able to realize their ambitions to raise living standards within a period of time that they themselves would consider reasonable? Are they now making progress at a rate they would consider adequate?

NATIONALISM AND DEVELOPMENT

The difficulty is that the political nationalism of the small developing countries is at odds with their economic weakness. For a variety of reasons, they are unable to make rapid progress within the existing economic framework based mainly on agriculture. Acceleration of the growth process necessitates industrial development. Indeed, the greater the progress in agriculture, the greater the surplus of labor released to seek productive employment in industry.

Modern industry is large scale and needs a certain minimum scale of operations for peak efficiency. This in itself would not matter if there were no barriers to world trade. Switzerland was able to build a viable economy without joining up with any other country. So were Belgium, Norway, and Sweden. But these countries took their first steps on the road to development in the days when specialization was possible because of relatively easy access to world markets. Switzerland could specialize in watches, Belgium in steel, Norway in shipping.

Today, the barriers to trade make it impossible for the newly emerging countries to risk specialization. For specialization means vulnerability, and these countries are all too vulnerable already. Few of them, in establishing manufacturing industries at the present time, could count on significant export markets. Markets in the industrial countries are closed to them partly because by now the technological lag is so great that, even though in developing countries wages are much lower, total costs per unit of output are generally higher because of such factors as low productivity of labor, lack of complementary facilities, or high costs of raw materials, power, or transport. Wherever this is not so, industrial countries themselves take steps to protect themselves against so-called unfair competition.

Markets in other developing countries are also closed to them. Where other developing countries have competing industries of their own, they have generally protected them up to the hilt in the home market. Where they do not have competing industries of their own, they would rather buy low-cost imports from North America and Western Europe than high-cost imports from their neighbors.

MARKETS TOO RESTRICTED

While the importance of economies of scale is sometimes exaggerated, it seems clear that the national markets of most of the smaller developing countries are too restricted to provide an adequate volume of demand for mass-production industries. Productivity in any one country is likely to be lower the greater the number of different industrial products or varieties that it attempts to manufacture, and the more its industries are limited to production for the home market alone. Where productivity is low and costs high, the tendency is for industry to seek—and obtain—correspondingly high protection. Yet if each industry in each country is separately entitled to the amount of protection it requires to survive while operating under conditions of low output and high costs, the tendency to regional specialization is necessarily inhibited. Protected inefficiency within small, self-contained markets becomes the rule.

Because of the failure of economic nationalism to provide a satisfactory solution for the problems of small countries, we are now witnessing a number of experiments in combining political nationalism with economic regionalism. It is too soon to say whether this approach can succeed, but the endeavor is certainly a valiant one.

In approaching the question of economic regionalism, the first thing people think of, not unnaturally, is lowering the barriers to regional trade. It is, of course, common ground among economists that protection may be a necessary condition for economic development at the national level. The question that now arises is whether group protection offers any advantages over national protection in stimulating the rate of growth. Those who favor regional groupings of developing countries do so because they see great advantages in securing, for the agricultural and industrial producers of each country, protected access to a region-wide market, instead of being confined within the limitations of narrow national markets. Protected access is secured by the lowering of internal barriers to trade at the same time as the outer ring of tariff and quota restrictions on imports from the rest of the world is maintained and perhaps even reinforced.

Such protected access would, it is thought, make it possible (a) for countries to use existing agricultural and industrial capacities more fully in supplying one another's needs; (b) for new investment to take place in industries that would not be viable if confined to individual national markets; and (c) for both old and new industries to reduce costs by benefiting from the economies of scale and specialization: in some cases this might help the industries concerned in the process of becoming fully competitive in world markets, including the markets of developed countries.

THE CASE FOR REGIONAL GROUPING

Stated in its simplest terms, the case for regional groupings of developing countries is that future economic growth presupposes a large amount of industrial development and that such development would be facilitated if the barriers to trade within each region could be reduced or eliminated.

A major difficulty facing the developing countries, however, is that the release of market forces through the reduction of regional trade barriers cannot be relied on to bring about comparable rates of development for all countries. In the past the free market system developed the world unevenly, concentrating industry and technical progress in limited areas of the globe. And just as, in the past, worldwide free trade led to great and growing inequality between continents, so now would intra-regional free trade be in danger of leading to or intensifying corresponding inequality between countries. Yet if the cohesiveness of a regional trading agreement is to be maintained or strengthened, it is vital that all participating countries should gain from the arrangement more than they could have gained without it; and highly desirable that any inequality in gains by various member countries should be held within reasonably narrow limits.

This does not mean, of course, that a sound development policy inevitably requires the equalization of growth rates throughout the area considered. It may well be that for any area regarded as a single unit, the most efficient way of developing may lie through deliberately unequal rates of growth in various districts and an intentional concentration of effort in the richer and more advanced regions. This may apply particularly where one starts from a very low level of development and encounters major indivisibilities, especially in outlays for social overhead investment.

Such a policy can, however, apply only to politically unified areas. It is not likely to be politically acceptable in an economic union, which cannot be regarded as a single unit for all purposes. Any one government can adopt policies which, while beneficial for the country as a whole— and leading to ultimate advancement for every part of the country—

nevertheless, leaves particular areas within the country behind, at any rate in the short run. But no government could possibly defend itself before its people if it allowed its own national interests to be submerged and compromised by the policies of the economic union of which it was a member, even where such policies were of demonstrable advantage to all other members of the union. Thus an economic union must study the interests of its constituent parts to an extent not required of a unified country. And where such a union is formed in the absence of strong federal loyalties among the mass of the people, the individual countries are likely to try and limit, as far as they can, the extent of any damage to their national interests caused by a powerful and perhaps zealous central authority.

In short, balanced and harmonious development of any group of countries is indispensable if the loyalty of all members to the group is to be maintained. And harmonious development can in turn be ensured only through concerted planning efforts based on agreement among the participating countries.

REDUCING TRADE BARRIERS

Experience in recent years has shown time and again that the process of tariff cutting which is regarded as the main feature in creating a customs union or free trade area among developed countries can only form part, and perhaps the less important part, of any program of integration among developing countries. At least equally important, for any grouping of developing countries, with the reduction of mutual tariffs, is the evolution of a mutually agreed program of development to which all countries are committed, and which provides for an adequate rate of growth for every one of them.

The failure of the Latin American Free Trade Association (LAFTA) to achieve its objectives has been attributed by some observers to the cumbersome process whereby annual negotiations were required for bringing about reductions in trade barriers. The European Economic Community (EEC) and the European Free Trade Association (EFTA) achieved major successes with across-the-board methods of tariff reduction in accordance with a predetermined and automatic schedule, and these are examples to which some observers believe that LAFTA should have conformed.

One can readily agree that automaticity, if attainable, would have led to more rapid tariff disarmament in LAFTA: this is too obvious to need laboring. But to stress automaticity as the answer to current difficulties is to mistake form for substance. The problem is precisely that governments do not want automaticity, and that the underlying political will and sense of common purpose needed for the application of automatic methods are still lacking in Latin America.

For one thing, automatic methods can be applied only where there is a presumption that such methods will lead to comparable benefits for all countries. While the Western European countries were sufficiently close to one another in levels of per capita income and production for such a presumption to provide a workable basis for action, the same cannot be said for Latin America or for other developing areas. The adoption of automatic methods in any group of developing countries, coupled with reliance on the spontaneous reaction of market forces to changes in tariff and quota restrictions, would be likely to benefit the strong as against the weak, and the industrially more advanced as against the industrially less developed.

As a matter of fact, even in Western Europe, one of the indispensable conditions for automatic dismantling of tariffs was that other steps, of a nonautomatic character, were taken to solve the problems of agriculture side by side with those of industry. At one point, in October 1964, France felt compelled to issue a warning that it would withdraw from the EEC if the agricultural market were not organized in the way that had been agreed. The agreement on a common price for grain that was reached two months later was thus an indispensable prerequisite for the continuation of the EEC tariff reduction program.

NATIONAL AND REGIONAL PLANNING

The problems of agriculture in Western Europe have this much in common with the general problems of both agriculture and industry in developing areas—that they cannot be solved exclusively through automatic arrangements operating alongside market forces. The modernization of agriculture in Western Europe is to be handled with direct support from governments and the same goes for economic development generally in the developing areas. In both cases the need is for national and regional planning for the most effective utilization of resources in meeting future demands.

The fact is that the simple process of liberating market forces within a regional framework of free trade cannot be relied upon in developing countries as a means of generating new investment in industry or of providing the networks of transport and communications and other elements of infrastructure that a thriving regional economy demands. What is needed is a much more deliberate intergovernmental promotion and stimulation of growth, with an equitable distribution of benefits throughout the region. Adequate joint planning arrangements are indispensable if a program along these lines is to be realized.

The real question, therefore, in Latin America and in other developing regions is this: Have the peoples and their governments reached the stage at which they are prepared to undertake both national and co-operative planning of their economic development? Are they ready to plan their own national development? And assuming that they are, will they be prepared to try to dovetail their national plans with those of other countries so as to achieve consistent overall targets for the region as a whole?

Assuming that the answers to these questions are in the affirmative, the next problem is how to secure a coordinated program of industrial development providing adequate advancement for each of the member countries of a regional grouping. It must be admitted that one cannot point to much experience of successful intercountry joint planning. Pioneer attempts to regulate industrial development on a region-wide basis in Central America and East Africa have not thus far yielded particularly encouraging results. Joint planning among members of the EEC has thus far been frustrated by opposition to the concept of planning as such. Even the countries of Eastern Europe have faced immense difficulties in coordinating their national plans of development.

Despite the limited success thus far of the program for coordinated industrial development in Central America, it may well be that certain features of this program do hold a key to the solution of the problem. The original intention of the program was that agreement would be reached among the five member countries on the distribution of new industries among them requiring access to the combined market of the whole area. These new industries were called "integration industries." Once the agreed upon integration industries were set up, they were to enjoy the benefits of free trade within the region. Any other plants in the same industry not qualifying for integration status would benefit only from annual reductions of 10 percent in the import duties applied to their products. This implied, however, that they likewise would gain free entry to the whole regional market at the end of ten years from the date specified in the protocol establishing the integration plant. Thus the preferential treatment given to the designated integration plants was to be strictly limited in duration.

A system basically similar to the Central American system was agreed to at ministerial level among Kenya, Tanganyika, and Uganda in April

1964, at Kampala. The ministers agreed that certain industries should be scheduled under the Territorial Industrial Licensing Acts, and a declaration was made in favor of an exclusive license to a firm operating in the agreed territory. Tanganyika was to have exclusive rights to assemble and manufacture Land Rovers, radios, and motor vehicle tires and tubes. Uganda was to have sole rights in the manufacture of bicycles and nitrogenous fertilizers. Kenya was to have similar rights for electric light bulbs.

DISTRIBUTION OF INDUSTRY

Three main arguments have been advanced against any program of intergovernmental agreements on the distribution of industry: that it would interfere with the optimum location of industry; that it would impede the establishment of small-scale factories catering to local markets; and that it would encourage monopoly.

It is contended that strictly industrial considerations based on the principle of comparative advantage would cause new factories to be located in regions providing the best combination of transport and power facilities, trained labor, and ample raw materials and intermediate products. The licensing of industry approach, on the other hand, would retard industrial efficiency insofar as new plants would have to be located in countries or areas that were less suitable than the best sites available.

The weakness of this argument lies in the static concept of the principle of comparative advantage that is implied. If, indeed, this static point of view were pressed to its logical conclusion, one would have to say that most of the new plants probably should not be placed anywhere in the less developed areas, but rather in North America or Western Europe. If, on the other hand, the principle of comparative advantage is reinterpreted within a dynamic framework, there is every reason to expect that even those countries that are industrially least developed at the present time will be operating viable industries in the long run.

It is also apparent that concentration of new industries in only one or two countries of a regional grouping would quickly cause the grouping to break up for lack of any incentive for the less-favored countries to stay in. In the case of Central America, for example, there is no reason why Honduras should agree to import manufactured goods from El Salvador or Guatemala at prices higher than those at which it could buy them from the United States, unless El Salvador and Guatemala are in turn prepared to take manufactures from Honduras. For industrial development is just as indispensable an ingredient in the solution of the economic problems of Honduras as it is in the advancement of El Salvador and Guatemala. The same considerations have prompted Tanganyika and Uganda to ensure that they obtain their fair share of the overall industrial development of the East African Common Market, where free market forces operating without restraint would tend to locate most industry in Kenya.

A second objection to the establishment of integration industries on a regional basis is that it would be likely to prejudice the development of small-scale factories supplying local markets. It would thereby discourage local initiative and enterprise.

It is odd to see this objection set side by side with the emphasis on free market forces operating in accordance with the principle of comparative advantage noted earlier. For if efficiency is regarded as the principal criterion relevant in taking decisions about the location of new industries, why is it not also the main consideration in determining the size of these industries?

A much more significant objection to intergovernmental licensing of industry is that it might tend to create regional monopolies, and it is probably this consideration that has been most influential in the reluctance of national and international financing agencies to aid this approach. Even if economies of scale were achieved by setting up only one plant catering to the whole of the Central American or East African region, what reason is there to believe that the benefits would be passed on to the consumer in the form of lower prices? Might not monopoly profits simply generate additional demand for luxury imports?

COMPETITION VERSUS MONOPOLY

It should first be noted that the general assumption that a single-firm situation is invariably bad and a multi-firm situation invariably good is not as clearly established in fact as some have supposed. One firm may dominate a market and yet be very go-ahead in discovering and applying new technologies; and in another market there may be a competitive battle so intense that no resources are devoted to research and development because of the general state of uncertainty induced thereby. Quite commonly, in developing as in developed countries, where there is more than one producer in an industry, the various companies get together and reach understandings about their respective shares of the local market; and the stalemate brought about by such understandings may be even more inimical to technical progress and dynamism than monopoly would be. Thus a doctrinaire approach to the problem of monopoly and competition is not likely to prove even relevant, let alone successful.

At the same time there is no doubt that the creation of new monopolies in groupings of developing countries could have an adverse effect upon their economies: it was for this reason that the Central American Agreement on Integration Industries provided for the protection of consumers by various means, including the establishment of an intergovernmental commission to supervise the program. The way was left open for the stipulation of quality standards and possibly even the regulation of prices. Moreover, the special advantages available to the designated integration industries were to be progressively reduced year by year and eliminated within ten years, as noted earlier.

In the industrially advanced countries the answer to this problem has been sought in the public regulation of monopoly, and this may be one of the best ways of approaching the matter. The public interest can always be safeguarded in the last resort, through the degree of protection afforded to local monopolies against competition from abroad. In other words, the government can always force the hand of a recalcitrant monopoly by lowering import duties.

In any case, if there are profitable business opportunities, failure to act along the lines of the integration industry approach will not necessarily prevent the creation of monopolies. It may merely leave the field open for foreign companies to set up the monopolies in question. Obviously it is much more difficult for developing countries to control foreign owned monopolies than those domestically owned.

For these reasons there appears to be a strong case for the joint planning of industrial development by groupings of small developing countries, employing some form of agreed policy of distribution of industry on a regional basis.

It should, perhaps, be emphasized that no distribution of industry policy can be based on a purely political decision. Any such policy would be bound to run into difficulties if it did not take account of all relevant economic considerations. While due allowance must be made for the fact that the current money costs of establishing new industries in less developed regions may be much higher than the social costs, there must be a reasonable expectation that in the long run any industry established will be able to stand on its own feet without special subsidy or support. The economic and technical basis for intergovernmental agreements on industrial location should therefore be as solid as modern methods of analysis can make it. If industries are to be sited in locations that are less than optimal, it is essential to know what additional costs will be incurred thereby, and how long it will take for the industries in question to become fully competitive. Once these facts are known, informed decisions can be taken at the political level. Such decisions should not, however, be left simply to the pull and push of political pressure, although it would be naive to imagine that such pressure can be avoided altogether.

There are, perhaps, grounds for a certain optimism regarding the long-run prospects of industries located even in the least advanced regions. The advance of modern technology is constantly reducing the relative importance of natural advantages in the location of manufacturing industries. Provided that the necessary skills can be learned and infrastructure provided, as they obviously can and will be, there is no reason why even the countries that are least industrialized today should not look forward to a high level of industrial development in the future.

It will not, however, be easy to decide how to balance present facts against future prospects. There will always be room for honest differences of opinion as to the long-run prospects for particular industries in particular countries, especially since the tools that we have in hand for evaluating such prospects are far from perfect or ideally suited to their purpose. Moreover, there are bound to be instances of diverging as well as of converging national interests. Where such basic questions of national economic interest are involved, there is an obvious need for effective institutional arrangements whereby national interests can be harmonized. Anything in the nature of joint planning and joint development is bound to call for the creation of fairly powerful institutions able to provide for consultation, conciliation, and policymaking.

One possible solution would be to take a leaf out of the EEC book, and provide for the creation of a strong council of ministers, and an executive on the lines of the EEC Commission. Here, however, we come back to the question of political nationalism—are such institutions, with their supranational overtones, compatible with the long-run independence of the member countries? Or is it a necessary condition of establishing such institutions that the countries concerned be prepared ultimately to envisage political as well as economic union? Experience to date does not provide us with a clear answer to this question.

Policy Issues on Services*

Professor Nau advises the newly industrializing countries (NICS) to recognize that including new issues, such as trade in services, in the Uru-

---

*Paper presented to the North-South Roundtable on Trade, Geneva, and originally published in *Linking the World: Trade Policies for the Future* (Islamabad: North-South Roundtable, 1988).

guay Round is a bargaining and not a theological matter.[5] This question was settled at Punta del Este along Solomonic lines by providing for parallel negotiations on trade in goods and in services, with the group on services reporting to the Trade Negotiations Committee. This degree of agreement was sufficient to permit the Contracting Parties to proceed to the next stage, but it did not, of course, constitute even a beginning to the solution of the underlying problems. Nor did it indicate what kind of negotiations would constitute "bargaining" and what "theology."

Professor Nau is undoubtedly well aware of the difficulties with his own approach. "The more the developing countries give in on services and other new sectors, particularly intellectual property," he says, "the more carrots the United States should offer by way of restraining its actions outside the GATT." The trouble with this, of course, is that it appears to imply that the NICS, or perhaps the developing countries as a whole, should provide material incentives to the United States and other industrial countries to comply with an international agreement, namely GATT, that they had freely and voluntarily accepted, and to discontinue activities inconsistent with that agreement.

Perhaps the above objection comes under the heading of what Professor Nau would regard as "theology." The objection is, nevertheless, quite a rational one (not all theologians are irrational) and what Professor Nau is proposing is moral hazard: once there is a case in which concessions are extracted as the price of compliance with the law, the incentive to further violations is obvious. The point that Professor Nau makes about encouraging the U.S. Congress is no doubt well taken, and he could also have said that the United States is prepared to drive a hard bargain on this matter. But facts are stubborn things, and the difficulty of restoring the rule of law in world trade is bound to be complicated by bargaining conducted on the above lines.

The Commonwealth Secretariat has described the background to the services issue as follows:

Over the past five years, the U.S.A. has persistently sought the extension of coverage of the GATT to include trade in services. This was prompted by the importance of services to the U.S. economy and by the implicit U.S. belief that this was an area in which it has a comparative advantage at a time when its competitiveness in agriculture and manufacturing is in decline. Secondly, the U.S. authorities took the view that there are barriers to trade in services which could be reduced by multilateral action.[6]

The Commonwealth Secretariat further describes the positions of various countries on this matter. At one end of the spectrum the United

States, supported by Canada, the EEC, and Japan, has been calling for negotiations on an "umbrella agreement" covering all services and under which specific sector agreements would be negotiated. The main elements proposed for this "umbrella" include transparency of regulatory procedures; competitiveness of public monopolies and the right to sell; national treatment and market access; investment and rights of establishment; and a dispute settlement mechanism.

The Commonwealth Secretariat suggests that the majority of GATT Contracting Parties, both developed and developing, have been taking a middle position. They are concerned by the lack of agreement on definition of the sector, the paucity of technical information, and uncertainty as to the scope of barriers to trade in services, as well as by implications for national sovereignty. They appear, however, to accept that certain GATT principles (MFN treatment, transparency, national treatment, and dispute settlement) might eventually be extended to services and are therefore more or less willing to explore the matter further in a longer time frame but without holding up the resolution of outstanding issues in the field of trade.

At the other end of the spectrum, according to the Commonwealth Secretariat, are a number of developing countries that are opposed to any extension of GATT to cover trade in services. Their concerns are national sovereignty, the possible demands of reciprocity, infant industry agreements, and the role of transnational corporations (TNCs) in the services sector. They consider that GATT is not the appropriate institution for discussion of this matter, which should be dealt with rather in the United Nations Conference on Trade and Development (UNCTAD) or in sector-specific bodies such as the International Telecommunication Union (ITU) or the International Civil Aviation Organization (ICAO).

One does not necessarily have to agree with the third group of countries mentioned above to recognize that proposals for trade in services raise a whole complex of issues that go well beyond the usual scope of a trade negotiation in GATT. This results in part from the fact that exports of services by the industrial countries are, on the whole, only a small percentage of the sales of services abroad by foreign affiliates of TNCs headquartered within those countries. It has been estimated that U.S. exports of private, nonfactor services in 1982 amounted to about $33 billion, compared to approximately $178 billion of sales by foreign affiliates of U.S. TNCs. Similarly, U.S. imports of services in 1982 amounted to about $33 billion, compared to approximately $125 billion of sales by foreign affiliates of non-U.S. TNCs in the United States.[7] Estimates for Canada, Japan, and the United Kingdom suggest that the volume of sales of foreign affiliates of TNCs headquartered in these countries is about twice as high as the volume of their service exports: in the Federal Republic of Germany the sales of service affiliates exceeded exports from the home country, though by a smaller margin. Thus for several of the industrial countries, and particularly for the United States, conventional trade in services is far less important than the overseas sales of services by affiliates of home-based TNCs.

Consequently any process of bargaining about the service sectors, whether in GATT or anywhere else, cannot fail to raise a whole host of issues connected with the overseas operations of TNCs. These are questions that have occupied various agencies of the United Nations for many years, and relatively few of these issues can be said to have been settled. If the same issues are taken up in GATT, the same disputes will arise, and the same ground and bargaining process will have to be retraced.

It is, of course, true that certain kinds of leverage may be available in GATT that were not available in the UN agencies dealing with these matters. Presumably the carrots referred to by Professor Nau will be brought into play, and perhaps some sticks as well. Time will tell.

It would, however, be a mistake to suppose that negotiations were at a standstill in the agencies involved, and that it was necessary to bring the matter to GATT in order to achieve a solution. Despite the carrots and sticks, there is a danger that attempts to reinvent the wheel by government trade representatives who have not previously had contact with TNC-related issues in a multilateral setting will put the clock back instead of advancing matters.

A good example is provided by the negotiations on a code of conduct on TNCs that are taking place in the UN Commission on Transnational Corporations. In his article on "A Simple Plan for Negotiations on Trade in Services," written in 1982, Ambassador William Brock listed a number of principles derived from GATT that might guide future negotiations on trade in services. These included, among others, the following:

- restrictive regulations should be applied on a "national treatment" basis;
- consultations and dispute settlement should be provided for;
- regulations and alterations in them should be transparent;
- a negotiated framework should entail both rights and obligations, with especially the right of renegotiation, compensation, or retaliation provided in cases of breach of agreements.

All of these issues have been thoroughly discussed in the UN Commission on TNCs. In some of them full agreement has been reached, while on others initial differences in position have been substantially reduced. The OECD countries have stated repeatedly in informal discussions that residual differences on these and other matters could be solved fairly quickly provided that there were agreement on one other issue not included in Ambassador Brock's list. That issue relates to the applicability of international law to matters dealt with in the code. In the view of several OECD countries customary international law contains, for example, provisions regarding approaches to be adopted in cases of nationalization, including dispute settlement and standards of compensation. One version of a text on this issue that is acceptable to the United States and some other OECD countries is the following: "In all matters relating to the code, States shall fulfil in good faith their obligations under international law."

This matter is, however, still in dispute because the developing countries do not agree that customary international law includes provisions along the above lines. While they are prepared to accept a text that would allow the industrial countries to maintain their position of principle on this matter in the event of disputes arising, they are unwilling to concede the point of principle itself. A proposal has been tabled by France that seems to have met with widespread but not universal support among both developed and developing countries. It reads as follows: "In all matters relating to the code, States shall fulfil in good faith their international obligations."

None of the related questions can be solved without overcoming the above stumbling block. On the other hand, it is doubtful whether restarting the discussion in GATT is the best way forward.

On the question of national treatment (namely that entities of TNCs should be given by the countries in which they operate treatment no less favorable than that accorded to domestic enterprises), the point of principle has been accepted on all sides, but the developing countries wish to introduce qualifications relating to the safeguarding of national security and the promotion of economic development. Both of these qualifications have in turn been accepted in principle by the developed countries, but the drafting of the development qualification has encountered the difficulty of how to recognize the validity of the development objective without in effect undermining the principle of national treatment itself. Here again it is by no means obvious that a solution of the problem will be reached more easily if it is transferred to GATT.

Similar questions arise in relation to the work of UNCTAD on restrictive business practices (RBPS) and the transfer of technology (TOT). As far as RBPS are concerned, a code was adopted by unanimous vote of the UN General Assembly in December 1980. It will clearly not be necessary for

GATT to reconsider the matters covered in the RBP Code, though it may conceivably be necessary to deal with additional questions not covered in that Code. The Code lays down standards of behavior for corporations and governments, and provides for a continuing program of activities at the international level to improve the control of RBPS. However, UNCTAD has not been given the power to investigate allegations of anticompetitive behavior or to review the antitrust policies of a particular country. The fact remains that an international agreement on RBPS does exist and that it contains provisions that permit evolution. As pointed out by Joel Davidow, who has represented the United States in UNCTAD's work both on RBPS and on TOT, world trade tensions have made protectionism and national industrial policy strategies more popular than liberal pro-competitive approaches such as antitrust. Also, the conflict between regulatory and laissez-faire approaches to TNCS and investment has been intensified, according to Davidow, by the strict defense of laissez-faire by the Reagan administration.[8] Further progress would seem to depend on an improvement in general economic conditions and a new spirit of compromise.

In the case of TOT, the situation is somewhat paradoxical. On the one hand, the benefits of free trade in high technology services are being recommended to the developing countries for the Uruguay Round. On the other hand, it has proved impossible thus far to reach agreement on the prohibition of restrictive licensing practices in the proposed code of conduct on TOT. As regards the latter, the developed countries have insisted on a commercial "rule of reason" to justify many licensing restrictions. The developing countries, on the other hand, reject this approach and wish to leave it to national authorities to make exceptions. Alternatively, these countries seek a standard for judgment under which the development interests of the recipient country would weigh far more heavily than the commercial interests of the licensing enterprises.

In addition, the developing countries have for many years insisted on an absolute ban on export restrictions while the OECD countries have urged that export restrictions are justified in a variety of situations, such as where they are designed to protect the exclusivity of rights being granted or utilized in other countries.[9]

The above illustrates rather neatly the point made by Harald Malmgren to the effect that information has value only if it is not freely available, and that the more restricted the access to information, the more valuable is it likely to be.[10] It is hardly surprising that the developing countries are reluctant to forego the creation of their own capabilities in high technology service industries if they cannot rely on gaining access to such technology through the free market. One striking illustration of this problem occurred in India, where IBM decided to discontinue its activities rather than comply with a new Indian law requiring majority domestic ownership of TNC affiliates unless the latter were engaged in substantial transfer of technology. In the view of the Indian government, IBM was not transferring technology to the extent that would have been needed to qualify as an exception to the rule.

Even the industrial countries have had difficulties with one another over this kind of issue, as evidenced by the concern expressed by Lord Kearton, former chairman of the British National Oil Company, that foreign companies operating in the North Sea were not transferring their technology to the United Kingdom, so that in the event that they gave up their holdings, the United Kingdom would have difficulty in taking over from them.

Thus in many countries, developed as well as developing, there is concern about the potential costs and benefits of a liberalization of international services, particularly since much depends on the policies pursued by the respective TNCs, and the extent to which such TNCs would seek to exploit the advantages flowing from liberalization. Many countries see the need for some kind of regulatory framework, and since there is for the time being little chance of the establishment of such a framework at the international level, they feel that it is all the more necessary to maintain their national rules and restrictions. That does not mean that negotiations could not take place on an easing of restrictions on both sides, but the types of negotiation that would have to take place on TOT, transborder data flows, and other complex matters would not necessarily lead to the best results if conducted in the environment of GATT preoccupations rather than in the institutions that have been dealing with these questions for many years. It should not be beyond the bounds of human ingenuity to devise an arrangement whereby the GATT negotiations could rely, to the extent necessary, on other institutions in dealing with some of the questions arising under Part II of the Punta del Este Ministerial Declaration relating to services.

The above discussion has thus far not taken full account of the case for infant industry protection of high technology industries in some of the developing countries nor of the problems of national economic management that would arise if banking services were liberalized. It is often taken for granted that because the industrial countries have a long head start in telecommunications, informatics, and related high technology service industries, they also have a long-run comparative advantage in these areas. As Rachel McCulloch has pointed out:

Moreover, while scale economies increase the potential benefits from liberalization, they also complicate the issue of how these benefits are shared. In particular, the possibility that a given nation may lose by expanding trade even though global efficiency is improved is more difficult to rule out when scale economies are important. Mutual gains are assured only if each country is able, on average, to expand production in industries with scale economies. Information-based and knowledge-based services are the areas in which U.S. firms and U.S. policymakers seem most confident of expanding global sales. These services are likely to exhibit strong economies of scale. The theoretical analysis of comparative advantage and gains from trade suggests both that the apparent U.S. advantage in these industries (as measured by domestic prices) may be overstated under current conditions and that the cautious approach of other nations toward the liberalization of trade in services may have a firm economic basis.[11]

The stakes are high in banking and insurance also. In the case of insurance, for developing countries it is a simple question of retaining domestic savings for use at home, although there are certain areas of reinsurance in which costs and risks may be sufficiently high to justify recourse to TNCs in one or more of the industrial centers. In banking, the integrity of national macroeconomic management is involved but, in addition, countries are bound to be concerned as to how far domestic savings may be drawn off or may be diverted away from domestic priorities. This is a case where the desire of TNCs for "national treatment" within the host country encounters particular difficulty. If TNCs had access to local banking resources not less favorable than that available to domestic companies, there might well be a serious diversion of domestic resources to the TNCs, if only because of the greater confidence of banks in the creditworthiness of the foreign companies. Moreover, countries under severe balance-of-payments pressure would have considerable grounds for concern that the TNCs might have an incentive to borrow in the local market while transferring the profits earned abroad.

The essential point of the foregoing discussion is not to say that negotiations in the service sector are impossible, but rather that the complexity and variety of nontrade issues involved argue for not limiting the negotiations to the Uruguay Round per se.

5
Foreign Investment

Can Foreign Investment Revitalize the Third World?

INTRODUCTION

Widespread hopes have been expressed by spokesmen for both the North and the South that private foreign investment can take up the slack in capital inflow into the Third World caused by the virtual cessation of voluntary lending by the commercial banks. The South is today much more receptive to foreign investment than it was in the 1960s and 1970s and has liberalized many of the legislative and regulatory obstacles. Expectations are, however, likely to be frustrated in the immediate future because of poor business prospects in the Third World, while in the longer run the pendulum of opinion in the South could swing back again unless some of the problems that caused confrontation with the transnationals in earlier years are resolved.

THE PERIOD OF TENSION

"Name any country you want to where you find trouble and somebody has made money out of the people." So said Senator Hubert Humphrey in May 1955 during hearings of the U.S. Senate Foreign Relations Committee that dealt, among other things, with Bolivia's expropriation of the tin mines belonging to Patiño Mines Enterprises Consolidated, Inc., of Delaware. "I hope they haven't gotten a nickel back," he said, referring to Patiño. And Republican Senator Aiken told the committee that up to the time that the mines were nationalized, "the people of Bolivia were given nothing at all out of that tin."[1] If these were the sentiments of highly respected members of the U.S. Senate from both political parties in 1955, it is not difficult to imagine what the views of the people of Bolivia must have been. Even if one assumes that the performance of this particular company was much worse than the average, which it may well

This essay was written specially for this volume, in 1989.

have been, a few well-known cases of this type could not fail to generate profound misgivings in developing countries about foreign corporations operating within their borders.

According to the UN Centre on Transnational Corporations, the annual rate of expropriations of foreign companies gradually increased during the 1960s, then built up rapidly to a peak of eighty-three instances in 1975, after which there was an equally steep decline during the rest of the decade of the 1970s. During the 1980s expropriation of foreign enterprises became a relatively rare event—only one case worldwide being reported in each of the years 1982, 1984, and 1985.

A number of scholars in the industrial countries were inclined to think that developing countries had valid grounds for their concern about private foreign investment. In 1969 Professor Albert Hirschman went so far as to write a Princeton monograph entitled, "How to Divest in Latin America and Why," referring to private investment as "an increasingly mixed blessing." His reasoning, to which we shall have occasion to return subsequently, was that so far from bringing benefits to the less developed countries, foreign investment might well be having a "retarding influence."[2]

VIEWS AND OBJECTIVES OF THE DEVELOPING COUNTRIES

The developing countries themselves did not go so far as to seek the withdrawal of foreign investment: cases of nationalization, particularly in the oil industry, were often due much more to a determination to take control of the commanding heights of the economy than to any particular dissatisfaction with the foreign corporations concerned. In the International Development Strategy adopted by the UN General Assembly in October 1970, developing countries explicitly agreed to "adopt appropriate measures for inviting, stimulating and making effective use of foreign private capital" which should, however, operate "in a manner consistent with the development objectives and priorities established in their national plans." The latter meant that measures were needed to increase local participation in management and administration, and promote the employment and training of local labor as well as the participation of local capital and reinvestment of profits.[3]

Less than two years later, in May 1972, the third general conference of UNCTAD, at the behest of the developing countries, expressed its concern "not only at the total amount of the financial outflow brought about by private foreign investment but also at its excessive utilization of local financial resources as well as the effect of certain marketing contracts among foreign companies that disrupt competition in the domestic markets, and their possible effects on the economic development of developing countries."

These concerns were reflected even more strongly in some of the statements made at the hearings conducted by the Group of Eminent Persons in 1973–74. The Group had been set up by the United Nations after complaints by the representative of Chile about damage caused by interference in his country's affairs by the International Telephone and Telegraph Corporation (ITT). The Group consisted of leading personalities selected by the Secretary-General of the United Nations, after consultation with governments, as representative of all the major regions of the world as well as of governmental, business, academic, and other interests. Addressing the Group, the Under-Secretary for Industry and Commerce of Mexico, José Campillo Sainz, stated, "The accelerated growth of transnational corporations . . . signals to the developing countries a new form of domination and new ways in which the legislation and policies of the home countries may be imposed upon them."[4]

The Group of Eminent Persons itself noted in its report the concerns of host countries about "the ownership and control of key economic sectors by foreign enterprises, the excessive cost to the domestic economy which their operations may entail, the extent to which they may encroach upon political sovereignty and their possible adverse influence on socio-cultural values."[5]

THE TRANSNATIONALS AT BAY

Although the Group's report did not make explicit reference to the complaint about the behavior of ITT that had led to its establishment, there is no doubt that wide publicity about ITT activities had a considerable influence on thinking both within and outside the United Nations. These activities were documented in a collection of confidential ITT memoranda published in the *Congressional Record*, together with other documents and testimony obtained by the Senate Multinationals Subcommittee chaired by Senator Church. The record appeared to show that ITT had taken initiatives, including offers of money, to prevent Salvador Allende from becoming President of Chile; and that, as Anthony Sampson put it, ITT's dealings with Chile had shown "in a magnified form the familiar characteristics of the company—the corporate arrogance, the inexorable lobbying, the two-faced attitudes, the corrupted communications."[6]

The distinguished international lawyer Professor Seymour Rubin, who subsequently headed the U.S. delegation to the Commission on Transnational Corporations for a number of years, had the following comments on these matters in 1974: "The multinational finds itself under steady assault from host and home government alike. . . . A share of the troubles can be laid to the ineptitude and greed of some multinationals, and a good many reasonably run, reasonably sensitive corporations must be groaning at being tarred with the brush of such episodes as the ITT/Allende affair."[7] And Professor Rubin cited a report of the Senate Multinationals Subcommittee indicating that at a time when a glut of oil on the world market was feared, a consortium of five Western oil companies had drilled wells in Iraq to the wrong depths in the hope of "hoodwinking the Baghdad government."[8] The same subcommittee released a copy of a memorandum written by the economists of a major oil company in 1968 suggesting that an anticipated threat to stable oil prices should be forestalled by reducing U.S. production, cutting imports into the United States from Canada, and slicing production in various oil producing nations to accommodate the expectations of increased shipments from Iran and Saudi Arabia. As Professor Rubin pointed out, such a revelation at any time would have come as a shock in a country (that is, the United States) with a tradition of opposition to restrictive business practices, and which was favoring the oil companies with advantageous tax rulings as well as mandatory oil import restrictions. "In the context of an oil shortage complicated by a revolution of rising prices," he said, "the shock is akin to trauma."[9]

In view of the opinions cited above from people of the caliber and independence of mind of Senators George Aiken and Hubert Humphrey, and of Professors Albert Hirschman and Seymour Rubin, it should not come as any surprise that host countries—developed and developing alike—had mixed feelings about their relationships with TNCs and considered it necessary to regulate their behavior so as to improve the prospects of benefiting from those relationships.

There was, nevertheless, a certain lack of comprehension and even a sense of resentment on the part of those in the home countries who felt that the host countries ought to be more appreciative of the favors being bestowed upon them by the TNCs. At the very time that more and more evidence was emerging of the damage that TNCs were capable of inflicting on host countries, fears were being expressed in the home countries that efforts by recipients of foreign investment to ensure that they would benefit thereby could not fail to generate international friction and even conflict. Indeed, in an article in *Foreign Affairs* in October 1974, C. Fred Bergsten advanced strong objections to a decision by the Canadian government to permit only those foreign investments to enter

Canada that would bring "significant benefit" to that country. Such requirements, Bergsten felt, would make international conflict "certain" and would ultimately lead to what he called "investment wars." His fears and expectations fortunately proved to be exaggerated, but the basic issue remains a live one and we shall come back to it.

THE POSITION BEFORE THE OIL CRISIS

To sum up the position in the early 1970s—a period during which the rate of expropriation of foreign enterprise reached its peak—there was great concern about TNCs among host countries in the Third World:

– fears of neocolonialism accompanied by political interference, corruption, pollution, and disturbance of social traditions;
– fears of the distortion of economic priorities, inadequacy of benefits derived from foreign exploitation of nonrenewable natural resources, displacement of domestic enterprise, inappropriate technologies, maldistribution of income, and pressure on the balance of payments.

The solutions to these problems were thought to be as follows:

– the assertion of domestic sovereignty, especially over natural resources;
– the introduction or tightening of regulations, controls, and monitoring devices;
– legislative and administrative measures designed to ensure compatibility of the activities of TNCs with national political, social, and economic objectives;
– legislative and administrative measures designed to ensure a fairer distribution of benefits, with particular emphasis on improving the terms of agreements negotiated with the TNCs and the prevention of abuses, such as manipulative transfer pricing and evasion of taxes and exchange controls;
– the creation of UN machinery (the Commission and Centre on TNCs) to negotiate a code of conduct on TNCs; to improve the flow of information to the Third World on the capabilities and limitations of the TNCs; and to provide technical support to strengthen the negotiating capabilities of developing countries.

Although the home countries considered themselves threatened by some of the strategies that were being developed in the Third World, they were not without their own problems in dealing with the TNCs. Their concerns (in a lower key than in the Third World) were with

- the loss of domestic employment thought to result from foreign investment intended to transfer production capacity abroad;
- performance requirements and other measures imposed on the TNCs by host countries and designed to turn the balance of advantage in favor of the host countries, against which the home countries would have to retaliate (Bergsten's "investment wars");
- the prevention of tax avoidance and evasion by the TNCs;
- the prevention of foreign takeovers or control of key domestic industries.

The industrial countries, while taking a much more permissive attitude to the TNCs than Third World host countries, also saw a need for a code of conduct for the corporations, which they introduced under the rubric of OECD Guidelines. Relatively little was done to prevent the transfer of production and associated employment abroad. Tax administrations adopted various methods for improving home country tax revenue collection from the TNCs. And a number of countries attempted to counter the alienation of ownership and control of key domestic industries, with varying degrees of success.

THE NEW OUTLOOK IN THE 1980S

Since the onset of the world debt crisis in the second half of 1982, Third World attitudes to private foreign investment and TNCs have changed radically. The sudden collapse of commercial bank lending to most of the major debtors of the Third World created nothing short of an economic upheaval in many countries that had been relying on the banks for most of their inflow of capital ever since the first oil crisis in 1973–74. Many of these countries found themselves in the position of having to run trade surpluses with the creditor countries in order to service their debts. Instead of being able to rely on foreign savings to finance part of their own investment requirements, they were now having to draw on domestic savings to service their foreign debts. This resulted in a sharp decline in their ability to invest in the expansion of domestic capacity, which is a primary goal for any country seeking to develop. Moreover, as the IMF pointed out in its *Annual Report, 1987* (p. 12), "The fall in living standards has been pervasive and large in the Western Hemisphere and in Africa, as countries in these regions have struggled to correct domestic and external imbalances in the face of an often unfavorable external environment."

It is unlikely that the peoples of these countries will be willing to accept indefinitely a situation in which their living standards and long-term economic prospects have to take second place in national priorities, while the servicing of debt takes first place in preempting available resources. As Fritz Leutwiler, former President of the Swiss National Bank and of the Bank for International Settlements put it: "But quite a different bomb might explode, namely a political or social one. This will explode when these debtor developing countries have to conduct a policy of austerity over too long a period simply in order to service their debt. That is a bomb with a built-in time fuse." [10] Recent moves by major commercial banks in the creditor countries to write down part of these debts, and build up their loan loss reserves, reflect a growing recognition that the debts cannot be repaid in full under the conditions now prevailing.

Much has been made, therefore, in recent years of the need for a major increase in nondebt creating capital flows to the Third World to replace the commercial bank lending that had predominated prior to 1982. U.S. Secretary of the Treasury James A. Baker III, during a major address to the annual meetings of the IMF and World Bank held in Seoul in October 1985, proposed a plan for dealing with the international debt problem on a basis that would permit debtors to maintain adequate rates of growth and thereby break away from the economic depression that had been forced upon them by the existing international debt strategy. He made the following point, among others: "There are essentially two kinds of capital inflows: loans and equity investments. Foreign borrowings have to be repaid—with interest. Equity investment, on the other hand, has a degree of permanence, and is not debt-creating. Moreover, it can have a compounding effect on growth, bring innovation and technology, and help to keep capital at home." Debtor countries should therefore, in his view, adopt "market-opening measures" to encourage foreign direct investment. Subsequently, in his statement to the annual meetings in September 1987, he further proposed the inclusion, within a "menu of financial options," the issuance of notes or bonds that would be convertible into local equity, and debt/equity swaps, both of which would improve the debt/equity mix in the foreign obligations of the debtor countries.[11]

THIRD WORLD ATTITUDES

The attitudes of developing countries toward foreign investment had already become much more receptive long before the announcement of the Baker Plan at Seoul.

At least four factors probably contributed to this. In the first place, most of the important foreign-owned, mineral-extracting companies in developing countries had either already been nationalized by the mid-1970s or had accepted a degree of local participation in ownership sufficient to satisfy the aspirations of the host countries concerned. Secondly, host governments began to realize that their development and revenue objectives could often best be secured by means other than nationalization—for example, by entering into advantageous agreements with TNCs prepared to take a long view and conduct their affairs as good corporate citizens of the host countries. Thirdly, the bargaining strength of host countries was seriously weakened by pressures on their balances of payments resulting particularly from the debt problem, and these countries therefore sought to avoid policies that might have adverse effects on the inflow of capital, whether public or private. Moreover, although they did not do away with the regulatory controls they had created, developing countries frequently liberalized and simplified the applicable legislation and the screening of project proposals was generally speeded up.

On the other hand, TNCs and other foreign investors, particularly in the resource sector, became more aware of and sensitive to host country objectives and often adapted their policies to those objectives by readiness to reduce their own equity participation while relying to a greater extent on fees, royalties, and other forms of nonequity income. Finally, cases of blatant political interference in the domestic affairs of host countries appear to have become infrequent, and efforts of foreign corporations to make known their interests to domestic authorities were undertaken with greater circumspection. Even ITT fell into line, with management issuing new and stringent rules under which activities of the kind prevalent in the company in the early 1970s would render those responsible subject to summary dismissal. Large-scale bribery by TNCs as well as by local entities persisted, but major scandals were not particularly frequent and there were, in any case, few if any host governments prepared to take a stand against it.

A striking illustration of the extent of the change in Third World attitudes is to be found in the course taken by the UN negotiations on a code of conduct on TNCs. When these negotiations began in January 1977, developing countries envisaged the code as being limited to provisions regarding standards of behavior of TNCs. The OECD countries, on the other hand, insisted that the code must be a balanced one in the sense of defining the obligations not only of the corporations to the host countries but of the host countries to the corporations as well. This was at first entirely unacceptable to the Third World. It was felt by many that there was a certain impropriety in placing host country governments and foreign corporations on an equal footing with one another in prescribing norms for conduct.

In 1980, however, the group of developing countries as a whole reversed itself, and agreed to a "balanced" code, overcoming the objections of certain influential delegations in their midst that continued to feel that it would be a mistake to do so. This formal recognition of the existence of host country obligations to TNCs marks a new stage in the evolution of the Third World's outlook on these matters.

THE PROSPECTS

Despite the notable convergence of views between North and South on the desirability of enhanced flows of direct investment to the developing countries, a substantial upturn is unlikely to be realized in the near future. The potential for new flows of private direct investment to the Third World has been greatly exaggerated. Much has been written about the great need for such flows and about the fact that equity capital has considerable advantages over loan capital from the standpoint of the recipient country. In particular, while loans have to be serviced regardless of whether the projects they finance are profitable, equity capital generates returns to the investor only if the project is a successful one. This gives the investor a strong stake in success, and means that the transfer of profits and dividends can always be financed out of the net company earnings from which they are derived.

But the fact that equity capital is "needed" provides no guarantee that it will be forthcoming to all those who need it. Precisely the same factors that are responsible for the reluctance of the commercial banks to make new loans to the debtor countries act likewise as a deterrent to new direct investment. If countries are not in sufficiently good economic health to assure payment of debt service on the funds they have borrowed, are they likely to be any more successful in remitting the dividends that become due to foreign owners of equity capital? It is true that a successful project is one that yields a profit on the capital invested in it. But the fact that a particular project is profitable does not mean that the overall balance of payments of the host country will be sufficiently strong to permit profits and dividends to be remitted. If interest is not being paid on loans received the chances are that the transfer of profits and dividends will be affected likewise.

In other words, the selfsame conditions of economic depression in the Third World that make it difficult for these countries to attract new commercial loans are an obstacle to new direct investment as well. The data on actual flows bear this out. Net flows of direct investment to net debtor developing countries reached a peak of $13.2 billion in 1981—the year in which borrowing from the commercial banks also attained its maximum. From that point direct investment flows dropped to $8.9 billion in 1983 and remained at approximately this level for the next three years. There was a recovery in 1987–88, but this was probably concentrated in the countries not experiencing severe debt servicing difficulties.[12]

Even if the recent recovery in direct investment benefited all the net debtor countries it would not make much difference to their import capacity, and it is their constrained import capacity that is the most important single obstacle to the restoration of a satisfactory rate of growth for these countries and to the recovery of their living standards. The fact is that the net external borrowing of net debtor developing countries from private sources and short-term flows fell from $76 billion in 1981 to only $6 billion in 1988. To compensate merely for one-half of this drastic decline direct investment would have to triple from its current level.[13] This is obviously out of the question in the near term.

The economic depression among the Third World debtors is only partly due to their debt overhang. Much of the trouble lies in the slack state of the world economy resulting from the macroeconomic policies of the industrial countries. It has been generally agreed in the multilateral financial institutions and the economics profession that one of the main factors on which the economic viability of the debtor countries depends is the maintenance of an average annual rate of growth by the OECD countries of at least 3 percent or, preferably, better.[14] This is because a growth rate at least that high is necessary to sustain the imports of the OECD group and hence the export earnings that the debtor countries need for meeting their debt service commitments. In fact, however, according to IMF data, the OECD countries did not reach the 3 percent threshold in five out of the ten years from 1980 to 1989. The performance of the European Community was particularly bad, falling short of 3 percent in eight out of the ten years. This distribution of growth rates among the industrial countries had an especially depressing effect on OECD imports because imports are a larger proportion of national output in the EC than in the United States and Japan. This has meant a weak market for the primary commodities that are the principal exports of the developing countries— so weak that commodity prices have repeatedly slumped to record lows for the postwar period. Thus the industrial countries themselves were in a sense partly responsible both for making it impossible for the debtor countries to achieve the level of export earnings needed to finance their debt service payments, and for creating an economic environment in which there was no inducement for private foreign investment flows to recover.

THE CONCENTRATION OF FLOWS

Direct investment is in any case of limited help in promoting Third World development because it is highly concentrated geographically, just as commercial bank lending was in the 1970s. For obvious business reasons it tends to concentrate on high-income and, to a lesser extent, middle-income countries.

About three-quarters of the flows are channeled within the OECD group itself, with only the remaining one-quarter going to developing countries. Within the group of developing countries, those with the highest per capita GNP (over $1,000 in 1979) account for two-thirds of the investment flows while low-income countries (under $380 in 1979) account for less than 5 percent. A mere six countries (Argentina, Brazil, Hong Kong, Malaysia, Mexico, and Singapore) consistently accounted for between one-half and three-quarters of direct investment flows to all developing countries in the latter years of the 1970s. For the low-income group the ratio of foreign direct investment to GNP was considerably less than 0.1 percent at the end of the 1970s, while even for high-income countries it was only around 0.6 percent.[15] TNCs are, quite naturally, interested only in countries that offer important profit-making opportunities. Among the low-income countries such opportunities are limited to those with exportable solid mineral deposits or petroleum. Foreign investment cannot therefore be a solution for the problems of the great majority of developing countries and cannot in any case substitute for official aid to the low-income countries. It may, however, be useful in bringing new technologies and managerial skills to the relatively few countries whose markets or economic potential are of interest to the TNCs.

THE COST OF FOREIGN INVESTMENT

A key point that seems to have been forgotten in the drive to substitute direct investment flows for loan capital is that one of the reasons for recourse to commercial borrowing in the 1970s was the attempt to deal with what the Group of Eminent Persons had referred to as the "excessive cost" of the activities of foreign corporations.[16] The Group devoted particular attention to the extent to which developing countries could acquire the capacity to purchase the package of resources provided by TNCs—namely technology, management, capital, and access to markets—at the lowest possible total cost. The most costly decision a host country could make, said the Group, was to choose the wrong package of resources and much therefore depended on the ability to determine which package it would be advantageous to purchase and how best to reshape it so that it could be integrated into the country's total strategy for development. One alternative to the package deal was the separate purchase of individual components of the package and it was here that access to commercial borrowing was seen to be helpful. Many TNCs, moreover, were and are willing to accept forms of operation in which ownership rights are reduced, including management and service contracts, turnkey operations, joint ventures, and coproduction agreements based on national ownership. But many of these forms of operation presuppose that the host country does not depend on TNCs for the capital needed, but has access to foreign borrowing facilities or other sources.

Unfortunately, under the conditions prevailing at the present time, and likely to prevail for some years to come, in which commercial borrowing capacity is not available to most debtor countries, it might be much more difficult to pick and choose the elements of the package to be purchased. The TNC is, therefore, in a stronger position to insist on maintaining the integrity of the package as a whole.

There is a serious lack of information as to just how "excessive" the costs of foreign direct investment to the host countries really are. This is due not only to the limited amount of data available in this field—data on costs of the type that all corporations naturally wish to keep confidential—but to conceptual difficulties in the analysis of the data. The problem is that actual costs have to be compared with some alternative situation which is in the nature of the case hypothetical. If a particular activity of a foreign corporation had not existed what would the alternative situation have been? Would the country have dispensed with domestic production and supplied its needs entirely through imports? Or would a local firm have moved into the industry and if so at what level of efficiency and costs? Or would there have been some combination of these two approaches, possibly through the kind of "unpackaging" discussed earlier? There is no way of getting precise answers to these questions, and the analyst therefore has to rely largely on common sense and his or her best judgment.

The best available study in this area comes to relatively few empirical conclusions, and the authors, Sanjaya Lall and Paul Streeten, are frank in pointing to the difficulties that they faced in reaching even these conclusions.[17] Their study relates to 159 sample firms, in six developing countries: the sample included a variety of firms, some wholly owned or partially owned abroad and some with local ownership. One of their major findings was that the large majority of manufacturing investments, domestic or foreign, have negative direct effects on the balances of payments of the countries concerned, but that foreign-controlled firms have worse average effects than do locally controlled firms. Foreign control does not generally seem to provide any stimulus to exports and may even inhibit them: there is "ample evidence," say the authors, that restrictive practices affecting exports abound where foreign investment and foreign technological agreements are involved. Lall and Streeten did not find any significant difference between foreign and locally controlled corporations as regards import propensities, but more recent studies by the UN Centre on Transnational Corporations have concluded that the import propensities of foreign-controlled firms tend to be higher than those of locally controlled firms, so that in this respect too the direct balance-of-payments effects are negative.

A second finding by Lall and Streeten is that the purely financial contribution of foreign direct investment appears to be negligible or negative. This, they say, is not an unexpected finding since "it is, after all, generally admitted that direct investment *is usually a rather expensive way to get funds as such*" (emphasis added).[18] What their findings mean, they say, is that "It would, in other words, have been cheaper for the countries concerned—had the loans, and in some cases technology, been available abroad—to borrow the money and buy out the foreign investments, or to divert local capital from other uses."[19] The corollary of the above is, of course, that a shift from borrowed to direct investment inflows would tend to have adverse financial consequences for the countries concerned.

The authors point out that the above results take no account of transfer pricing. Though they do not say so, it is likely that allowance for transfer pricing, if such allowance could be made, would considerably reinforce the authors' conclusions since transfer pricing is almost invariably designed to increase the "take" of the foreign corporation at the expense of local entities—the government, local shareholders, wage earners, and so forth.

THE BURDEN OF TRANSFER PRICING

"Transfer pricing" is the term used to denote the pricing of inputs and outputs within a company, and becomes a matter of concern to governments when intra-company transactions cross national frontiers. By arbitrary or abusive transfer pricing, a TNC may shift income from one country to another in response to a variety of factors including, for example, intercountry differences in corporate tax rates. Abusive transfer pricing is also used by some TNCs to shift income out of countries with strong exchange controls. In this area home countries and host countries frequently have common interests, especially where a TNC shifts income from both home and host countries to the so-called tax havens. There is growing cooperation among industrial countries in tracking down abusive transfer pricing by TNCs, but relatively little cooperation in this field exists between industrial and developing countries.

Even the U.S. government, with the large investigative resources that it has at its disposal, experiences difficulty in tracking down abusive transfer pricing. As a study prepared by the U.S. Internal Revenue Service observed, "We are severely hampered by the lack of information" about TNCs as well as by the fact that affiliates of these corporations, together with their books and records, are scattered throughout the world.[20] Moreover, according to the U.S. Comptroller General, in modern business conditions "a true arm's length price (such as is necessary for checking transfer prices) can rarely be identified."[21] A study by the Canadian tax authorities states that profit transfers to a tax haven usually involve the use of a special distributing or sales company in a tax haven to minimize income attributable to, say, a Canadian affiliate. "It is our belief," says Revenue Canada, Taxation, "that this method is prevalent throughout many industries."[22]

The problems of home and host countries in relation to transfer pricing are also encountered by subsidiary tax authorities within these countries. For example, owing to the possibility of abusive transfer pricing the individual states of the United States have difficulty in determining how much taxable income is generated within each state by companies with country-wide or worldwide affiliations. For this reason several U.S. states introduced systems of unitary taxation, whereby the taxable income of a TNC within each state would be determined on the basis of a formula. For example, the state of California decided to tax a share of any company's worldwide income equal to the average of the fractions of the company's worldwide property, payroll, and sales reported for California alone. This method was challenged on various grounds all the way to the U.S. Supreme Court, which upheld the system of unitary taxation, thereby accepting California's approach to the determination of taxable income generated within the state as fair and reasonable.[23]

The Supreme Court's decision was followed by a sharp reaction from European and Japanese TNCs. The *New York Times* reported, "From 1984 to 1986 the Florida and California legislatures were bombarded with threats by foreign companies to shift their facilities elsewhere unless they repealed their unitary taxes."[24] The companies mobilized their home governments on this matter and strong government-to-government pressure was applied at the highest level. Ultimately some of the states that had adopted systems of unitary taxation felt compelled to give way. But the issue remains a live one, and in January 1990 the U.S. Supreme Court issued a further ruling in favor of the state of California and against Alcan Aluminium and Imperial Chemical Industries (ICI).[25] Moreover, the facts remained unchallenged—namely that, as the Supreme Court had recognized, the states did not and do not have an adequate basis for the determination of the taxable income of TNCs. And what is true for the states of California and Florida is true also for many developing countries.

ASSESSING PERFORMANCE

The question of performance criteria has become an issue between home countries and host countries—the latter including certain developed as well as developing countries. Particular objection is taken by home countries to host country efforts to regulate the proportion of a TNC's output that is exported or the maximum import content of locally produced goods or the proportion of equity that is held locally. A statement of U.S. government policy on this matter indicates that the United States opposes the use of government practices that distort, restrict, or place unreasonable burdens on direct investment. The United States, the statement says, intends to continue its efforts to reduce or eliminate such practices and will make a particular effort to prevent the introduction by other countries of new measures of this type. While the United States will continue to attempt to deal with this issue on a multilateral basis, "non-multilateral approaches may be appropriate on a case-by-case basis."[26]

One major example of this "non-multilateral approach" was the direct pressure exerted on India under the 1988 Omnibus Trade and Competitiveness Act to abolish an array of investment regulations alleged to distort trade. If agreement with India on this matter as well as on certain other matters such as the opening up of the Indian insurance market to U.S. companies were not reached by June 16, 1990, the law required that the United States retaliate. According to the *New York Times* of April 28, 1990, such retaliation could take the form of 100 percent duties on selected imports from India.

This question is presently under discussion in GATT in the context of the Uruguay Round. On the one hand it is entirely legitimate for host countries to seek assurances of satisfactory performance by TNCs. Some of the main features of such performance are set out below. On the other hand, home countries also have a legitimate interest in protecting their fair share of the taxable income of TNCs or their affiliates operating within their borders, and in avoiding, if they can, a loss of employment opportunities resulting from excessive inducements offered by host countries or potential host countries to TNCs. But home countries are not entitled to prescribe the types of foreign investment regulation that a host country may impose or whether a host country may be required to open up particular domestic markets to foreign competition, and there is really no reason why GATT should claim jurisdiction in this field in place of the UN Commission on TNCs, which has been dealing with it for many years. It is particularly open to question whether home countries are entitled under GATT to threaten individual host countries or trading partners with retaliation if they do not comply with home country demands. The use of this weapon has drawn virtually unanimous condemnation among GATT members.

As long as the question of performance criteria is not treated as one of fundamental principle there seems to be no reason why appropriate accommodations should not be negotiated between the parties, as has already occurred in a successfully resolved dispute between the United States and Canada in this field that was brought before GATT. On the other hand, if the position were taken that all government efforts to supervise the performance of TNCs are illegitimate in and of themselves, since they constitute a form of "distortion" of the market, a solution might be much more difficult to find.

CONCLUSION

Thus far there has been a certain lack of realism about expectations for the revival of private foreign investment. The assumption seems to have been that foreign investors would rush in where the commercial banks feared to tread. But immediate prospects for direct investment flows to most developing countries are distinctly modest, not because developing countries would not welcome such flows but because profitable investment opportunities are limited. The external capital requirements of debtor countries, which are very great at this stage owing to the virtual cessation of voluntary lending by commercial banks, will have to be met by channeling funds through bilateral and multilateral official institutions, whose resources need to be greatly increased.

There is no doubt that in the longer run many of the TNCs have it within their power to make important contributions to growth and development in those developing countries in which they recognize attractive profit-making opportunities. Unfortunately only a small minority of the developing countries have been of interest to the TNCs in the past, even under favorable business conditions. But perhaps one can look forward to a gradual enlargement of the number if potential host countries demonstrate a strong commitment to development by mobilizing their own resources more effectively to that end, and if the international community provides the necessary support through trade and aid and a return to policies for a more vigorously expanding world economy. For the time being traditional North-South conflicts relating to foreign investment have subsided, partly because the South is under severe balance-of-payments pressure and does not wish to jeopardize whatever prospects there may be of larger inflows. But these issues are probably only quiescent. There is no reason to expect any large-scale resumption of major confrontations over expropriation because most of the important mineral-extracting companies in developing countries have already been taken over or have accepted a degree of local participation in ownership sufficient to satisfy the host countries concerned.

Other issues that arose in the past, however, may well recur once larger and more adequate flows of foreign investment are resumed and developing countries feel that they have less cause for anxiety about the availability of external finance in the aggregate.

At that stage the extent of the additional impetus to development given by the TNCs will depend on

- refraining, or continuing to refrain, from interference in purely domestic affairs;
- making deliberate efforts to ensure that company strategies and operations are fully consistent with national objectives and policies;
- showing flexibility in dealing with requests for local participation in ownership and control;
- bringing in capital from abroad rather than preempting local financial resources;
- effectively transferring technologies adapted to Third World conditions and opportunities;
- maximizing the utilization of local labor and other inputs and permitting local participation in the capital and management of local affiliates;
- promoting export capacity and efficient domestic substitution for imports;
- abstaining from tax evasion and abusive transfer pricing;
- behaving in general as good corporate citizens.

Much benefit could be gained by bringing the negotiations on a UN Code of Conduct on TNCS to a successful conclusion. The few issues remaining do not pose great difficulties and compromise formulae to deal with them already command wide support within each of the major groups of negotiators. In fact the expert advisers to the negotiating body, who include representatives of the TNCS, have themselves jointly proposed perfectly workable solutions to the outstanding questions.

A major difficulty is that several home countries believe that they can get more favorable terms in bilaterally negotiated investment agreements than in a UN Code. This may be true in some cases but the agreements are admittedly one-sided and key clauses are likely to be repudiated or ignored in cases of serious difficulty between the parties. A multilaterally agreed Code will almost certainly command much greater respect than bilateral agreements signed under the pressure of the greatly superior bargaining power of home countries.

It is noticeable that as the home countries become more involved with one another as recipients as well as suppliers of direct investment, some of the same concerns are emerging among them as have arisen between North and South. Thus Sir Michael Butler, former U.K. representative to the EC, wrote an article in February 1986 entitled, "How Europe Can Fight the Multinationals." He expressed the view that U.S. and Japanese multinationals operating in Europe would seek to knock out or take over the European competition, after which they would be free to shift the balance of their investments in plant and research toward their home bases or other markets yet to be conquered.[27]

Similar fears are expressed more and more frequently in the United States. Consider the following statement, for example: "We are a dependent nation that is beginning to lose control of its fate. . . . I can foresee a time . . . when our foreign creditors and foreign owners will demand concessions from us. . . . These concessions will undermine our independence." This was not a statement by an official from Brazil or Mexico. It is a statement by Dale Bumpers, U.S. Democratic Senator from Arkansas.[28]

The wider dissemination of such views in the North may make it easier for people to understand the concerns about private direct investment expressed from time to time in the past in the South. Such awareness and understanding of the concerns of other countries may clear the road for the creation of a new modus vivendi going beyond a Code of Conduct to the mutual advantage of the North, the South, and the TNCS. This possibility is for the future, but it is worth working for.

6

The International Debt Crisis

Crisis Management and the International Debt Problem*

Despite the extraordinary effort, skill, and ingenuity displayed in dealing with the world debt crisis of the 1980s, a great opportunity was lost. A forward-looking strategy of crisis management would have taken every possible advantage of the common interest of all the parties involved in ensuring the quickest possible recovery of the debtors and hence of their autonomous capacity to service their debts. The measures adopted had the effect instead of promoting an adversary relationship between creditors and debtors and of delaying and prolonging the recovery process unnecessarily to the late 1980s or even beyond. The crisis, therefore, persists: the forms that it takes may, for the moment, be less dramatic than previously, but may become even more threatening than before as resentment builds among the populations of the debtor countries.

CRISIS AND CONFLICT

The handling of the world debt problem since August 1982 is widely regarded in the international financial community as a tour de force of crisis management. A series of major debtor countries found themselves unable to meet their debt service obligations falling due. In certain cases the payments involved were sufficiently sizable to be a significant element in the earnings of large commercial banks. In these instances failure to pay on the due dates could have led to a collapse of public confidence in the banking systems of the lending countries, had it not been for the alertness of national and international authorities in improvising hurried rescue operations that provided loans to the debtor countries with which to make the payments falling due. In announcing the $500 million rescue operation for Argentina at the end of March 1984, for example, the U.S.

*This essay was originally published in *International Journal* 40 (Autumn 1985). The author gratefully acknowledges valuable comments received from Christine Bindert, Michael Dell, Gerald Helleiner, Richard Jolly, Pedro Malan, and Frances Stewart.

Secretary of the Treasury remarked that in helping the government of Argentina the United States was seeking to avert an international banking crisis: "If you want to look over the cliff and see the chasm down below," he said, "that is the sort of thing that might happen."[1]

International attention has been concentrated chiefly on the tensions between debtor country entities, whether public or private, and the commercial banks that had provided them with syndicated loans during the 1970s. But there is another group of countries, generally at lower-income levels, which encountered equally pressing problems associated with the burden of servicing debts due to foreign governments and international financial institutions. While the debts of low-income countries to official institutions were much smaller in the aggregate than the corresponding debts of middle-income, developing countries to private banks, the ratio of debt service to exports in many of the former group of countries was and is at least as large if not larger than the corresponding debt service ratios of countries such as Argentina, Brazil, Mexico, and the Philippines.

It will not be possible here to discuss all the various sources of conflict, domestic and international, associated with the debt crisis, or the effectiveness of crisis management in dealing with them. The main emphasis will have to be on the management of relationships between debtors and creditors, their respective home countries and the international community. Other elements of the problem will be mentioned only as they bear directly on the principal theme.

WHEN A CRISIS IS NOT A CRISIS

Not all debt servicing emergencies are considered sufficiently important to warrant the use of the big guns of the international artillery. When steps were taken in February 1983 to augment the resources potentially available to the IMF under the General Arrangements to Borrow (GAB) stringent limitations were placed on their use.

The GAB was an arrangement originally established in 1962 to permit the ten leading industrial countries to make supplementary resources available to the Fund for on-lending to one or more members of the ten so as "to forestall or cope with an impairment of the international monetary system."[2] In 1962 it did not seem likely that any such impairment could result from developments in the balances of payments of countries other than the ten participants in the GAB. The crisis of 1982 showed that a number of developing countries had reached the stage where their ability to service their debts was a matter of great importance for some of the biggest and most powerful banks in the world. Accordingly, the text of the GAB was revised to permit participants in it, together with "parallel creditors" (such as Saudi Arabia), to make resources available to the Fund for on-lending to nonparticipants as well as to participants. The activation of the GAB in this way was to depend on a finding by the Managing Director, subsequently endorsed by GAB participants as well as by the Executive Board of the Fund, that the Fund's resources were not adequate "to meet actual and expected requests for financing that reflect the existence of an exceptional situation associated with balance-of-payments problems of members of a character or aggregate size that could threaten the stability of the international monetary system."[3] Obviously the number of developing countries whose debt service obligations were sufficiently large or important to qualify as such a threat was quite small—perhaps half-dozen or so.

Up to mid-1985 it had not proved necessary to activate the GAB in their new form, but attitudes to the debt crisis clearly reflected the distinction drawn in the GAB.[4] The current mood of optimism about the handling of the international debt crisis since 1982 is based on experience with the half-dozen or so largest debtors. It does not take account of the persistent crises encountered in the smaller debtors of the Third World—in Africa, Latin America, and elsewhere—many of which, as noted earlier, have a burden of debt that, in relation to their export earnings, is comparable with or higher than that of the large debtors.

RESPONSIBILITY FOR THE CRISIS

It could be argued that once the debt problem reached crisis proportions, it did not much matter who was responsible for it. It was in any case necessary to create conditions under which payments of interest and principal falling due could be made at the appropriate times.

In view of the intense controversy over the fairness of the debt rescheduling arrangements made, however, the question of responsibility for the crisis cannot be altogether avoided. It is of considerable interest in this context that in 1984 Michel Camdessus, the former President of the Paris Club, expressed the opinion that "poverty or mismanagement is not, in most cases, the main cause of serious debt problems."[5] There is, moreover, a large measure of agreement, even among those who regard the rescheduling arrangements as entirely equitable, that while the borrowers were often imprudent in the extent of their borrowing, the lending banks cannot escape their own responsibility in the matter.

Indeed, the commercial banks went to great lengths during the 1970s, under the conditions of excess liquidity created by the huge accumulations of petrodollars deposited in the Eurodollar market, to press their loans upon any countries that could meet minimum standards of creditworthiness. The same is not true of the lending of official institutions to low-income countries, but by the same token these countries cannot be accused of overborrowing, if only because of the limitations on foreign aid imposed by the lenders.

In assessing responsibility for the massive buildup of debt during the 1970s the first point to note is that it took place not by chance but as the result of a deliberate decision by the lenders and the borrowers—a decision supported by the entire membership of the IMF. The rise in oil prices had resulted in the oil exporting countries accumulating large savings which it was well beyond their capacity to use productively within their own countries alone. Simultaneously, the real incomes and savings of the oil importing countries had been correspondingly reduced. Unless the surplus resources in the hands of the oil exporting countries could somehow be channeled elsewhere, there was a danger that the world economy as a whole would be thrown into a deflationary spiral, to the detriment of oil exporters and oil importers alike. Consequently, the Fund membership decided unanimously that special measures were required to offset the potentially deflationary effects of the increase in oil prices. To this end, oil facilities were established by the Fund to provide loans at low conditionality to countries needing them in order to sustain their level of economic activity. In fact the only condition laid down by the IMF for making these loans was that the borrowers should undertake to maintain their levels of business activity and not to cause difficulties for others by restricting imports in the effort to counter pressures on the balance of payments.

The financial resources available to the Fund for this purpose were, however, very small in relation to the scale of the problem created by the rise in oil prices. Most of the requisite channeling of financial resources from surplus to deficit countries was therefore undertaken by the commercial banks, which thereby, in effect, took over the major part of IMF responsibilities for providing balance-of-payments support. In the first few years of this process the loans were made at relatively low nominal rates of interest, and real rates were often actually negative. Later, however, interest rates rose to unprecedented levels as a result of monetary policies adopted by the industrial countries to counter inflation. While the cost of servicing accumulated debts soared, the export earnings of the debtor countries dropped sharply as their export prices and volumes reacted to slackening business activity in the main industrial countries. This in turn led to a collapse of new lending by the commercial banks.

There is no doubt that in individual cases debtor countries compounded their own problems through lax fiscal and monetary policies and, in some cases, extravagant expenditure on investment and consumption, including military outlays. But it is not possible to account for the sudden upsurge in the number of countries coming under severe balance-of-payments pressure in the early 1980s on the basis of mismanagement alone. Jacques de Larosière, the Managing Director of the IMF, stated recently that during the period from 1981 to mid-1984 fifty-eight countries encountered debt servicing difficulties in the sense that they incurred external payments arrears or had to reschedule their debts—a far larger number than in any previous period of comparable length.[6] As the former Brazilian Minister of Finance, Mário Henrique Simonsen, has pointed out:

> The chances of widespread crises being precipitated by the errors of a large number of *independent* actors are minute. A plausible explanation for the debt crisis must rely on either some external factor, or the inadequacy of the recycling system or both. Hence, the witch-hunting investigation might well be left aside, were it not for the insistent charges by conservative-populist politicians and by poorly informed observers.[7]

It should also be noted that many of those who now rejoice in the wisdom of hindsight cannot be said to have foreseen the crisis or to have proposed, in good time, measures for preventing or avoiding it. Neither of the Bretton Woods institutions sounded the alarm in an effective manner. As late as May 1980 the IMF was playing down the increase that was taking place in the ratio of debt to GNP:

> As far as financing is concerned, the question of whether a country should seek further credit should not be answered by reference to statistical measures, such as the ratio of debt to GNP, but by consideration of the profitability of the investment financed with borrowed funds. As long as the expected return on investment over the longer run exceeds the cost of borrowing abroad, higher foreign indebtedness is sound policy for both lender and borrower because the higher level of investment financed by foreign borrowing will eventually be reflected in additional net export capacity. From a global perspective, it is apparent that it would be desirable to match the

higher current account surplus of the oil exporting countries, which represents an increase in their savings, with maintained or even increased investment in the rest of the world. From this viewpoint, and because overall liquidity in international financial markets will in all likelihood be increased through the oil exporting countries' placements, it would seem that the notion of what is a reasonable amount of foreign indebtedness should be revised upward for at least some non-oil developing countries.[8]

Similar arguments were used in several World Bank publications. *World Development Report 1982*, for example, stated that "although there have been misjudgments by borrowers and lenders alike . . . on the whole, flows from private sources have gone to those countries best able to use these additions to domestic savings."[9]

A study of debt and adjustment in selected developing countries during the 1970s, prepared by members of the World Bank staff in 1984, came to the conclusion that apart from certain specific cases, resources borrowed from abroad had been "for the most part appropriately used." Investment rates had risen, incremental capital-output ratios had remained at about their earlier levels, growth momentum had been maintained despite the recession of 1974–75 among the industrial nations, and the rapid expansion of exports had contributed to the maintenance of acceptable debt service ratios. Externally, the deficit on the trade balance had been reduced as a proportion of GNP from 1974–75 to 1976–78 and internally, the rate of growth of consumption had been brought into line with the reduced rate of growth of domestic income. Carlos Diaz-Alejandro made much the same kind of survey for the Latin American countries alone, reaching the conclusion that, generally speaking, "1980 debt indicators and aggregate measures of creditworthiness did not look significantly worse than they did in 1973." Not until 1980–81 could it have been said that a need for adjustment and reform had emerged, and even then "nothing in the situation called for traumatic depressions."[10]

As to the factors leading to the deterioration in the balance of payments of non-oil developing countries in the early 1980s, analyses by the IMF have been quite clear and consistent. The Fund's *Annual Report 1983*, for example, explained the sharp setback in the total current account balance of these countries from 1978 to 1981 as follows:

The key consideration here is the generally unfavorable nature of the external economic and financial environment faced by these countries in recent years and the importance of certain major adverse influences almost wholly beyond their own control. The global recession, of course, has undermined the buoyancy of export markets in volume terms and has brought severe weakness in export prices for primary commodities. Meanwhile, continued increases in the import prices faced by non-oil developing countries had already contributed to the prolonged deterioration of their terms of trade (1982 having been the fifth consecutive year of such deterioration). Finally, the upsurge of interest rates that followed the general shift toward monetary restraint in the major industrial countries in 1979 imposed an unexpectedly heavy and lasting burden on this group of countries, whose balance of payments structures already featured quite sizable debt service charges. . . .

For the oil importing developing countries, the entire deterioration of their combined current account balance from 1978 to 1981 can be ascribed to essentially the three adverse factors just enumerated.[11]

The IMF staff has pointed out that wherever external payments imbalances are not transitory or reversible, the countries concerned have to adjust, regardless of whether they themselves are responsible for the imbalances. This is clearly correct, but it does not settle the question of how the burden of adjustment should be shared between debtor and creditor countries. The purpose of the "witch-hunting" referred to by Simonsen is precisely to provide a rationale for placing virtually the entire burden of adjustment to the debt crisis on the shoulders of the debtor countries, which are now alleged to have brought about their own undoing through mismanagement. But if the latter assertion is less than a half-truth, as the Fund's 1983 report quoted above demonstrates beyond doubt, present burden-sharing between debtors and creditors appears grossly inequitable. Many of the debtor countries have sustained reductions in real income of one-third or more in recent years, while the creditor banks have been able, as will be seen, to raise the earnings on their loans to developing countries on the grounds that the reduced creditworthiness of the debtors necessitates higher margins on loans as well as increased fees and commissions.

THE CONTRAST BETWEEN NATIONAL AND INTERNATIONAL APPROACHES

There is a remarkable contrast between the treatment afforded to debtors faced with difficulties at the national and international levels. At the national level it is by no means accepted that the debtor must invariably be saddled with the entire burden arising from his inability to pay. On the contrary, it is recognized as in the interests of the creditors themselves that debtors should be enabled to work their way out of their difficulties by rebuilding the capacity to service their debts. To this end protection is provided against the possible onslaughts of overanxious, overzealous, or over-greedy creditors. In the United States, under chapter 11 of the Bankruptcy Reform Act of 1978, provision is made for judicial review of plans for reorganization negotiated between creditors and debtors in cases in which debtors file pursuant to that chapter. Standards are laid down to guide judges in deciding whether particular plans of reorganization should be confirmed. These standards include, for example, a requirement that plans of reorganization shall be "feasible" in the sense that they are not likely to be followed by a subsequent need for further reorganization. Judges are endowed with broad equitable powers and in evaluating feasibility may decide whether the schedule of payments and the associated charges are consistent with the purpose of the reorganization.

The United States is not the only country which has adopted special provisions to safeguard the well-being and rehabilitation of the domestic debtor, although it may have taken the most far-reaching steps to this end. Most industrial countries have felt themselves compelled to reject a strictly legalistic approach to indebtedness and have adopted measures that reduce the predominance of the creditor and give considerable weight to the needs and interests of the domestic debtor.

Very different is the state of the art at the international level, where the predominance of the creditor is perhaps more marked than at any time during the past century.[12] Unlike the situation under U.S. domestic law, there is no strong judicial or even quasi-judicial authority at the international level responsible for assessing the feasibility of programs of rescheduling and for ensuring that such programs will rebuild the autonomy and productive capacity of the debtor as quickly as possible, and be so structured as to avoid any need for a repetition of such rescheduling.

Despite the adoption by commercial banks of multiyear rescheduling programs for a number of debtor countries in 1984–85, the debt service obligations of these countries remain unreasonably high, and there is considerable doubt as to their ability to continue meeting these obligations over the long run. Both official and private creditors at the international level seem to be much less aware of their own best interests than at the national level where it is recognized that a debtor who is allowed sufficient breathing space to restore the viability of his enterprise is more likely to be able to effect repayment than a debtor who is driven to the wall.

A CASE HISTORY

This contrast between national and international approaches to debt problems is not a purely academic one. In April 1984 the U.S. Court of Appeals for the Second Circuit in New York upheld a lower court ruling in favor of three Costa Rican banks which, under orders from the central bank of the republic, had suspended payment in 1981 on a loan from a thirty-nine-bank syndicate, and dismissed claims by a U.S. bank which had declined to accept a rescheduling agreement reached by the other thirty-eight banks. The Court of Appeals held that:

> The actions of Costa Rica that resulted in the prohibition of payments on external debt are consistent with the law and policy of the United States. In Canada Southern Railway Co. v. Gebhard, 109 U.S. 527 (1883), the Supreme Court bound New York bondholders to the Canadian government's reorganization of the debts of the government owned Canada Southern Railway. In ordering the dismissal of the bondholders' suit on the old bonds, the Court stated: "[The plan] is in entire harmony with the spirit of bankrupt laws, the binding force of which, upon those who are subject to the jurisdiction, is recognized by all civilized nations. It is not in conflict with the Constitution of the United States, which, although prohibiting States from passing laws impairing the obligation of contracts, allows Congress 'to establish . . . uniform laws on the subject of bankruptcy throughout the United States.' . . . Under these circumstances the true spirit of international comity requires that schemes of this character, legalized at home, should be recognized in other countries." Similarly, Costa Rica's prohibition of payment of its external debts is analogous to the reorganization of a business pursuant to Chapter 11 of our Bankruptcy Code, 11 U.S.C.§§1101-74 (1982). Under Chapter 11, all collection actions against a business filing an application for reorganization are automatically stayed to allow the business to prepare an acceptable plan for the reorganization of its debts, 11 U.S.C.§§103(a), 362, 901(a) (1982). See In re Frigitemp Corp., 8 B.R. 284 (S.D.N.Y. 1981) (purpose of §362 is to give insolvent debtor opportunity to formulate plans for repayment and reorganization with protection from mad scramble of creditors for assets). Costa Rica's prohibition of payment of debt was not a repudiation of the debt but rather was

merely a deferral of payments while it attempted in good faith to renegotiate its obligations.[13]

In March 1985, after rehearing the case, the same court reversed itself and found for the plaintiff. It explained the reversal as follows:

In our previous decision, we affirmed the district court's dismissal. We did not address the question of whether the act of state doctrine applied because . . . we determined that the actions of the Costa Rican government which precipitated the default of the Costa Rican banks were fully consistent with the law and policy of the United States. . . . We therefore concluded that principles of comity compelled us to recognize as valid the Costa Rican directives. Our interpretation of United States policy, however, arose primarily from our belief that the legislative and executive branches of our government fully supported Costa Rica's actions and all of the economic ramifications. On rehearing, the Executive Branch of the United States joined this litigation as amicus curiae and respectfully disputed our reasoning. The Justice Department brief gave the following explanation of our government's support for the debt resolution procedure that operates through the auspices of the International Monetary Fund (IMF). Guided by the IMF, this long-established approach encourages the cooperative adjustment of international debt problems. The entire strategy is grounded in the understanding that, while parties may agree to renegotiate conditions of payment, the underlying obligations to pay nevertheless remain valid and enforceable. Costa Rica's attempted unilateral restructuring of private obligations, the United States contends, was inconsistent with this system of international cooperation and negotiation and thus inconsistent with United States policy. The United States government further explains that its position on private international debt is not inconsistent with either its own willingness to restructure Costa Rica's intergovernmental obligations or with continued United States aid to the economically distressed Central American country. Our previous conclusion that the Costa Rican decrees were consistent with United States policy was premised on these two circumstances.

In light of the government's elucidation of its position, we believe that our earlier interpretation of United States policy . . . was wrong.[14]

This case history reinforces the point that there is a marked contrast between the policies of creditor countries relating to domestic as against external debt problems. And it shows that but for this divergence in policies, the analogy between domestic and foreign debts would, even on a strict legal interpretation, be a sustainable one, as indicated by no less a body than the Supreme Court of the United States.

THE CASE-BY-CASE APPROACH

At the international level the application of a corpus of enlightened general principles to the debt problem is conspicuous by its absence. Indeed, an elaborate argument has been developed to justify the belief that every debt crisis is unique and cannot be compared with any other case. Consequently, the view prevails that no general conclusions can be deduced and no minimum standards of relief applied. Indeed, the very exercise of trying to draw up general principles and minimum standards would, it is said, encourage countries to seek relief in circumstances in which they were not entitled to it. In a study entitled, "External Debt of Developing Countries," published by the OECD in 1981, the conclusion was reached that "there is no general debt problem calling for general solutions. Acute debt-servicing difficulties have remained exceptional, have affected only a few countries, and have been effectively dealt with on a case-by-case basis in a multilateral framework." [15] This statement received the support of the Managing Director of the IMF in 1983 as follows: "there can be no uniform solutions to the debt problems. Rather, their resolution requires forceful and well-crafted adjustment programs geared to the individual circumstances and needs of each debtor country and supported in each case by judicious and coordinated financing arrangements." [16]

There is, of course, no dispute that each case of debt crisis has its own special characteristics that need to be taken into account in devising adjustment programs. In exactly the same way domestic programs for the reorganization of companies that are in difficulties have to be "geared to the individual circumstances and needs" (to use De Larosière's words) of each particular debtor. But individually crafted domestic programs are subject to careful judicial scrutiny in accordance with a body of law establishing criteria for assessment of the feasibility and viability of the measures to be adopted, thereby protecting debtors against unreasonable demands by creditors. Indeed in many cases debtors are relieved of past contractual obligations freely entered into where this is deemed necessary for a successful reorganization of the enterprise. Exaggerated emphasis at the international level on the case-by-case approach tends to prevent the establishment of such a body of law or of generally accepted principles. And in their absence, the case-by-case approach means that the terms and conditions of each rescheduling operation are set by a lengthy bargaining process and hence ultimately by the leverage that each party to the process is able to mobilize in its own favor.

The case-by-case approach also has the effect of enforcing the isolation of debtors at the same time as it permits the cartelization of creditors, a development that obviously loads the dice heavily in favor of the creditors.[17] One reason for the resistance of the creditors and of the IMF to any kind of general dialogue between creditors and debtors is the fear of the former that this might encourage threats of collective default by the debtors in support of policy positions unacceptable to the creditors. The fact is, however, that the debtors have behaved with the utmost prudence and restraint, despite draconic reductions in real incomes, and have avoided any kind of threats against the creditors: in this respect they have been much more circumspect than their predecessors during the past century or more, many of whom not only threatened to default but did default, repeatedly. The refusal of the creditors to countenance a general dialogue on debt, or the adoption of general principles for debt relief, may prove in the long run to be shortsighted and self-defeating. By failing to create a forum in which the difficulties encountered by debtors can be reviewed in their generality, the creditors are in effect isolating themselves from the realities of the situation and are reducing their own capability for responding to the imperatives dictated by circumstances as they arise. They thereby run the risk that resentments will build up to the point at which it would be too late for them to generate a response that would avoid damage to their own interests as well as to those of the debtors.

THE RESCUE OPERATIONS

It is not possible here to analyze the specifics of each of the successive major debt crises and the ways in which they were variously handled. The creditors considered it important to avoid giving the impression that a crisis could be regarded as a routine matter for which standard procedures could be laid down in advance. Consequently, each situation led to its own forms of improvisation. But the basic methods of dealing with each crisis had many more similarities than differences. Indeed, the irony of the insistence by crisis managers that every case was unique, and that there were therefore no uniform solutions, was that in practice the approach of all the various IMF stabilization programs was virtually identical.

The linchpin of every major negotiation was an austerity program laid down in an agreement between the debtor country and the IMF. The program invariably required severe compression of aggregate demand, notably through curtailment of budget deficits, and reductions in real wages in terms of tradable goods, through devaluation, supported by restriction of the money supply. The primary purpose of these measures was to reduce the domestic demand for exportable goods as well as for imports, and thereby to make it possible to achieve the excess of exports over imports required for servicing the external debt. Currency devaluation was seen as an additional means of improving the trade balance, and its potentially deflationary effects were viewed as an offset to the accelerated cost inflation that it was likely to induce. Every program had to be such as to satisfy the IMF that the overall outcome of the measures adopted would be a satisfactory rate of improvement in the balance of payments.

The adoption of an agreement was a precondition for enabling the debtor country to draw on the resources of the Fund in a series of installments, each of which depended on the implementation, in stages, of the measures agreed upon. Moreover, the Fund's "seal of approval" for the behavior of the debtor countries was taken as a signal by the commercial banks for rolling over loans falling due and providing modest amounts of new money. To the extent necessary, bridging finance was provided by the leading industrial countries and, in the early stages of the crisis, by the Bank for International Settlements, while longer-term government finance took the form of export credits.

The many low-income countries whose debts were owed mainly to official institutions took their rescheduling problems to the Paris Club, but there too it was the agreement with the IMF that was taken as the key to unlocking debt relief and even official development assistance.

The virtuosity of crisis management related mainly to the task of getting agreement by and among the commercial banks. There is no doubt that the difficulties—in the case of the large debtor countries—of securing a common approach by several hundred banks from various parts of the world were formidable. Much more ingenuity and innovativeness were applied to dealing with those difficulties than in seeking viable and equitable solutions to the devastating problems facing the debtor countries.

One of the issues for the banks was the IMF's insistence on new money for the debtor countries, despite the inability of the latter to meet existing commitments. In the case of Mexico the Managing Director of the IMF is reported to have told the banks that unless they provided $5 billion in new money, he would not recommend acceptance of the $3.9 billion

Fund program for Mexico by his Executive Board. This was an important departure for the IMF, because it was the first time that that institution had made its own lending conditional upon that of other entities. De Larosière's warning was a persuasive one, because without the IMF program the entire rescue operation was bound to fail, and Mexico would be left with no choice but to default. The dilemma that this created for the banks was immediately alleviated by the chairman of the U.S. Federal Reserve Board, Paul Volcker, who announced that "where new loans facilitate the adjustment process and enable a country to strengthen its economy and service its international debt in an orderly manner, new credits should not be subject to supervisory criticism."[18]

The new principle involved here was a potentially important one. To the extent that the IMF was in a position to take the initiative in mobilizing resources other than its own in support of the balance of payments of a member country, this meant that the IMF had some discretion in determining, in a particular case, the trade-off between immediate adjustment and financing. The only question was—how far was Mexico a special case, or how far were all the major debtors special cases? Would the IMF look for additional resources for the many countries whose balance-of-payments difficulties were not important enough to endanger the international monetary and financial system? And would the chairman of the Federal Reserve Board bend the rules for the latter countries as well as for the former?

A serious obstacle to the new approach arose from the sharp differences of interest between the major creditor banks, on the one hand, and the smaller regional and local banks, on the other. The latter were far less exposed, both absolutely and relatively, and sought to clear their portfolios of Third World loans as quickly as possible.[19] They had been minor and subordinate participants in the massive syndicated loans of the 1970s and saw no advantage for themselves in prolonging their involvement. The leading banks of the syndicates, however, knew that for them there was no way out—they could not abandon the debtors without damaging their own financial stability. For them it was important to cajole or compel the smaller banks to share the burden that they themselves were unable to escape. Every kind of direct and indirect pressure was applied in the United States, Western Europe, and Japan to maintain the solidarity of the banks. Joseph Kraft reports that the chairman of Lloyds Bank raised contributions from British banks at a session compared by one of those present to a church charity drive. The Fund's Managing Director intervened personally to acquire funds from an Italian bank. And so it went on.

It seems, however, that all this activity was less productive than had been hoped. In May 1985 Volcker reported that private bank lending to developing countries which were not members of the Organization of the Petroleum Exporting Countries (OPEC) had increased less than 5 percent in 1983 and less than 3 percent in 1984; the corresponding figures for U.S. banks only being 3 percent and 0.5 percent, respectively.[20] Optimistic appraisals of prospects for the world debt problem have generally involved the assumption that such lending would rise not less than 7 percent per annum.

The banks that did cooperate in the rescue operations charged a high price for doing so: the premiums that they exacted from the debtors in the form of enlarged profit margins, front-end fees, and the like were exorbitant. As the chief Mexican negotiator, José Angel Gurría, put it: "The banks did fabulously well on the deal. They played the good Samaritan and did their best business. They made 70 to 90 percent on their capital. Restructuring turned out to be good business for them."[21] It also set an excellent precedent for subsequent negotiations with Brazil, Argentina, and other countries. The banks could, moreover, claim that they had acted under pressure from the IMF and their respective governments: no government that had pressed the banks to maintain or increase their exposure to the debtor countries would be able to stand aside in the event of trouble. Thus the banks actually stood to make higher profits at lower risk. One could well say with Polonius: "Though this be madness, yet there is method in't."

In the event, Mexico's performance under its various agreements was rated so highly by its creditors that it became possible in August 1984 for Mexico to renegotiate the repayment of its debt over a much longer period and at a lower interest rate, and Venezuela and a number of other countries subsequently achieved a similar result.

These developments were undoubtedly important steps in the right direction, but their significance was greatly exaggerated. The banks had known all along that they would, if necessary, have to roll over repayments of principal and this was not in itself a matter of great concern to them so long as interest was being paid in line with contractual obligations. It is, after all, the business of banks to lend. The reduction in interest costs was more to the point, but here the gain to the debtor countries was relatively small. The premium charged over London market rates was reduced, but nothing was done about the fact that the market rates themselves were still much too high.

It was also somewhat strange that the easing of terms was represented by high officials of the international banking community as a "reward" for good behavior and performance. Here again the extraordinary contrast between domestic and international practice comes to the surface. On the domestic scene, any effort to impose upon a company undergoing reorganization unduly high interest rates, commissions and front-end fees, and excessively short maturities would be regarded as incompatible with the very purposes of the reorganization. But at the international level they are par for the course until the debtor has demonstrated his good faith. As Gurría pointed out: "It wasn't really logical to charge us rates that made money at the time, but made it harder for us to pay back later. But the banks thought they could stick it to us."[22]

It is difficult to resist the impression (admittedly with the benefit of hindsight) that however hard-pressed the officials of the creditor institutions may have been, and however close to the precipice they may have felt the situation to be, crisis management should have included more effective resistance to the placing of unreasonable demands upon the debtors. This impression is all the stronger in the light of the considerations set out elsewhere about the absence of any effort to bring about a reasonable sharing of the burden of adjustment to the crisis.

The Mexican renegotiation also enhanced the role of the IMF. Under existing procedures the IMF holds annual consultations with all member countries and reports confidentially to each country on the outcome of these consultations. Under the agreement of August 1984 with Mexico the IMF conducts two reviews of Mexico's economy annually and submits reports to creditor banks assessing the country's prospects for growth and debt servicing. This is regarded as a logical extension of the IMF "seal of approval" given implicitly in adopting an agreement with a member country for providing balance-of-payments support. But it goes much further, because the semi-annual reports are apparently to continue even after Mexico's program with the Fund comes to an end. In effect, the Fund would be contributing to the decision whether or not commercial banks should continue lending to Mexico. The agreement is widely interpreted as politicizing commercial bank lending to the Third World by involving governments more deeply than ever before, particularly the governments having the preponderance of votes within the IMF.[23] Moreover, insofar as the banks rely on the IMF in determining their lending policies, they will no doubt feel that they should also be able to depend on IMF and hence governmental support in the event that difficulties arise as a result of following IMF advice. While IMF advice will certainly be worded with the utmost care and with a minimum of commitment, it could hardly avoid pointing in one direction or another, however tentatively, if it is to be of any use to the recipients.

THE SMALLER AND POORER COUNTRIES

Although the smaller and poorer countries are not likely to set off a world-scale economic crisis, many of them have individually been faced with a series of destructive debt crises over the past decade. Such crises could easily lead to political upheaval on a scale that would have worldwide repercussions. For the purposes of this discussion a distinction may be made between those cases in which the debt arises mainly in connection with syndicated lending by commercial banks and those in which a substantial amount of official development assistance (ODA) is involved in addition to export credits and trade arrears.

Typical of the latter group are the low-income countries of all regions, particularly Africa. In many of these countries debt service ratios to exports are as large as, or larger than, corresponding ratios in the major debtor countries. In 1984 the World Bank reported that in the case of the Sudan, even if arrears currently outstanding were consolidated and rescheduled on 1983 Paris Club terms with a 10 percent interest rate, the Sudan would face debt service ratios averaging 80 to 90 percent for the rest of the 1980s.[24] Countries such as the Central African Republic, Madagascar, Somalia, and Zaire face similar difficulties. These impossible situations arise, according to the World Bank, because rescheduling in the last few years, mostly on conventional terms, gave short-term relief, but at the expense of increasing the debt service burden from 1984 onward. This should provide a sobering lesson for other countries. Repurchases and charges on loans from the IMF to sub-Saharan countries will total $3.5 billion during 1985–87, and new aid from bilateral donors is already being used, at least in part, to repay the IMF. Moreover, some OECD members of the IMF are beginning to argue that the IMF has no business lending to most of the African countries at all, because IMF loans are supposed to be short-term and these countries may well be unable to repay within the time limits required. The World Bank concludes that "unless corrective measures are taken, the external resource position of sub-Saharan Africa is likely to become disastrous in the next few years."[25] In other words, in the case of sub-Saharan Africa, there is no sign that debt problems are in the process of being overcome.

Debt difficulties in the low-income countries go back to the 1970s. In 1978 the Trade and Development Board of the United Nations Conference on Trade and Development adopted by consensus resolution 165(S-IX) providing for the retroactive easing of terms on official debt, including in the case of the least developed countries, conversion of outstanding loans into grants. Thus far seventeen creditor countries have reported measures favoring fifty-eight individual developing countries and entities in amounts totaling $6.2 billion, of which $3.5 billion represents debt cancellation. Despite these steps, conditions have generally deteriorated in these countries, which have been severely affected by the weakness of commodity exports and the slowdown in new ODA flows, as well as by natural disasters, especially in Africa.

Meanwhile the plight of the first group of countries, those with large debts to the commercial banks, has also been given relatively low priority by those who are preoccupied with the problems of the major debtors.[26] Some of these countries have, for all practical purposes, defaulted, though without as yet drawing upon themselves declarations of default. But the exposure of the commercial banks to these countries is relatively small: at the end of September 1984 U.S. banks were owed $69.4 billion by Argentina, Brazil, Mexico, and Venezuela, as against $19.3 billion by Caribbean and other Latin American countries. Most of these small debtor countries obtained rescheduling terms that were much less favorable than those for the Big Four. Grace and repayment periods were shorter, fees and spreads much higher, and only two countries—Ecuador and Honduras—were granted multi-year reschedulings.

One wonders whether the differences in terms and conditions between the minor and major debtors are explicable in terms of the case-by-case approach so staunchly defended by the IMF and the creditor countries. Or are they due simply to the limited leverage of the smaller countries, so that good performance is only a secondary consideration—if, indeed, it is a consideration at all? Would it not have been helpful to the smaller countries if, without abandoning the case-by-case approach, general standards and guidelines for terms and conditions had been laid down by a competent authority? The reader will no doubt draw his or her own conclusions.

CRISIS MANAGEMENT AND THE POOR

The large reductions in real national income required under stabilization programs have tended to sustain or accelerate inflationary price spirals in the countries concerned as various income groups have tried to escape their share of the burden by raising the prices of their own services. Workers seek to protect themselves by demanding higher money wages, but any increases granted tend to be offset by higher prices so that the effort to maintain real wages fails. The wages of the unorganized and generally poor workers tend to lag behind those of organized workers with the result that the real wages of the former group lose ground both absolutely and relatively. The real value of incomes fixed in terms of money falls even further.

Moreover, where, as in Africa, the fall in total consumption is accompanied by a decline in food supply, the stimulus to inflation is even greater. As real incomes fall the demand for food rises in relation to total demand as well as in relation to total income at the same time as the supply of food is falling in relation to total supply. This has a particularly depressing effect on the real incomes and consumption of the low-income groups except insofar as poor farmers benefit from a shift of real income from industrial workers.

Governments often attempt to offset the adverse distributional effects of a decline in real incomes by such devices as food subsidies, the rationing of foodstuffs in short supply, and the use of direct controls on imports to conserve scarce foreign exchange for purchasing essential supplies for consumption and for high priority investment. Government welfare payments to low-income groups may also be stepped up. But, in the course of negotiations associated with stabilization programs, efforts are usually made to induce governments to cut back the share of the public sector in total national expenditure and to abandon direct controls of the type required for rationing food and imports. Insufficient account is thereby taken of the social and political risks associated with such measures, to say nothing of the potentially disruptive effects of abrupt changes in the distribution of income in accelerating inflationary spirals.

Thus, although it would in principle be possible to protect low-income groups against having to shoulder more than their fair share of a reduction in total real income and consumption, and thereby limit the socially divisive effects of stabilization programs, the fashionable dogmas of the day are frequently invoked against the kinds of government intervention that would be needed for this purpose. UNICEF has drawn the attention of the international community to the particularly damaging effects that such programs may have, in the absence of special efforts to the contrary, on the welfare, health, and nutrition of children and other vulnerable groups.

THE NEED FOR A BROAD-BASED DIALOGUE

A group of Latin American countries—the signatories of the Cartagena Consensus—in a statement addressed to a meeting of the Fund's Interim Committee in April 1985—called for a "political dialogue . . . between the creditor and debtor countries, a dialogue which must be structured and pursued in an appropriate forum so that the specific problem posed to both sides by the crisis of development and of the external indebtedness of the developing countries can be addressed."[27]

The meaning of the term "political dialogue" was not spelled out and is obviously open to several interpretations. It would appear, however, that the Cartegena group had in mind the creation of an intergovernmental forum in which it would be possible to discuss certain aspects of the debt problem that go beyond the competence and responsibility of the commercial banks. There was no doubt that legitimate subjects for a dialogue of this nature existed. For example, negotiations with the commercial banks could, within limits, affect the income sought by the banks on new and rescheduled loans as well as their fees and commissions. But the banks were not in a position to do anything about the general level of interest rates which was by far the most important single factor in determining the overall magnitude of debt service obligations. Nor could the banks negotiate on the requirements of the regulatory authorities regarding such matters as the reporting of payments deemed to be overdue. In this regard European banks are able to take a much more flexible position on various proposals for "capping" interest—rephasing interest payments according to some pre-agreed formula—than are the U.S. banks because of differences between the reporting requirements of their respective regulatory authorities. Insofar as IMF policies affect the behavior of the banks, these too are beyond the terms of reference of a dialogue limited to debtor countries and the banks alone. Official loans in the form of bridging finance and export credits and their relationship to the funds provided by the banks might also come up for consideration. With the best will in the world, debtor countries cannot make good on their debt commitments unless their exports are accepted in the markets of the creditor countries in the amounts required. This depends partly on the level of import demand, and hence of general business activity in the creditor countries, and partly on the maintenance of a liberal policy on trade restrictions in these same countries.

Finally, and above all, the Cartegena group considered it essential to achieve a meeting of minds between creditors and debtors on the long-run perspective for solving the debt problem and on the need for the creation of conditions under which the growth of domestic investment and consumption in the debtor countries could be resumed. Even on the most optimistic assumptions envisaged by the economic forecasters of the IMF and of other public and private agencies, it appears that many debtor countries will not be able to regain their pre-crisis levels of per capita real income until the late 1980s or early 1990s. Moreover, as Helleiner has pointed out, the need for further structural adjustment to improve export performance and substitute for imports is being prejudiced by the contraction of investment and output designed to attain short- to medium-term external balance.[28] The crucial question is whether such a prospect is sustainable, either politically or economically. That this question has still not been fully addressed is in itself an indication of the shortcomings of crisis management to date.

ALTERNATIVE STRATEGIES

One might ask what alternative strategies would have been needed—or would now be needed—to create a viable and equitable basis for solution of the debt problem. A basic premise for any satisfactory strategy would have to be that debtor countries should be enabled not only to meet their debt service obligations (at whatever level and rate those obligations were set in agreement with creditors), but to sustain an adequate rate of growth of domestic consumption and investment as well.

Obviously there is no unique solution to this problem. For example, it is a question of judgment what an adequate rate of growth of consumption and investment in particular countries would be: what is clear is that those rates are dangerously low or negative at the present time. At any given rate of growth of consumption, investment, and imports in the debtor countries, debt servicing capability depends on the relationship between the rate of interest on debt and the rate of growth of exports. The higher the rate of interest on debt the greater would the rate of expansion of exports have to be to ensure the capability to service the debt. Dornbusch and Fischer have pointed out that with a rate of growth of exports of 8 percent annually and a rate of interest of 5 percent the debt problem would disappear.[29] This is not the only viable relationship that can be envisaged, but what is important is that creditors and debtors should reach agreement on a mutually acceptable framework for the solution of the debt problem, a framework that establishes internally consistent objectives for trade, debt service, and the flow of new capital.

In light of the realistic prospects for the future expansion of exports from the debtor countries, it seems unlikely that the world debt problem can be solved unless real and nominal interest rates are reduced to normal historical levels. This implies the need for a reversal of the policy stance of the industrial countries of the past several years whereby economic management relied heavily on tight monetary constraints, without regard to international repercussions.

Export growth has been limited by the depression in commodity prices which is itself related to excessive interest rates as well as to inadequate domestic growth rates in several of the major industrial countries and the pressure for expansion of commodity export volumes from hard-pressed supplying countries. Some important successes have been achieved by debtor countries in a position to export manufactures, but this has been associated with an exceptional growth in the trade deficit of the United States which is unlikely to continue. A concerted strategy for the expansion of the overall growth and imports of the industrial countries, coupled with more effective resistance to protectionism, are indispensable elements of any long-run solution to the debt problem.

Finally, provision would need to be made for a major expansion of new capital flows to debtor countries (both low-income and middle-income). It has been true for some time that developing countries could have made effective and profitable use of a much larger inflow of capital than was available to them, and as matters now stand this situation seems likely to continue in the absence of deliberate policy decisions to the contrary. It is generally agreed that commercial bank flows on the scale of the 1970s will not be repeated, at least in the near future; and while developing countries have liberalized their regimes for foreign direct investment considerably, any idea that transnational corporations are anxious to bring about a significant expansion of such investment at current low levels of economic activity in the debtor countries and in the light of persistent weakness in commodity markets is simply wishful thinking.

The conclusion is inescapable that a major increase in the resources of the multilateral financial institutions is indispensable in building a viable framework for the solution of the debt problem. Recent experience has thrown doubt on the legitimacy as well as the efficiency and reliability of balance-of-payments support by commercial banks. The IMF has had to bring strong pressure on the banks to cooperate in dealing with the debt crisis in a manner acceptable to the international community, and even then the total effort of the banks has nevertheless fallen far short of the Managing Director's target. This clearly indicates that the short-term motivation and objectives of the banks could lead them, at times of crisis, to act in a manner that would be disruptive of internationally agreed policies. The commercial banks are not an effective instrument for crisis management. The IMF should be enabled through a major expansion of its resources to take back from the banks the responsibility for balance-of-payments support that it lost to them during the 1970s— a role in which the banks are neither qualified nor comfortable. And the World Bank and regional development banks should be given both the concessional and nonconcessional resources needed to fuel the recovery process in capital-short countries. It must be recognized that there is formidable opposition to any such expansion of the resources and powers of the Bretton Woods institutions, but there would appear to be no alternative way of supplying the additional resources that are indispensable if the heavily indebted countries, large and small, are to maintain political and economic stability during the next several years.[30]

THE SUCCESSES AND FAILURES OF CRISIS MANAGEMENT

1. A number of rescue operations have been carried out since the early 1980s as a means of avoiding default by major debtor countries which, if allowed to occur, might well have caused a collapse of public confidence in certain leading banks.

2. Considerable resourcefulness, energy, and institutional innovation contributed to the short-term success of these rescue operations. Up to mid-1985, however, little had been done to resolve the emerging long-term problems, and even the multiyear rescheduling resorted to in the cases of Mexico, Venezuela, and other countries in 1984–85 fell far short of adequate treatment of the problem.

3. The most serious shortcoming of crisis management was the failure to recognize that all the parties concerned had fundamental long-run interests in common that were much more important than the points on which their interests diverged. In this all-important respect the approach of the international crisis managers was much less enlightened and sophisticated than that of the authorities responsible for dealing with similar problems arising within each country. The creditors are, after all, just as interested as the debtors that the latter shall be enabled to recover from their difficulties as quickly as possible, and with a minimum of dislocation, and this is just as true at the international as at the national level. In fact, however, an adversary relationship quickly developed between creditors and debtors which was reflected in the strategy of crisis management that was adopted. Since the debtors were obviously in a much weaker bargaining position than the creditors, the entire burden of adjustment was placed on the debtor countries, even though their difficulties had been caused, to a major extent, by factors beyond their control.

4. Unlike the situation prevailing in the domestic economies of the creditor countries, no independent judicial or quasi-judicial authority was available internationally to protect debtors against unreasonable demands and to ensure that the conditions imposed on each and every debtor were not incompatible with as rapid a recovery and rehabili-

tation as possible. Under ideal conditions the IMF might itself have played such a role, but it proved difficult to escape the conflicts of interest inherent in the preponderant weight that creditor countries have in the Fund's decisionmaking process.

5. The method adopted for securing the requisite release of resources by debtor countries for payment of debt service was to bring about sharp reductions in incomes and production in these countries through deflationary fiscal and monetary policies. This was designed to free resources for export and to cut the demand for imports as well as domestic consumption and investment. Insufficient effort was made to create the conditions under which adjustment could have been achieved by expansion rather than contraction. Moreover, the declines in investment were prejudicial to the creation of the new export and import-substituting capacities needed for the attainment of balance-of-payments viability in the long run. The widespread recessions inevitably fed upon one another, compounding the problems involved. Furthermore, the devaluations that primary producers were required to introduce, combined with pressure to increase export volumes, had the effect of depressing commodity prices, thereby adding to the real burden of debt service.

6. One of the most important single factors in the world debt crisis was the unprecedented rise in interest rates from 1978 onward. This was the result of efforts to contain inflation in the industrial countries by relying entirely on tight monetary policies, without giving due weight to the international repercussions of such policies. Effective crisis management would have required, and still requires, international agreement to reduce interest rates to more normal levels, especially in view of the subsiding of inflation in the industrial countries.[31]

7. Among other shortcomings of crisis management were the following. First, there was a failure to prevent the escalation of protectionism in the industrial countries, even though the ability of debtor countries to service their debts depended on the successful marketing of their exports in the industrial countries. In other words, the creditor countries were and are themselves partly frustrating the efforts of the debtor countries to meet their debt service obligations. Second, the growing involvement of the IMF with the commercial banks, including the latter's decisionmaking process, tended to prejudice the independence and authority of the Fund and its ability to take impartial positions on current problems. Third, although creditor country governments, in cooperation with the IMF, clearly had some leverage over the commercial banks, that leverage was not used to limit the

excessive costs imposed on the debtors by the banks until the restructuring for Mexico, Venezuela, and some other countries in 1984–85. Even then the setting of appropriate terms, conditions, and maturities for lending was envisaged as a reward for good behavior rather than as a common interest of all debtors and creditors, and the smaller countries were generally unable to secure terms as favorable as those granted to the countries in the limelight.

8. The distinction drawn between countries whose debts to commercial banks were large enough to constitute a potential danger to the international monetary system and all other debtor countries, whether indebted to the banks or to official institutions or both, resulted in inadequate attention being given to the problems of the latter countries, even though many of them were in even greater difficulties than the large debtors. In many cases the rescheduling procedures employed gave only short-term relief, at the cost of building up a crushing burden of debt service from 1984 onward.

9. Thus far the creditor countries have strongly resisted proposals for an intergovernmental dialogue on the world debt problem. They are content with existing arrangements and prospects and see no need to run the risk that might, in their view, emerge at meetings at which political issues may be raised and efforts made to obtain additional financial support from creditor country governments. But many of the multiplicity of interdependent factors involved in the world debt problem (including trade as well as money and finance) are the sole responsibility of governments. Only in an intergovernmental dialogue will it be possible to bring together, in a single negotiation and decisionmaking process, all those having the right to tackle an agenda as broad as the scope of the problem itself.

The Debt Problem: Strategies and Solutions[*]

HISTORICAL PARALLELS

International debt crises have occurred periodically in the past, and while the current crisis has its own special characteristics, the similarities with past experience are striking. Robert Solomon, former adviser to the Board of the U.S. Federal Reserve System, has pointed to strong

[*]Shortened and revised version of a paper originally presented to the International Conference on External Debt of Developing Countries, Kingston, Jamaica, January 28–29, 1988.

similarities between the experience of the United States as a debtor in the nineteenth century and that of the debtor countries of recent times. When, for example, recession struck in Britain in the nineteenth century, the prices and volume of exports of the United States would fall, thereby depressing the tax revenues of the sovereign borrowers and the income of the railways and other private debtors. "The result," says Robert Solomon, "was often suspension of interest payments, often referred to as default. . . . This has a familiar ring. It is similar to the experiences of Brazil, Mexico, and other borrowers in recent times."[32]

Similarly, Barry Eichengreen and Richard Portes point out that the debt-servicing difficulties experienced in recent years by many Latin American and other countries represent only the latest in a series of similar episodes stretching back over a period of centuries. Moreover, the problems encountered by sovereign borrowers culminated in default "not infrequently," and "Quite often, defaulting debtors were able to re-enter the international capital market only to default again."[33] Indeed, it could be said that the most important difference between the debt crises of the 1980s and those of the past is that in recent years debtors have gone to great lengths to avoid default for fear of being blacklisted by capital markets and the governments of creditor countries.

STRATEGIES FOR LOW-INCOME COUNTRIES

In principle the debt problems of low-income countries should not be difficult to solve because most of the debt is owed to official creditors—governments and international institutions. The governments of the creditor countries are well aware of the exceptional difficulties facing African countries, and as long ago as 1978 resolution 165 (S-IX) adopted in UNCTAD by consensus provided for the retroactive easing of terms on official debt, including, in the case of the least developed countries, conversion of outstanding loans into grants. While a measure of debt relief was in fact provided under this resolution, compliance was far from complete, and by early 1987 it was becoming clear that recovery efforts in Africa were being undermined by a deteriorating financial situation and that additional action was needed.

Accordingly the UN Secretary-General, after consultation with interested governments as well as with the World Bank and IMF, appointed an advisory group of eminent persons which met under the chairmanship of Sir Douglas Wass. The group reported its findings and recommendations in February 1988, the most important of which were the following:

1. Almost all of sub-Saharan Africa was suffering from import strangulation, and a spirit of despair was pervading the continent.
2. While the implementation of programs of reform worked out with the Bank and Fund was indispensable, the reforms would not succeed unless more international assistance was provided.
3. Debt relief should be provided, including the conversion of official loans into grants in low-income countries that were unlikely to become creditworthy, and substantial easing of terms in other cases.
4. Existing flows of assistance as of the middle of 1987 should be increased by $5 billion a year for the next few years—this amount being necessary simply to restore the prospects for development and growth as of the early 1980s. The group added that this assessment was "conservative": as happens frequently in such cases, the amount finally selected by the members of the group was determined at least as much by their judgment as to what would be acceptable to the donors as by any objective assessment of African requirements for development and growth.[34]

There cannot be any doubt of the gravity of the debt problem in Africa. It may not be as much of a threat to the international banking system as the debt of the middle-income countries, but it is certainly a threat to the debtor countries themselves. It has been estimated that the aggregate external debt of the sub-Saharan countries, excluding arrears, grew from an estimated $6 billion in 1970 to more than $136 billion at the end of 1988, more than a 630 percent increase in constant (1980) U.S. dollar terms. Over the same period the real gross domestic product per capita of the sub-Saharan countries fell by about 10 percent. Scheduled debt service obligations approached 50 percent of exports of goods and services during 1986 and 1987, though debt relief and arrears limited debt service payments to about 30 percent of exports.[35]

Various initiatives by governments and international institutions in recent years have sought to deal with the debt problems of sub-Saharan Africa but the amounts involved have been small in relation to the debt service obligations of the debtor countries, and relatively little has been done to reduce the stock of debt. Under the best of conditions it will take enormous efforts on the part of African governments to bring about a recovery of the region. Without further debt relief and assistance of at least the magnitude recommended by the Wass group, the prospects for sub-Saharan Africa would indeed be grim.

STRATEGIES FOR INTERMEDIATE COUNTRIES

A number of countries are in danger of falling between two stools. They do not qualify for treatment as low-income countries and their problems are not due primarily to borrowing from commercial banks. Their difficulties arise largely from the fact that much of their debt is owed to the Bank and Fund, which are unwilling to reschedule their past loans. In the case of the Bank this is due to concern that rescheduling might affect the Bank's credit rating and hence the cost of borrowing.

A way should, nevertheless, be found to overcome the consequences of the privileged creditor status of the World Bank and IMF insofar as waivers or rearrangements of claims are concerned. Former Prime Minister Seaga of Jamaica proposed the creation of a refinancing facility in the Fund, which seems to be a moderate and unexceptionable proposal that should be applicable to the World Bank as well. Moreover, this is not only a problem for Jamaica and the intermediate group but for the low-income borrowers as well. In both cases the World Bank ought to be prepared to renegotiate the terms of past loans wherever, with hindsight, one can see that the terms were too hard. Certainly new lending should be on softer terms. It is unlikely that this would endanger the rating of the World Bank's bonds. There is no reason why the market should take a different view of the prudent treatment of a sovereign debtor in difficulties for reasons beyond its control than a commercial bank would in the case of a domestic debtor in analogous circumstances. What counts is the guarantee by the industrial countries of the World Bank's obligations to the market, not the Bank's treatment of individual debtors that happen to be in severe difficulties for reasons beyond their control.

STRATEGIES FOR MARKET BORROWERS

After years of efforts to deal with the world commercial debt crisis, there is still no agreement on a basic strategy for the future. Insofar as a strategy was implicit in the ad hoc arrangements made from year to year since 1982, it was that the debtor countries would eventually grow out of the commercial debt problem and that all that was needed to this end was a favorable world economic environment and responsible policies on the part of the debtors.

Although criticisms could be made of the performance of some debtor countries, there is general agreement among responsible observers that these countries applied policies of severe retrenchment with considerable vigor, thereby reducing current account deficits (for the aggregate of countries with recent debt servicing problems) from $72.3 billion in 1981 to $22.8 billion in 1986. The IMF's *Annual Report 1987* noted the heavy price that had been paid for this achievement: "The fall in living standards has been pervasive and large in the Western Hemisphere and in Africa, as countries in these regions have struggled to correct domestic and external imbalances *in the face of an often unfavorable external environment*" (page 12, emphasis added). Meanwhile, in these same countries, total external debt, which had been equivalent to somewhat less than double the value of their exports of goods and services in 1981, reached a level in excess of three times such exports in 1986. Despite the postponement of amortization and declines in nominal interest rates, debt service payments were still preempting 42.7 percent of export receipts in 1986 compared with 32.9 percent in 1981.

The sacrifices of living standards, and of levels of business activity and employment have not resulted in a restoration of the creditworthiness of the debtors as had been hoped and expected. With the drying up of the most important sources of capital inflow, the debtors were compelled to allocate substantial proportions of their domestic savings for the payment of debt service. This led to a decline in the ratio of gross capital formation in the above group of countries from 25.3 percent in 1981 to 19.2 percent in 1986—a particularly damaging result because so far from current sacrifices building a more viable future for these countries, their long-run development was being steadily undermined.

It is, therefore, quite clear that the existing strategy is a failure in the short run and long run alike. The strategy could have succeeded if the international environment required as a complement to that strategy had been put in place. In that case, at the very least the debtor countries would have been able to earn sufficient foreign exchange to permit an expansion of imports along with the payment of debt service, and that expansion of imports might have made it possible to prevent the collapse of investment. But international policies did not permit this, and all the international agencies foresee a deterioration in the world economic environment, owing mainly to a slowdown in business activity in the industrial countries.

This being the case, there seems to be no choice but to reverse the present strategy and seek to reduce the stock of debt instead of adding to it. Until recently this was not a negotiable proposition. More than 100 proposals have been made by distinguished authors for dealing with the debt problem, and the great majority of them take it for granted that nothing can be done to reduce the stock of debt other than through repayment of principal.[36] Efforts should, they feel, be concentrated rather on bringing about a faster rise in the GDP and exports than in the stock of debt, so as to reduce the ratio of the latter to the former. As we have seen, the actual trends have been the exact opposite of this. Nevertheless, to many observers debt relief is anathema.

THE CASE AGAINST DEBT RELIEF

The case against debt relief has been stated by Fred Bergsten, William Cline, and John Williamson as follows:

(a) Debt relief may well be to the disadvantage of the debtors themselves because it would jeopardize their future access to credit.

(b) Widespread debt relief granted by the commercial banks would have a devastating impact on their earnings and even their solvency, which could easily redound to the disadvantage of the debtors as well as of the banks.

(c) Because of these two considerations, debt relief should be restricted to cases of "insolvency" and avoided when the problem is merely "illiquidity."

(d) A readiness to grant debt relief even in cases of insolvency might have demonstration effects on less marginal debtors that could ultimately threaten the banking system because of point (b).[37]

The assumption of Bergsten and associates that access to credit is within reach for debtor countries as long as they are not given debt relief cannot be sustained. Even where the international community has acknowledged outstanding performance by particular debtor countries, the expected restoration of access to private capital markets on a voluntary basis has not materialized.

Whether or not "widespread debt relief" would have a "devastating impact" on the commercial banks depends on how one defines "widespread." The banks have in fact already sold significant amounts of their claims on developing countries at substantial discounts in the secondary market—discounts that increased continuously in 1985, 1986, and especially during 1987.

Disaster scenarios for the commercial banks usually rest on the assumption that losses from the writing down of debt would have to be absorbed instantaneously and that the total amount of such losses could, in adverse circumstances, exceed the capital of the banks by a substantial margin. The argument has, for example, been advanced that even if the major U.S. creditor banks handed over their entire equity capital to the principal Latin American debtors, that would not make much of a dent in the stock of debt owed by the latter. But this is beside the point. With appropriate adjustment of the rules, where necessary, the banks could undertake a major write-down of their Third World debt over an extended period of years without damage to their financial stability.[38]

Nor does it necessarily follow that because a country has been granted debt relief it will be denied access to private capital markets indefinitely: even the IMF staff has acknowledged this. For many years the IMF was firm in asserting that if an external imbalance was persistent, the fact that it was due to factors beyond the control of the country concerned was of secondary importance. It is only recently that some signs of a reconsideration of the above doctrine have emerged. The last paragraph of the IMF's *World Economic Outlook October 1987* includes the following statement:

> . . . attitudes toward arrangements that are perceived to be equivalent to debt forgiveness are likely to be heavily conditioned by perceptions of the basic causes of the countries' debt servicing difficulties. To the extent that these stem from developments perceived to be beyond the authorities' control, such as a change in the terms of trade, investors may, in effect, write off any losses to misfortune and let bygones be bygones when making future investment decisions. If, on the other hand, countries' difficulties are perceived to stem from their own mismanagement, then resolution of the difficulties via schemes that lower the contractual value of debt rather than via increases in its market value, such as through improved domestic policies, is likely to affect future financing flows and growth prospects adversely [p. 30].

In other words, according to the IMF staff if countries are in difficulties that are not of their own making investors may in effect write off losses as due to misfortune.

The above consideration also disposes of the concern frequently expressed about moral hazard, which is in any case farfetched since no country would willingly go through a prolonged depression simply for the sake of being able to default. Nothing is so likely to restore investor confidence as a clear indication that debtors are no longer overwhelmed by unrealistic debt service obligations that make it impossible for them to raise their own level of business activity and economic growth. What is needed for this to come about is a cooperative effort by debtor countries, creditor countries, the multilateral financial institutions, and the commercial banks to negotiate a strategy and burden-sharing exercise for solution of the debt problem.

Even if it were true that countries might lose their access to private capital markets for a prolonged period, this does not mean that debt relief should be ruled out. As noted earlier, there is no other option so long as the creditor countries insist on constraining their economies well below their economic potential. Those countries denied direct access to private capital markets would have to obtain such access through the World Bank and regional development banks. That, after all, is still a basic function of the World Bank. At Bretton Woods it was taken for granted that private capital markets would not be able or might not be willing to provide sufficient resources for reconstruction and development, and it was therefore up to the World Bank to channel the requisite resources for these purposes by borrowing them from private investors and relending them to the countries in need of additional finance. The role of the World Bank must in any case be expanded, as has been recognized by the industrial countries including the United States, and the extent of that expansion should be adjusted to the requirements of the situation. To that end the international agencies, including the Bank, the Fund, and UNCTAD, should be requested to assess the capital requirements of the debtor countries to achieve adjustment with growth.

The suggestion made above that creditor countries should participate in the burden-sharing exercise will no doubt encounter the objection that at a time of budget stringency public funds cannot be mobilized for debt relief and that such funds should in any case not be used for what would, in effect, be a bailing out of the commercial banks. The idea that the creditor country governments themselves contributed to the original problem is not well understood let alone accepted.

There are at least two reasons why, in addition to the commercial banks, the governments of the creditor countries should make some contribution to debt relief. In the first place it was these governments that were originally responsible for curbing the amount of official recycling of petrodollars through the IMF—which Managing Director Witteveen had strongly advocated in 1974. One of the main reasons for this decision was the view, as expressed at the time by the United States, that private channels should be used to the maximum extent possible for financing oil deficits and that the Fund should not finance deficits that could be handled by private commercial banks.[39] It was this unfortunate decision that led to the piling up of commercial debt and the transference of the interest rate risk to the debtors. While reliance on official rather than private recycling would not have entirely obviated the difficulties that arose for the debtors subsequently, it would certainly have alleviated them considerably, if only because it is likely that the interest rate risk would have been shared more fairly between creditors and debtors instead of being transferred entirely to the debtors.

There is, however, an even more important reason for the creditor country governments to assume a significant share of the burden of writing down the debt. It is their macroeconomic policies that have held the rates of growth of the creditor countries to levels substantially below their potential. The creditor countries thereby failed to sustain an international environment conducive to the reconciliation of debt service obligations with satisfactory rates of growth for the debtor countries. In other words, the creditor countries have as much stake as the debtor countries in a revival and further expansion of the world economy, and their taxpayers should be prepared to bear an appropriate share of the cost of bringing this expansion about.

Although legislatures are often blamed for "aid fatigue," it is noteworthy that the Subcommittee on International Development Institutions and Finance of the U.S. House of Representatives has stated quite clearly that a solution to the debt crisis "will require burden sharing by all parties, *both private and governmental*" (emphasis added). Moreover, the subcommittee recommended over two years ago that the World Bank should develop an "explicit action plan" for dealing with the debt crisis "as rapidly as possible"; a plan that would recognize "the long-term unsustainability of recessionary austerity measures in developing countries." Already at that time the subcommittee called for "outright debt relief," specifying also that "Options to protect the integrity of private banks affected by any such debt relief should also be identified, including those regulatory changes which might facilitate a restructuring of private loan portfolios with developing nations." [40]

Attitudes to debt relief have therefore been changing for some time, and the applicability of the principle of debt relief to commercial debt now appears to have gained widespread acceptance both by banks and by the governments of creditor countries, including the United States.

THE BRADY PROPOSAL

In March 1989 U.S. Treasury Secretary Brady announced a major step in U.S. governmental thinking about the debt problem. He acknowledged that it was a "truly international problem" which "contains economic, political, and social elements." In other words, it had ramifications extending far beyond the contractual obligations laid down in the relevant loan agreements. Particularly important was Secretary Brady's statement urging creditors "to achieve both debt and debt service reduction." He did not spell out the details of what he had in mind, particularly as regards the magnitude of financial resources to be provided and the sources from which they might be obtained. It appeared, however, that there were expectations of major participation by the Japanese government in providing the necessary funds, but that other OECD governments wished to minimize their new commitments. U.S. Treasury Under-Secretary Mulford informed Congressional committees that the present capital resources should be "ample" over the next two years to support an expanded role by the IMF and World Bank in assisting voluntary debt reduction programs by the most indebted countries. Mulford stated that U.S. Treasury estimates suggested that the new debt reduction policy could cut the total owed by thirty-nine developing countries by $70 billion, or roughly 20 percent, over three years, while making a reduction of more than $20 billion, also about 20 percent, in these countries' interest payments over the same period. The estimates assumed that these reductions would be achieved with a total of between $20 billion and $25 billion provided by the World Bank and IMF which would encourage the commercial banks to reduce the principal and interest payments due to them.[41] It is, however, not clear to what extent the above amounts are additional to those that the countries concerned might have expected to receive in any case. It is, moreover, unlikely that a 20 percent reduction in interest payments would suffice to permit the debtor countries concerned to resume vigorous growth.

It is, therefore, of the highest importance for the World Bank to initiate, as soon as possible, thoroughgoing studies of the amount of capital required to permit developing countries, whether heavily indebted or not, and whether middle-income or low-income, to achieve and maintain substantial growth rates. Although some exercises along these lines have been undertaken by several of the international agencies, there is an urgent need to review and update them in the light of the new policy position set forth by the United States and endorsed by the Interim and Joint Development Committees meeting in Washington in April 1989. In conducting the new studies, substantial allowance should be made for the fact that many countries will be seeking to put behind them a long period of economic depression. The import requirements associated with such a major shift in economic outlook and performance cannot be derived simply from import elasticities based on normal trend rates of growth. There is undoubtedly a large pent-up demand for new investment of all kinds, including both fixed capital and inventories, as well as for reversing the heavy deterioration of infrastructure caused by long years of inadequate maintenance and replacement. Nor should essential consumption requirements be overlooked, particularly in view of the many cases identified by UNICEF in which children and other vulnerable groups have been suffering acutely from the effects of economic depression.

PROPOSALS FOR DEBT RELIEF

The literature on the debt problem contains a considerable number of useful suggestions for debt relief that are worthy of consideration as a means of following up on the Brady proposal. Many of these suggestions provide for some national or international institution to take over the nonperforming claims of the commercial banks at a substantial discount, and provide debt relief to the borrowing countries by converting short-term and medium-term floating rate loans to long-term bonds of lesser face value at low fixed rates.

Lever and Huhne, while favoring the writing down of debt, have reservations about proposals of the above type.[42] They point out that an essential objective of any solution to the debt problem must be to promote new flows of money to the debtor countries, so as to reverse the present net transfer of resources by these countries. And they raise the question whether any of the banks selling existing Third World debt to some national or international agency would be willing thereafter to extend further loans to the indebted countries. "The agency and its discounts," they say, "would be a continuing and sharp reproof to any director on the board of a major bank who proposed new lending to one of the debtors."[43]

Consequently, they propose that the governments of the industrial countries should guarantee new lending to the developing countries, including any loans needed for the payment of continuing interest obligations. The provision of such a guarantee should be dependent on the agreement of the banks that they would each year write down, according to circumstances, that part of their existing debt which was judged "bad or doubtful." They would also have to agree to long-term rescheduling of interest on the written-down debt. The guarantees could be provided by such institutions as the Export-Import Bank in the United States and the Export Credit Guarantee Department in the United Kingdom. The banks should be given "many years" to write off old debts "without excessively impairing their profitability, capital position or ability to lend."[44]

There can be no doubt of the need to reverse the net transfer of resources from developing countries. The question is whether the best way of doing this is through government guarantees to new lending by the commercial banks. The banks were never qualified for the role assigned to them in the 1970s for recycling petrodollars and there is no evidence that they have acquired that capability since. If the ultimate responsibility has to be shouldered by the governments themselves why should it not be the governments that do the lending either directly or through the World Bank and other multilateral financial institutions?

A number of proposals provide for central banks to take over nonperforming commercial bank loans to the Third World. A recent proposal along these lines by Paul Davidson is for central banks to stand ready to accept a significant proportion of the international loan portfolio of commercial banks in exchange for stock in the central bank.[45] The central bank would in turn sell these loan securities to its government in exchange for government bonds. The government would then negotiate a write-down of debt with each debtor country. These matters would be the subject of an International Conference of Creditor and Debtor Nations—"away from the eyes of the media (similar to Bretton Woods)."[46]

Under this scheme, whatever burdens had to be shouldered on the creditor side would be borne by the governments, and the commercial banks would not share in those burdens at all since it is argued that the private banks do not have the financial strength to bear any substantial part of the burden, and that it is important to protect them against decapitalization. However, the implicit judgment that public opinion in the creditor countries would agree to such a wholesale bailout of the commercial banks is open to question. It is likely to be difficult enough to get general agreement on even modest government support for the banks.

The case for action by individual central banks rather than by an international agency such as the World Bank may rest on several considerations. There are substantial differences between countries both in the degree of exposure of the commercial banks to the most vulnerable debtors and in the ability of the banks to cope with the effects of default or near default, including the capital provision they have made or may have to make against possible losses. Thus the central bank of each country is bound to be in a better position to assess the needs of its member banks and the extent of action required to meet them than any international agency. On the other hand, there is also a need for international policy coherence and consistency and for rough justice in the sharing of burdens. These latter objectives may be more readily attained through an international institution applying an internationally negotiated set of rules and norms.

The best known of the proposals for action by an international agency is that by Felix Rohatyn, of Lazard Frères and Company, the investment banking firm. Interestingly enough, his is also the most radical of the proposals that have been made in terms of the writing down of debt, but it should be borne in mind that his credentials include the major contribution that he made toward restoring the creditworthiness of New York City after a period of near bankruptcy.

Under the Rohatyn proposal an agency analogous to the Municipal Assistance Corporation of New York would be established either as an independent entity or as a subsidiary of the IMF or World Bank. The posing of these alternatives may have reflected an awareness that the IMF and World Bank, being creditors themselves, might be deemed by some to be unable to function in the capacity envisaged without conflict of interest.

The objective of the proposal would be to provide the amount of debt relief required to reduce debt service to the equivalent of 25 to 30 percent of exports. The agency, which would require government guarantees, would make mandatory purchases of bank loans in exchange for low-interest bearing long-term bonds. The agency would in turn make loans at 6 percent interest over periods of fifteen to thirty years. The losses implicit in these arrangements would be subject to negotiation between debtor countries, taxpayers, and bank stockholders.[47]

Much emphasis has been placed by the governments of the industrial countries on the need for any acceptable solution to be "voluntary." At the same time they insist that there should be no transfer of risk from the private sector to the public sector. These two objectives are probably incompatible, and certainly the search for "voluntary" solutions for a large number of debtors is likely to take so long that the debtors may be forced to take matters into their own hands.

One of the great merits of the Rohatyn proposal, therefore, is its provision for compulsory purchases of bank loans. However, the idea of mandatory debt reduction has been criticized on the grounds that it would prevent or at least delay the reestablishment of confidence in the debtor countries, so that commercial banks would be unwilling to return to voluntary lending to them. This argument is even less persuasive now than it was when it was used previously to oppose debt reduction of any kind, including voluntary. As Eichengreen and Portes have shown, historical experience indicates that debtor countries that met their debt service obligations in full under crisis conditions gained no advantage thereby as regards access to capital markets over countries that defaulted.[48] This should apply a fortiori in the present context since we are not assuming default but merely debt reduction.

Mandatory debt reduction (and, indeed, voluntary reduction also if that were the method chosen) would have to be large enough to permit the debtor country to resume economic growth in line with its capacity. Once the capability for significant growth is regained, it is only a matter of time before the commercial banks would seek to rebuild their positions in the countries whose creditworthiness is restored.

In the absence of a measure of compulsion and the imposition of deadlines for decisionmaking, the process of negotiating debt reduction for a large number of countries would at best be subject to endless maneuvering and procrastination, thereby possibly forcing a number of countries faced with growing domestic unrest into default. Moreover, individual banks with large exposures would have a strong incentive to hold back from negotiating seriously in the expectation that firm settlements by other banks would generate an increase in the market value of the remaining claims. Even banks prepared to negotiate seriously for debt reduction would be deterred from doing so if they had reason to believe that their competitors were holding back. It is, therefore, in the interests of the banks themselves that collective debt reduction should be made mandatory, thereby avoiding altogether the problem of "free riders."

There is already a widespread awareness that, left to themselves, the banks are not likely to act expeditiously. And the need, therefore, to bring pressure on the banks has been recognized by authorizing the IMF to begin disbursements against its own loans without waiting for the banks to make their contributions. Perhaps the signal that this gives to the banks is sufficient, but it is more likely that stronger pressures will have to be applied to encourage the banks to engage in major collective reduction of their outstanding claims.

The mandatory phase could, however, be preceded by a negotiation in which debtors, commercial banks, creditor country governments, and international financial institutions were all participants. The honest broker at such a negotiation could be a specially created Bank-Fund affiliate. A major question is whether the Bank and Fund are too set in their ways to deal with the problem as efficiently and expeditiously as circumstances require. The main reason for this is that they have both become locked into a conceptual framework that predisposes them to seek far-reaching policy changes and adjustments in debtor countries without providing the financial resources that would allow adjustment to take place in a context of growth. There is a tendency to greatly underestimate the magnitude of resources required for bringing about a speedy recovery of both low-income and middle-income countries.

The blame for the one-sided approach hitherto adopted by the Bretton Woods institutions should not be placed exclusively on the managements of these institutions. Their freedom of action was narrowly circumscribed by the strong views held by their major shareholders regarding the policy reforms needed in the debtor countries, side by side with a reluctance on the part of the creditor countries to face up to the financial requirements of a thoroughgoing solution to the debt problem. It could be argued, therefore, that since the member governments and the voting structure will be the same, regardless of whether a new facility were operated by one of the existing institutions or by an agency created specifically to deal with the debt overhang, there is no reason to prefer a new agency to an existing one. If there is a case for a new facility it would have to depend on a recognition by key governments of the need for prompt and effective measures to deal with the debt overhang without insisting on an immediate commitment by debtor countries to policy changes that they consider controversial. It may be thought quite unlikely that the major creditor countries would agree to such a modification of conditionality in conjunction with debt reduction: and it may well be unrealistic to expect any relaxation of conditionality unless the views of the creditor countries change markedly.

The search for a solution may depend on the outcome of the negotiations between the parties involved, as mentioned above. The Group of Twenty-Four has been trying for some time to persuade the Group of Ten to enter into such a dialogue, and one can only hope that the advantages of such a dialogue will become apparent to all in the near future.

7
The Adjustment Process

Conceptions and Misconceptions of Adjustment*

In the course of his masterly address on the "Current Crisis in International Economic Co-operation" to the Association of Banks in Malaysia in honor of Tun Ismail Ali, Dr. I. G. Patel summed up as follows:

> What all this adds up to is a pretty somber picture necessitating more imaginative cooperative as well as purely national endeavors. What we find instead is a retreat from shared responsibility and adherence to a philosophy which takes us back even before the days of laissez-faire to a policy of what I can only describe as a kind of vindictiveness toward what are considered to be recalcitrant segments of society combined with an aggressive attack on anything which goes beyond a narrowly commercial ethic. It is not an accident that a less compassionate policy at home and a so-called hard-headed approach abroad have been revived at the same time. The idealism born out of adversity during the Second World War seems to have spent itself; and a new arrogance and indifference born out of plenty seem to be in the ascendant.[1]

This somber passage, should, of course, be viewed in the context of the achievements of the early postwar period which Dr. Patel described in the same lecture, and which provided an indication of the constructive endeavor of which the international community was capable when the will was there and the auspices were favorable. The stark characterization cited above relates to the severe setback in international economic cooperation during the last few years and the purpose of the lecture is to provoke a reexamination of the factors underlying recent trends with a view to restoring cooperation, if possible at an even higher level than before.

*This essay was originally published in *Essays on Economic Progress and Welfare*, ed. S. Guhan and Manu Shroff (Delhi: Oxford University Press, 1986). Valuable comments by V. B. Kadam are gratefully acknowledged.

DISTRIBUTION OF THE BURDEN

Nowhere is such a reexamination more urgently required than in relation to the so-called adjustment process. This term has been so much used and abused that one is apt to forget what it is supposed to mean. Indeed, adjustment is now usually regarded as something that the other fellow has to do when things go wrong. Any idea that every international economic relationship is a two-sided affair seems to have vanished from sight, except where deficit countries have some leverage of their own, as will be shown subsequently. Generally speaking, if someone is in trouble, the presumption is that it must be exclusively his own fault, and he is likely to get short shrift unless he puts his house in order. The approach to the problem of distribution of the burden of adjustment to balance-of-payments disequilibrium is above all a question of power politics.

The United States, at the time of the Committee of Twenty's efforts to reform the international monetary system, went so far as to argue that "Deficit countries would in any case be unable to restore equilibrium unless surplus countries at least followed policies consistent with a reduction of the net surplus in their payments positions."[2] In other words, the sharing of responsibility for adjustment between deficit and surplus countries was not merely desirable but indispensable, since in the absence of consistent policies by the two groups of countries, equilibrium could not be restored.

There is no controversy about the desirability, in principle, of symmetry in the adjustment process, and all pay lip service to it. As a practical matter, however, adjustment is almost invariably treated as involving unilateral actions by deficit countries—unless they happen to be reserve currency countries. There is little, if any, practical concern even as to whether unilateral acts of adjustment by deficit countries are being frustrated by countervailing activities of surplus countries, let alone as to whether the surplus countries are themselves taking steps to promote a return to equilibrium. The neglect of symmetry may be understandable in cases where deficits are relatively small and randomly distributed among countries, and where they are principally the result of domestic mismanagement. But where deficits are massive and system-wide, and result from common factors applying across the board to all or most countries, pressure for unilateral adjustment of the type seen in 1982–84 is not only inequitable but self-defeating. Simultaneous deflation by a large number of deficit countries is bound to compound their problems, not only because of the consequential contraction in reciprocal demand but also because of the depressing effect on the level of activity—and hence import demand—of the surplus countries. If, moreover, deflation undertaken by deficit countries to deal with balance-of-payments disequilibrium is accompanied by deflation by surplus countries undertaken as a counter to inflation, the stage is set for a cumulative downward spiral of economic activity.

In responding to critics of unduly harsh IMF conditionality, the point is often made that the measures required to restore external balance in a deficit country are dictated not by the Fund but by the objective situation confronting the country concerned, including, in particular, its capacity for mobilizing foreign exchange from its own resources or by borrowing. Given the availability of foreign exchange, the stringency of the measures required follows as inexorably as night follows day.

ADJUSTMENT AND THE DEBT CRISIS

The basis for this contention has, however, been put in question by the measures adopted in dealing with the balance-of-payments difficulties that faced a number of major debtor countries beginning in 1982. The availability of foreign exchange was certainly not taken for granted in these cases—on the contrary, it was part and parcel of the negotiations undertaken. The IMF management acted in effect as an arbitrator between the deficit countries and their creditors (including the IMF itself as well as the commercial banks) in bringing about what was considered to be an appropriate relationship between the amount of belt-tightening required of the debtors and the amount of finance to be provided by the creditors. The arbitration was based essentially on political, or at least noneconomic, considerations. The political capacity of the debtors to withstand various possible degrees of retrenchment had to be measured against the degree of flexibility of the creditors in regard to the amount of financial resources to be provided. Thus the relationship of finance to adjustment was at the heart of the bargaining process—it was not a question simply of determining the amount of adjustment required in the light of a predetermined fixed volume of available finance.

This was no doubt an exceedingly crude and imperfect way of trying to introduce an element of symmetry into the adjustment process (always bearing in mind that the term "adjustment process" as used here is very far from implying the kind of structural adaptation that the situation demanded and continues to demand). In terms of the logic that the U.S. delegation, headed by Paul Volcker, employed during the deliberations of the Committee of Twenty in 1972, the concept of "symmetry," as applied to the situation in 1982–84, would have to involve, at the least, a deliberate and substantial reduction in the interest rates on foreign lending, and a rolling back of protectionist restrictions on imports from the debtor countries. It is true that nominal interest rates did fall to some extent in 1983, but not as a deliberate act of government policy, and not sufficiently to meet the needs of the situation. Moreover, since nominal rates remained high while inflation decelerated appreciably in several major industrial countries, real rates of interest actually moved upward.

Nor should one exaggerate the extent of the concessions made to the big debtor countries in 1982–83. In particular, the charges made by the commercial banks for rescheduling were exorbitant in terms of both interest premiums and front-end fees. The toleration by the international community of the rapacity of the banks was indeed deplorable.

Nonetheless, the negotiations between the principal debtors and their creditors in 1982–83 did involve an implicit, albeit minimal, element of symmetry. The clearest indication of this, perhaps, was the fact that when certain commercial banks showed signs of trying to avoid new commitments to the debtors, they were warned by the IMF in unmistakable terms that unless they made their contribution to the financial provisions required, the Fund itself would not be in a position to enter into the necessary stabilization agreements, with the result that the debtors would not be able to honor their obligations to the commercial banks among others.

MAJOR AND MINOR DEBTORS

This minimal symmetry was, however, reserved for the major debtors—those whose difficulties were important enough in terms of magnitude to endanger the international monetary system as a whole, and more particularly, the financial health of the countries to which the major lending banks belonged. No such special provision was deemed necessary in cases that were not considered as posing such a danger. Indeed the difference between minor and major cases was deliberately institutionalized under the revision and expansion of the General Arrangements to Borrow (GAB) undertaken in February 1983. Under the new dispensation, nonparticipants in GAB may obtain access to GAB financing on a finding by the IMF Managing Director, endorsed by the GAB participants, that the Fund faces an inadequacy of resources to deal with expected drawings by nonparticipants and that an exceptional situation exists associated with balance-of-payments problems of a character or size that could threaten the stability of the international monetary system.

If the difference between minor and major cases were simply a matter of the quantitative demands on IMF resources involved, special arrangements for mobilizing resources would be understandable, although even here it is arguable that under the Articles of Agreement of the Fund such resources should have been provided through the requisite enlargement of the quotas of all members rather than through ad hoc measures designed only for a particular category of members. But the main point is that the kind of negotiations undertaken by the Fund for the big debtors, and the margin of flexibility involved in such negotiations, are not available to countries that do not have access to the private international capital market for balance-of-payments support and that must therefore rely entirely on the Fund for such support. The volume of finance available to such countries is limited by the size of their quotas unless the Fund is prepared to waive quota limitations. This it cannot do under the constraints on IMF resources imposed by the industrial countries, which is itself a reflection of the weakening of the spirit of international cooperation and the adherence to a narrow commercial ethic so clearly analyzed by Dr. Patel. Moreover, even if valid arguments could be adduced in support of the refusal by industrial countries to provide for an adequate enlargement of quotas and of access by members to Fund resources, there was no reason why the Fund should not be permitted to borrow on a much larger scale from governments and private markets.

There is no question, in the case of low-income countries in balance-of-payments difficulties, of negotiating an appropriate relationship between the amount of retrenchment to be undertaken by the deficit countries and the amount of finance to be provided by the creditors. In these cases the amount of finance available is narrowly determined by the size of quotas, and the countries concerned have no choice but to live within the resources thus available. They must do this regardless of what it may mean in terms of disruption of the economy and of development programs, and regardless also of the degree of responsibility of surplus countries for aggravating the problem through restriction of imports from the deficit countries, or through the deterioration of the terms of trade inflicted on the deficit countries by the deflationary policies adopted by the surplus countries.

It would be wrong to conclude from the foregoing that the large debtor countries have obtained more favorable treatment from the international community than other countries. The stabilization programs required of the big debtors as a condition for balance-of-payments support have involved large sacrifices for them, and it would be difficult to measure those sacrifices against those of the low-income countries. Proportionally the sacrifices of the heavily indebted countries may have been as large as or even larger than those of the low-income countries during the period following mid-1982. On the other hand, countries at a lower level of income were bound to be more severely affected by any given percentage of decline in real income, and these countries had not gone through a preceding period of rapid growth and development as many of the large debtors had.

BRINGING PRESSURE ON THE CREDITORS

The important point is a different one. It is that in the case of the major debtor countries international coercion was applied to creditors as well as debtors in 1982–83 and that this was a new experience in the negotiation of stabilization programs. It was an experience that demonstrated that the posture of the creditors does not have to be taken as a given datum in such negotiations, but that the creditors themselves may be called upon to make an accommodation with the debtors. By "creditors," of course, is meant, in this particular context, the commercial banks, but there is no reason, in principle, why the same considerations should not apply to the governments of creditor countries.

Consequently, it is necessary to reconsider the traditional argument that the degree of adjustment required of a particular deficit country is a simple function of the foreign exchange resources available to it, including a borrowing capacity that is fixed within fairly narrow limits. There are circumstances in which even the most tough-minded creditors may be prevailed upon to be flexible in their willingness to lend. Such flexibility has, of course, been demonstrated mainly in cases where creditors considered that the integrity of their own major banks was endangered, so that they themselves had something to lose. The implicit evidence of the GAB negotiations is that creditors are certainly not, at the present time, prepared to apply the same reasoning to the small debtors as to the large ones. But the principle has been established just the same—namely, that the burden of adjustment should be shared by creditors as well as debtors—and there are obvious reasons why that principle should be applied on a nondiscriminatory basis instead of on a basis that implies that small debtors are less worthy of consideration than large ones.

ENHANCING THE ROLE OF THE IMF

A further conclusion from recent experience relates to the role of commercial banks in the international monetary system. The very fact that in order to bring the commercial banks into line the IMF had to threaten them with dire consequences demonstrates quite clearly that the private banks are unsuited to the task of providing balance-of-payments support. They had assumed this responsibility immediately after the first oil crisis because the resources position of the IMF had been steadily undermined since the 1960s by the refusal of the industrial countries to keep increasing Fund quotas in line with world trade. The commercial banks, awash with liquid resources deposited with them by the capital surplus OPEC countries, were only too happy to be able to press their loans upon the creditworthy oil importing countries, both developed and developing. They filled a vacuum at a time when there were no alternative institutions ready to undertake the recycling of surplus funds that was required if worldwide deflation was to be avoided. But an institution having pretensions in the field of balance-of-payments support must be prepared to supply resources in bad times as well as good, and no financial institution whose principal purpose is profit-making can be expected to place the objectives of the international community above those of its shareholders, especially if significant risks are involved. There is, therefore, a strong case for rebuilding the resources of the IMF to the point at which it would take back the task of balance-of-payments financing from the commercial banks, and thereby regain the importance that it had during the 1950s and 1960s as a source of balance-of-payments financing.

ADJUSTMENT AND GROWTH

Thus far we have discussed questions of equity and efficiency that arise when adjustment is unilateral rather than two-sided, and the differences in the treatment of deficit countries that depend on whether their situations are believed to constitute a threat to the stability of the international monetary system.

A further key question is the following: how far is the kind of adjustment now being undertaken by developing countries appropriate in the light of their own economic situation as well as that of the world economy as a whole?

If one steps back from the body of dubious doctrine relating to this subject, it will be apparent that the term "adjustment" should include the concept of improving the ability of an organism to thrive in the particular environment in which it finds itself. In the case of balance-of-payments disequilibrium, to the extent that adjustment is required in a deficit country, it involves, or should involve, a process of change that reduces the chances that such a disequilibrium will recur. In other words, adjustment implies structural adaptation of a kind that will restore external equilibrium at a normal level and rate of growth of economic activity.

In practice, however, the adjustment process is viewed in a much more limited perspective. The main objective is considered to be the restoration of external balance without much regard to the general business conditions under which such restoration is achieved. For this purpose a reduction of aggregate demand suffices. This position is sometimes defended by the argument that elimination of external disequilibrium through demand management will release the inherent forces making for resumption of growth. But a mere reduction of aggregate demand does not improve the functioning of the economy in a manner that will make it possible to maintain external balance at a high level of activity. Thus any effort by a country that has restored external equilibrium by demand management alone to revive the level of activity and hence of demand may simply founder on a recurrence of the selfsame difficulties that led to the original measures of deflation, wrongly entitled "adjustment."

In other words, there is a tendency to treat the "adjustment process" as if it consisted of nothing more or less than a reduction of aggregate demand. While such a reduction may well be an important component of an overall program of adjustment, in and of itself it contributes little or nothing to the adaptation of the economy to changing conditions. In fact there is a sense in which the effects of deflation and of adjustment are in opposite directions. Deflation tends to reduce the ability of an economy to adjust because it slows down the momentum of investment which is indispensable to adaptation and change.

THE SEARCH FOR NEW APPROACHES

For a time, in 1980 and 1981, the IMF experimented with policies that took greater cognizance of the structural aspects of external deficits than had previously been customary. This was accompanied by a major increase in the supply of resources, both gross and net, to developing countries. The Fund began advocating what it called "supply-oriented adjustment policies." Two approaches were envisaged. The first was designed to promote efficiency at a given level of aggregate nominal demand by reducing what were regarded as distortions caused by price and exchange rate rigidities, monopolies, taxes, subsidies, and trade restrictions. The second approach aimed at enhancing the long-run rate of growth of full-capacity output through incentives to saving and industrial investment, expansion of education and training, stimulation of technical innovation, and limitation of the size of the government sector.

These first approaches by the Fund toward the analysis of structural elements in balance-of-payments disequilibrium were welcome, even though they fell far short of what was needed. In particular they gave inadequate attention to sectoral imbalances, and exaggerated the importance of prices and incentives as against the promotion of adjustment through investment and growth in key sectors of the economy. Alignment of domestic prices with world levels was assumed to be advantageous in all cases, often without any effort to assess the social costs that could result from too doctrinaire an approach to this subject. The penchant for limiting the size of the government sector smacked more of politics than of economics, especially where the government sector accounted for a significantly smaller proportion of GNP than in most of the industrial countries. But it is, perhaps, churlish to criticize a palpable effort by those concerned to make a positive and constructive response to the demand for recognition of structural change as a key factor in a sound adjustment process.

THE SIGNIFICANCE OF THE INDIAN LOAN

It was during this brief interval of IMF experimentation with new approaches to the adjustment process that a new IMF loan to India came up for consideration. The history of this loan is of great interest despite the fact that in many ways it was the exception that proved the rule. The conditions applied by the IMF to the Indian loan did not call for deflation: on the contrary the Indian economy was envisaged as continuing to grow throughout the period during which drawings on the loan were to be made. But the Indian program was the subject of strong criticism by the United States, with the result that the period of IMF experimentation with supply-oriented adjustment was brought to an abrupt end, and subsequent stabilization programs in other countries reverted to the traditional deflationary model.

India approached the IMF for balance-of-payments support early in 1981, at a time when its external position was giving grounds for some concern, but had not yet reached critical dimensions. This kind of early approach to the Fund was fully in line with previous declarations by its Managing Director regarding the behavior of deficit countries. In responding to criticisms of IMF conditionality, the Managing Director had argued that deficit countries were apt to leave it to the last possible moment to approach the Fund for help, and by that time the situation had often deteriorated to the point at which harsh measures were unavoidable. It would be better, the Managing Director had said, for countries to consult with the Fund at an early stage of any deterioration in their balances of payments since this would make it possible to forestall a major crisis and thereby avoid unduly severe measures of retrenchment. These views on the need for early approaches to the Fund had been fully endorsed by the industrial countries, including the United States.

Developing countries generally were not inclined to place themselves in the hands of the Fund prematurely, but the Indian approach was certainly justified in terms of the policies that had been enunciated by the Fund management. The adjustment process agreed upon between India and the Fund involved government investment in the energy and transport sectors within a general context of growth and at a high level of public and private savings and investment. It was envisaged that the requisite restructuring of supply, especially in the energy and transport sectors, would be firmly launched during the first two or three years of the program and that the investments contemplated would put temporary pressure on the balance of payments, calling for access to Fund financing. This kind of program was in full conformity with the requirements of the Extended Fund Facility (EFF) which had been established in 1974 to deal with cases involving the correction of structural imbalance.

THE REJECTION OF THE INDIAN PRECEDENT

The United States, however, was critical of the Indian program which, it felt, would establish an undesirable precedent. Acceptance of the Indian program would amount to changing the whole character of the IMF, turning it into a "medium-term financial intermediary" instead of a monetary institution designed to provide temporary balance-of-payments support to member countries standing in need of such support. It was not the purpose of EFF to help countries to maintain high growth rates. India could perfectly well reduce its deficit on current account by adopting a less ambitious investment program. The United States considered that if India insisted on maintaining such a program it should seek the requisite funds from the private international capital market, especially having regard to the low level of India's debt service obligations. It was in any case not the function of the IMF to provide member countries with the resources required to sustain high levels of investment. The Fund should not act as a financial intermediary but only as a "lender of last resort," analogous to the central banks of member countries.

In the event, the Indian loan was approved despite U.S. objections. It did not, however, set a precedent for Fund programs. On the contrary, while other developed countries had decided to support the Indian loan on an exceptional basis, they joined the United States in opposing any liberalization of IMF conditionality. In the latter part of 1981 it became clear that the leading industrial countries basically supported the philosophy underlying the position that the United States had taken on the Indian loan, and that they would not be prepared to go along with a general application of the approach that had been taken in the Indian case.

THE ABANDONMENT OF NEW APPROACHES

This led immediately to abandonment of the search for new approaches to the adjustment process, and little further was heard of "supply-oriented adjustment policies." The conditions imposed for IMF lending were tightened once again, and continued to be hardened further on the argument that Fund liquidity had been reduced by the impact of the debt crisis beginning in the second half of 1982. As noted earlier, this argument was largely specious, since Fund resources were being artificially restricted under deliberate policies of the industrial countries.

As a result, adjustment programs reverted to the traditional deflationary pattern. Moreover, countries were increasingly required to comply with certain "preconditions" which were to be satisfied prior to submission of programs to the Executive Board for approval. Although this was not a new practice, it had been employed only occasionally in the past. Now it became a customary feature of Fund programs. Although the preconditions are ultimately reported to the Executive Board, the board's control is, in effect, preempted except after the event. Yet the preconditions may include measures of fundamental importance to the economy, including even exchange rate adjustments and the elimination of commodity subsidies.

Further tightening of conditionality is to be seen in the policy whereby a country that does not succeed in effecting the structural adjustment called for under an EFF program is not allowed to renegotiate that program even where failure is due to circumstances beyond its control. Additional IMF assistance, if available at all, is provided only under a stand-by arrangement.

As recently as June 1981 the Fund staff had been arguing in favor of stabilization programs that utilize foreign borrowing to permit "higher levels of expenditures—as well as higher growth rates over the medium term." These, together with the fulfillment of IMF performance criteria, would ensure that "the flow of output out of a given stock of resources is maximized."[3] This perception seems like a vision of Utopia when viewed in the perspective of the draconian stabilization programs of 1983–84.

Gone is any thought of symmetry or burden-sharing in the adjustment process. The concept of structural adjustment, to the extent that it is used in current discussion of balance-of-payments problems, has been deprived of all meaning, just as the concept of adjustment itself has. The World Bank, likewise, has not been able to make much practical sense of the concept, partly because of the entirely inadequate resources that it can devote to this purpose, and partly because Bank conditions for structural adjustment lending are normally superimposed on Fund conditions that leave no room for sustaining, let alone enhancing, the growth process. And one must say yet again that without investment and growth there cannot be adjustment in any genuine sense of that term.

One is forced back to Dr. Patel's indictment of the "retreat from shared responsibility" and his lament for an idealism that seems to have been lost.

The International Environment for Adjustment in Developing Countries*

THE CONTEXT OF ADJUSTMENT IN THE 1970S

The succession of crises in the world economy that began with the collapse of the Bretton Woods system in 1971 subjected the developing countries to the most severe test of their capacity for adjustment of the postwar period.

Many countries faced current deficits in their balances of payments of unprecedented magnitudes. While a significant proportion of these deficits reflected imbalances of domestic origin, there were major external elements for which the deficit countries were either not responsible, or were not wholly responsible. Moreover, the deficits, large as they were, did not reflect the full extent of the difficulties faced. The fact that countries were forced to reduce production and income below otherwise attainable levels so as to bring their external payments into balance meant that recorded surpluses and deficits were smaller than they would have been if the existence of such disequilibrium had not in itself caused a constriction of output and employment.

In effect, many of the developing countries were faced with a burden of adjustment out of all proportion to their degree of responsibility for the imbalances arising in the international payments system.

*Originally published in World Development 8, no. 11 (Oxford: Pergamon, 1980): 833–42, this essay draws extensively on a longer study by Sidney Dell and Roger Lawrence, The Balance-of-Payments Adjustment Process in Developing Countries (Oxford: Pergamon, 1980).

The principal sources of disequilibrium that were beyond the control of the deficit countries but which nevertheless imposed tremendous burdens upon them were the following:

- the sharp changes in the prices of primary commodities, especially in 1974–75, and the acceleration of the upward trend in prices of manufactured goods imported by developing countries;
- that part of developing country deficits that constituted the counterpart of structural surpluses in certain industrial and certain oil exporting countries;
- the shifting of balance-of-payments pressures from industrial countries to developing countries through the slackening of import demand in the former countries associated with the recession of 1974–75 and the period of low growth that ensued;
- the further shifting of pressures resulting from a growing wave of protectionism in the industrial countries directed particularly at imports from low-income countries.[4]

A comparison of movements in the trade balances of both developed and developing countries as between the periods 1962–72 and 1973–76 shows that in the latter period the frequency of increases in import volumes as a primary factor in explaining deterioration in trade balances diminished greatly.[5] At the same time, the frequency with which import price changes appear as a primary factor increased dramatically for all groups of countries, and the frequency of export price declines increased for all groups other than the large OECD countries. The sharp reduction in the frequency with which import volumes appear as a primary factor in deterioration in the trade balances of developing countries and the key importance of changes in foreign trade prices in this regard in 1973–76 suggest that during this period demand pressures emanating from domestic economies were far less important, relative to other causes of change in the trade balance, than had previously been the case. Consequently, policies, both at the national and international level, that assumed that excessive demand pressures were still the most important feature of payments problems were in need of review.

Owing to the inadequacy of official flows of finance, bilateral and multilateral, in relation to the balance-of-payments pressures encountered, a large proportion of the external financing provided during this period took the form of flows from private capital markets. This enabled the recipient countries to sustain a substantially higher level of economic activity and import demand than would otherwise have been possible. Private capital flows were, however, directed mainly to industrial countries and the more advanced of the developing countries. Many of the low-income countries were unable to secure access to private capital markets and borrowing in these markets in any case involved terms that were inappropriate for these countries. Consequently, there was a pronounced bias in the recycling process against the poorest countries, which were therefore required to bear more than their fair share of the burden of adjustment.

The problems arising from the increase in the general level of international prices and, for most non-oil exporting developing countries, from the sharp deterioration in terms of trade, were compounded by the additional pressures that were brought to bear on their balances of payments as a result of the 1974–75 recession in the industrial countries and the slackness of the recovery that followed. This created an obstacle to the growth of exports from developing countries, especially where the weakness of external demand had the effect of depressing export prices.

These difficulties were further aggravated by the wave of protectionism that accompanied, and was stimulated by, the economic slowdown in the industrial countries. The recent Multifibre Arrangement expands the scope and increases the intensity of discriminatory restraints on shipments of textiles from developing countries to developed countries. These restraints date back to 1962, when the first international agreement of this kind, limited to cotton textiles only, was adopted as a temporary measure to be applied "during the next few years." Thus adjustment in the textile industry under broad international supervision has already lasted more than sixteen years on a temporary basis, and the end is not yet in sight. Moreover, the restrictions affect supplies not only from the major exporters but also from the poorer countries such as Bangladesh, Indonesia, and Sri Lanka, where textile products account for a high proportion of manufactured exports.[6]

Quota restrictions have also been introduced or intensified in relation to other products of interest to exporters in developing countries in a broad spectrum ranging from petrochemicals to footwear, to bicycle tires and tubes. Major barriers have also been applied increasingly to developing country exports of beef, sugar, vegetables, tobacco, and grains, as well as of manufactured food products of various types.[7]

Thus while the international community often requires prompt adjustment in countries with balance-of-payments deficits, it tolerates increasingly restrictive trade measures that frustrate the efforts of the deficit countries to adjust. Similarly, while great emphasis is placed on exchange rate realignment as a means of correcting external imbalance, by improving the export competitiveness of developing countries, the efficacy of the exchange rate weapon is continually eroded through the removal of products from the influence of the price mechanism and the forces of competition by direct control.

Thus the environment for adjustment was unfavorable. Too little of the adjustment of deficits took the form of rising exports. This was due partly to the relatively limited capacity of a number of developing countries to raise their earnings from traditional exports and/or to develop new types of export. But it was due also to the general slackness of world markets and protectionist policies that depressed the demand for products exported by developing countries, and, in some cases, the prices of these products.

What was required in these circumstances was the provision of financial support on a scale sufficient to permit the necessary adjustments to be made in a context of growth, thus tiding over the effects of unfavorable and reversible world market conditions. The financial support that was forthcoming was, however, insufficient, despite considerable expansion and innovation in the provision of official payments finance. Consequently, in most countries an inordinate share of the burden of adjustment fell on imports, and import compression became a significant avenue through which external disturbances were transmitted to the domestic economy, thereby disrupting the development process.

IMPACT ON DEVELOPING COUNTRIES

The disturbances in the international economy were transmitted to the domestic economies of developing countries through a variety of channels. Sharp increases in export prices in 1973–74 expanded the purchasing power of the private and often also of the public sector, while subsequent declines had the opposite effect. Increases in import prices led to an acceleration in domestic price inflation from the cost side. In particular, cost-push pressures had a considerable influence on real wage rates and earnings. In several countries the rates of decline in real wages were unprecedented, amounting in some cases to as much as 20 to 40 percent over relatively short periods. Although direct evidence is lacking, there is a strong presumption that in many countries the reduction was accompanied by a deterioration in the distribution of income.

Particularly important was the impact on the capacity to import. In many developing countries imports play a crucial role both in sustaining the utilization of existing productive capabilities and in expanding productive capacity.

Available data show that in those countries in which the growth rate of imports in 1973–76 was equal to or greater than that experienced in

1965–73 average rates of growth of GDP and its major components were generally higher in 1973–76 than in the earlier period. On the other hand, where import growth in 1973–76 fell below the level of preceding years, GDP growth also declined. While not all of the differences in performance of the two groups can be attributed to differences in import availabilities, the latter factor was an important determinant of changes in economic performance.

It should be noted that the capacity for adjustment is far from uniform among countries. The elasticity of an economy, especially of its foreign trade sector, and the mobility of its resources, and hence its capability for withstanding external shocks tend, on the whole, to be related to its level of development. There are marked differences in the ability of countries to raise export earnings, particularly by expanding exports of manufactures or of other nontraditional products such as processed foodstuffs. Similarly, countries differ considerably in the extent to which they can compress imports without suffering adverse effects. Much depends on the degree and promptness with which a country can shift resources from domestic consumption to exports and provide domestic substitutes for imports. This kind of mobility and flexibility is in turn a function of the stage of development attained and, in particular, of the size of the industrial sector. It is the relatively more developed countries that have the advantage in minimizing the costs and maximizing the benefits of the adjustment process. An equitable distribution of the burden of adjustment would take these factors into account, whereas in practice the burden has tended to weigh more heavily on the developing countries, and particularly upon the poorest among these countries.

The experience of individual developing countries during the crisis period was conditioned by two fundamental and interrelated factors: their capacity to adjust by expanding export earnings and their ability to attract and mobilize external resources in support of the development process.

Some countries had experienced a fairly rapid expansion of import capacity during the years before the crisis, and deliberately sought to maintain import and GDP growth from 1974 onward by borrowing from private capital markets. Several of these countries had reached a relatively advanced stage of development, and here a high capacity to adjust was accompanied by a relatively high capacity to finance deficits, and these two factors came together in a way that limited disruption of the growth process.

In a considerable number of other countries, capacities to adjust were moderate or low, and many of these countries entered the period 1974–76 with earned import capacities below the levels achieved in 1970. Long-term lending generally played little role in supporting import capacity. Reserve availability and payments finance were also inadequate, and at best cushioned declines in import capacity during the first year in which they occurred: it was the poorest countries, in particular, that were least able to sustain import purchasing power by borrowing from private capital markets. The declines in earned import capacity that occurred were thus passed through to the economy in the form of a reduction in imports of such magnitude that compression of developmental imports was unavoidable.

The consequences of these events were detrimental to growth and development. Those sectors most sensitive to foreign exchange availabilities, in particular manufacturing, experienced a decided deceleration in rates of growth of output. Apart from the decline in real wages referred to earlier, investment declined noticeably in many cases, and a number of countries experienced one or more years of net disinvestment. In such cases the inability to provide to the domestic economy minimal protection from external disturbance stunted the growth of productive capacity, or even reduced that capacity.

Although payments imbalances were substantially reversed in 1976 and 1977, the period of disequilibrium left a legacy of lower growth rates in the world economy, especially in developing countries, as well as of increased vulnerability of developing countries to external shocks. Stagflation in the developed countries accompanied by the new protectionism has limited the growth of developing country exports, so that improvements in trade balances have had to be achieved through reductions in the growth of imports in real terms. Even those countries that enjoyed ready access to private capital markets in the past cannot necessarily rely on additional financing of the same magnitude from those sources in the immediate future, especially where substantial increases in debt service ratios have occurred. Moreover, the ratio of reserves to imports has fallen substantially in a large number of developing countries. For all these reasons, the problem of maintaining a reasonably sound external position in a context of adequate growth in GDP will continue to encounter difficulties.

THE ROLE OF THE IMF

Mention has already been made of the inadequacy of official balance-of-payments support in relation to the severity of the external pressures encountered. While part of the reason for this inadequacy was the limited size of Fund quotas in relation to balance-of-payments deficits, many countries hesitated to make use of regular Fund facilities even when they were under the most intense pressure both in their external accounts and in their domestic economies because of the conditions imposed on drawings. There were only ten cases of drawings beyond the first credit tranche in 1974–76 among the entire Fund membership. Thus quite apart from questions of the general adequacy of international official resources for balance-of-payments support, and as to whether the present balance between official and commercial sources of balance-of-payments finance can be regarded as satisfactory, there is a further question as to whether the official resources that do exist are sufficiently "available" for the purposes intended.

There is no disagreement among governments on the broad principle of conditionality in the Fund. The issue arises rather from the practical application of Fund policies relating to conditionality. There is a widespread feeling among developing countries that the quota resources available in the Fund are too small to justify the considerable changes in economic plans and policies that might have to be made in order to be allowed to draw on these resources, except as a last resort.

This in turn reflects a concern as to the diagnosis usually made of balance-of-payments problems and the performance obligations required in the light of that diagnosis.

As to diagnosis, the *Fund History, 1966–71,* describes the Fund's approach to financial programming whereby a set of monetary and fiscal policies can be determined for the next twelve to eighteen months "that would reconcile resource availabilities with resource needs in such a way as to produce minimum strain on the member's domestic price level and a desired balance of payments result."[8] Advanced econometric techniques are employed with a view to summarizing the monetary picture of a country in terms of a few aggregate figures: this makes it possible for the Fund to work with members to devise specific credit ceilings and targets suitable for inclusion in stand-by arrangements and to review the performance of members under these arrangements.

The Fund is itself well aware of the many legitimate questions that may be raised concerning the methodology employed. The *Fund History, 1966–71,* for example, indicates that much remains to be done in considering such questions as: To what extent is a monetarist approach—that is, one based the assumption that changes in the stock of money are a primary determinant of changes in total spending—valid for all countries? Are there not important intercountry differences in the manner in which monetary influences affect real output, employment, and the price level? How do programs based on credit ceilings affect domestic employment and the distribution of income? Are aggregative techniques useful for achieving such socioeconomic objectives as enhancing employment and redistributing income?[9] Further questions emerge from a highly important article published by the Fund suggesting that the monetary approach to the balance of payments "needs blending with other lines of analysis."[10]

It is particularly important for the methodology employed to be capable of distinguishing cases in which the predominant feature is excess aggregate demand from cases in which cost-induced inflation or wage price spirals are the key element. Often these factors may be present together in a given country at a particular time, but it is still necessary to ascertain as accurately as possible the relative importance of each. There is a danger inherent in the effort, characteristic of stabilization programs, to sum up the economic performance of a country in terms of a few monetary aggregates. Moreover, the selection of quantitative monetary targets for performance criteria that will be used to justify drawings on Fund resources itself largely determines the character of the adjustment to be undertaken. The most important target is usually considered to be a ceiling on domestic credit expansion and the corresponding policies involve global fiscal and monetary restraint, regardless of the source of balance-of-payments pressure. To the extent that a balance-of-payments deficit is due to excess pressure of demand on domestic resources, it is natural that the solution should be sought in a general curb on demand. But in many cases a significant and often major proportion of the deficit is due to factors that do not lend themselves to treatment by generalized deflation.

Such factors may be either of external or of internal origin. Reference has already been made to some of the external factors causing pressure on the balances of payments of developing countries in the 1970s, which clearly could not be dealt with by generalized deflation in the deficit countries. These included extraordinary price movements that were generated externally; the slackening of business activity and hence of import demand in the industrial countries; and protectionist restrictions on imports from developing countries.

An additional external factor of major significance results from structural surpluses in the balances of payments of other countries. For example, the government of the Federal Republic of Germany has advanced the idea that the German surplus is structural, and that adjustment is bound to take time and organizational imagination. Although the international community has, de facto, accepted the persistence of chronic surpluses in the system, the implications for the treatment of counterpart deficits have been ignored. Pressure is brought upon the deficit countries to eliminate their deficits completely within a relatively short period of time, despite the fact that little or nothing is being done to bring corresponding pressure to bear upon the surplus countries. The result is that deficit countries are being required to adjust to an extent that goes far beyond the degree of their responsibility for their deficit positions. Of course the inevitable outcome of forcing excessive retrenchment on deficit countries while surplus countries continue to maintain their surpluses is that deficits are simply shifted from country to country. And the cumulative deflation thus brought about by the adjustment process is thereby superimposed on, and reinforces, the primary deflation resulting from business recession in the industrial countries.

There are also internal problems for which the remedy cannot be sought in generalized deflation. These include sectoral imbalances in the domestic economy due, for example, to a need to bring about the kinds of reforms in agriculture that would lead to an expansion of food supplies and to shift to cheaper and less import-intensive forms of energy. Adjustment to such imbalances calls for specific policies and measures adapted to the particular problem. In such circumstances reliance on global monetary and fiscal policies as the main instruments for balance-of-payments adjustment may necessitate a higher proportional decline in real income for a given improvement in the balance of payments than would otherwise be required. In most developing countries exportable supplies are increased relatively little by monetary and fiscal contraction while imports are not easily compressed, especially where they have already been limited by direct controls, so that it takes a relatively large cutback in domestic income to achieve the further reduction in imports needed for external balance. In other words, a cost-benefit analysis of general deflationary measures intended to improve the trade balance by cutting domestic consumption would yield one set of results in a country where exports were not consumed domestically and imported consumer goods consisted mainly of basic foodstuffs, and a different set of results when a substantial proportion of exportables is consumed domestically and there is a wide range of imported consumer goods.

The Fund considers that restrictions on trade are not an acceptable means of tackling balance-of-payments pressures, and that such restrictions may, in fact, be said to compound the problem of adjustment instead of dealing with it. While it is recognized that certain long-standing restrictions may be difficult to remove in the short term, because of the effect that this would have on production and employment, the Fund requires that stabilization programs should provide for removal of restrictions newly imposed for balance-of-payments reasons, and for renunciation of any further recourse to them.

The Fund's position on this matter dates back to the period of trade liberalization immediately after World War II. But the general climate of world trade is no longer expansionist, and developing countries can no longer rely on being able to redeploy their resources into sectors with an export potential. Moreover, even where a country has attained the level of development at which such redeployment would be feasible, it can rarely be expected to yield results within the time frame of a stand-by arrangement of one year any more than a redeployment away from the textile industry has been considered feasible in the industrial countries within such a period. In many of the least developed countries, moreover, export diversification will be achieved only as part of the long-run process of development. There are, therefore, many cases in which an intensification of trade restrictions provides the only option for achieving the requisite import reduction without an excessive decline in real income and employment.

Exchange rate changes are one of the essential instruments for adjustment, and all countries need to make such changes from time to time. As in the case of monetary and fiscal policy, however, there are no standard formulas that can be applied: the usefulness of exchange rate adjustment depends greatly on the particular circumstances of each case.

The case for exchange rate adjustment is clearest where world market prices do not cover the domestic costs of export products, including a reasonable margin of profit, at current exchange rates. Beyond this point, however, the usefulness of the exchange rate weapon varies considerably from country to country depending on the degree of elasticity and diversification of the economy concerned. Quite moderate devaluations may achieve some success in countries where trade flows react sensitively to exchange rate changes—though even here experience suggests that time lags may be considerable, so that in the short run the external balance may deteriorate. But where trade flows are not very responsive to exchange rate changes, the degree of devaluation needed to secure equilibrium in the balance of payments will be large. So many of the basic costs of developing countries are tied to import prices that it may be impossible to prevent devaluations of large magnitude from setting off severe cost-induced inflationary spirals—with all the attendant economic, social, and political dangers that this entails. Thus great care is required in assessing the need for exchange rate changes, especially in countries where trade flows are relatively inelastic with respect to such changes, as is the case particularly of the least developed countries.

More attention is also needed to the determination of the desirable *rate* of adjustment, which, for present purposes, may be defined as the rate that minimizes cost in terms of output or growth potential foregone, including the frictional costs of reallocating resources. Moreover, the factors to be taken into account go beyond purely economic considerations: the political and social costs of unduly rapid adjustment may be very high. While other costs may be assessed correctly, the costs of social strife are often overlooked, or not foreseen.[11]

It is natural and appropriate for international agencies to limit themselves to the technical aspects of problems as far as they can. They have no mandate to take political factors explicitly into account. Unfortunately, technical and political aspects can, in the last resort, rarely be separated. The very act of pressing a technically valid solution to the limit may be unwise in a larger political context. It is important that international agencies should not directly or indirectly substitute their own political judgment for that of their member governments.

The Fund recognizes that the optimum rate of adjustment depends very much on the extent of imbalance and on the degree of redeployment of resources required. In the past, when it was apparent that the adjustment needed could not be effected within the time frame of a one-year, stand-by arrangement, the rate of adjustment could be moderated through a series of successive arrangements over several years. More recently it has become possible to adopt stand-by arrangements covering periods of up to two years, or arrangements under the EFF which are at present available for periods of up to three years, with repayment falling due within a period of four to ten years.

While the new approaches are a move in the right direction, they do not as yet amount to a full recognition of the nature or dimensions of the problem. The Fund still considers the one-year, stand-by arrangement to be the normal procedure to be adopted, and the longer-term arrangements as exceptional. While there are cases in which a substantial degree of adjustment can be effected within the space of one year, there are many other instances in which the imbalance is large and persistent, and the remedies involve longer-term structural change. The Fund did recognize the existence of such a problem in instituting the oil facility. The problem of adaptation to the change in oil prices is, however, only one example of a whole series of structural problems with balance-of-payments implications. There is, therefore, a strong case for bridging the gap between short-term balance-of-payments accommodation and long-term development finance of the type provided by the World Bank.

If a slower rate of adjustment is to be envisaged under certain conditions, the question of the adequacy of resources for balance-of-payments support comes to the fore. Fund quotas declined from the equivalent of approximately 10 percent of the imports of member countries in the early 1950s to about 3 percent in 1977, and the ratio is not expected to change significantly in the near future, despite quota increases.

It is true that relations between the Fund and the private banking system have recently become much closer, so that in a sense agreement between a member country and the Fund on the conditions for a drawing may be said to bring with it the possibility of a larger volume of balance-of-payments support than that provided by the Fund alone, though commercial borrowing is usually subject to a ceiling in countries that already have a substantial burden of debt service. Borrowing from private banks is, however, at best a poor substitute for adequate resources in the Fund, especially in view of the fact that there are great inequalities in the access of member countries to the private banking system and that the terms and conditions of private bank lending are inappropriate for low-income countries. Fund resources form a much higher proportion of the total balance-of-payments financing available to the weakest and—in terms of the narrow criteria of private capital markets—least creditworthy countries than they do for other Fund members. The weakest countries are those that can least afford to hold fully owned reserves, and also those most likely to require Fund assistance and come under Fund surveillance. They are, therefore, in multiple jeopardy—they tend, through the process of shifting mentioned earlier, to attract more than their share of the pressures on the balance of payments exerted by structural current account surpluses in the system, as well as a less than proportional share of the capital flows that these surpluses generate; they are least likely to be able to finance such deficits out of owned reserves or by borrowing from nonofficial sources; they are, therefore, most likely to have to comply with constraints upon their economies, the extent of which is a function of the inadequacy of available official financing; and they have the least capacity for adjustment because of the rigidity and lack of diversification of their economies.

THE NEED FOR REFORM

The main conclusions suggested by the preceding discussion are the following:

- Generalized deflation should not be regarded as the standard remedy for balance-of-payments difficulties, especially where such difficulties are accompanied by falling production and employment, by supply bottlenecks in particular sectors, or by factors of external origin for which the deficit country is not responsible.
- Stabilization programs should indicate objectives and directions for the economy but should avoid standard formulas and pinpoint targetry.
- The package of measures for adjustment should be sensitive to the particular situation of each country, including the political and social philosophy underlying its development program, the level of development and degree of flexibility and diversification of its economy, the extent to which its balance-of-payments difficulties are of internal or external origin, and the impact of the package on long-run development prospects.
- The conditions required for drawings on the regular facilities of the Fund have become too demanding in relation to the amount of resources made available, and countries are now reluctant to approach the Fund except in the most extreme circumstances. Both for this reason, and on the merits of the case, an easing of conditions seems justified.

The changes needed at the international level in order to secure a more effective and less disruptive adjustment process in developing countries may be listed under three headings:

- a more favorable international environment, notably as regards markets for developing country exports and the flow of capital to these countries;
- improvement in the diagnosis of balance-of-payments problems and the adaptation of remedies to problems;
- avoidance of disruptive conditions for international balance-of-payments support, coupled with an increase in the official resources available for such support.

Improvement in the adjustment process calls for the creation of an international environment in which developing countries pursuing effective development programs would be able to rely on a steady expansion of export markets in the developed countries with reasonable stability of prices and absence of trade barriers, particularly of a discriminatory kind. Similarly, an expansion of the flow of long-term capital would make it possible for adjustment to take place at a higher level of economic activity than would otherwise prevail, and would facilitate the redeployment of resources needed to improve the flexibility and responsiveness of the economies of developing countries.

Shortcomings in the diagnosis of balance-of-payments problems have already been reviewed. Apart from adequate differentiation of the various types and sources of balance-of-payments pressure, there is a need for measures to tackle the basic causes of disequilibrium and the long-run obstacles to growth along with the proximate phenomena of inflation and balance-of-payments pressure that accompany it. Indeed, one of the key elements in working out an appropriate stabilization strategy should be a review of the development plan or program of the country concerned, and a main objective of stabilization should be minimum disruption of long-run development. One of the most disturbing features of the experience of the 1970s is the large number of cases in which there were major declines in investment growth. At the very minimum, one would expect that provision should be made for investment targets to play an essential role in stabilization programs. Although it would not be appropriate to include such targets among the Fund's performance criteria because governments do not control the level of private investment, and because of the uncertainties involved, stabilization programs should explicitly consider the manner in which investment will be sustained, and will be oriented so as to deal with the sources of current difficulties. A decline in productive investment of more than temporary significance should be taken as a prima facie indication that a stabilization program is not achieving one of its principal goals. Moreover, where balance-of-payments difficulties are due to factors other than excessive pressure of domestic demand, sectoral policies may be a much more important object of concern than the rate of domestic credit expansion.

To the extent that deficits are due to, or are compounded by, structural surpluses in the system, or reflect a shifting of balance-of-payments pressures from other countries as a result of business recession or import restrictions, remedial measures should be required of the industrial countries concerned. Furthermore, if the application of such remedial measures extends over a long period, adjustment in the deficit countries should be programmed over similarly extended time periods, and appropriate finance should be provided accordingly.

It is also necessary to balance considerations of monetary and payments stability with those of equity. Explicit attention to the distribution of the burden of adjustment among various segments of the population is needed. For example, a tight monetary policy tends to favor those who are in a position to obtain loans abroad: apart from the fact that those who borrow abroad may virtually escape the effects of the tightening of credit, they may also make large profits by taking advantage of interest rate differentials associated with steep increases in domestic rates. Likewise devaluation may bring windfall profits to primary producers at the expense of the urban and rural poor. In some countries particular objections have been raised by the Fund to the continuation at existing levels of subsidies on essential foodstuffs because of the heavy costs to the government budget. While a reduction of subsidies may be effective in reducing the budget deficit as well as imports, it tends to bring about a deterioration in the distribution of real income and consumption at a time when international development agencies are calling for greater concentration of resources on satisfying the basic needs of the poorest countries, and of the poorest communities within these countries.

The adaptation of remedies to problems should also take account of the broad political and economic philosophy of the governments concerned. For example, objections have been raised to the use of direct controls on the economy, including price controls. This, however, is a matter that cannot be settled on the basis of conventional economic logic alone. For example, where price controls are employed as an integral element of the planning mechanism for the allocation of income and resources, their elimination is not a technical question, but a question of basic political and economic strategy that is properly a matter for decision by the government alone.

The experience of the 1970s dramatized the adverse effects on long-term growth that can occur as a result of the disruption of development programs brought about by the compression of the balance-of-payments adjustment process into an unduly brief period of time. It is clear that the period of adjustment was much too short for many countries, and that a lack of adequate official resources for medium-term balance-of-payments support was severely felt. There is, therefore, a strong case for stretching out the period of adjustment in appropriate cases and for easing the terms and conditions of the balance-of-payments support provided by the Fund, especially in cases where structural changes have to be made. This in turn implies a corresponding increase in the financial resources of the Fund.

To sum up, the following proposals emerge from the preceding discussion:

– Improvement of the adjustment process in developing countries requires the creation of an international environment conducive to this end, particularly the creation of favorable conditions for trade and the flow of capital.

- The conditions applied for drawings on the Fund should be as flexible and responsive as possible, with a view to permitting deficit countries to phase the adjustment process over longer periods when necessary, to undertake the structural changes required to achieve balance-of-payments equilibrium, and to avoid the disruption of development programs.
- Determination of the magnitude of adjustment, the kind of balance-of-payments support required, and the conditions for drawings on the Fund should take into account the extent to which a deficit is due to factors within the responsibility of the country concerned as against factors beyond its control.
- The adjustment process should be placed firmly in the broader context of long-run development, and stabilization programs should explicitly address the question of ensuring consistency between short-run and long-run objectives.
- In order to permit the programming of the adjustment process over longer periods, where necessary, the resources of the Fund should be expanded. This could be done by making the supplementary financing facility permanent, as well as easing the conditions and lengthening the repayment period applicable to that facility. Alternatively a medium-term facility should be established at a substantial level of resources to provide balance-of-payments support over periods of five to ten years. Interest subsidies should be provided to the countries already eligible for such subsidies under the Fund's oil facility.
- Surplus countries have a special responsibility for channeling resources through multilateral lending agencies in a manner that would ensure a recycling of resources that would be equitable as between those countries that do and those countries that do not have access to other sources of finance, including private capital markets.
- In the longer run it should be an objective of the Fund that the ratio of Fund quotas to the imports of members should regain the level of the 1950s, that is a level of 10 percent.
- Where pressure on the balance of payments of a developing member country builds up due in part to factors beyond its control and adjustment becomes unavoidable, it should be recognized that there may be a need for the imposition of import restrictions by the government in the context of a satisfactory program of adjustment agreed with the Fund, if such measures are required to avert or mitigate a decline in real per capita output or income.

8

Stabilization, Conditionality, and Cross-Conditionality

Stabilization: The Political Economy of Overkill*

INTRODUCTION

In the course of his remarkable essay on stabilization plans in the Southern Cone of Latin America, Diaz-Alejandro (1981) suggests that these plans were a case of "overkill," in the sense that the economic retrenchment that they brought about went much further than was strictly necessary in terms of what could have been regarded as reasonable objectives.

The term "overkill" used by Diaz-Alejandro could well be used much more generally to describe the national and international programs of adjustment adopted in the 1970s and early 1980s. The following discussion deals first with international aspects of this process of overkill, and later with some of the national aspects.

INTERNATIONAL ASPECTS

The Distortion of Priorities

The purposes of the IMF are set out in the first of its Articles of Agreement. Six such purposes are defined, including international monetary cooperation, the expansion and balanced growth of international trade, the promotion of exchange stability and of a multilateral system of payments, the mitigation of disequilibrium in balances of payments, and the provision of resources to facilitate the correction of such disequilibrium.

The fundamental objectives underlying these purposes are described in Article I (ii) as being "the promotion and maintenance of high levels of

*This essay was originally presented to the Conference on IMF Conditionality held by the Institute for International Economics in March 1982. It was first published in *World Development* 10, no. 8 (Oxford: Pergamon, 1982): 597–612, and subsequently reprinted in *IMF Conditionality*, John Williamson, ed. (Washington, D.C.: Institute for International Economics, 1983).

employment and real income and . . . the development of the productive resources of all members as primary objectives of economic policy." Further reference to these primary objectives is made in Article I (v) which lays down that the correction of maladjustments in the balance of payments should be undertaken "without resorting to measures destructive of national or international prosperity."

The international community seems to have strayed quite far from these "primary objectives of economic policy." In a situation of increasingly inadequate effective demand, growing underutilization of productive capacity, and soaring unemployment, the pressure continues for even greater reductions of demand, which are likely to increase the volume of idle capacity and unemployment still further. The single-mindedness of the attack on inflation seems to have gone beyond the point at which trade-offs with other objectives are even considered, so that monetary restriction has almost become an end in itself.[1] This is a distortion of IMF priorities, as well as the priorities of Article 55 of the United Nations Charter and of the International Development Strategy drawn up under that Charter.[2]

There is irony in the fact that the first industrial country to express any sense of alarm about the current situation is precisely the one that, throughout the postwar period, had maintained the strongest orthodoxy in fiscal and monetary matters, and that on past occasions had invariably resisted proposals for economic expansion that might carry with them the smallest risk of inflation. On the insistence of Chancellor Schmidt, the Washington communiqué of January 6, 1982 contained the following warning: "The Chancellor referred to the danger of a worldwide depression."

In the circumstances it might have been expected that world leadership would be concerned at the present time with charting a program of economic recovery and with seeking international cooperation in such a program. In fact, however, the IMF management takes the position that:

> The fight against inflation must continue to concentrate heavily on demand management for although the increase in oil prices was earlier an important contributing factor, oil prices have recently softened and the major impulse behind inflation in both industrial and developing countries has come from expansionary financial policies mainly associated with large budgetary deficits and from a complex of cost-push factors and expectations [Dale, 1982].

This statement exemplifies the fundamental error of much current thinking about the world economy as well as about the problems faced by individual countries, industrial and developing.

It is interesting to examine this statement in the context of the United States, whose economy is still so large in relative terms as to play the leading role in determining the level of activity of the industrial countries as a whole and hence, to a considerable extent, of the developing countries as well.

In April 1982 unemployment in the United States was at a level of approximately 9 percent and rising. There was idle productive capacity in every sector of the economy and the rate of utilization of capacity had fallen to a level of 70 percent or lower in manufacturing industry. If it is true that current financial policy in the United States is expansionary as a result of the large budget deficit, why is it that output is not rising? Why, on the contrary, has real GNP been falling at a rate of no less than 4.5 percent per annum for the past six months? And if real income, and hence real demand, is falling, what sense does it make to say that the fight against inflation is essentially a problem of demand management?

The mistake here is twofold. In the first place a budget deficit per se tells us nothing about whether aggregate demand is excessive or not. It is only when we consider the budget deficit in conjunction with other demands on private saving—namely gross investment and net exports— that we can tell whether aggregate demand is excessive.

Secondly, under conditions of substantial unemployment and excess capacity, one must distinguish between that part of a budget deficit which is an automatic response to the low level of business activity, leading to reduced government revenues and higher government transfers, and the rest of the deficit which would add to demand even at a high level of employment. Despite the ascendancy of monetarism, the U.S. Department of Commerce continues to estimate the high employment budget deficit at regular intervals, and not long ago it issued a revised series going all the way back to 1955. Unfortunately the department has over the years progressively raised the percentage of unemployment used as a basis for defining the concept of high employment, so that that percentage now stands at 5.1, a level that seems much too high. Nevertheless, even at this level, the high employment budget was in surplus in the United States in 1979, 1980, and the first three quarters of 1981, while the deficit in the fourth quarter of 1981 was equivalent to considerably less than 1 percent of GNP—well within the order of error of the estimates. Now if the high employment budget was balanced or in surplus throughout the period from 1979 to 1981, it can hardly be said that inflation in the United States during that period was due to "expansionary financial policies mainly associated with large budgetary deficits." Clearly the source of inflation must be sought elsewhere. Even for 1982, available projections indicate that the expansionary thrust of the deficit, adjusted for the level of employment, is likely to be small or negligible.

Although the notion of a high employment budget deficit cannot be transferred mechanically to developing countries because of conceptual problems connected with the definitions of unemployment and excess capacity, it is just as true in these countries as in the industrial countries that at reduced levels of activity budget deficits increase because of the associated declines in government revenue. Consequently the expansionary thrust of a budget deficit in a developing country, as in an industrial country, cannot be assessed without allowing for the level of economic activity.

It has been necessary to dwell upon this matter because it is typical of the errors of diagnosis that so often lead to the disorientation of stabilization programs and hence to the process of overkill. Deflationary policies, however essential they may be in cases where balance-of-payments disequilibrium is due primarily to excess demand, should not be regarded as a panacea for all problems. Nor should the explicit injunction of Article I (v) be forgotten, that is, that measures to restore external equilibrium should not be "destructive of national or international prosperity." In many cases measures that carry the obvious risk of being destructive of national prosperity are nevertheless considered indispensable in overcoming inflation, or in restoring external balance, or both. Moreover, such measures are commonplace not only in countries where balance-of-payments support is being sought, but in many other countries also.

Some comfort is derived from the recent slowing down of cost inflation, as though this single measure of economic health could be given priority and ascendancy over all others. No one ever doubted that with sufficient determination it would be possible to cut back the level of business activity to the point at which demand inflation would be eliminated and cost inflation at least slowed down. The question was rather that of determining whether it was really necessary to burn down the house in order to discover roast pig; and whether there was not some better way of doing things that would give higher priority to "national and international prosperity" and somewhat less importance to the rate of increase in prices.

That is not to say that inflation is a matter that can be neglected. On the contrary, it is clear that inflation can seriously distort the development process by encouraging the use of resources in socially undesirable ways and by intensifying inequity in the distribution of income. But if the real problem is cost-induced inflation, and the remedy applied is demand deflation, the cure is likely to prove worse than the disease. Instead of reducing social tension it is likely to aggravate it, and even if the cost inflation is slowed down temporarily, the benefits are likely to last only as long as demand is maintained at subnormal levels.

A permanent solution to the problem of cost inflation cannot be obtained by seeking to play on the fear of rising unemployment among those who try to protect themselves against increases in the cost of living by demanding higher wages. Where a cut in living standards is unavoidable, price stability in a democratic society depends on general agreement as to the way in which the burden should be shared. Intimidation through unemployment is likely to make any long-lasting agreement on burden sharing more difficult to achieve, not less.

The ultimate futility of the deflationary approach becomes particularly clear in the prospects for the world economy foreseen by the adherents of this approach. After a decade of stagnation their program of action calls for little but further stagnation for some time to come, so as to ensure that the inflationary psychology is broken. Such stagnation seriously prejudices the adjustment process, since adjustment is always easier in an expanding economy. But the real danger is more fundamental. Sooner or later persistent deflation, whether monetary, fiscal, or both, is bound to cause a crisis of confidence, and it is this that Chancellor Schmidt no doubt has in mind in speaking of the danger of depression. If such a depression were to come, it would be the first to be brought about deliberately, on the misguided view that this is the only way of dealing with inflation.

The Problem of Symmetry

The Fund continues to insist that the origin of a balance-of-payments deficit, whether internal or external, has no bearing on the adjustment measures required. On this view, the only valid question is whether a deficit is temporary or persistent; and if it is persistent there is only one way of dealing with it.

In taking this position, the Fund appears to shrug off its responsibility for ensuring that the burden of adjustment is distributed equitably and efficiently among countries. Since the underlying principle seems to have been forgotten, it is perhaps worth restating it—and, in fact, putting it in the terms in which it has been advanced in the past by some of the industrial countries that are now most insistent in pressing for unilateral adjustment by deficit developing countries.

The need for equity and efficiency in the distribution of the burden of adjustment was advanced with particular emphasis by Paul Volcker, representing the U.S. government in the Committee of Twenty at Deputy level. The *Economic Report of the President* for January 1973 sets out the essential elements of the case argued before the committee by Volcker as well as the text of a memorandum on this matter submitted to the committee in November 1972.

The point was made that there had been nothing in the Bretton Woods system to assure compatibility of the balance-of-payments objectives of various countries, and that the breakdown of the system could be attributed to the failure to induce the adjustments required to achieve equilibrium. In the light of this experience the U.S. proposals for a new system were designed "to apply equivalent incentives for adjustment evenhandedly to all countries" (*Economic Report of the President 1973*, pp. 161–62).

Symmetry in the adjustment process was seen as partly a question of equity, in the sense of sharing the political and economic costs of adjustment. But it was also necessary for efficiency:

> If countries on both the deficit and the surplus side of a payments imbalance follow active policies for the restoration of equilibrium the process is likely to be easier than if the deficit countries try to bring about adjustment by themselves. Deficit countries would in any case be unable to restore equilibrium unless surplus countries at least followed policies consistent with a reduction of the net surplus in their payments positions [pp. 124–25].

The U.S. view as to what was the main shortcoming in the adjustment process was not, of course, shared by the European countries, which regarded the asymmetry between the reserve center and the rest of the world as the crucial problem, and asset settlement as the solution of that problem. But as Williamson (1977) has pointed out, there was no necessary contradiction between these two approaches and it would have been possible to construct a system that incorporated both. Unfortunately the system (if system it can be called) that actually emerged incorporates neither approach.

The Parallel of the 1980s and 1970s

The combined current account deficit of net oil importing developing countries rose from $30 billion in 1978 to $80 billion in 1981. As against this increase of $50 billion, their bill for oil and interest payments alone increased by close to $70 billion. In fact, despite the world recession, the net oil importing developing countries achieved a remarkable improvement in their exports, and actually moved into surplus on their non-oil trade accounts (De Larosière, 1981). This refutes the assertion often made that the developing countries did not adjust after the first oil crisis. They certainly did adjust, and on an impressive scale. The deterioration in their current account that occurred in 1979–81, despite these significant efforts of adjustment, was due entirely to factors beyond their control—namely the further rise in oil prices and the new upsurge in interest rates.

During the first oil crisis, the IMF decided to establish an oil facility to provide balance-of-payments support at low conditionality in 1974–75. Any Fund member drawing on the oil facility was required "to cooperate with the Fund in order to find appropriate solutions for its balance-of-payments problem." This requirement of cooperation with the Fund was the same as that applicable to the compensatory financing facility, but the character of the conditionality involved was quite different. Under the relevant decisions of the Executive Board on this matter member countries drawing on the oil facility were required to avoid "competitive depreciation and the escalation of restrictions on trade and payments," and to pursue "policies that would sustain appropriate levels of economic activity and employment, while minimizing inflation."[3]

It is apparent that in the view of responsible Fund authorities the situation in the 1980s is quite different from that prevailing in the 1970s and is therefore not susceptible to the same treatment. The reasons for this view are, however, not altogether clear. At times it appears to be suggested that the surpluses of the oil exporting countries are likely to be more persistent in the 1980s than in the 1970s.[4] Consequently, on the grounds that persistent imbalance calls for adjustment regardless of its character and origin, it is argued that a much greater effort of adjustment is required in the 1980s than in the 1970s.

The expectation that the oil surpluses will be more persistent in the 1980s is, however, open to question. While the recent decline in the real price of oil is no doubt attributable to a substantial extent to the slackening of business activity, there appears to be evidence also of increased capacity for the supply of oil as well as, in the words of the Interim Committee, "a break in the previous close link between economic growth and oil consumption" (IMF, 1981, p. 200). In addition, the import demand of OPEC countries associated with development and defense has shown tendencies to increase faster than expected. A continuation of recent downward trends in oil prices, and in the relationship between oil consumption and GNP in the industrial countries, together with further expansion in the import demand of OPEC countries would eliminate the OPEC current account surplus in the near future. Relevant also is the fact that the long-term component of the financing of OPEC countries' current account surpluses has been increasing significantly. For all these reasons there are grounds for doubting whether the evolution of the balance-of-payments positions of the OPEC countries in the early 1980s calls for a greater degree of adjustment by deficit countries than occurred in the 1970s—and the latter, as shown earlier, was itself quite impressive.

The Burden of Unilateral Adjustment

The downward pressure of the adjustment process on non-oil developing countries in 1980–81 was much heavier than necessary in the circumstances in which these countries found themselves. In analyzing the situation of these countries in October 1979 the Interim Committee stated:

> It was especially important, in the Committee's view, that the industrial countries, in the design of their economic policies, pay particular attention to the economic needs of developing countries. In this connection, a wide range of policies was seen to be relevant, including the reduction of protectionist measures; the opening of import markets to exports of manufactures and commodities from developing countries and of capital markets to outflows of funds to such countries; and measures to give new impetus to the flow of official development assistance, which had stagnated in recent years [IMF, 1980b, p. 153].

The fact that protectionist measures were actually intensified, that the flow of official development assistance continued to stagnate and that private capital flows leveled off added greatly to the burdens imposed on the developing countries. Moreover, the particular mix of fiscal and monetary policies employed by the industrial countries, without regard to international consequences, in dealing with inflation, aggravated the imbalances still further by steeply raising the interest cost of foreign borrowing from both private and public institutions, including the Fund, the World Bank, and the regional development banks.

Here again the policy stance of the IMF is inconsistent. On the one hand, it seeks to encourage export supply in the developing countries through adjustment of exchange rates and other "outward-looking" policies. On the other hand, it advocates further reductions in aggregate demand, and hence in the demand for imports, in the industrial countries that provide the principal markets for the additional export supplies thus generated. The Fund has been outspoken on the subject of protectionism, but its admonitions in this respect are more than nullified by its insistence that the industrial countries balance their budgets at low levels of employment and maintain or strengthen their policies of monetary restriction. After all, it is precisely the low level of employment that encourages protectionism.

Further inconsistency can be seen in the emphasis placed by the IMF on the need for governments to create market and other incentives for structural change while at the same time recommending deflationary policies that destroy any inducement to incur the risks of the investment in the new capacity that would be required.

The Doctrine of Persistence

The logic of the IMF's position is, of course, that if the protectionism and other policy developments in the industrial countries mentioned earlier appear to be of a persistent character, there is no choice for the deficit countries but to adjust accordingly. In fact the doctrine of persistence would appear to imply that even if the policies pursued by one group of member countries were of a deliberately "beggar-my-neighbor" character, and looked like continuing indefinitely, and if other countries encountering consequential deficits were to seek balance-of-payments support, the IMF would be compelled to insist on whatever degree of adjustment was called for in the circumstances, as a condition of providing such support. But does this not raise the question whether the IMF thereby becomes, albeit unwillingly, an accomplice in the "beggar-my-neighbor" policies in question?

It should be noted further that under current conditions of long-lasting business stagnation, the line to be drawn between persistent and temporary imbalance becomes indeterminate. In the past, deficits caused by slackening of import demand owing to a business recession in major markets would have been regarded as coming unequivocally within the category of "temporary" and therefore eligible for financing without adjustment. This was because recessions had hitherto been of relatively brief duration, and self-reversing. At the present time, however, recessions are not necessarily temporary. As far as is known, it has not yet been suggested that a country should be declared ineligible for compensatory financing if its export shortfall is due to a decline in import demand in other countries resulting from a downturn in business activity that is expected to persist. Yet this is the logic of the IMF position, and it would also be required if the wording of the decision establishing the facility, which is intended only for cases of temporary shortfalls, were taken literally.[5] For the time being, efforts to neutralize the intent and effectiveness of the facility are taking the form of proposals to tighten the regime of conditionality that is applied.

Thus a new situation may be approaching in which all deficits are considered to be of a character that calls for adjustment, and in which even the compensatory financing facility becomes otiose.

The Basis of Conditionality

But what is it that requires the Fund to insist on stringent upper credit tranche conditionality, regardless of whether a borrowing country is responsible for the deficit confronting it, and regardless even of whether the factors contributing to the deficit (such as protectionism) are compatible with the Fund's own purposes and primary objectives?

Originally the imposition of conditions on a potential borrower was considered to be justified largely in terms of the need to ensure prompt repayment of drawings so as to safeguard the revolving character of the Fund's resources. Thus Article I (v) provides for "making the general resources of the Fund temporarily available to [members] under adequate safeguards."

But, as Killick (1984, p. 184) has pointed out, "the stringency of conditionality has sometimes seemed disproportionate to the need to safeguard the repayment of Fund credits—credits which in the past have often been small relative to a country's total foreign exchange supplies." There is, moreover, no method of correlating the conditions imposed with the capacity to repay, if only because circumstances can change drastically over the period of the loan. For example, no matter how severe the conditions imposed on a primary producing country may be, the capacity to repay will inevitably deteriorate if the price of its principal export falls significantly, as happens not infrequently.

The World Bank and regional development banks have not hitherto made demands on borrowing countries of the type characteristic of Fund programs, and yet no one imagines that repayment of their loans is less assured than of the loans made by the Fund. It is true that the projects for which financial support is obtained from the multilateral banks are appraised so as to determine that they will yield a return adequate to service the loans. But this does not provide any guarantee that foreign exchange will in fact be available in the amounts and at the times required. In practice, repayment to the multilateral banks is ensured, not by project appraisal but by the fact that no country would willingly risk the drastic consequences for its access to all forms of credit that would result from a default to any of these banks. And the same consideration applies to repayments to the Fund, whether or not the loans involved carry upper credit tranche conditionality.

In justifying its policies on conditionality, the IMF now relies relatively less on the idea that this will safeguard the revolving character of its resources and relatively more on its responsibility, under Article V. 3(a), for assisting members "to solve their balance-of-payments problems in a manner consistent with the provisions of this Agreement." Moreover, Article IV. 3(a) requires the Fund to "oversee the international monetary system in order to ensure its effective operation." While this provision is included in the Article concerning exchange arrangements, its significance may be regarded as being of a general character.

The Fund's Mandate

Thus the IMF may be said to have a general mandate for watching over the international monetary system and for seeking viable and consistent balance-of-payments policies among its members. In carrying out this mandate, the Fund has at its disposal resources calling for various levels of conditionality. However, as shown elsewhere (pp. 252–53 in this volume), the low conditionality resources happen, at the present time, to constitute an abnormally low proportion of the total, because of the particular method that members have adopted for enlarging access to the Fund's resources—that is, by increasing access as a percentage of quota rather than by increasing quotas themselves. The effect of this is that, of the cumulative 600 percent of quota available to members for drawings, only 25 percent is provided at low (first credit tranche) conditionality; whereas if quotas had been increased sixfold, which would have been the normal way of proceeding, first credit tranche conditionality would have applied to the equivalent of 150 percent of current quotas.

All this does not, however, mean that the Fund lacks discretion in determining the stringency of conditions to be applied, even if it is established that a source of imbalance is persistent. As we have seen, the compulsion on a member to repay its drawings on the Fund is not derived from the provisions of the stand-by arrangement but is based on the profound interest of sovereign governments in maintaining their creditworthiness, not only with the Fund but with all other potential creditors.

Nor do the more general responsibilities of the Fund in relation to the international monetary system require it to impose conditions on a deficit country that ignore the degree of responsibility of that country for the imbalance arising. On the contrary, the Fund has an implied responsibility *not* to act in a manner that appears to condone behavior on the part of other countries that is incompatible with the Fund's purposes and with "primary objectives of economic policy." In particular, the Fund has an obligation to do all it can to assist a member that is suffering the effects of events beyond its control or of injurious policies pursued by other members.

The Fund has itself pointed out that the effort of non-oil developing countries to adjust to increased oil prices "is hampered by the slowing in the pace of industrial activity in the rest of the world, as well as by protectionist barriers to certain types of their exports to the industrial countries" (IMF, 1980b, p. 51). An additional obstacle mentioned by the Fund is the effect of unusually high rates of interest on external debt. As noted earlier, this resulted from the particular constellation of domestic fiscal and monetary policies employed by the industrial countries in attempting to deal with inflation, without regard to international repercussions.

In the light of these findings, the idea that the Fund's options are limited to a determination whether a deficit is temporary or persistent is farfetched. The Fund cannot, of course, supply more resources than are available to it. But, subject to that constraint, there is much that the Fund can do to lighten the burden of adjustment and avoid the application of severe and peremptory measures, especially of a deflationary character.

Developing countries must, of course, adjust to irreversible changes—this issue is not in dispute. But in determining the appropriate policy mix, including the amount of balance-of-payments support to be provided, the conditions required for the provision of that support, and the period over which adjustment should be programmed, it is important to distinguish between those elements of a balance-of-payments deficit for which a developing country is itself responsible and those elements that are due to factors beyond its control.

A Possible Solution: Liberalization of CFF?

This is not a revolutionary idea. At one time levels of activity had to be cut back even where external imbalance was due to a temporary decline in foreign demand for exports. The introduction by the IMF of the Compensatory Financing Facility (CFF) and later of the oil facilities indicated clear recognition of the principle that it is improper to force standard adjustment policies on member countries in circumstances for which they are not responsible. What is now proposed is an extension of that principle to all external sources of disturbance in the balance of payments.

Indeed, the Fund is itself well aware of the shortcomings of CFF and has taken a number of steps to improve its coverage and relevance. The facility was established in 1963, but only fifty-seven drawings, totaling SDR 1.2 billion were made under the restrictive provisions that applied during its first thirteen years. A turning point was the liberalization of the facility in 1975. From January 1976 to December 1981 there were drawings totaling SDR 5.9 billion under the facility; these accounted for 32 percent of total drawings by non-oil exporting developing countries during that period (Goreux, 1980, pp. 2–3, updated by the IMF).

Important as the liberalization of December 1975 was, the facility was still subject to major shortcomings. Although CFF drawing rights were increased progressively from 50 to 75 percent and later to 100 percent of quota in any one year, even the latter amount was in many cases insufficient to finance the full amount of export shortfalls, especially if they persisted over periods longer than a year. Moreover, the reasoning that had been applied to export shortfalls was still not applied to import overages resulting from factors beyond the control of particular countries. In May 1981 a first and very limited step toward the latter objective was taken by the Fund when it agreed to extend financial assistance at low conditionality "to members that encounter a balance of payments difficulty produced by an excess in the cost of their cereal imports." As in the case of export shortfalls, the Fund must be satisfied that the source of difficulty is short-term in character and is "largely attributable to circumstances beyond the control of the member."[6]

It thus took no less than eighteen years for the Fund to reach the conclusion that the logic that it had introduced with respect to export shortfalls in 1963 was applicable also to import overages. And even then, in 1981, the step forward that was taken was extremely limited and inadequate in scope.

There is, nevertheless, still hope that the next stages of the process of liberalization can be accelerated and that the low conditionality facility of the Fund will be enlarged so as to be applicable to all imports and so as to provide drawing rights that are much larger in relation to potential shortfalls and overages than they are today.

If this were done, the Fund would have at its disposal, at last, an array of facilities that would allow it to adjust the volume and conditions of the balance-of-payments support that it provides to the circumstances of each case, including particularly the degree of responsibility of the country concerned for the difficulty encountered.

It has been suggested by William Dale, Deputy Managing Director of the IMF (1983), that what he calls "pure intermediation" by the Fund is unnecessary because there is no longer any uncertainty about the adequacy of finance for that purpose. The implication here, presumably, is that "pure intermediation" is a function of the commercial banks only. In that case, however, the only countries entitled to have access to "pure intermediation" would be those that the commercial banks deem to be creditworthy in their terms—the industrial countries together with a minority of developing countries, as matters now stand.

As noted earlier, if the Fund had enlarged access to its resources by raising quotas instead of by increasing drawing rights as a percentage of existing quotas, the volume of resources available to members on first credit tranche terms would have been six times as large as they are under the method actually employed. The Interim Committee and the IMF management have stated repeatedly that the correct method of enlarging Fund resources is by increasing quotas. The Fund authorities must therefore see a role for a much increased volume of first credit tranche resources, whether one calls it "pure intermediation" or anything else.

NATIONAL ASPECTS

Even-Handedness or Discrimination?

The IMF approach to the balance-of-payments problems of developing countries starts out from three basic assumptions. The first of these is that there is sufficient flexibility in the economies of these countries to permit them to respond to standard adjustment formulae without undue cost. The second is that by and large the problems are of a short-term character that can and should be handled within a relatively short time frame. The third is that within the framework of appropriate government policies it is generally best to rely on market forces to bring about the requisite adjustment.

These basic assumptions are considered equally valid for all members of the Fund, and even-handed treatment of Fund members therefore requires that stabilization programs should be of roughly similar design, regardless of what countries are involved. This does not, of course, mean that the content of programs has to be the same from country to country: obviously the degree of devaluation, if any, required in a particular case will depend on the circumstances of that case, and similar considerations apply to all other stabilization measures involved. On the other hand, given the degree of balance-of-payments pressure and the factors responsible for that pressure in any particular country, the stabilization measures required would be approximately the same, regardless of whether the country were developed or developing.

This may seem to imply even-handed treatment of Fund members, but it is not necessarily so in practice. Indeed, even-handed treatment as seen from the standpoint of the lender can and frequently does involve inequality of burden sharing among borrowers. This can be illustrated by a hypothetical case involving two countries suspected of having overvalued exchange rates, one of which is completely dependent on primary commodities for its export revenues while the other obtains most of such revenues from sales of diversified manufactures. Standard purchasing power parity calculations may show the degree of devaluation required to be the same in both cases. But the burden of such devaluation will be much greater for the exporter of primary commodities than for the exporter of manufactures because of the much smaller responsiveness of exports to be expected in the former case: in fact, the impact on primary exports may be perverse. In that case the entire burden of correcting the disequilibrium falls on imports and hence on the curtailment of domestic consumption or investment or both. The country exporting manufactures, on the other hand, may find itself in a position to correct its external balance entirely through an increase in exports and hence in the level of business activity. If unutilized labor and capital are available, such a country may actually be able to improve its situation even from the standpoint of domestic consumption and investment.

More generally, any approach to stabilization policies that overlooks the much lower mobility of resources in developing than in developed countries is bound to discriminate against the former if standard formulae are applied to purely monetary measures of internal and external disequilibrium. Moreover, correction of present imbalances calls for structural adjustment over periods longer than traditional Fund programs. While the need for medium-term structural adjustment has been accepted in principle in statements by the Interim Committee and the IMF management, it is unclear how far the requirements of such adjustment are recognized in practice. The very fact that adjustment is programmed over a longer period would appear to imply a less rigorous and demanding program of stabilization than if the same degree of adjustment had to be achieved within a shorter period. It has nevertheless been stated by the Fund that on average resources are now being provided at a much more exacting level of conditionality than they were in the mid-1970s, and that while, in the mid-1970s, approximately three-quarters of the resources provided by the Fund to its members were at low conditionality, three-quarters of current new lending commitments involve upper credit tranche programs.[7]

Finally, the effort to induce developing countries to rely on market forces in the adjustment process contrasts oddly with the steady increase in the number of products exported by developing countries that have been removed from the influence of market forces through restrictive measures adopted by the industrial countries.

If free market conditions were the key to development, there would be no dichotomy between developed and underdeveloped economies, since government intervention in the latter economies is a relatively recent phenomenon, following accession to economic independence. There is not a single industrial country that did not employ vigorous protection at some stage in its history. Among the much applauded, newly industrializing countries (NICS), the most important have highly regulated economies. Even so highly industrialized a country as Japan, the miracle economy of the century, continues to this day to protect its industrial development in a variety of ways. While Japan is under great pressure to dismantle this protection, the important lesson of Japan for developing countries and for the Fund is that properly managed protection, so far from being an obstacle to growth, is an indispensable instrument in promoting growth.

Where there is a case against regulation, it depends not on any inherent superiority of market forces, but on the much simpler consideration that many developing countries do not have the administrative resources required for extensive or detailed regulation and control; and that even where such resources do exist, it is often difficult to ensure that regulation and control are exercised in the interests of the public at large and not merely in the interests of the regulators and controllers. But that does not mean that developing countries should do away with all controls—only that they should limit themselves to those key controls that they are able to operate efficiently.

The Capacity for Adjustment

Mention was made earlier of intercountry differences in the elasticity of supply of exports as a factor in explaining differences in the effectiveness of adjustment. This is one example—perhaps the most important—of a more general differentiation between countries in their capacity for adjustment. For example, countries differ considerably in the extent to which they can compress imports without suffering adverse effects. On the one hand, some countries are better equipped than others in terms of the availability of skills and resources for developing substitutes for imports. On the other hand, while in some countries imports may include a substantial share of nonessentials that can be readily restricted without serious economic injury, in others they may consist entirely of essential foodstuffs, raw materials, and equipment, the curtailment of which would have damaging effects on basic consumption, investment, or production.

In the UNDP/UNCTAD study (Dell and Lawrence, 1980) it was found that much of the intercountry variation in performance during the 1970s could be attributed to differences in the capacity for adjustment. It was also suggested that adjustment programs and policies should be adapted to the particular capabilities for adjustment of each country. Mention has already been made of the potentially very different effects of devaluation in various countries, depending on the responsiveness of actual or potential exports to such a step in the short and medium term. Similarly, a cost-benefit analysis of general measures to improve the trade balance by cutting consumption would yield one set of results in a country in which exported goods were not consumed domestically and imported consumer goods consisted mainly of basic foodstuffs, and a different set of results when a substantial proportion of exportables was consumed domestically and there was a wide range of imported consumer goods.

Exchange Rate Policies

Perhaps the greatest difficulties in relation to stabilization programs have arisen in the area of exchange rate adjustment. It is here that the effect of government intervention in the economy is particularly visible. Moreover, the effect of that intervention is usually to bring about a decline in domestic consumption and a shift in the distribution of income.[8] In many cases, in fact, it is precisely the fall in real income and the shift in income distribution that are the main goals of exchange rate adjustments, especially where supply and demand elasticities in foreign trade are relatively low.

It is not uncommon for exchange rate adjustments exceeding 50 percent to be proposed, often on the basis of the crudest purchasing power parity calculations. It is not merely that the data themselves have serious shortcomings. There is also the problem of determining the composition and weighting of the two price or cost series to be compared, for which there is no unique solution. No doubt in extreme cases the need for exchange rate adjustment is clear enough on the basis of any reasonable grouping of the available data. But establishing the required direction of change is not the same thing as determining the precise degree of adjustment needed.

More serious, however, is the fact that, as Kaldor has pointed out, it cannot be taken for granted that the internal distribution of income, which is the outcome of complex political forces, can be effectively changed by devaluation. A large-scale devaluation may be followed by a price upheaval that ends up by reproducing, at a much higher level of prices, the same price and cost relationships as had prevailed before the devaluation (Kaldor, 1987).

A study of Tanzanian experience in the 1970s for the UNDP/UNCTAD project showed that Tanzania had resisted devaluation on the grounds that any attempt by that country to raise its share of export markets for primary commodities would have provoked retaliation; and that there was a preference for using import controls and selective indirect taxation for limiting imports since those were the instruments of choice in the overall planning process. On the other hand, devaluation was regarded as far too unselective a means of demand management that would tend to shift income from the relatively poor producers of food to the relatively richer exporters of cash crops, which was inconsistent with Tanzania's social objectives and the goal of raising food production. Tanzania nevertheless devalued in 1971 and 1975 when absolute cuts in domestic export prices or major export subsidies would otherwise have been needed.

Devaluations in Zambia in 1976 and 1978 were designed to maintain the profitability of the mining companies in the face of rising external costs (equivalent to 60 to 70 percent of total costs) and falling copper prices. The difficulty seen in the devaluation strategy, however, was that to the extent that it succeeded, it tended to increase excess supplies and, hence, depress prices still further, thereby making it necessary to undertake recurrent devaluations.

Doubts about the effectiveness of the exchange rate weapon are, however, not limited to low-income primary producing countries. Brailovsky (1981) studied the impact of exchange rate changes during the 1960s and 1970s in a group of thirteen countries, of which seven are among the leading industrial country exporters of manufactures—Canada, France, the Federal Republic of Germany, Italy, Japan, the Netherlands, and the United Kingdom—while the remaining six are the more successful exporters of manufactures among the developing countries—Argentina, Brazil, Hong Kong, the Republic of Korea, Mexico, and Singapore.

The data presented by Brailovsky suggest that changes in nominal exchange rates resulted in relatively small changes in real exchange rates during the periods examined, and it is therefore not surprising that they account for only a small proportion of the shifts in market shares. The main impact of changes in nominal exchange rates was on rates of domestic inflation rather than on real exchange rates.[9]

The Role of Monetarism

Despite a certain eclecticism to be found in the published IMF literature, most Fund programs are established within a common framework. According to members of the Fund staff, "In this framework there is a fairly well-defined relationship between money, the balance of payments, and domestic prices, in which the supply of and demand for money play a central linking role" (Khan and Knight, 1981, p. 3).

A distinction is often drawn between what is called the new monetarism and the old monetarism, and between their respective prescriptions for stabilization. The important point, however, is not the differences but the similarities, particularly the incorrect diagnosis of problems, and the consequent shortcomings of would-be remedial programs.

The Case Against Monetarism

This is not the place to elaborate on the case against monetarism—there is an abundant and growing literature (see particularly Hicks, 1975, 1976, and Kaldor 1964, 1978, 1981) in support of the propositions that:

– Correlations between the supply of money and levels of expenditure do not indicate the direction of causality, even if there is a time lag between the former series and the latter.
– While narrow definitions of the money supply are not very useful for most purposes, broad definitions are arbitrary, and money supply broadly defined is surrounded by a halo of liquid assets that are not included but are nevertheless close substitutes for assets that *are* included.
– It is not the money supply, however defined, that is relevant to spending decisions but liquidity in the widest sense, including not only money but money substitutes. And liquidity in this widest sense is not under the control of the monetary authorities.
– In a credit economy, the fact that a substantial proportion of bank money is idle breaks the link between the total quantity of money and that part of it which is circulating. Insofar as monetary controls are

effective at all, it is the rate of interest that is important and not the total quantity of money, however defined.

- If output is below capacity levels, it is likely that an increase in money supply will be noninflationary and that the effect will be a rise in output.
- Goodhart's law: any measure of the money supply that is used as a basis for an attempt at official control quickly loses its meaning.
- It is incorrect to group all forms of inflation together as being induced by a single factor—an increase in the money supply. In deciding on the remedy for inflation, it is essential, as noted earlier, to distinguish between demand inflation and cost inflation, and to adapt the remedies accordingly.

Perhaps the single most important economic reason why the management of national economies is in disarray throughout the developed as well as the developing world at the present time is that problems of cost inflation are being attacked by measures to deflate demand, even in situations where economies are operating at 20 percent or more below capacity. As Killick (1984, p. 204) concludes on the basis of replies to questionnaires addressed to IMF staff, "it appears on this evidence that the Fund is no less likely to require demand restraint even in countries where its own staff do not believe excess demand to be a principal cause of the payments problems." Demand deflation, if taken far enough, will ultimately have an impact on cost inflation—there is no dispute about this. What is in question is the need for the heavy social and economic costs that are involved.

The Policy of Sackcloth and Ashes

As Diaz-Alejandro (1981, p. 125) has pointed out in examining the stabilization plans of the Southern Cone countries of Latin America:

Even in cases where excess demand was a plausible explanation for the high rates of inflation during the preplan period, its explanatory power declines as the months go by and excess capacity and foreign exchange reserves pile up. Remaining fiscal deficits and/or high rates of increase in the money supply provide weak explanations under conditions of declining output and of shrinking real credit and cash balances. Excessive trade union power can hardly be blamed when real wages collapse and union leaders are jailed, or worse.

Despite continuing retrenchment, inflation rates were not brough down below the 15 to 20 percent level. The situation became one of "over kill," in the sense that reductions in aggregate demand went beyonc what was required to make room for an expansion in the production o exportables and of those importables and nontraded goods benefitin from the new constellation of relative prices. The curtailment of deman brought with it severe weakness in capital formation as reductions ir public investment were accompanied by lack of confidence on the par of the private sector. Diaz-Alejandro suggests that the process of overkil cannot be fully explained without reference to the authorities' wish tc discipline the labor force by creating a soft labor market.

The situation thus described is characteristic of many countries ir other parts of the developing, and, indeed, of the developed world. Ir some developing countries stabilization programs in the 1970s induce declines in real wages of the order of 20 to 40 percent over relativel short periods (Dell and Lawrence, 1980, p. 64). It should be noted tha programs of this type were by no means limited to countries enterin into stand-by arrangements with the IMF. The wave of exaggerated eco nomic retrenchment was and is an almost worldwide phenomenon, anc in many cases where adjustment policies of great severity were applie under stand-by arrangements the government itself was at least as keer to cut back as the IMF mission involved. Moreover, as is well known in a not inconsiderable number of cases ministries of finance and cen tral banks welcomed the support given by IMF missions to policies o retrenchment that the former were having difficulty in persuading othe sectors of the government to accept.

Is evidence of the type cited earlier relevant? Williamson (1983, pp 130–31) points out quite correctly that a comparison of "what is" with "what was" is "conceptually inappropriate" if one is trying to asses policy results and economic performance. What is implied here, how ever, is that alternative methods of adjustment were available that woulc not have involved so large a reduction in real income, and in some case perhaps no reduction at all. Such methods would have required cor rect identification of the sources of cost inflation and the mobilizatior of the social consensus required to slow down and ultimately halt th struggle between social groups to safeguard their respective shares o real income. Given such social consensus, the need for demand deflatior would have been correspondingly reduced; devaluations, where the occurred, could have been much less drastic, and the fall in real wage would have been correspondingly smaller. In cases where idle resource could be shifted to exportables facing open markets abroad, the adjustment process could even have been carried out without loss of output and income—as did in fact occur in countries such as Brazil and the Republic of Korea where access to the international capital market made it possible to escape the standard deflationary remedies, at least for a time. More recently, in the face of mounting debt and soaring interest rates in the international market, even Brazil has felt compelled to deflate.

As to why the sackcloth and ashes approach to adjustment was preferred, the reasons lie more in the realm of politics than of economics. Many governments, developing as well as developed, were seeking radical solutions to what they regarded as long-standing problems of income distribution and trade union militancy, and came to the conclusion that their goals were too far from existing realities to be realized through the normal processes of negotiation and compromise required for the attainment of social consensus.

At the international level the radical solution envisaged by developed countries takes the form of reducing, so far as possible, the transfer of concessional resources to developing countries and relying on market incentives to generate the flows of private capital required to supplement the domestic efforts of these countries and provide them with balance-of-payments support when needed. Under this concept, the role of the Bretton Woods institutions is to support the basic thrust of the aforementioned strategy by cooperating more closely with the private sector, and negotiating the kind of stabilization programs that would help deficit countries to attract balance-of-payments support from the only source capable as matters stand of providing it in the volume required—namely, the commercial banking system.

This strategy, of course, leaves out all those countries that are unable to attract large-scale commercial bank loans *under any conditions*. For them the Fund is the lender of both first and last resort. Thus the concept of the Fund as primarily a stimulus to and guarantor of the creditworthiness of developing countries, and only a residual provider of balance-of-payments support in its own right, is completely unacceptable to the low-income countries that have no other source of such support available to them. The strategy is also unwelcome to other developing countries, if only because the country limits for lending set by commercial banks for prudential reasons do not, in the aggregate, reflect an appropriate measure of the borrowing capacity of the countries concerned, especially under conditions of artificially high interest rates.

Pinpoint Targetry

One advantage of monetarist theories is that they make it possible to devise straightforward performance criteria in the form of precise monetary targets that can be readily monitored by the IMF. This creates an apparently objective basis for determining whether member countries that have entered into stand-by arrangements with the Fund are performing sufficiently well to establish an entitlement to successive phased drawings on the lines of credit established by the Fund under these arrangements.

Killick (1984, p. 201) finds that "In economic terms, by far the strongest evidence of a stereotyped approach is the almost universal inclusion of ceilings on bank credit, which in many cases are the chief test the government must pass," though he notes also that "there is a considerable diversity in the forms which these take" to suit local conditions. Almost all stand-by arrangements include limits on the amount of new bank credit which could be extended to both the public and private sectors.

The fact is, however, that neither the developed nor the developing countries have had much success in achieving quantitative monetary targets, even when they have set the targets for themselves. The Governor of the Bank of England (Bank of England, 1978, pp. 36–38) has reported that from 1974 to the beginning of 1978 the mean error of forecasts of the Public-Sector Borrowing Requirement (PSBR) made at the beginning of each financial year in the United Kingdom was of the order of 3 billion pounds sterling: the average annual level of the PSBR from 1974/1975 to 1977/1978 was 8.2 billion pounds sterling. For this and other reasons the Governor was sharply critical of procedures requiring a particular numerical target to be reached by a particular date: "Firm deadlines can force one either to adjust too fast to an unforeseen trend developing late in the period, or to appear to accept a failure to reach one's target."

Similar problems have arisen in the United States. As reported by Governor Henry Wallich (1980, pp. 12–13) of the Board of Governors of the Federal Reserve System:

Since mid-1974, a whole collection of standard money-demand functions used routinely in econometric models has misperformed on a large scale by overpredicting the amount of money that would be demanded at given levels of income and interest rates. By late 1979 this overprediction amounted to anywhere from 9 to 17 percent of M-1A or M-1B, or something like $35–70 billion. This overprediction of the amount of money required made the Federal Reserve's targets, which seemed quite restrictive, turn out relatively unrestrictive. . . . The uncertainties inherent in this approach underline the advisability of stating money-supply targets in terms of a range rather than of a single number.

Wallich suggests further that "it may be risky to become irrevocably committed to a numerical set of targets." And he points out that the most successful countries in conducting noninflationary monetary policies have been the Federal Republic of Germany and Switzerland, and that both these countries have been "quite relaxed about their adherence to [money supply] targets."

Incidentally, the Federal Reserve study prompted Wallich to conclude further that "monetary restraint, however steady, cannot quickly bring down inflation nor interest rates. The most plausible view is that the main impact of monetary restraint on prices occurs with a two-year lag." This is not a very promising time horizon even for stabilization programs based on IMF extended arrangements, let alone for standard one-year programs.

The Breakdown of Stand-by Arrangements

The IMF is, of course, not "irrevocably committed" (to use Wallich's phrase) to precise monetary targets. Killick (1984, pp. 202–3) reports that on the average as many as one-third of the Fund's stand-by arrangements are amended as a result of minor deviations from targets that are regarded as temporary or reversible, or that result from unexpected changes in circumstances.

More serious, however, are the many cases in which credit ceilings are exceeded, or other targets breached, by margins that cannot be dealt with by waivers. Here the member government automatically loses its right to draw outstanding installments of its line of credit without, as Sir Joseph Gold (Horsefield [ed.], 1969, 2:533) has pointed out, the need for a decision by, or even notice to, the Executive Board.

The government always has the option in such cases of negotiating a new understanding with the Fund, but there is no guarantee that such negotiations will succeed or that the new targets will be more easily achieved than the previous ones. Moreover, in many cases some of the damage done by the breakdown of the agreement may be irreversible, especially if it leads to a general loss of confidence and the government is forced into costly alternative courses of action.

The frequency of breakdowns indicates in itself that there is something wrong with the system of pinpoint targetry. Can so many governments all be guilty of incompetence or mismanagement? In some cases the time lags involved in the preparation of the necessary statistics are such that the negotiators on both sides are unaware that the targets under discussion are already out of date and impossible of achievement. Even where this is not the case, the aforementioned experience of the United Kingdom and the United States indicates that reliance on precise quantitative targets is full of pitfalls, and that the errors of estimation may be of very large orders of magnitude.

These shortcomings would be serious even if it were clear that monetary targets were the right targets on which to concentrate. But this is not necessarily the case even if the primary objective is demand management: where demand is excessive it may be much more important and effective to raise taxes than to restrict credit. In the many instances in which improvements in the balance of payments depend primarily on structural change, monetary targets may be at best of limited importance and at worst entirely irrelevant.

A good example of destabilizing error resulting from the uncertainties of forecasting is to be found in the experience of Peru in 1978–79. Peru was compelled to negotiate for an IMF stand-by in the third quarter of 1978, and had to accept stringent obligations to deflate the economy— less severely than the unrealistic agreement of December 1977 had provided, but still harsh enough.

Yet if one examines the balance-of-payments projections agreed upon as a basis for the stand-by negotiations, it is immediately apparent that had the negotiators known that the price of copper would recover from 58 cents per pound in July 1978 to 90 cents per pound in March 1979, they would have realized that that fact alone would come close to restoring external balance without any cutting down of the economy at all. By April 1979 the Peruvian balance of payments was so strong and the inflow of capital so massive that the *Financial Times* was reporting "an embarrassingly large inflation-inducing surfeit of dollars."

Mistakes of forecasting are, of course, unavoidable and a case of this kind underlines the dangers of pinpoint targetry. A more important source of concern is that here was a case in which the projected external imbalance was largely due to a temporary and reversible factor— namely the low price of copper. The cost to Peru in terms of lost output and investment was out of all proportion to the magnitude of the external problem that had been encountered. It is disquieting that the economy of a country such as Peru—which by developing country standards has relatively diversified exports—can still be at the mercy of the volatility of a single commodity. And it is alarming that such a country can find itself compelled to endure lasting damage to its economy on account of circumstances that are reversible, through an inability to mobilize balance-of-payments support on a scale sufficient to avoid such damage.

CONCLUSION

A number of forward-looking steps have been taken. The IMF (1980a, p. 42) has stated that:

> In view of the size of the current deficits and of the difficulties that may arise in private intermediation, the Fund must be prepared, when necessary, to lend in larger amounts than in the past. Also, the structural problems faced by many countries may require that adjustment take place over a longer period than has been typical in the framework of Fund programs in the past. Further, lending by the Fund must reflect the sort of flexibility, with an awareness of the circumstances of members, that is called for in the Executive Board's current guidelines on conditionality.

More recent developments, notably the severe tightening of conditionality, raise some doubts as to whether the promise of the above statement is being or will be realized. The concept of unilateral adjustment, with one group of countries at best neutral toward, and at worst frustrating, the adjustment process of the other group, is not an acceptable basis for IMF supervision of the international monetary system. There is a pressing need for the Fund to reconsider its position on this basic issue.

Furthermore, care should be taken to avoid overkill in determining the degree and character of adjustment needed in stabilization programs. This will require setting aside monetarist doctrines that lead to mistakes in the diagnosis of problems and in the specification of solutions, especially where problems of structural adjustment over the medium term are involved.

One useful device for dealing with some aspects of both these problems would be to liberalize and enlarge the compensatory financing facility with the objective of applying the same kind of regime to imports as to exports. This would have the effect of providing the Fund with an array of facilities at low and high conditionality that would make it possible to design stabilization programs in a manner that would be more responsive to the particular situations of individual countries.

On Being Grandmotherly: The Evolution of IMF Conditionality*

INTRODUCTION

On March 2, 1979, the International Monetary Fund adopted a set of guidelines regarding the conditions to be accepted by member countries wishing to draw on the resources of the Fund. The guidelines were intended as a positive response to previous expressions of concern by the developing countries on this matter, but they were only the first step in a process of change. As Sir Joseph Gold, former General Counsel of the Fund, put it in his 1979 Fund pamphlet on conditionality: "There is no reason to believe . . . that debate on this subject is at an end."

This essay is intended as a contribution to that debate. It deals with the history of conditionality, emphasizing particularly those aspects that seem to have a special bearing on current concerns. It then proceeds to an analysis of the contemporary issues and makes a tentative evaluation of the recent evolution of Fund policies.

THE HISTORY

The Prelude to Bretton Woods

Writing in January 1944, before the Bretton Woods Conference, Lord Keynes described the views of the U.S. government on the future character of the International Monetary Fund as follows: "In their eyes it should have wide discretionary and policing powers and should exercise something of the same measure of grandmotherly influence and control over the central banks of the member countries, that these central banks in turn are accustomed to exercise over the other banks within their own countries" (Moggridge, 1980, 25:404).

Keynes believed, however, that as a result of the Anglo-American discussions on this and related matters, "the American representatives were persuaded of the inacceptability of such a scheme of things, of the undesirability of starting off by giving so much authority to an untried institution, and of the importance of giving the member countries as much certainty as possible about what they had to expect from the new

*This essay was originally published in the Princeton series, *Essays in International Finance*, no. 144 (October 1981, copyright 1981). Reprinted by permission of the International Finance Section of Princeton University.

institution and about the amount of facilities which would be at their full disposal" (Moggridge, 1980, 25:404–5). Keynes thought he had gained acceptance for the view that the Fund's "initiative and discretion" should be limited "to cases where the rules and purposes of the institution are in risk of infringement" and that the Fund should be "entirely passive in all normal circumstances, the right of initiative being reserved to the central banks of the member countries" (Moggridge, 1980, 25:404).[10]

It is particularly interesting, in the light of present-day controversy about the policies of the IMF, that in the Anglo-American discussions preceding Bretton Woods, the U.K. negotiators were under explicit instructions from Churchill's War Cabinet that a deficit country should not be required to introduce "a deflationary policy, enforced by dear money and similar measures, having the effect of causing unemployment; for this would amount to restoring, subject to insufficient safeguards, the evils of the old automatic gold standard" (Moggridge, 1980, 25:143).

As it turned out later, the U.S. government had by no means abandoned the idea of a "grandmotherly" Fund; still less had it acquiesced in the concept of a "passive" Fund. It is also clear that Keynes was far from being alone in his views—and that the United Kingdom had the support of virtually all countries other than the United States in wishing to place strict limitations on the Fund's responsibilities vis-à-vis the economic policies of its members. From an American standpoint, of course, the United Kingdom and most of the countries supporting its views were potential deficit countries seeking to obtain assured access to postwar balance-of-payments support, which could be provided—in the early postwar years at any rate—only from the real resources of the United States.

The Atlantic City Debate

An important episode in the legislative history of Fund conditionality occurred in the course of meetings of the Pre-Bretton Woods Conference Agenda Committee, which were held in Atlantic City at the end of June 1944 and in which seventeen countries participated. The documentation for this meeting included a combined draft in which the Joint Statement by Experts on the Establishment of an International Monetary Fund (prepared jointly by U.S. and U.K. officials and published in April 1944) was reproduced in conjunction with various amendments that had been proposed (Horsefield, ed., 1969, 3:131–35).

There was considerable discussion at Atlantic City about the wording of what later became Article V of the original Fund Agreement.[11] Two phrases in that Article had a crucial bearing on the conditions governing the use of Fund resources. The Joint Statement had provided that:

> A member *shall be entitled to buy* another member's currency from the Fund in exchange for its own currency on the following conditions: (a) The member *represents that the currency demanded is presently needed* for making payments in that currency which are consistent with the purposes of the Fund [emphasis supplied].

The United States proposed an Alternative A to replace the above text, in which the following changes were made in the italicized words:

> A member country *may buy* the currency of another member country from the Fund in exchange for its own currency subject to the following conditions:
> (1) The member country initiating the purchase *needs the currency requested* for making payments in that currency which are consistent with the purposes and policies of the Fund [emphasis supplied; (NARS, Box 1, File A-3)].

When the Agenda Committee discussed this matter, Lord Keynes said that the wording of Alternative A left it unclear whether it was the Fund or the member country that would decide whether the payments for which a country sought to purchase currency from the Fund were consistent with the purposes and policies of the Fund. Countries must, he said, have an unqualified right to purchase foreign exchange within the prescribed quantitative limits, subject to the provisions of the Fund Agreement. He therefore favored the wording of the Joint Statement, which made it clear that the decision on a drawing would be that of the member country, not of the Fund.

Edward M. Bernstein replied for the United States that the fact that a country informed the Fund that it needed foreign exchange for purposes and policies consistent with the Fund Agreement did not provide sufficient protection for the Fund against misuse of its resources. The Fund must be in a position to question a country's statement on this point. The U.S. proposal to change "represents" to "needs" had been made because, in the event that a member's use of Fund resources was for purposes inconsistent with the Agreement, the Fund must be able to invoke the subsection of the same Article under which a member could be suspended from making further use of the resources of the Fund.

The U.K. position on this matter was supported by other delegations. Leslie G. Melville, speaking for Australia, took the view that a central bank must be certain that the resources it had counted upon would be available as required. J. W. Beyen of the Netherlands considered that there could be no question of having to convince the Fund on such matters and that the wording of Alternative A was "impossible."

In the event, the two draft amendments proposed by the United States were dropped, and the key words "entitled" and "represents" were included in the final text of the Bretton Woods Agreement.[12]

Given the foregoing legislative history, most countries probably ratified the Bretton Woods Agreement in the belief that British views on conditionality had prevailed and that the Fund would have no right to challenge a member's "representation" that it needed to draw resources from the Fund in order to effect payments consistent with the Agreement. In the Fund history, Horsefield (1969, p. 72) argues that Keynes had recognized in October 1943 that the use of the word "represents" did not imply that the Fund would automatically accept such a representation. He bases his argument on a cable to London in which Keynes mentioned as being still unresolved the question whether the Fund would be able to discipline a country's use of Fund facilities within the relevant quantitative limits. This does not mean, however, that Keynes accepted the U.S. view on the interpretation to be given to the word "represents." In any case, the developments at Atlantic City and Bretton Woods had clearly altered the situation, and it was understandable that Keynes and others should have thought that the British view of the matter had won the day.

When the Executive Board of the Fund eventually came to consider the interpretation of the word "represents" in May 1947, it was decided, in spite of the legislative history, that a member's representation under Article V, Section 3(a)(i), could be challenged by the Fund "for good reasons." As Horsefield (1969, p. 189) points out, in reaching this decision the board was effectively rejecting the concept of an automatic right to draw within the quantitative limitations specified in the Articles.[13] The decision was therefore a turning point in the campaign for conditionality.

Silence at Bretton Woods

At a meeting held on July 1, 1944, at which members of the American delegation to the Bretton Woods Conference were briefed by Harry Dexter White, Assistant to the Secretary of the U.S. Treasury, on the U.S. government's position on questions likely to arise, the continuing conflict of views on conditionality was made clear, as was the fact that the United States stood virtually alone on this matter. White informed the delegation that "the foreign countries always speak of [drawings on the Fund] as a matter of right." He also acknowledged that the text of the Agreement was not clear on this point: "It reads in a way that is not too easy to see if you read it quickly." He was confident that the U.S. position was fully safeguarded by a number of provisions, including those, for example, of Article V, Section 5. This Section would enable the Fund to limit a member's right to draw if the member were found to be "using the resources of the Fund in a manner contrary to the purposes of the Fund." "Our lawyers," said White, "have taken the position that beyond question that gives adequate powers." Other delegations, he said, had tried to make it difficult for any Fund management to challenge the right of a member country to draw. But the U.S. negotiators had never yielded on this point, although (as a colleague, Ansel Luxford, pointed out) "we have tried to avoid emphasizing [this] any more than you have to" (NARS, Box 28, File W-5).

In view of the failure in Atlantic City to reach a common position on conditionality, it might have been expected that the subject would generate some lively controversy at the conference proper. In fact, however, the question was scarcely even mentioned at the conference, and certainly not debated.

Since none of the records thus far declassified throws any light on the reason for this silence, any explanation that could be offered is at best conjectural. One possible version might run as follows: The U.S. delegation, having encountered strong opposition in Atlantic City, was anxious that the conflict on conditionality should not surface at Bretton Woods. The fact that other countries interpreted the draft Agreement as authorizing unconditional drawings within certain quantitative limits, would, it might well have been felt, be bound to endanger the prospects of ratification by Congress. Congress was well aware that the United States would, for some time to come, be the only possible source of substantial net credit to the system. Prospects for ratification were already uncertain because of strong opposition to the idea of a Fund by the American Bankers' Association.

On the other hand, the delegations opposed to Fund conditionality had every reason to believe, after Atlantic City, that they had won their point and that, as long as the key words of the Joint Statement were maintained, there was no need to engage in another confrontation with the Americans on the matter. Moreover, Keynes had decided that he would raise as few issues as possible that might be embarrassing to the United States, because he was aware of the administration's difficulties with Congress and was unwilling to add to them.[14]

One indication that nearly all countries other than the United States assumed that the question of conditionality had been settled along the lines of the view that had prevailed in Atlantic City is given by the fact that, although reservations were filed by governments on many provisions of the Articles of Agreement, there was not a single reservation on conditionality.

Another point of some interest is that, strong as the position of the United States on the principle of conditionality undoubtedly was, its objectives were clearly limited at this time. Members of the U.S. delegation at Bretton Woods might have been surprised if they could have peered into the future and read the text of a typical IMF stand-by arrangement. In intergovernmental discussions, the U.S. negotiators repeatedly emphasized that "no restrictions should be imposed [by the Fund] unless misbehavior is flagrant," as White put it at a meeting in October 1943. For example:

> The Fund's facilities should not be used to finance either a flight of capital or the issue of foreign loans by a country which could not afford to undertake foreign lending. Again, the Fund would be justified in intervening where a country was using its quota for rearmament. On the other hand, *it would not be justified in the case of an unbalanced budget. In general the Fund would intervene only in extreme cases of violation of qualitative rules, and would bear the burden of proof* [emphasis supplied; Horsefield, 1969, p.69].

Similarly, at the private meeting held to brief the U.S. delegation on July 1, 1944, there was no suggestion by any of the participants that the Fund's conditions for drawings would be onerous. A striking remark by White was, "I don't think the Fund should butt into every country's business and say 'We don't like this or that.'"

On the latter point, the wording of Article IV, Section 5(f), of the original IMF Agreement is of particular interest. This subparagraph stated that, so long as the Fund was satisfied that a change in the par value of a particular member's currency was necessary to correct a fundamental disequilibrium, "it shall not object to a proposed change because of the domestic social or political policies of the member proposing the change." This wording (as pointed out to the author by Bernstein) makes it clear that the intention of the Agreement as a whole was to preclude Fund interference with domestic policies having social objectives, such as the subsidization of food or other essential consumption goods, for the protection of low-income groups.

At a later stage, when the Bretton Woods Agreement came up for ratification by Congress, Professor Raymond Mikesell drafted the response to be made to the expected congressional criticism that the Fund would give member countries a virtually automatic right to borrow. Mikesell's brief, used by White, was categorical in asserting the right of the Fund, under the Articles, to refuse a drawing. But it also provided an answer to the question why the Articles did not explicitly authorize the Fund to pass on each request for a drawing or to require guarantees of good performance from members seeking drawings:

> The reason is that if a member agrees not to impose exchange re-strictions on current transactions, and not to depreciate its currency, it must be given assurance of assistance in periods of adversity. . . . If countries are asked to come to the Fund "hat-in-hand" each time they find themselves in need of reasonable amounts of foreign ex-change, they are not going to be willing to forego those exchange practices which in the past they have been forced to employ for the protection of their economies. [NARS, Box 8, File E-204; draft dated June 29, 1945.]

An explanatory document issued to the press on July 21, 1944, at Bretton Woods included the following passage:

> There are many safeguards provided in the Fund to protect its re-sources from uses that are excessive in amount or in duration. . . . No safeguard provided for the Fund is more important than the provi-sion that the countries' request for foreign currencies must indicate that the uses to which these currencies will be put are consistent with the purposes of the Fund. This means that countries which con-duct their affairs in good faith in accordance with the undertaking to act in conformity with the purposes of the Fund will not in any cir-cumstances divert the resources of the Fund to inappropriate uses. *In international agreements between sovereign States no method of enforce-ment can be as important as reliance on the good faith of the participants* [emphasis supplied; U.S. Department of State, 1948, 2:1212–13.]

The Early Years of the Fund

The United States was fully aware that the battle for a grandmotherly Fund had not been won at Bretton Woods. Once the Fund was a going concern, however, its Executive Board might be persuaded to introduce the implementing regulations or interpretations necessary to give the institution supervisory functions. Without such safeguards, the United States would not agree to the release of Fund resources. At a meeting of the board in May 1946, the U.K. Executive Director, George Bolton, put forward his view of the "semi-automatic character of Fund facilities." The U.S. Executive Director, Harry Dexter White, on the other hand, while conceding that the text of the Articles of Agreement did not specifically authorize the Fund to exercise supervision, considered that there would have to be some check on the right of a Fund member to draw. He suggested that all applications in excess of a ceiling figure, to be determined later, should come before the board for comment and decision.[15]

Speaking for Canada, Louis Rasminsky, later Governor of the Central Bank of Canada from 1961 to 1973, argued that the Fund could not operate if every transaction were to be regarded as an application to the board. If a member gave the necessary guarantees and carried out its undertakings in good faith, it must be able to use its quota with assurance. Quantitative limitations on drawings had already been set out clearly in the Articles of Agreement, and if a member was fulfilling its undertakings by not purchasing foreign exchange for purposes inconsistent with the Articles, it should not be questioned. The Fund should be aware of the behavior of members and should be prepared to be courageous in its criticisms. But large-scale drawings should be regarded as no more than danger signals (PRO Treasury File 236/1162).

In a statement to the Executive Board on August 29, 1946, the Managing Director, Camille Gutt, said that the Fund could be considered as "a sort of automatic machine selling foreign exchange to members within certain limits and on certain terms, and repurchasing this foreign exchange within certain limits and on certain terms." The Fund could, however, issue warnings to members and, in certain circumstances, declare a member ineligible to draw. In Gutt's view an Executive Board composed of high-level officials was required not so much for the discharge of such functions as to constitute "a most important monetary policy-making body, consulted by and advising its members during the critical periods they may pass through" (PRO Treasury File 236/1162).

In November 1946 a report to the Bank of England by the U.K. Executive Director stated, "For the time being there is no reason to fear a policy of persistent and irresponsible interference in the domestic affairs of members" (PRO Foreign Office File 371/62340). As late as September 1947 the Treasury brief for the U.K. delegation attending the second Annual Meeting of the Board of Governors of the IMF suggested that the "battle for 'automaticity' may be largely regarded as won" and pointed out the failure of the United States to have the French economic situation discussed by the Executive Board before allowing additional French drawings (PRO Treasury File 236/1174).

But the situation was in reality quite different.[16] The Europeans had the best of the argument, perhaps, but it was the United States that had the resources, and it was resources that counted, especially in the immediate aftermath of World War II. By 1950 the Fund had come to a complete standstill, there being no drawings at all in that year. As the Fund history points out, "Many people, both inside the Fund and in member countries, were disturbed at the small extent to which drawings were being made available to assist member countries in the kind of difficulties which the Articles had envisaged" (Horsefield, 1969, 1:276).[17]

The decline in Fund operations was partly due to the so-called "ERP Decision," adopted over European opposition, whereby countries receiving assistance under the European Recovery Program were only exceptionally to request the purchase of U.S. dollars from the Fund. But an additional factor was the continuing insistence of the U.S. Executive Director that the use of the resources of the Fund must be subjected to close scrutiny. This contention was used to challenge requests for drawings not only by the Netherlands, which had withdrawn its informal undertaking not to draw on the Fund, but by a number of other countries such as Nicaragua and South Africa (Horsefield, ed., 1969, 2:398).[18]

Deploring "the current tendency to write off the Fund as moribund," Gutt made a proposal in November 1950 to break the deadlock by linking drawings to an engagement by members to take specific steps to overcome balance-of-payments difficulties. The legality of this proposal was immediately challenged by European and other members of the Executive Board. In the end, however, only France and the United Kingdom withheld their approval, the remaining countries considering, as the Fund history puts it, that the Managing Director's plan "offered a useful technique for enabling members to resume drawing from the Fund" (Horsefield, 1969, 1:281).

Similarly, an earlier proposal by the United States to establish a maximum period of five years for the repayment of drawings was adopted despite initial opposition, on legal as well as policy grounds, by most members of the Executive Board (Horsefield, ed., 1969, 2:399–400). The view of the Fund staff on this matter was that the board had no legal authority to set a term for repayment of drawings unless it distinguished between members. If at the time of drawing it seemed to the board inherently likely that repayment could be made reasonably soon, the board had no power to impose conditions. If such repayment could not be foreseen, the proper course was to refuse to allow the member to draw at all (Horsefield, 1969, 1:278).

The Principle of Conditionality Conceded

Thus, it was a desire to enlist the cooperation of the United States as the principal source of credit that prompted other Fund members to give way to American views on the question of conditionality, rather than any conviction on their part that adoption of the U.S. concept of conditionality was indispensable for a successfully functioning IMF. As the former General Counsel of the Fund, Sir Joseph Gold, wryly put it: "The [Executive Board's] decision of February 13, 1952 [adopting the principle of conditionality] was intended to reinvigorate the Fund by encouraging members to believe that they would be able to use its resources" (Horsefield, ed., 1969, 2:524).

Among the main points of this decision were the following:

– The Fund's attitude toward the request of a member for assistance would turn on "whether the problem to be met is of a temporary nature and whether the policies the member will pursue will be adequate to overcome the problem within such a period."
– Drawings should be for periods "within an outside range of three to five years."
– "A member can count on receiving the overwhelming benefit of any doubt" respecting drawings in the gold tranche.
– Stand-by arrangements might be envisaged, whereby a member would enter into discussions with the Fund, not for an immediate drawing "but in order to ensure that it would be able to draw if, within a period of say 6 to 12 months, the need presented itself" (Horsefield, ed., 1969, 3:228–30).

In 1955 the policy of differentiating between drawings in the successive credit tranches was embodied in the further principle that "the larger the drawing in relation to a member's quota the stronger is the justification required of the member," but it was noted that in practice the Fund's attitude toward drawings in the first credit tranche would be "liberal" (Horsefield, ed., 1969, 2:404).

The Substance of Conditionality

It follows from the above that the conditions a member must satisfy in order to be eligible for a drawing on the Fund's ordinary resources, or for a stand-by arrangement, vary according to the size of the drawing in relation to the quota. The main concern of the Fund has been to protect the revolving character of its resources, and it was this consideration that prompted the adoption of the three- to five-year limit for repayment of drawings. Linked to the capacity to repay, of course, is the need for the country concerned to adopt policies and measures that will help to restore and maintain balance-of-payments equilibrium.

Such policies and measures have in the past focused on the restoration of a balance between the aggregate demand for and aggregate supply of resources, making use of monetary and fiscal policies to this end. Where the balance-of-payments problem was thought to be due in part to distortions in the price structure, the measures required for reestablishing equilibrium might be held to include changes in exchange rates, interest rates, and other prices and incomes. Limitations on the accumulation of new foreign debt might also have to be considered.

It is obviously not possible, within the scope of this essay, to undertake a thoroughgoing review of the manner in which the Fund's policy requirements have been worked out and applied, although certain aspects will be touched on subsequently in connection with the examination of some of the main issues that have arisen in relation to conditionality. One point, however, may be noted even at this stage. As Gold (1979b) has pointed out, the Fund maintains a deliberate relationship between the resources it makes available unconditionally, or on the basis of mild conditionality, and the resources for which it applies stronger conditionality. At times the Fund has leaned in the direction of milder conditionality (as in the mid-1970s, when it established oil facilities at low conditionality), while at others (as in the early 1980s) it has imposed more exacting conditions. "The relationship," says Sir Joseph, "is not fixed, and a prevailing balance may be modified in favor of milder conditionality if circumstances make this change advisable."

Particularly striking from this point of view were the Fund's decisions whereby the conditions relating to gold subscriptions arising out of quota increases were relaxed in the case of members encountering "undue payments difficulties." On the occasion of the fourth review of quotas in 1965, the Fund declared that "the representation of a member with respect to undue payments difficulties . . . would not be challenged by the Fund except where it was clearly evident that the representation was without basis." Sir Joseph draws the conclusion from this experience that the Fund evidently considered that it had the authority to adopt policies on the unconditional use of its resources quite apart from its gold tranche policy.

The Proliferation of Limitations and Targets

From 1952 onward the stand-by arrangement was developed as the main instrument for conditionality applicable to drawings beyond the first credit tranche. Two stages in the evolution of stand-by arrangements may be noted. In 1956 phasing was introduced; in other words, drawings were authorized in installments over a period of time, each installment being approved in the light of satisfactory performance by the drawing country. Binding performance conditions evolved gradually, beginning in 1958. In that year a drawing by Paraguay was made conditional on observance of a credit ceiling and of maximum commitment levels for budget expenditure and public works programs. When this matter was reviewed in the Executive Board, the Executive Director for the United Kingdom asked that it be recorded that the performance conditions required of Paraguay on this occasion should not be regarded as a precedent for general application (Horsefield, ed., 1969, 2:485). In 1959 Haiti undertook a broader range of policy conditions, and this time several Executive Directors expressed reservations.

These developments were followed by further elaboration of performance conditions. As the Fund history puts it, "There has been a tendency toward the proliferation of specific limitations and targets" (Horsefield, ed., 1969, 2:486). There is some difference of opinion as to the significance of this "proliferation."

On the one hand, Gold has argued that the progressive "refinement" of stand-by arrangements "should not be understood to mean that the provisions of stand-by arrangements have become stricter with each development in the Fund's policies" (Horsefield, ed., 1969, 2:534). It was essential, on this view, that the assurance of access to Fund resources given to a member country entering into a stand-by arrangement be balanced by equally firm assurance by the member country of consistency with Fund policies.

A quite different view was taken by the developing countries and, in the earlier years, by some of the developed countries as well. It was felt that, in the nature of the case, a proliferation of limitations and targets would be bound to have the effect of increasing the stringency of the conditions imposed, because the freedom of action of the monetary authorities of member countries would thereby be reduced still further. It was for this reason that in September 1968 the Executive Board decided that the number of performance criteria to be applied in cases of drawings beyond the first credit tranche should be limited to those considered truly necessary for determining whether the objectives of a member's stabilization program were being achieved.

The steps that led up to this decision are of considerable interest. A relatively large stand-by arrangement for the United Kingdom was approved in November 1967 with a minimum of conditions, causing particular concern among developing countries represented on the Executive Board as to equality of treatment of member countries.[19] The Executive Director from Brazil, Alexandre Kafka, while supporting the proposed arrangement, drew attention to the fact that it contained no provision for phasing, no performance clauses, and relatively few monetary or credit ceilings. In other words, although this stand-by arrangement was in the highest credit tranches and should therefore have involved stringent performance conditions, it lacked both a quantitatively defined program and other clauses customarily included in stand-by arrangements. Instead, it contained unusually far-reaching provisions for consultations, the significance of which in terms of performance conditions was far from clear. Kafka went on to say that many countries might wish that any stand-by arrangement approved for them should be modeled on the same lines as that for the United Kingdom. His position was supported by nearly all the Executive Directors from developing countries.

This episode touched off a general review of the Fund's policy on the use of its resources under stand-by arrangements, which took place in August and September 1968. In the course of this discussion, the U.K. Alternate Executive Director, Guy Huntrods, defended the absence of specific safeguards in the U.K. stand-by arrangement on the grounds that the U.K. economy was the subject of close examination by the Fund and the terms of the arrangement were therefore, in his view, no less stringent than arrangements for other members. Moreover, performance criteria had been expressed largely in qualitative rather than quantitative terms because the difficulties of accurate forecasting were particularly marked in the case of the United Kingdom.

Developing-country members, on the other hand, no doubt considered that, however great the difficulties of accurate forecasting might be in the United Kingdom, they were considerably greater in developing countries. Yet the information placed before the Executive Board by the IMF staff showed that the number of performance criteria in stand-by arrangements for members in Latin America and Asia had on average been much greater than for members in Europe. Executive Directors for developing countries noted the view expressed by the Fund staff that one of the reasons for not setting fiscal targets as performance criteria was that fiscal data were not sufficiently reliable. But since monetary ceilings and targets could also not be forecast accurately, how, they asked, could it be supposed that these would be any more useful in performance clauses than fiscal targets?

On September 20, 1968, a comprehensive decision was adopted that has, with minor modifications, provided the basis for Fund policy since that time. These were the main elements of the decision:

- Clauses requiring the member to remain in consultation with the Fund were to be included in all stand-by arrangements. Periodic consultations were also to be required in all cases of drawings beyond the first credit tranche, whether under a stand-by arrangement or otherwise.
- In stand-by arrangements limited to the first credit tranche, no provision would be made for phasing of amounts drawn or for the achievement of performance criteria as a condition of each additional drawing. Such provision would, however, "normally be included" in all other stand-by arrangements but would be applicable only to purchases beyond the first credit tranche.
- Performance clauses would be limited to stipulating criteria necessary to evaluate the implementation of a member's stabilization program. (De Vries, 1976, p. 347).

Notwithstanding this development and codification of Fund practice, it was not until 1969 that the principle of conditionality was given explicit legal sanction through amendment of the Articles of Agreement. Among other things, it was made explicit in Article V that "A representation by a member under (a) above shall be examined by the Fund to determine whether the proposed purchase would be consistent with the provisions of this Agreement and with the policies adopted under them, with the exception that proposed gold tranche purchases shall not be subject to challenge" (Articles of Agreement of the International Monetary Fund, as amended effective July 28, 1969, Art. V, Sec. 3(d)).

THE ISSUES

Conditionality and the Access to Resources

An obvious question is whether any useful purpose is served by reviving the old debates about automaticity and conditionality. There is now no disagreement among governments, whether from developed or developing countries, on the broad principle of conditionality in the Fund. Moreover, as noted above, an amendment to the Fund's Articles of Agreement adopted in 1969 explicitly recognizes the principle of conditionality.

It is useful, nevertheless, at a time when the application of the principle of conditionality is being reexamined inside as well as outside the IMF, to bear in mind that there is a role for both conditional and unconditional resources within the Fund, and that there are compelling reasons for a major increase in the proportion of resources made available unconditionally or at low conditionality. These reasons will be set out in the course of the following discussion.

Another reason for going back over the historical record is the startling similarity between the views held today by developing country members of the Fund and the views that were being vigorously advocated by the Europeans at a time when they, too, had to face major balance-of-payments pressures of a structural character. If the monetary authorities of countries such as France, the Netherlands, and the United Kingdom would like to gain a better understanding of the current insistence by the developing countries on the need for access to a larger volume of unconditional resources, they have only to look back at their own files and position papers of the early postwar period. What was sauce for the goose in the late 1940s and early 1950s should, perhaps, be sauce for the gander in the 1980s.

Even the United States, concerned as it was at the end of World War II not to expose itself to excessive external demands on its resources, and unyielding as it therefore was on the basic principle of conditionality, had quite limited objectives at the time of Bretton Woods on the policing of Fund lending, as has been shown above.

The fact that Keynes was opposed to the idea of a "grandmotherly" Fund does not mean that he thought all drawings on the Fund should be automatic. On the contrary, it is worth looking at Keynes's own proposal for an International Clearing Union. Not only did it limit the rate of drawing on the Union and provide in certain circumstances for the deposit of collateral, but it empowered the Governing Board, as a condition of allowing a member to increase its debit balance to a figure in excess of one-half of its quota, to require the member to devalue, to control the outflow of capital, and to surrender gold or foreign exchange in appropriate reduction of its debit balance. The Governing Board could also recommend "internal measures affecting [the member's] domestic economy" (Horsefield, ed., 1969, 3:23). Where a member's debit balance had exceeded three-quarters of its quota on the average for at least a year, the member could be "asked by the Governing Board to take measures to improve its position," and if appropriate improvement had not occurred within two years, the member could be declared in default and lose its entitlement to draw further (ibid., 3:23–24).

One of the most important points of contrast between the British (Keynes) plan and the American (White) plan was in the size of member-country quotas. The Clearing Union proposal appears to have envisaged total quotas on the order of $30 billion or more, equivalent to one-half or more of world imports.[20] The American proposal adopted at Bretton Woods, on the other hand, was for aggregate quotas of $10 billion. In particular cases, of course, quota limitations could be set aside by a waiver procedure. But in global terms, at the lower level of quotas proposed by the Americans, it became much more important, in Keynes's view, to provide for a larger unconditional element in drawing rights on the Fund. Otherwise, countries would not have the assurance they needed of access to a sufficient volume of balance-of-payments support, in case of need, to give them a minimal degree of freedom of action in their economic policies. In October 1943 Keynes wrote to Professor Jacob Viner that, on second thought, he felt that the Clearing Union "policing" provisions may have been too strict, "though this was actually balanced under the Clearing Union by the much greater size of quotas" (Moggridge, 1980, 25:333).

Similar considerations apply a fortiori to the present situation in the IMF. While IMF quotas averaged about 16 percent of total imports in 1948, the proportion had fallen to less than 3 percent in 1980. For non-oil developing countries the percentage was a little higher—between 4 and 5 percent. The proportion of quota now available unconditionally, or at low conditionality, includes not only the reserve tranche and the first credit tranche but drawings under the combined compensatory financing and cereal import facility of up to 125 percent of quota. (Drawings for the financing of buffer stocks are also available at low conditionality.) The combined facility, however, deals only with balance-of-payments difficulties due to export shortfalls or to excess import costs for cereals, and many other factors outside the control of these countries—such as increases in import prices for commodities other than cereals—can exert balance-of-payments pressure.

On the whole, therefore, the capacity of the Fund to provide balance-of-payments support to developing countries unconditionally, or at low conditionality, has declined substantially. At the same time, drawings in the upper credit tranches are subject to stringent conditions. Such expansion of Fund resources as has taken place recently, as noted below, has added to the lending capacity of the Fund only at high conditionality, while the low conditionality resources previously available through the oil facility and from sales of gold have come to an end.

Conditionality and the Burden of Adjustment

As is well known, the distribution of the burden of adjustment tends to be highly inequitable between countries. During the Great Depression, the term "beggar-my-neighbor" was used to describe the policies whereby countries sought to shift the burden of adjustment to one another, and it was generally the stronger countries that achieved the greatest success. Keynes summed up the historical experience of the functioning of the adjustment process as follows:

> It is characteristic of a freely convertible international standard that it throws the main burden of adjustment on the country which is in the *debtor* position on the international balance of payments. . . . Thus it has been an inherent characteristic of the automatic international metallic currency (apart from special circumstances) to force adjustments in the direction most disruptive of social order, and to throw the burden on the countries least able to support it, making the poor poorer [Moggridge, 1980, 25:27, 29].

As Keynes points out, the process of adjustment is compulsory for the debtor and voluntary for the creditor. Moreover, most of the means of adjustment open to the debtor country are apt to have adverse effects on its terms of trade, and in the case of the poorer countries—exporting mainly primary products—the adverse price effects may be large enough to offset, or more than offset, any favorable movement in trade volumes.[21]

Experience since Keynes's time amply confirms his assessment. Strong international pressure has frequently been brought to bear upon deficit countries, while surplus countries have been under little or no pressure to adjust. Developing countries that are in deficit are frequently accused of mismanagement of their affairs, but the same term is never used to describe the policies of surplus countries. Surplus countries may be faulted for unwillingness to share the burden of adjustment but never for mismanagement. On the contrary, recent years have seen a revival of mercantilist policies among the industrial countries aimed at the attainment of surplus positions all round.

It would be difficult in these days to point to a country, developed or developing, that is *not* vulnerable to the charge of economic mismanagement from some point of view or other, so that the common use of the term mainly to describe the conduct of developing countries is hardly objective, to say the least. But there is a more subtle abuse in the indiscriminate use of the term "mismanagement" to describe the alleged sins of developing countries. For once it can be shown that a country has made some error of economic management, there is a tendency to assume that this fact alone can be held responsible for the entire balance-of-payments deficit with which the country is confronted. This may be far from the case. A country may have made errors of economic management, and yet the more important factors contributing to external imbalance may be a deterioration in terms of trade or the imposition by other countries of import restrictions affecting its exports. Under current practice, it is not a standard requirement that allowance be made in stabilization programs for factors outside the control of the deficit countries concerned, other than those arising in cases where shortfalls in export earnings are involved. Once there is a prima facie showing of mismanagement—and few if any countries are completely innocent of it—the conclusion is generally drawn that the elimination of the entire deficit is the exclusive responsibility of the deficit country.

In defense of this position it has been suggested that, despite all the hopes for effective exchange rate surveillance, the Fund still does not have any mechanism for compelling a surplus country to adjust. Given this fact, and given a situation where a country is faced with a balance-of-payments deficit of more than temporary duration, adjustment cannot be avoided. This reasoning is inescapable as far as it goes, but it does not go far enough. It certainly does not justify the application of standard upper credit tranche conditionality to a country finding itself in the situation described. As matters now stand, whether or not a country is compelled to accept exacting Fund conditions does not depend upon the character of its balance-of-payments problem or upon the degree of its responsibility for that problem. It depends simply on whether its cumulative drawings on the Fund have risen beyond the level of the first credit tranche.

As noted earlier, owing to the failure over the years to increase Fund quotas in line with world trade, the ratio of quotas to trade has fallen to an exceedingly low level. In most of the countries that have to rely mainly on the Fund for balance-of-payments support, it does not take a very large deficit to move the country from the first credit tranche, where conditionality is low, to the upper credit tranches.

Clearly, the situation of a country whose deficit is merely the mirror image of a structural surplus elsewhere in the system is vastly different from that of a country in which domestic expenditure is excessive. There are no rational grounds for compelling the former country to undergo all the rigors of standard upper credit tranche conditionality. On the contrary, precisely because of its inability to carry out the mandate of the Articles of Agreement in relation to surplus countries, the Fund might be expected to lean over backward to ease the difficulties of countries that are suffering the effects of that shortcoming. The Fund cannot, of course, supply more resources than are available to it. But, subject to that constraint, there is much that the Fund can do to lighten the burden of adjustment and avoid the application of severe measures, especially of a deflationary character.

The Fund, however, has rejected the idea that the origin of a deficit should be taken into account in determining the degree of conditionality imposed. In justifying this position, it is pointed out that both internal and external factors may be present in many situations. Moreover, in terms of adjustment, it is suggested, a more important consideration is whether the imbalance is transitory, and therefore self-reversing, or is likely to persist. If it is likely to persist, the country will need to undertake adjustment regardless of the internal or exogenous character of the deficit.

Here again the reasoning is valid but incomplete. It is quite true that in real life a balance-of-payments deficit may have elements of both internal and external origin and that where the deficit is persistent, adjustment is inescapable. But it is also true that, within the resources available to it, the Fund has sufficient degrees of freedom in the application of conditionality to be able to distinguish between a country whose deficit is mainly self-generated and a country whose deficit is mainly due to external factors. In particular, there is no reason why a country that has already sustained a decline in real income because of a deterioration in terms of trade for reasons beyond its control should be called upon to lower its income still further by means of devaluation or fiscal and monetary contraction unless there are specific indications of a genuine need for such measures. The Fund should seek rather to support the kind of solution that is consistent with an expansion of output and employment.

Conditionality and Self-Generated Imbalance

There are reasons for questioning the Fund's methods of applying the principle of conditionality even in conventional cases where countries themselves are primarily responsible for their balance-of-payments difficulties—for example, where there is excess pressure of domestic demand.[22] So far as the diagnosis of problems of imbalance is concerned, the Fund history has itself pointed to the questions that arise regarding the validity and applicability of the monetarist approach to the balance-of-payments employed by the Fund (De Vries, 1976, p. 368). There are also dangers inherent in the characteristic effort of stabilization programs to sum up the economic performance of a country in terms of a few monetary aggregates. Moreover, the use of quantitative monetary targets as performance criteria tends to determine the character of the adjustment to be undertaken even though other forms of adjustment may be more appropriate.

Foremost among the basic assumptions underlying IMF stabilization strategy, as pointed out by John Williamson (1984), is that "the least-cost way of satisfying a budget constraint is to let the market decide how it is to be done, except where there are specific reasons for believing that there are divergences between private and social costs and benefits." It is on these grounds that the Fund seeks to promote the liberalization of trade and payments, and prefers exchange rate changes to the intensification of controls when expenditure switching is called for. While sharing the general viewpoint on which the Fund's preferred strategy is based, Williamson sees difficulties in avoiding controls in cases where reliance on the market would lead to what he calls "peremptory (or, even worse, oscillating) adjustment."

A further consideration is that the magnitude of social costs and benefits is rarely quantifiable and there is therefore a tendency to ignore them. From the standpoint of a country committed, for political and social reasons, to planned development, any proposal for a stabilization program that would, in effect, take major decisions out of the hands of the planners and rely instead on determinations by the market inevitably appears to involve a political judgment outside the competence or responsibility of the IMF. (For a strong reaction to such proposals, see Nyerere, 1980.) The IMF's own guidelines on conditionality imply that the Fund ought to be able to adapt its policy prescriptions to the social and political objectives of individual member countries.[23] Yet, while the Fund has made an effort to adapt stabilization programs to the goals of centrally planned economies, it has tended to assume that for all other countries market forces are likely to yield the best results.

Even on purely economic grounds, there are many cases in which the wisdom of exchange rate changes or of the liberalization of trade and payments is open to serious doubt. As two members of the Fund staff have put the matter:

Where trade flows are responsive to price factors (as, for example, for developing countries which have a substantial manufacturing sector) there is more likely to be a balance of advantage in rate flexibility. . . . In other cases, however, where trade flows are not very responsive to exchange rate changes (because export prices are determined in world markets and there are no close domestic substitutes for imports), the exchange rate changes needed to secure equilibrium in the balance of payments will be large. For these countries, the repercussions of exchange rate variability on domestic objectives, such as investment promotion and income distribution, may be a more potent factor on the negative side [Crockett and Nsouli, 1977].

For countries whose exports consist mainly of primary products, moreover, it cannot be assumed that an increased share of the market can invariably be obtained by cutting export prices in terms of foreign currency, with or without devaluation. Any such move is bound to put pressure on other producers to retaliate in defense of their own market shares. The result is a loss for all producers, and this loss is aggravated where a series of devaluations leads to a rise in the output of primary products and hence a further deterioration in the terms of trade. Devaluation is justified only where domestic costs have risen so high that it has become unprofitable to export traditional primary commodities, or where dropping the exchange rate can reasonably be expected to generate a major expansion in nontraditional exports, particularly manufactures.

The liberalization of trade restrictions is another policy approach that should not be insisted on indiscriminately. The case for maintaining and even reinforcing trade controls is particularly strong where a country would otherwise be forced into substantial deflation and unemployment as a means of reducing imports, when the same goal could be achieved with a lesser decline in real income and employment through the use of trade controls.

Even in the many situations where member countries themselves prefer to rely on decisionmaking by market forces, the use of pinpoint monetary targets raises serious difficulties. The setting of such targets is far from being as scientific a process as is usually implied in the literature on this subject, particularly in view of the historical evidence cited by the IMF staff itself. The evidence does not support the presumption that the velocity of circulation of money remains steady when domestic credit is manipulated for policy purposes (see Fleming and Boissonneault, 1977, and Park, 1970). There is also the practical difficulty that huge errors in short-term forecasting are commonplace even in regard to monetary aggregates presumed to be under government control, let alone in relation to the private sector.

It is true that program ceilings can be, and often are, modified by the Fund to take account of unforeseen events or incorrect assumptions. But frequently this cannot be done until after the mistaken targets have been in operation for some time and significant damage has already occurred. Analysis of recent experience of monetary targets in industrially developed countries with advanced statistical underpinning has shown the extraordinary difficulties that arise even in selecting and quantifying the appropriate monetary target, let alone in exercising the control required to achieve that target. The Governor of the Bank of England is among those who have been sharply critical of procedures that require a particular numerical target to be reached by a particular date (Bank of England, 1978). An important statement dealing with this matter and entitled "Measures to Combat Inflation" was issued on April 14, 1981, by the Group of Thirty. This nonofficial group of leading bankers, central bankers, economists, and businessmen meeting under the chairmanship of Johannes Witteveen, former Managing Director of the IMF, expressed the view that "It is perhaps time to review critically recent experience with the use of strict quantitative targets for growth in the money supply, whether it is broadly or narrowly defined."

In some cases it is felt that the situation calls for shock treatment in the form of a drastic change in the exchange rate or a major cutback in real income. Where economic chaos appears imminent, such treatment may be almost unavoidable. Moreover, if internal political and social relationships are cohesive, such measures may be accepted without political upheaval. But there are at least as many cases in which such cohesion is lacking, so that shock treatment may be compatible only with authoritarian government. In such cases international pressure for drastic measures may have consequences that are incompatible with other international objectives.

Conditionality and Externally Generated Imbalance

If there is a need for reconsideration of certain features of traditional stabilization programs even in cases of self-generated imbalance, the validity of such programs is still more questionable where balance-of-payments problems are of external origin or of a structural nature.

The Fund's *Annual Report* for 1979 (p. 23) noted that the entire increase in the balance-of-payments deficit of non-oil developing countries from 1977 to 1979, estimated at some $22 billion, was due to two factors: the deterioration in terms of trade and the rise in the cost of servicing external debt. Both of these developments were the result of forces outside the control of the developing countries concerned, including the mounting export prices of the industrial and oil exporting countries and the increases in interest rates associated with efforts by the industrial countries to curb inflation by means of monetary restrictions.

The situation in 1979–81 is reminiscent of that in 1974–75. At that time, too, developing countries, as well as many developed countries, encountered very large deficits in their balances of payments, owing mainly to a deterioration in terms of trade. In a note presented to the Committee of Twenty at its Rome meeting in January 1974, the Managing Director of the IMF indicated that oil importing countries would, in the short run, have to accept the deterioration of the current account of the balance of payments since, "Attempts to eliminate the additional current deficit caused by higher oil prices through deflationary demand policies, import restrictions, and general resort to exchange rate depreciation would serve only to shift the payments problem from one oil importing country to another and to damage world trade and economic activity" (IMF, 1974, pp. 25–26). Subsequently, in its communiqué of June 13, 1974, the Committee of Twenty noted, "As a result of inflation, the energy situation, and other unsettled conditions, many countries are experiencing large current account deficits that need to be financed. . . . Sustained cooperation would be needed to ensure appropriate financing without endangering the smooth functioning of private financial markets and *to avert the danger of adjustment action that merely shifts the problem to other countries*" (emphasis supplied; Committee of Twenty, 1974, p. 221).

These were the considerations underlying the decision to establish an oil facility to provide balance-of-payments support at low conditionality in 1974–75. Any Fund member drawing on the oil facility was required "to cooperate with the Fund to find appropriate solutions for its balance of payments problem." This was the same level of conditionality that was applicable to the compensatory financing facility.

Very similar considerations applied to the situation in 1981–82. Here again, the upsurge in oil prices, coupled with general inflation, had a major effect on the balances of payments of a large number of countries. And once more, as in 1974–75, it was important that deficit countries not adopt policies that would merely aggravate the problems of other countries. But while in 1974–75 it was recognized that countries incurring balance-of-payments deficits due to oil-price increases should not be forced into immediate adjustment, in 1981–82 the resources provided by the Fund brought with them all the rigors of upper credit tranche conditionality. Yet it was as true in 1981–82 as it was in 1974–75 that the inevitable outcome of forcing excessive retrenchment on deficit countries while the surpluses of oil exporting countries were maintained was that deficits were simply shifted from country to country. The cumulative deflation brought about by the adjustment process was thereby superimposed on, and reinforced, the primary deflation resulting from business recession in the industrial countries.

Adjustment to the new increases in oil prices, in any real and lasting sense, could not be achieved within a short period of time. The kind of shock treatment often considered advisable in cutting back excess demand was virtually useless in the above circumstances, which called for the adaptation of the economy to a new level of the energy terms of trade.

In some respects the situation in 1981–82 and subsequent years was even more difficult that in 1974–75. Countries that had obtained ready access to private capital markets in 1974–75 could not count on accommodation on the same scale in the period ahead because of mounting concern among commercial banks about the risks involved and the tightening of credit in major industrial countries.[24] And the lowest-income countries had to rely on official sources of finance, which had been subject to curtailment as part of a process of budget cutting in donor countries. These considerations pointed to the need for a substantial increase in the flow of resources to developing countries from the multilateral institutions—the Fund, the World Bank, and the regional development banks—on terms and conditions that would permit rates of growth to be maintained and programs of structural adjustment accelerated.

Despite important conceptual advances in policy statements by the Fund management, to which reference will be made below, there was and is a continuing reluctance within the Fund to accept the proposition that the origin of balance-of-payments disturbances is a highly relevant factor in determining the appropriate way of dealing with them. There is no dispute that permanent changes, such as in the energy terms of trade, call for adjustment by the deficit countries. But the crucial point is that the adjustment process required of them is not of the classical variety designed to curb excessive domestic demand. It is concerned much more with the need for structural changes in the economy—changes that will bring about savings in the use of imported fuels, for example, or that will redeploy domestic resources in a manner that can achieve external balance without undue disturbance to domestic growth and employment. The experience of the 1970s dramatized the adverse effects on long-term growth and development that can occur through compression of the balance-of-payments adjustment process into an unduly brief period of time. It is clear that the period of adjustment was much too short for many countries, and that a lack of adequate official resources for medium-term balance-of-payments support was severely felt.[25]

Objectives of the Developing Countries

Since 1978 the Fund has come under strong pressure from the developing countries to liberalize its conditions for lending. Such use of Fund credit as did occur during the middle and later 1970s was concentrated almost entirely on the facilities available on relatively easy conditions— the oil facility, the compensatory financing facility, and the reserve and first credit tranches. Even where countries were under the most intense pressure both in their external accounts and in their domestic economies, they hesitated to make use of the upper tranches of their quotas in the Fund and avoided such drawings if they could. There were only ten cases of drawings beyond the first credit tranche in 1974–76 among the entire Fund membership.

There was a widespread feeling among developing countries that the quota resources available in the Fund were too small to justify the considerable changes in economic plans and policies that might have to be made in order to be allowed to draw on them, except as a last resort in circumstances leaving no other option. A relationship existed, therefore, between the willingness of countries to accept Fund conditions and the amount of resources that the Fund was able to make available to them. By the same token, the larger the resources that could be provided and the longer the period over which they could be made available, the less abrupt did the adjustment process have to be and the less exacting the conditions imposed.

Beginning in September 1978, the Group of Twenty-Four—representing developing-country members of the IMF—held a series of meetings at which issues were raised that were considered to be of key importance. At its meeting in September 1978 the Group expressed concern about the multiplicity of performance criteria and some other forms of conditionality that were inhibiting access to Fund resources by member countries. The Group urged the Executive Board of the IMF to set appropriate guidelines designed to limit the performance criteria only to relevant macroeconomic variables, paying due regard to the need for sustained growth in the developing countries (Group of Twenty-Four, 1978, p. 306, para. 12).

A further meeting held on March 6, 1979, expressed agreement with the fundamental conclusion of a study that had been prepared for the Group, to the effect that "in determining the volume and conditionality governing balance of payments assistance, a clearer distinction needs to be made between the causal factors attributable to the domestic policies of the developing countries and the external elements beyond their control" (Group of Twenty-Four, 1979a, p. 87, para. 9).

The following September, at a meeting in Belgrade, the Group of Seventy-Seven, meeting for the first time at Finance Minister level, adopted a program of international monetary reform submitted to it by the Group of Twenty-Four.[26] The program included support for the establishment of a medium-term balance-of-payments facility to respond to the particular needs of developing countries. It was proposed that the new facility should have sufficient resources at its disposal to permit a volume of support that would be significant in relation to current levels of deficits. It should, moreover, carry "minimum conditionality, since it is responding to an externally induced balance of payments deficit, and should provide support on longer-term maturity." Finally, an interest subsidy should be provided to low-income developing countries. It was proposed further that existing IMF facilities should be adapted so as to lengthen repayment periods, provide for larger amounts, and set conditionality "with due regard to causes of deficits" (Group of Twenty-Four, 1979b, p. 322, paras. 9–10).

The Response of the Fund

These meetings and proposals gave rise to a corresponding series of meetings of the Executive Board of the Fund at which the various issues were discussed and, in some instances, decisions made. Some of the issues were also examined at ministerial level by the Fund's Interim Committee, notably at its meeting in Washington on September 28, 1980, when there was a first discussion of the proposals for international monetary reform advanced by the developing countries.

In response to the representations made on conditionality, on March 2, 1979, the Executive Board adopted a set of guidelines providing, among other things, for the Fund to "pay due regard to the domestic social and political objectives, the economic priorities, and the circumstances of members, including the causes of their balance of payments problems." Moreover, performance criteria were to be limited to those necessary to evaluate implementation of stabilization programs, and were normally to be confined to macroeconomic variables and those necessary to implement specific provisions of the Articles or policies adopted under them (Gold, 1979b, pp. 22, 30).

While useful in certain respects, there was relatively little that was new in the guidelines. Their significance was described as follows by Gold (1979b, p. 15): "Most of the decision is declaratory of the practice that has emerged since 1968, but the decision includes certain new or clarified elements, largely in deference to the views of developing countries. There is no reason to believe, however, that debate on this subject is at an end."

Sir Joseph's implicit recognition that the new guidelines did not dispose of the fundamental issues is noteworthy. In particular, the guidelines did not deal with the question of the applicability of the Fund's standard performance criteria to the particular types of structural balance-of-payments problems experienced in recent years. It is true that the Fund had already, in 1974, begun to address problems of structural imbalance. It had established an extended facility to deal with structural maladjustments in production and trade due to persistent cost and price distortions, and those involving a combination of slow growth and an inherently weak external sector. The Extended Fund Facility (EFF) assured members of Fund assistance for up to three years in a maximum amount equivalent to 140 percent of quota, as against the normal stand-by arrangement for up to twelve months and 100 percent of quota. In consideration of EFF assistance, a member country was required to present a one-year program of measures to correct structural imbalance, to be followed by corresponding programs for the second and third years. The three- to five-year repayment period of stand-by arrangements was extended to a period of four to eight years, which was in turn subsequently extended further to ten years. Repayments were, however, to be accelerated in case of improvements in the balance of payments, involving a potential source of uncertainty for the borrowing country. In the first few years after the introduction of the facility, there were relatively few EFF drawings because of difficulties in reaching agreement on the programs to be implemented by the governments concerned.

The need for special arrangements to deal with structural problems became still more pressing following the second round of increases in oil prices and the accompanying deterioration in terms of trade in oil importing developing countries. Moreover, the volume of balance-of-payments support required was greatly increased. As a result, the Fund agreed to lend in substantially larger amounts than in the past. As the Managing Director pointed out:

> Traditionally, a member using the Fund's ordinary resources used to be able to borrow from us a maximum cumulative amount equal to 100 percent of its quota in the Fund. As circumstances have changed,

we have progressively adopted policies whereby a member may now draw on ordinary resources and on resources borrowed by the Fund up to a cumulative amount of 600 percent of its quota. In 1980 alone the Fund's new lending commitments under adjustment programs agreed with members reached SDR 7.2 billion, more than double the average level of the three preceding years [*IMF Survey*, February 9, 1981, p. 35].[27]

The Fund also recognized that pressures on the balance of payments of developing countries under current conditions called for structural changes in the economy, involving, for example, the need to economize on oil and develop additional sources of energy. The Managing Director acknowledged that structural changes of this type may take longer than the one to three years normally set as the length of Fund programs. "Thus, while we continue to stress the importance of appropriate demand management, we now systematically emphasize the development of the productive base of the economy and we contemplate that countries may, therefore, need our financing for longer periods" (*IMF Survey*, February 9, 1981, p. 35).

A New Departure?

It is not clear to what extent, if any, the new developments in Fund thinking involve an easing of conditionality. Recent cases can be cited in which certain countries appear to have been able to obtain large drawings on apparently easy terms, while in others, involving broadly similar circumstances, the performance requirements seem to be no different from those associated in the past with standard deflationary programs.

Whatever disposition there may be to increase the proportion of balance-of-payments assistance to developing countries that is provided at low conditionality encounters strong resistance from the major industrial countries—including those that fought hard for that selfsame objective in the 1940s and early 1950s. In part this resistance probably reflects a basic distrust of the ability of developing countries to manage their own affairs, as well as a suspicion of what the industrial countries regard as newfangled concepts of structural adjustment. These concepts do not fit easily into the traditional categories of fiscal and monetary balance.

The Minister of Finance of the Federal Republic of Germany, Hans Matthoefer, was undoubtedly speaking for other major industrial countries as well as for his own when he told the Annual Meeting of the IMF on September 30, 1980: "The IMF was created as the guardian of internal and external monetary stability. It should resist all attempts that might call this mandate in question. The conditionality of its lending must be maintained."[28]

It is well known that all governments, developed and developing, are now in agreement on the principle of conditionality and that there is no proposal before the IMF to change that principle. It is, therefore, important to try to identify the nature of the concerns that gave rise to Matthoefer's statement. There are two areas in which he may have seen difficulty. One is the suggestion by developing countries that the total financing available to them for balance-of-payments support includes too small a proportion of unconditional as against conditional resources. The second is the contention of developing countries that, so far as conditional resources are concerned, the conditions applied should be adjusted in the light of the character and origin of the balance-of-payments deficits involved, taking structural factors into account. This carries the implication that fiscal and monetary restraints should be applied only where, and to the extent that the circumstances require them.

The first of these areas of difficulty involves a question of judgment but certainly not of principle. It is even more unusual today than it was in the past for developed countries to seek access to the conditional resources of the Fund, because they have a variety of other borrowing facilities at their disposal. But for those developing countries that are unable to obtain balance-of-payments support from the international private banking system, the resources available from the Fund are crucial. In fact, Fund upper credit tranche lending may in the future be virtually confined to developing countries, simply because developed countries no longer have any need for it. In these circumstances it is important for the Fund to be able to provide an array and distribution of resources— at zero-level, low-level, and high-level conditionality—that is not too dissimilar from the corresponding array and distribution available to developed countries. Since this is not the case, and since developed countries have access to a much higher proportion of unconditional or low conditional resources than do the developing countries, there is serious inequity in the system. Moreover, the imbalance is accentuated by the huge unearned increment to the reserves of developed countries resulting from the rise in the price of gold. At a gold price of $400 per ounce, the unearned increment accounted for over one-half of the total developed-country reserves at the end of 1980, as against a proportion of less than one-quarter for the non-oil developing countries.

Mention was made earlier of the IMF decision to allow members to draw on Fund resources up to a cumulative amount of 600 percent of quota exclusive of drawings under the compensatory financing and buffer stock facilities. This enlargement of access to Fund resources represented an important step forward, but the form of the increase had a major shortcoming. The very fact that it became necessary to establish drawing rights at so large a multiple of quotas highlights the severe lag in quotas in relation to world trade to which reference was made earlier. By providing for the expansion of access in this way, governments escaped the need, under the Articles of Agreement, to provide additional subscriptions to the Fund equivalent to 25 percent of whatever increase in quotas would otherwise have been required. But the result is that of the 600 percent of quota thus made available, only 25 percent of quota is provided at low conditionality—the conditionality of the first credit tranche. In a sense this is contrary to the spirit of the Articles of Agreement, since if quotas had been adjusted in line with world trade, and had therefore been increased sixfold, first credit tranche conditionality would have applied to the equivalent of 150 percent of current quotas instead of only 25 percent. The method of expanding access that has been chosen has the effect of forcing member countries into upper credit tranche conditionality much sooner than would occur if quotas had been adjusted appropriately. This is one of the factors responsible for the hardening of conditions on Fund drawings to which the Managing Director has referred, as noted below.

One way of offsetting this deterioration in the conditions for borrowing from the Fund would be to make substantial allocations of SDRS. The international liquidity explosion of the 1970s, in the form of reserve-currency creation and the rise in the price of gold, redounded mainly to the benefit of the developed countries. Yet, from 1973 to 1978, the liquidity explosion was used as a basis for refusing new allocations of SDRS that would have benefited developing countries at least to the extent of their share in Fund quotas—the basis of SDR distribution. The failure to maintain allocations of SDRS led to a decline in the share of the SDR in world reserves, notwithstanding the injunction in the Articles of Agreement that the SDR was to become the principal international reserve asset. Thus a strong case can be made on several grounds for major new allocations of SDRS. (A more complete statement of the case is contained in Legarda et al., 1987.)

As for the second major area in which the views of industrial countries may diverge from those of the developing countries, there is no question of abandoning conditionality but rather of adapting it to the circumstances. Diagnosis and treatment should bear some relationship to one another. If a balance-of-payments deficit is due to structural deficiencies in the energy sector, there is little point in applying a crash program of monetary and fiscal deflation. On the other hand, where demand is excessive, compression of demand is indispensable. And where both phenomena are present, both kinds of remedy can be and should be invoked.

The conceptual lag is such, however, that few if any developed countries are prepared for the time being to envisage any change that could be regarded as departing from conventional ideas about standard upper credit tranche conditionality. Nevertheless, the availability of larger resources in the Fund, together with the decision to permit adjustment over longer periods than in the past, should, in principle, make for a less drastic adjustment process than would have been required if the restoration of equilibrium had been sought in a one- or two-year period with a minimum volume of resources. On the other hand, while it has been announced that the Fund envisages a borrowing program of SDR 6 to 7 billion in 1981, the Fund's total resources will remain small in relation to projected balance-of-payments deficits of developing countries, though substantial in past perspective.

For middle- and upper-income developing countries with access to international capital markets, additional borrowing facilities afforded by the Fund may do no more than compensate for any shortfall in borrowing from commercial banks resulting from the constraints referred to earlier. For the low-income developing countries, on the other hand, the interest rates on borrowing from the Fund may be a serious deterrent, even if they are lower than would apply to loans obtained elsewhere. An important new factor is the subsidy account established by the Fund in December 1980 in connection with drawings by low-income countries under the supplementary financing facility (*IMF Survey*, January 12, 1981, p. 1). Unfortunately, such subsidies will apparently not be available in the near future on any resources that the Fund may obtain by other means. In view of the exceptional difficulties in maintaining the ability of the low-income countries to import at a time of severe externally generated pressures on their balances of payments, the policy of interest subsidization accepted by the Fund should clearly be given broader application.

Overall, there is no doubt that the conditions now required by the Fund in connection with the balance-of-payments support it is providing are, on average, much more stringent than they were at a similar period during the mid-1970s. In the words of the Managing Director:

In the period following the first oil shock, approximately three-quarters of the resources provided by the Fund to its members were made available on terms involving a low degree of conditionality. At present, by contrast, some three-quarters of our new lending commitments involve "upper credit tranche" programs, that is to say, they require rigorous adjustment policies [*IMF Survey*, February 9, 1981, p. 35].

Some Tentative Conclusions

The new concepts of the IMF management represent an important step forward, indicating a readiness to reexamine some of the basic assumptions underlying the Fund's treatment of stabilization programs in the past. At the same time additional clarification will be needed before the new ideas can be translated into operational guidelines. One suspects that particular difficulty will be encountered in establishing performance criteria in line with the new concepts. For example, the most important single performance criterion in most, if not all, stand-by arrangements of the past was a ceiling on the net domestic assets of the central bank or the banking system, accompanied usually by a subceiling for credit supplied to the government by the central bank or the banking system.

The monitoring of country performance in terms of compliance with a set of quantitative targets is a traditional element in IMF supervision of stabilization programs. It cannot readily be adapted to a different kind of approach in which structural adjustment rather than the curtailment of effective demand is the basic objective. There may well be a tendency for the Fund to continue relying on indicators of demand management even in situations where the primary objective of a stabilization program is quite different. Even where the need for structural adjustment is recognized, there appears to be a tendency to emphasize the importance of pricing policies, exchange rates, and tax regimes, as against more direct measures such as the sectoral allocation of investment.

Certainly, structural adjustment does not lend itself to the kind of quantitative measurement and pinpoint targetry that the money supply does. To the extent that the Fund engages in a new type of balance-of-payments support, new methods of monitoring will be needed accordingly.

The idea advanced above that a reasonable balance should be struck between the low conditional and high conditional resources provided by the IMF is fully consistent with the credit tranche policies of the Fund itself—policies that have been distorted by the failure of the Fund membership to raise quotas in line with world trade. Such a balance is also essential as a means of giving developing countries at least some of the freedom of maneuver in the management of their economies that developed countries have under similar conditions. It is not in the interests of the international community that developing countries should be continually hemmed in by the policy prescriptions of an international organization, however well motivated those prescriptions may be. Developing countries should have access to balance-of-payments support, especially in cases of externally generated imbalance, on conditions that are appropriate to their circumstances. This is not an argument for unconditional Fund programs but for forms of conditionality that are clearly adapted to the specific character of the imbalances encountered.

Finally, the distribution of the burden of adjustment among countries cannot be separated from the question of responsibility for the factors making adjustment necessary. This basic idea was written into the Fund's Articles of Agreement in the form of the scarce-currency clause. It was this fundamental concept, likewise, that animated the Committee of Twenty's attempt to find an objective means of determining the distribution of adjustment obligations as between surplus and deficit countries, as well as between the reserve center and the rest of the world.

A passive attitude to the distribution of the burden of adjustment is by no means the same as an impartial or objective attitude. To suggest, regardless of whether a disturbance is of domestic or foreign origin, that it is the deficit country that must accept the full burden of adjustment is to settle the question of responsibility as decisively as if the matter had been addressed directly instead of indirectly. Such an attitude is tantamount to saying that those countries that have the power to shift the burden are entitled to do so. And it is precisely this approach that in the 1970s resulted in the imposition of a burden of adjustment on the poorest and weakest countries out of all proportion to their responsibility for the disequilibrium that had arisen.

The step forward that the Fund management has taken in its latest thinking contains the potential for one of the most important and constructive changes in IMF policy since Bretton Woods. But the word "potential" should be stressed, because for the time being it is mainly concepts that have been developed, and those concepts have not yet been translated fully into practical action. The shift in approach is significant and the importance of structural adjustment in solving balance-of-payments problems has been acknowledged, but the new thinking does not yet fully accept the proposition that the difference between internally and externally generated disturbances is a crucial factor in assessing the form and content of conditionality required. While the Fund management has received the support of governments in its effort to provide larger volumes of balance-of-payments financing over longer periods, there is a reluctance to make any significant changes in conditionality. In fact, in global terms there has been a step backward: on average, resources are being provided at a much more exacting level of conditionality today than they were in the mid-1970s, even though the problems confronted in the two periods are very much alike.

The Fifth Credit Tranche[*]

The abolition of the Compensatory Financing Facility of the IMF—at any rate in its original incarnation—is a tragedy. An IMF decision of September 14, 1983, while it preserves the name CFF, destroys the basic purpose of the facility.

CFF was established in 1963. It was the result of a UN initiative: this was by far the most important case in which the United Nations was able to bring influence to bear upon IMF policies. In 1949 and again in 1953 UN expert groups had proposed compensatory financing in the form of countercyclical lending by the IMF, designed to offset pressures on the balances of payments of member countries resulting from fluctuations in the import demand of other members. A member of the 1953 group, F. G. Olano, in an appendix to the group's report, proposed the establishment of a system of mutual insurance whereby compensatory payments would be made out of an appropriate fund to countries experiencing "unjust, unfair and inequitable" terms of trade. Building upon these ideas, UN economists and subsequent expert and intergovernmental groups gradually developed a scheme for compensatory financing of export fluctuations. In May 1962 the UN Commission on International Commodity Trade (CICT) invited the IMF to present a report as to whether and in what way the Fund might undertake such a responsibility. As a result of this initiative, CFF was in fact established in the following year. Incidentally, when the industrial countries claim, as they frequently do, that the United Nations has no right to make recommendations to the IMF, they are overlooking, among other things, the history of CFF. The Fund official history makes it quite clear that CFF was "the Fund's response" to the above-mentioned invitation addressed to the IMF by CICT.[29] Moreover, after it was established, CFF was liberalized several times, as a result of recommendations emanating from UNCTAD.

*This essay was originally published in *World Development* 13, no. 2 (Oxford: Pergamon, 1985): 245–49.

The new facility provided that a compensatory drawing would be made available where (a) a shortfall in export receipts was of a short-term character and largely caused by circumstances beyond the member's control, and (b) the member was willing to cooperate with the Fund in an effort to find appropriate solutions for its balance-of-payments difficulties, where such solutions were needed. In order to identify shortfalls of a short-term character, the Fund, in conjunction with the member concerned, would seek to establish reasonable estimates of the medium-term trend of the country's exports; such estimates would be based partly on statistical data and partly on qualitative information regarding export prospects. Resources provided by the new facility were to be additional to those available from the credit tranches.[30]

In 1966 CFF became a "floating" facility, in the sense that drawings under CFF were no longer to be taken into account in determining the standing of members in the credit tranches. This was a particularly significant liberalization of CFF because it meant that no matter how large a drawing a member might make under CFF (within the limits prescribed) this would not have the effect of forcing the country into upper credit tranche conditionality.

During its early years CFF was of relatively little quantitative importance. Only fifty-seven drawings totaling SDR 1.2 billion were made during the first thirteen years. Use of the facility increased considerably in terms of numbers of Fund members making drawings as well as in absolute size and as a share of total Fund credit following a series of liberalizations of the facility as mentioned earlier. In particular, the maximum amount of outstanding drawings was raised progressively from 25 percent of quota, under the original mandate, to 50 percent of quota in 1966, 75 percent in 1975, and 100 percent in 1979. The 1979 decision also eliminated the additional constraint on drawings within a twelve-month period, which were limited to 25 percent of quota under the 1966 decision and 75 percent under the 1975 decision.[31]

As can be seen from table 1, drawings under CFF reached a peak in absolute terms of SDR 3.74 billion in the financial year ending April 30, 1983. During that year twenty-nine members made use of the facility in amounts ranging from 50 percent to 100 percent of quota. As of April 30, 1983, outstanding purchases amounted to SDR 6.8 billion by no less than sixty-seven members. Thirty-two members had drawings outstanding in excess of 50 percent of their quotas, of which eleven were at 100 percent or more of their quotas. A sharp drop in drawings occurred in 1983–84 when only thirteen members drew SDR 1.18 billion. While some of this decline may have been due to the recovery in import demand in some

Drawings under the Compensatory Financing Facility
(CFF), 1977–84 (billions of SDRs)

Financial Year Ending April 30	Total Drawings Under All Tranches and Facilities	Drawings Under CFF	CFF as Percentage of Total
1977	4.91	1.75	36
1978	2.50	0.32	13
1979	3.72	0.46	12
1980	2.43	0.86	35
1981	4.86	0.78	16
1982	8.04	1.63	20
1983	11.39	3.74	33
1984	11.52	1.18	10

Source: IMF, *Annual Report* (1983 and 1984).

of the industrial countries, commodity markets remained weak and it is likely that a considerable proportion of the decline may have reflected the impact of the deliberate cutback in CFF. It should be noted that although the Executive Board did not take its decision on CFF until September 1983, the Fund management had been applying the new policy for some time before that.

It will be seen from table 1 that while CFF drawings in 1983–84 reached a peak more than twice the level of preceding high points in 1976–77 and 1981–82, the share of these drawings in total credit extended by the Fund was slightly lower than in the two earlier years. Indeed, Louis Goreux, of the IMF staff, has stated that if Fund credit to the United Kingdom is excluded, CFF accounted for as much as 45 percent of total Fund credit extended from January 1976 to March 1980.[32] In relative terms, therefore, CFF had already passed its peak long before the decision of September 1983 and this too appears to reflect long-standing efforts to curb the facility.

The fatal blow to CFF under the decision of September 1983 was that the conditions under which CFF drawings could be made were changed in a fundamental way. Countries drawing the first 50 percent of quota under CFF were not hitherto required to receive a Fund mission because there was no question of negotiating conditions for drawing. On the contrary, as Goreux has pointed out, speed of operations was "a major concern in setting up and administering the compensatory financing facility" and telex was the usual means of communication.[33] After the member had provided the necessary data to establish the existence of a shortfall as defined under the terms of CFF, the IMF staff needed two weeks for analyzing them and preparing a report for submission to the Executive Board. The board in turn would decide on the request about two weeks after receiving the staff report, and if the request was approved, the country could draw within a matter of days. Thus the entire operation could be conducted in about a month.[34]

Moreover, while the first CFF drawing up to 50 percent of quota required hitherto only an indication of willingness on the part of the member country to "co-operate with the Fund in an effort to find, *where required*, appropriate solutions for its balance-of-payments difficulties" (emphasis added), the board now decreed that such readiness to cooperate "implies a willingness to receive Fund missions and to discuss, in good faith, the appropriateness of the member's policies and whether changes in the member's policies are necessary to deal with its balance-of-payments difficulties."[35] If such policies were considered "seriously deficient" or the country's recent record of cooperation were deemed unsatisfactory, the Fund would "expect the member to take action that gives, prior to submission of the request for the purchase, a reasonable assurance that policies corrective of the member's balance-of-payments problem will be adopted."[36]

Thus the fact that a country has established, to the satisfaction of the Fund, that it has experienced a temporary export shortfall (as defined by the Fund) for reasons beyond its control (and therefore for reasons having nothing to do with domestic policies) no longer provides sufficient grounds for a CFF drawing. Under the new ruling the Fund is entitled to send out a mission and to require the country to agree to make changes in domestic policies even before a request for a drawing is submitted to the Executive Board.

This appears to be a new departure of major dimensions in Fund policies. The traditional doctrine of the Fund regarding conditionality has been stated by a member of the Fund staff, Manuel Guitián, as follows: "In any examination of the rationale and concept of conditionality, a key feature of the international adjustment process needs to be underscored, which is that external payments imbalances have to be corrected *whenever they are not transitory or reversible*" (emphasis added).[37]

Moreover, in response to the contention in a study undertaken for the Group of Twenty-Four that the application of the principle of conditionality should take into account the extent to which balance-of-payments difficulties are due to factors beyond the control of the country concerned,[38] the Fund staff has recorded its position in the following terms:

Balance-of-payments problems may be due to a variety of factors that are often distinguished according to whether they are external or internal and to whether they are transient or enduring. While the particular strategies of adjustment may vary depending on whether the payments difficulties are due to developments inside a country's economy or to developments in the rest of the world, the fundamental question of whether adjustment is actually required hinges more on the assessment of the permanent or temporary character of the disturbance. Deficits stemming from adverse transitory (external or internal) factors typically call for temporary resort to financing. Mechanisms have been devised in the Fund and elsewhere to cope with situations of this sort—the Fund's compensatory financing and buffer stock facilities and the European Community's STABEX Fund [scheme for stabilization of export earnings] are examples of such mechanisms. However, if the imbalances (whether of external or internal origin) are due to permanent factors, appropriate measures of adjustment must be taken to remove them.[39]

The above statement indicates clearly that "appropriate measures of adjustment" should be viewed as applicable to cases involving "permanent factors" and not to cases (such as those qualifying for CFF) where deficits are temporary and reversible.

Until now the Fund was at least prepared to shield the weaker member countries against temporary external pressures attributable, for example, to cyclical fluctuations in the demand of industrial countries for imports of primary commodities. From now on the burden of adjustment may be shifted by the Fund entirely to the countries that are the victims of such external pressures. In consideration of being given permission to make a CFF drawing, countries may, it appears, be required, in advance of submission of their requests, to agree to devalue, to take steps to eliminate budget deficits, to restrict credit and to move toward opening up domestic markets by liberalizing imports and doing away with subsidies. Nothing is said in this context of any obligation of the country or countries undergoing the cyclical decline in import demand that is at the root of the problem, to take immediate steps to restore the level of such demand, or to take such other steps as would maintain the level of their external disbursements. Thus a new low is reached in breaching the principle of symmetry.

Drawings in the upper tranche of CFF—that is, the second tranche of 50 percent of quota—have always been subject to the additional and stricter criterion that "the Fund is satisfied that the member has been cooperating with the Fund in an effort to find, where required, appropriate solutions for its balance-of-payments difficulties." Under the new decision this criterion is interpreted as meaning that "in the light of action taken by the member and the balance-of-payments policies being pursued the Fund is satisfied with the member's record of cooperation." The decision continues as follows:

> The existence of a satisfactory balance-of-payments position (apart from the effects of the shortfall) or the existence of and broadly satisfactory performance under an arrangement with the Fund, or the adoption of such an arrangement at the time the request for a CFF purchase is made, will be considered to provide evidence of cooperation. However, the existence or the adoption of an arrangement is not a prerequisite. If a member's current and prospective policies were such as would, in the Fund's view, meet the criteria of the use of resources in the credit tranches, the member would be deemed to have been satisfactorily cooperating with the Fund, even though such use was not contemplated at the time of the CFF request.

Thus an upper credit tranche arrangement with the Fund is not a "prerequisite" for drawing the second 50 percent of quota under CFF, and any member able to satisfy the Fund that its balance-of-payments position is "satisfactory" apart from the effects of the shortfall should be eligible for a second tranche CFF drawing if other CFF conditions are met. The meaning to be ascribed to a "satisfactory" balance-of-payments position is not defined, but clearly the kind of assessment required for this purpose introduces a further element of uncertainty into the determination of eligibility to draw. For one thing, the statistical and qualitative information available at the time the export shortfall occurs are generally insufficient to answer the question how far that shortfall is responsible for the balance-of-payments difficulties being encountered and, therefore, whether the country would be in difficulties apart from the shortfall. Secondly, there are several ways in which a "satisfactory" balance of payments can be defined. For example, would a country that maintains quantitative controls on imports or a multiple currency practice ever be regarded as having a "satisfactory" balance of payments by the IMF? Such questions did not have to be addressed under the CFF policies of the Fund as they existed during the twenty years from 1963 to 1983.

As the IMF staff sees the matter, the new CFF rules are designed to deal with the present crisis situation in which export shortfalls arise almost invariably in conjunction with pressures on the balance of payments resulting from other factors connected with the crisis. It is, therefore, impossible, under current conditions, to separate the effects of general balance-of-payments difficulties from those of export shortfalls.

Perhaps it was the intention of the IMF merely to say that where a country has an upper credit tranche program the rigorous conditionality of that program will apply also to any simultaneous drawing on CFF. If this had been the purpose of the September 1983 decision, the Fund could have said so in simple and straightforward terms. The new decision would still have been a most unfortunate one but it would have been somewhat less destructive of the purpose of CFF in its original form. But the wording of the decision goes much further, implying as it does that the semiautomatic basis on which CFF drawings had hitherto been made has been abolished, regardless of whether the problem is a purely cyclical one or not. Thus, even if the present crisis were overcome, it would not be possible, as matters now stand, to go back to the CFF regime that prevailed before 1983.

A number of prestigious groups have recently advocated the strengthening of CFF, and the further liberalization of its provisions. The Commonwealth Study Group, for example, made a series of important proposals to enhance the contribution of CFF to balance-of-payments financing, so as "to provide adequate liquidity for those that need it most and, more generally, to assist developing countries to stabilize their imports."[40] Alas, at the very moment that these important recommendations were published (July 1983) the patient was already dying, although there were relatively few who were aware at the time of the full gravity of the illness.

The new decision also has the effect of downgrading the IMF still further from the status that was planned for it at Bretton Woods. Fund financing had already been greatly reduced in relative terms through the refusal of leading member countries to allow quotas to rise in line with world trade. And the Fund's Articles of Agreement had been set aside through a series of decisions against the issuance of SDRs, which is essential if the objective of Article XXII is to be achieved, namely to make the SDR "the principal reserve asset in the international monetary system."

A further severe blow has now been struck at the competence and responsibility of the IMF by depriving it of the major part of its low conditional resources. Even before the recent move, there were strong grounds for saying that the balance between low conditional and high conditional resources in the hands of the Fund was tilted too steeply in favor of the latter. Now there is little left of low conditional resources except the (unconditional) reserve tranche and the first credit tranche. This leaves the Fund without the flexibility that is indispensable in dealing with the wide variety of balance-of-payments needs that arise. In the view of its major shareholders the Fund's main role, it seems, is not so much to provide balance-of-payments support as to discipline member countries wishing to draw on Fund resources, regardless of whether the factors prompting such drawings are under their control or reflect cyclical fluctuations in export earnings for which they are in no way responsible. The end of CFF in its original form and concept has to be viewed against that background.

The Question of Cross-Conditionality[*]

SUMMARY AND CONCLUSIONS

All member countries of the Bretton Woods institutions (the International Monetary Fund and the World Bank) have an interest in close cooperation between the two institutions as well as in consistency and complementarity between their programs. Such cooperation has grown steadily, especially in recent years, as the degree of overlap in the operations of the two institutions has increased.[41]

Cooperation between the Bretton Woods institutions is being stepped up still further under the Fund's Structural Adjustment Facility (SAF), since although loans to SAF-eligible countries will continue to be negotiated and administered separately by the IMF and World Bank, they will have to be consistent with a "policy framework" previously agreed upon between the two institutions and the country concerned. There has also been a strengthening of cooperation between the Bank and Fund and other external sources of capital, particularly the regional development banks, the bilateral donors, and the commercial banks. Inevitably, the drawing together of these various agencies and the growing interdependence of their decisionmaking processes have greatly increased the complexity of the negotiating process for potential borrowers, and this consideration alone has caused delay in the approval and disbursement of loans. The costs of such delays to the borrowers are considerable, even where there are no disagreements between lenders and borrowers or among the lenders themselves.

[*]This paper was originally prepared at the request of the Commonwealth Secretariat and published in *World Development* 16, no. 5 (Oxford: Pergamon, 1988): 557–68.

The consequences of delays in the granting of loans by the development finance institutions have been especially severe in cases where disputes over the policies of member countries have been protracted. Damage to a country's economy may result not merely from the holding up of a single project, but from the consequential suspension of preparatory work on new projects, so that the project pipeline becomes depleted. Any subsequent resumption of lending, even after full agreement on policies has been attained, therefore becomes subject to aggravated delay.

While calling for closer cooperation between the Bank and the Fund, the Interim and Development Committees have made it clear that cross-conditionality is to be avoided without, however, defining that term. Although it is difficult for an outsider to obtain all the evidence needed for a thorough evaluation of the issues arising in connection with cross-conditionality, it does seem that there have been cases in which the above-mentioned injunction of the two committees has not been observed. It appears, however, that there have been relatively few, if any, cases in which formal cross-conditionality has occurred in the sense of a veto by one of the Bretton Woods institutions of a loan by the other. Rarely, if ever, does a case of cross-conditionality reach the Executive Board of either institution.

On the other hand, there appear to have been many cases of informal cross-conditionality whereby each of the Bretton Woods institutions has withheld loans to a member country, or has suspended a borrower's access to an existing loan, because the country concerned was in disagreement with the other institution on policies or performance. Ever since the adoption of the Extended Fund Facility (EFF) and multi-year, stand-by arrangements by the IMF, designed to promote structural adjustment, the Fund has relied on the World Bank for the evaluation of investment priorities and other factors affecting the efficiency of the use of resources in member countries. The counterpart of this is that Structural Adjustment Loans (SALS) by the World Bank have been made only to countries having stand-by arrangements with the IMF or to countries whose Article IV consultations with the Fund indicated satisfactory macroeconomic performance.

Periodic disagreements between one or other of the two institutions and some of their member countries, or between the two institutions themselves, should occasion no surprise in view of the fact that strategies for promoting development and balance-of-payments adjustment are far from being the subject of an exact science. People of goodwill and high expertise frequently come to widely different conclusions regarding these matters in the developed countries and there is no reason why similar differences of opinion should not be encountered in relation to developing countries also.

Thus the mere fact that one institution has been critical of policies or performance in a member country should not automatically constrain decisions by the other institution. If it is desired that decisions of the international community in a particular field should invariably be uniform, the corresponding responsibility should be undivided, and located in a single institution. If, on the other hand, there is a need for two or more institutions to operate in closely related, if not identical fields, common sense would suggest that each institution should have its own clearly defined responsibilities and the power to carry out those responsibilities on the basis of its own independent judgment.

It would not be consistent with the Articles of Agreement of either of the Bretton Woods institutions to surrender the power of decision on the use of its resources to any other institution. While close cooperation is to be encouraged, neither institution is entitled to abdicate its responsibility for reaching its own decisions on all aspects of its lending programs and policies—including those aspects that may be the primary responsibility of another institution.

Thus the Bank is entitled to say that, having considered the views presented to it by the Fund on relevant aspects of the policies or performance of a member country and after a full substantive examination of the issues involved, it has concluded that it is in agreement with the Fund's views. But even though the Fund has primary responsibility in certain fields, the Bank would not be fully discharging its own responsibilities under its charter if it simply accepted Fund views as a routine matter without examining them thoroughly in substance. The same considerations apply, mutatis mutandis, to the manner in which the Fund should take Bank views into account in connection with its own programs.

In the latest volumes of the Fund history, the Fund historian has described the disagreements that have arisen from time to time between Bank and Fund staff regarding the impact of stabilization programs on development prospects. Such disagreements should not be ruled out, and the Bank and Fund staffs should not be forced into artificial compromises in cases of disagreement, simply on the grounds of the need for consistency or for closer cooperation. The issues involved are too momentous, too complex, and subject to too much uncertainty to warrant the adoption of such methods.

Even where there is general agreement on the specific policies required for adjustment, differences of opinion can and do arise as to the timing of particular measures, and as to the overall rate of adjustment required. There are no technical answers to the choice between shock treatment and a more gradual approach to adjustment, so long as resources are adequate for either strategy. Such choices are a matter for political judgment for which the Bank and Fund have no special qualifications and no mandate under their charters. If the Bank and Fund differ as to the rate of adjustment appropriate for a particular country, there is no reason to compel them to settle their differences by insisting on uniformity at any price.

THE MEANING OF CROSS-CONDITIONALITY: IS THERE AN ISSUE?

The meaning of the word "conditionality" in the context of the IMF and, more recently, of the World Bank, is well known to those familiar with these two institutions, and there is a large and growing literature on the subject. Sir Joseph Gold has stated, "The word 'conditionality' in the IMF refers to the policies the Fund expects a member to follow in order to be able to use the Fund's general resources."[42] A similar interpretation of the word would presumably apply to policy-based lending by the World Bank.

The word "cross-conditionality," on the other hand, is of more recent vintage and there is no generally accepted definition of it, even though the word has appeared in communiqués of the Interim and Development Committees, as well as of the Group of Twenty-Four.[43] It would appear, however, that there are, conceptually, two main forms of cross-conditionality which might be roughly described as "formal" and "informal." Formal cross-conditionality arises, or might arise:

– if either of the Bretton Woods institutions exercised, or sought to exercise, a veto over a loan under consideration by the other or over a drawing against an existing loan;
– if there were a formal understanding between the two institutions that neither would make a loan to or an arrangement with any member country, or with a particular member country, except with the concurrence of the other institution;[44]
– if there were a formal understanding between the two institutions that neither would allow member countries, or a particular member country, continued access to a previously agreed loan or arrangement except with the concurrence of the other institution;

– if a formal action, notably a declaration of ineligibility by the Fund were, by previous arrangement between the two institutions, to interrupt access to a Bank loan.[45]

Informal cross-conditionality might then be said to arise in circumstances in which although there was no formal arrangement or understanding between the two institutions, the same outcome occurred as in the situations listed above through the unconstrained decision of each institution acting independently.

It would appear that formal cross-conditionality in the sense indicated above has been ruled out by the Bretton Woods institutions. It is agreed, for example, that it would be improper for either institution to exercise, or seek to exercise, a veto over a loan under consideration by the other. In fact, many would say not only that such a veto would be improper but that there has never been an occasion on which such a veto has occurred. In 1985 in the context of discussion of the use of Trust Fund reflows, the Fund's Interim Committee recommended, "Given the emphasis on structural adjustment, it was important that the Fund should work in close collaboration with the World Bank, while avoiding crossconditionality."[46]

The fact remains that cross-conditionality *is* an issue in the Bretton Woods institutions, an issue that has figured prominently in communiqués of the Group of Twenty-Four as shown below. It will be the objective of the following discussion to elucidate the nature of the controversy arising.

THE NATURE OF THE ISSUE

In practice, it is not the possible use of a formal veto that worries the Group of Twenty-Four. Their concern is rather with cases in which, allegedly, one of the Bretton Woods institutions succeeds in preventing or delaying a loan by the other without any formal action being taken, and certainly without any formal veto being cast.

As far as is known few, if any, cases involving explicit cross-conditionality have ever come before either of the Executive Boards. Those who believe that cross-conditionality is nevertheless a real problem contend that loans held up by cross-conditionality are not presented to the respective Executive Boards for consideration or decision until compliance with the requisite cross-conditions has been secured, and that the Executive Boards are not made officially aware of the existence of any cross-conditions.

Thus cross-conditionality does not, it is alleged, manifest itself in any very overt way. Indeed, the perception of those who argue that the question of cross-conditionality simply does not arise is that while the staffs of the Fund and Bank do consult together, each institution takes its own decisions in accordance with its own rules and procedures. No doubt the Fund staff attaches great weight to World Bank staff views on long-term development issues and policies and the Bank staff in turn takes due account of Fund staff views on adjustment problems and policies. But in the last resort each staff makes up its own mind on the basis of all views and evidence available to it, and the conclusions thus reached are reported to the appropriate Executive Board which, in turn, makes its own decisions in accordance with its own judgment.

If one institution influences the other, that, it is felt, is quite normal and legitimate and is, indeed, not inconsistent with the views of the Group of Twenty-Four, since the Group has itself recognized the importance of collaboration between the two institutions in ensuring "consistency and complementarity between their programs."

How then do the undoubted differences in perception regarding cross-conditionality arise, and why is there an issue at all?

THE VIEWS OF THE GROUP OF TWENTY-FOUR

Ministers of the Group held their thirty-first meeting in Washington on April 16, 1985. In paragraph 61 of their communiqué they made the following statement:

> Ministers expressed satisfaction at the decision not to establish any formal relationship between the Bank and the Fund or a joint committee of the two institutions and emphasized that coordination between the World Bank and International Monetary Fund should not become a means for enforcing any type of cross-conditionality but should help place developing countries on the path of growth and development.[47]

Subsequently, on March 27, 1986, it was announced that the Fund's Executive Board had established a new lending facility, known as the Structural Adjustment Facility (SAF), to provide balance-of-payments assistance to low-income countries on concessional terms. The board thereby gave effect to a recommendation made by the Interim Committee in Seoul in October 1985 regarding the use to be made of SDR 2.7 billion in Trust Fund reflows expected to become available during 1985–91. SAF loans were to be provided to eligible members presenting medium-term macroeconomic and structural adjustment programs intended to overcome protracted balance-of-payments problems and foster growth. Sixty countries were eligible for such loans, but China and India had declared that they would not avail themselves of the facility.[48]

An eligible member seeking to use resources of the new facility was required to develop a policy framework, describing the member's medium-term objectives and the main outlines of the policies to be followed in meeting these objectives. The press release on this matter stated:

> This medium-term policy framework will be developed jointly with the staffs of the Fund and the World Bank and will embody the general outlines of a three-year adjustment program including structural measures and delineation in broad terms of the expected path of macro-economic policies. The framework will contain an assessment of the country's financing needs and possible sources of finance to support comprehensive economic programs, including indicative levels of financing from the Structural Adjustment Facility and the World Bank Group.[49]

Even prior to the Executive Board decision establishing SAF, the Group of Twenty-Four was voicing concern regarding the trend of the board's discussion of the facility. The annotations to the agenda of the Group meeting held in Buenos Aires on March 6, 1986, included the observation that "an unacceptably high level of conditionality" was being considered for the use of SAF resources, that was "inconsistent with the spirit of the Trust Fund." The annotations continued as follows:

> On Fund-Bank collaboration, one industrial country proposed that the two institutions should visit the relevant country, agree on a "policy framework" and then jointly produce a paper to be simultaneously discussed and approved by the Executive Boards of the two institutions. While collaboration between the two institutions is necessary, if consistency and complementarity between their programs are to be ensured, developing countries noted that cross-conditionality would clearly emerge in the proposals discussed in the Boards.[50]

Group members accepted the "policy framework" with the greatest reluctance, judging that a refusal to go along with it would lead to unacceptable delay in the creation of SAF. They regarded the imposition of tight conditionality on the relending of Trust Fund reflows as a serious violation of the spirit of Article V, Section 12(f) (ii), of the Articles of Agreement. Under this provision, the resources now being used for

SAF—that is, resources of the IMF Special Disbursement Account obtained from the sale of gold—were to be available for providing "balance of payments assistance . . . on special terms to developing members in difficult circumstances." The special terms referred to in the Article were intended to be particularly favorable to the members concerned, whereas the terms of SAF were to be onerous.

The ministerial communiqué dealt with this matter as follows:

> Ministers deplored that recent developments in the IMF Board have shown that, through suggested changes in the 1980 decision on Trust Fund operations, it is likely that, in using Special Disbursement Account resources, more conditionality would be introduced and cross-conditionality would emerge, especially if a "general policy framework," worked out jointly by the Fund and the Bank, has to be a precondition before programs are approved.[51]

The following points emerge directly and indirectly from the foregoing discussion:

- The Group of Twenty-Four accepts the need for collaboration between the Bretton Woods institutions as a means of ensuring "consistency and complementarity between their programs."
- The Group of Twenty-Four emphasizes, however, that the Fund and Bank are different entities with different functions and responsibilities, and that collaboration should not lead to impairment of these distinct roles. Nor should it lead to complications in relations with member countries, or slow down the decisionmaking process, or introduce elements of inflexibility and cross-conditionality.
- Even prior to the establishment of SAF, it was the belief of the Group that instances of cross-conditionality had occurred and that the interests of the countries concerned had suffered as a result.
- The Group of Twenty-Four believes that while in the past cross-conditionality was only an occasional problem, with the establishment of SAF there is a danger that it may, in effect, be institutionalized.
- Now that the concept of a coordinated "policy-framework" has been adopted in the context of SAF, it is believed that efforts may be made, sooner or later, to apply the same concept to all Fund and Bank programs. In the view of the Group, this would be most undesirable.

THE BURDEN OF CROSS-CONDITIONALITY

In March 1986, at the twenty-third meeting of Central Bank Governors of the American Continent, Dr. Eduardo Lizano, President of the Central Bank of Costa Rica, presented a paper entitled, "La Condicionalidad Cruzada y la Deuda Externa" (Cross-conditionality and External Debt), jointly written by himself and Silvia Charpentier. The paper states that cross-conditionality is of growing importance, and is creating a new obstacle to relations between those seeking and those supplying external resources. It points to five considerable problems facing developing countries as a result of cross-conditionality:

– difficulties arising out of the greatly increased complexity of negotiations with external sources of finance that have strong linkages with one another;
– a major reduction in the freedom of action of borrowing countries in developing their own economic policies (especially the determination of targets and selection of instruments);
– unnecessary constraints on the execution of stabilization and development programs;
– the undermining of government authority resulting from the establishment of direct relations between foreign financial institutions and domestic groups (including political parties and associations of employers);[52]
– the preempting of substantial time and human resources in having to deal with the various problems arising.

Dr. David Ibarra, former Minister of Finance of Mexico, has summed the matter up as follows:

But the World Bank is establishing a new set of conditionality rules. Now, we have conditionality by the IMF, conditionality by the World Bank, and the process goes on. The bilateral agencies are also establishing their own conditionality. So after a while you end up with so many rules of conditionality and cross-conditionality that you give the government no leeway to decide a proper adjustment policy well adapted to their internal needs.[53]

CASES OF CROSS-CONDITIONALITY

Because of the circumstances in which cross-conditionality is believed to occur, and the fact that generally no objective evidence can be provided of its occurrence, it is not possible to document specific cases in a satisfactory manner. For this reason, the cases that are set out below are given in general stylized terms, without indication of the country involved. They are not hypothetical cases—they are actual cases described to the author by responsible senior officials of the countries concerned. It is recognized that in some, perhaps all, cases the observed facts could be explained in terms that do not include cross-conditionality. However, even if there had been no cross-conditionality in any one of the following cases, the fact that officials who are not otherwise ill-disposed toward the Fund or World Bank have the perception that the facts clearly indicate the existence of cross-conditionality is itself sufficient to constitute a problem of explaining Bank/Fund linkages to responsible officials in a more effective manner. It should be borne in mind that all of the following instances occurred long before the establishment of SAF or the creation of a medium-term policy framework.

The seventh case cited indicates that it is possible for cooperation between the Bank and Fund to result in a *more* favorable outcome for the member country. It is the impression of Group of Twenty-Four members that such cases are much less frequent than those in which the opposite occurs, but no evidence can be cited in this regard.

Case One. The country made a successful approach to the IMF for the establishment of a program under the EFF designed to relieve pressure on the balance of payments. This was to be achieved through a program of public investment, especially in the energy and transport sectors. When the program was presented to the Executive Board of the IMF, it was reported by the Fund staff that the World Bank fully endorsed the structural changes envisaged under the program. No difficulty arose in this case because World Bank endorsement of the structural changes in question antedated the EFF negotiations with the Fund, so that those negotiations were not held up in any way. The question raised by this case is what would have happened (a) if World Bank approval had not been given in due time, or (b) if the World Bank had withheld its approval.

Case Two. A proposal for an industrial sector loan for a certain country reached the loan committee of the World Bank with the full support of the responsible regional department of the Bank. The loan was, however, blocked on the grounds that the Fund was critical of the country's exchange rate policy, and of the accompanying trade restrictions. The loan proposal was later resubmitted to the loan committee, and turned down a second time.

Case Three. Drawings on an EFF loan by a certain country were suspended by the IMF because of failure to comply with the associated performance requirements. This led to the suspension by the World Bank of a second drawing on a SAL, and the holding up of a rescheduling operation by the Paris Club.

Case Four. A World Bank loan for the development of agriculture in a certain country was held up because the country had had difficulty in reaching agreement with the Fund on its exchange rate policy. As seen by the government of the country concerned, the Fund had exercised a de facto veto on the World Bank loan.

Case Five. A World Bank loan to finance emergency imports for a certain country to replenish its severely depleted inventories of certain essential items was held up on account of failure to reach agreement with the Fund on a program of adjustment.

Case Six. The staff of the World Bank had reached the conclusion that a certain country had adopted the macroeconomic policies regarded by the Bank as being sufficient to justify a structural adjustment loan. The Fund, however, was not satisfied, and called for more stringent policies, and the proposed World Bank loan was therefore held up. Eventually the problem was resolved and the World Bank loan was approved.

Case Seven. In this case, the World Bank staff was able to persuade the Fund staff that the conditions contemplated in connection with a prospective stand-by arrangement were unnecessarily severe, and the Fund staff agreed to ease the conditions accordingly.

The point has been made that there is a "selection bias" in the reporting of cases of cross-conditionality. In other words, the cases that come to light are those in which the country concerned believes that it has a grievance. This belief may or may not be justified, but it is argued that in any event the reporting of such incidents leaves out of account the much larger number of unreported cases in which countries feel either that their treatment was reasonable, or even that they gained from the cooperative efforts of the Bank and Fund, as in case seven.

It is impossible for an outsider to form a view on the validity of the above comment, since this would call for a thorough examination of at least a random sample of relevant case histories. In any event, the mandate of the present paper relates to the problem of cross-conditionality as such, regardless of the frequency with which that problem is encountered. It should also be borne in mind that even in cases where the cooperation of external capital-supplying agencies does not lead to a deliberate delay or interruption of assistance programs, the greatly increased complexity of the negotiations involved, as pointed out by Ibarra and Lizano, is itself a source of difficulty and delay.

THE RATIONALE OF BANK/FUND COOPERATION

Cooperation with other international organizations is provided for in Article X of the Fund's Articles of Agreement and in Article V, Section 8(a), of the World Bank's Articles. Cooperation is envisaged both with "any general international organization" and with "public international organizations having specialized responsibilities in related fields." Since the above provisions are applicable equally to organizations that do not as well as to those that do have "specialized responsibilities in related fields" they could hardly be regarded as authority for Bank/Fund cross-conditionality of any kind, formal or informal.

In the case of the World Bank, there is an additional provision that has no counterpart in the IMF Articles. Paragraph 8(b) of the World Bank Articles provides that "In making decisions on applications for loans or guarantees relating to matters directly within the competence of any international organization of the types specified in the preceding paragraph and participated in primarily by members of the Bank, the Bank shall give consideration to the views and recommendations of such organization." Two points may be noted here. First, while the World Bank is clearly required to "give consideration" to the views and recommendations of the IMF, there is no comparable obligation for the IMF under its Articles. Second, the Bank is not required, under Article V. 8(b), to do more than "give consideration" to the views and recommendations of the Fund. The Bank is certainly not bound by anything that the Fund may say or do. More generally, responsible legal opinion is that it would not be consistent with the Articles of Agreement of either of the Bretton Woods institutions to surrender the power of decision on the use of its resources to any other institution.

It is useful to distinguish between two stages in the evolution of Bank/ Fund cooperation. The dividing line between the two stages is set by the introduction of EFF by the Fund in 1974. Prior to this date the functional differences between the Bank and Fund were reasonably clear. The Fund was concerned with assisting its members in dealing with relatively short-term balance-of-payments problems, including the adoption of the macroeconomic policies required for this purpose, particularly policies with respect to exchange rates and the management of demand.[54] The Bank was concerned with the promotion of specific investment projects for development, with a much longer time horizon, and based mainly on micro-considerations. The principal exception to this division of labor was the program lending of the Bank, which was tantamount to balance-of-payments support.[55] But this was concentrated in a very few member countries.

In December 1966 the Bank and Fund agreed to define their respective areas of competence in dual memoranda that contained the following paragraphs:

4. As between the two institutions, the Bank is recognized as having primary responsibility for the composition and appropriateness of development programs and project evaluation, including development priorities. On those matters, the Fund, and particularly the field missions of the Fund, should inform themselves of the established views and positions of the Bank and adopt those views as a working basis for their own work. This does not preclude discussions between the Bank and the Fund as to those matters, but it does mean that the Fund (and Fund missions) will not engage in a critical review of those matters with member countries unless it is done with the prior consent of the Bank.

5. As between the two institutions, the Fund is recognized as having primary responsibility for exchange rates and restrictive systems, for adjustment of temporary balance of payments disequilibria and for evaluating and assisting members to work out stabilization programs as a sound basis for economic advance. On these matters, the Bank, and particularly the field missions of the Bank, should inform themselves of the established views and positions of the Fund and adopt those views as a working basis for their own work. This does not preclude discussion between the Bank and the Fund as to those matters but it does mean that the Bank (and Bank missions) will not engage in a critical review of those matters with member countries unless it is done with the prior consent of the Fund.[56]

A case could be made that the concordat of December 1966 was designed to prevent untoward effects of the independence of the two institutions rather than to promote cooperation between them. In fact, its chief purpose was to avoid the conflicting advice to member countries that could result from the independent and uncoordinated relationships between the two institutions and their member countries. By agreeing on a strict division of labor, the Bank and Fund left themselves free to continue on their separate courses without the need for close or tight coordination between them.

Traditionally, in fact, the two institutions have, by common consent, maintained a certain distance from one another.[57] Annual meetings of the two Boards of Governors are held jointly, but this is mainly for the convenience of the Governors and the meetings are not of great importance in the decisionmaking processes of the two institutions. There are, by contrast, no joint meetings of the Executive Directors of the two institutions, but an official of one institution is permitted to attend meetings of the Executive Board of the other institution when certain matters of common interest are on the agenda. Separate staffs are maintained, and only rarely have joint studies been prepared. Moreover, despite the above-mentioned provision of the Articles of the two institutions for cooperation with one another, relations, as pointed out by Sir Joseph Gold, "have not always been close, so that at times in the past the word independence was more apt than collaboration to describe the relationship."[58]

In these circumstances, the fact that under the concordat the Bank recognized the primary responsibility of the Fund in regard to exchange rate questions and that the Fund deferred to the Bank on the composition and appropriateness of development programs did not imply cross-conditionality. In fact, each institution specifically reserved the right to reach its own views on the entire range of issues with which it had to deal and to discuss them with the other institution whenever the subject matter so required. In practice there was usually considerable coherence of views, but also many cases of disagreement, as discussed further below. From time to time one or other institution would decide to go ahead with a loan to a member country, even though that country was for the time being unable to draw on the other institution because of policy disagreement, often on some quite major matter.

THE PROBLEM OF OVERLAPPING ROLES

Since 1974 the area of overlap between the two Bretton Woods institutions has progressively increased, first as a result of the Fund's introduction of EFF and subsequently owing to the Bank's entry into the field of policy-based lending with the SAL program. Further extension of the overlap is expected as a result of the SAF program recently adopted by the Fund. The Bank has been required, in connection with its responsibility for SALS, to expand its capability for the assessment of the macroeconomic policies of member countries in parallel with the Fund, while the Fund has recently established a Development Finance Division, despite repeated statements over the past twenty years by members holding a majority of the voting power that the Fund is not a development finance institution.

As recently as June 1985, deputies to the ministers and governors of the Group of Ten took the position that although they expected the Bank to engage in a variety of activities, including the support of medium-term structural adjustment, "primary emphasis must remain on project lending." Similarly, the Group of Ten has repeatedly argued that the Fund should not deviate from its main role of balance-of-payments support, and should not, in particular, become involved in the kind of programs that belong more properly in the realm of development finance. These lines of demarcation between Bank and Fund responsibilities have, however, become blurred as each institution has become progressively more involved in areas that had hitherto been dealt with almost exclusively by the other.

There is no doubt that the introduction of the EFF and SAL programs reflected genuine and important needs, particularly the need to assist countries in dealing with problems of structural adjustment in the longer term. And although the conditionality of SAF is a matter of controversy, the plight of low-income countries had rendered it urgent to arrange for effective use of the Trust Fund reflows.

This is not the place to examine the question whether the manner in which Bank and Fund activities were expanded to accommodate requirements for structural adjustment in the longer term and for special assistance to low-income countries was the most efficient that could have been devised. The fact is, however, that the expansion of activities took forms that greatly complicated the division of labor between the two institutions that had worked reasonably well during the 1950s and 1960s. And now that these complications exist, the attempt is being made to overcome the resulting difficulties through closer cooperation than had been considered necessary prior to 1974.

It is instructive to recall the reasons advanced by the American Bankers Association (ABA) in 1945 for opposing the establishment of a separate Bank and Fund. In addition to arguing that some stabilization programs would call for long-term loans,[59] the ABA pointed to "the prospect of divided authority and the likelihood of jurisdictional conflicts between two such institutions." The ABA went on to suggest:

> The Congress might well consider the potential confusion and extra burden upon the public of the activities of two institutions with pos-

sibly overlapping powers. Washington's wartime experience with multiple government agencies has shown us that where two agencies are created to work in the same general field the result is a tangle of red tape, increased expense, lost time, duplication of reports and decreased efficiency. . . . If the Congress should decide to create only a single institution, the Bank might by minor changes in its charter, as suggested later in this report, carry on the desirable functions of the Fund.[60]

If there is a need for two institutions to operate in closely related, if not identical, fields, common sense would suggest that each institution should have its own clearly defined responsibilities and the power to carry out those responsibilities on the basis of its own independent judgment. It would be very strange to give two institutions overlapping functions and then insist that they must always agree on everything before either of them did anything. This would simply be a recipe for the tangle of red tape, increased expense, lost time, and decreased efficiency about which the ABA expressed concern in 1945. If it is desired that decisions of the international community should invariably be uniform in a particular field, the corresponding responsibility in that field should be undivided, and located in a single institution. Divided responsibility is not compatible with uniformity in the decisionmaking process.

The Fund's historian, Margaret de Vries, has described some of the differences of opinion that have arisen from time to time between the staffs of the Fund and the Bank in the following terms:

Admittedly, cooperation between the two institutions did not always proceed smoothly. Disagreements among economists about the effectiveness of alternative economic policies were unavoidable and took place even among Fund staff. Differences of view continued on the emphasis to be given to the Fund's primary objectives for a member—achievement of internal financial stability and a stronger external payments position in the relatively short term, usually through tighter monetary and credit policies—and the World Bank's primary goals—achievement of economic growth over a longer period by fostering investment and larger productive capacity. At times, these points of view came into conflict, especially in instances where the Fund's conditionality involved curtailment of current consumption and investment. Fund staff saw such adjustment as the essential foundation for growth and development, but they were sometimes seen by World Bank staff as countering the Bank's development aims. These conflicts became sharper as the World Bank's management and staff oriented themselves increasingly to satisfying the basic needs of poverty-stricken populations, to increasing current employment, and to redistributing domestic income.[61]

UNIFORMITY OR DIVERSITY?

The above considerations lead to the question whether the Bretton Woods institutions should seek to promote uniformity of views between them so as to avoid the kind of disagreements noted by the Fund history. In particular, should the kind of "policy framework" now envisaged for countries drawing on SAF be regarded as a means of enforcing a common approach to each country by the two institutions?

It should be borne in mind that strategies for promoting development and balance-of-payments equilibrium are not the subject of an exact science. It is simply not the case that solutions to the difficult political, social, and economic problems involved can be laid out in the manner of a Euclidean theorem, to which all persons of goodwill can subscribe once they have worked through the reasoning involved.

The acceleration of development and the correction of balance-of-payments disequilibria involve complex political judgments on which the views of reasonable persons can differ widely. The questions at issue between the Bank and Fund recorded by Margaret de Vries on such matters as the role of income distribution in adjustment programs do not lend themselves to clear-cut yes or no answers based on a generally accepted analytical framework. It would be counterproductive to insist on uniquely defined solutions in these areas, or to suppress disagreement even within each of the two institutions, let alone between them. There is no virtue in uniformity for its own sake—institutions can be uniformly wrong as well as uniformly right.

Apart from political considerations, it cannot be said even at the technical economic level that there is a generally accepted way of dealing with each and every problem. Even the analysis of basic factual situations can be the subject of honest differences of opinion between experts that cannot be resolved with complete certainty because the underlying statistical information has inherent shortcomings. As for the economic projections on which decisions have generally to be based, one has only to examine statistical series projected in earlier periods with the actuals for the same periods—even for the most statistically advanced countries—to see how unreliable the data often are for the purposes of policy analysis and prescription. A noteworthy example is the universal failure of analysts, national and international, to foresee the length of the recession in major industrial countries in the early 1980s, and even the direction of change in output in some quarters. In such circumstances, a purely bureaucratic harmonization of data and views between two or more institutions would serve no useful purpose and could be harmful.

Even where there is general agreement on the specific policies required for adjustment, differences of opinion can and do arise as to the timing of particular measures, and as to the overall rate of adjustment required. There are no technical answers to the choice between shock treatment and a more gradual approach to adjustment, so long as resources are adequate for either strategy. Such choices are a matter for political judgment for which the Bank and Fund have no special qualifications and no mandate under their charters. If the Bank and Fund differ as to the rate of adjustment appropriate for a particular country, there is no reason to compel them to settle their differences by insisting on uniformity at any price.

There is also no reason to make any change in the arrangements whereby the project financing of the World Bank and the balance-of-payments financing of the IMF are determined on the basis of independent criteria and methodologies that can at times be favorable to the would-be borrower in the one case and unfavorable in the other. Moreover, the fact that the exchange rate, for example, may be critical for the long-run viability of a particular investment project does not mean that such projects should be held up by the World Bank until agreement is reached with the Fund on the current exchange rate. Some general understanding regarding exchange rate policy over the long run may be reasonable in some cases. But where a project will not begin operating until after several years of construction and other preparatory activities, as is often the case with World Bank projects, it does not seem reasonable to insist on a particular rate for the current year as a pre-condition for that project.

Even in the overlapping areas of policy-based lending, including sector lending as well as SALS, identity of views of the two institutions may be sought but should not be insisted upon as indispensable. Where one institution, after careful consideration of the views of the other, comes to the conclusion that it should take either a more favorable or less favorable position on a member country's performance, and hence on the attitude it should take to an additional policy-based loan, the member country should be allowed to benefit from the views of the more favorably inclined institution.

Similarly, the policy framework established for SAF drawings by eligible countries should not become a means for imposing delay or for suppressing interinstitutional differences. There appears to be considerable danger of such delay since it is envisaged, as noted earlier, that the Bank and Fund would enter into separate negotiations for drawings by member countries only after the preparation by Bank and Fund missions, working with country officials, of a "medium-term policy framework" for each country. Moreover, each country's "policy framework" would have to be submitted to the Executive Board of the Fund for approval, in the hope that similar Bank approval would be timed in such a way as not to hinder Fund programs under SAF, or the disbursement of SAF resources. There is obviously much potential for delay in so complex and cumbersome a procedure. The World Bank already has great difficulty in raising the volume of its lending, despite the urgent need for such expansion, because of the complexity of the loan conditions that it lays down.

THE DOMINO EFFECT

Mention was made earlier of the fact that there are growing links between the various sources of external capital. The lending of the Bank and Fund are linked not only to one another but also, increasingly, to that of the regional development banks, the bilateral donors, the commercial banks, and the loan rescheduling activities of Paris Club members. Thus a breakdown in arrangements between a member country and one of the above agencies—in particular the IMF or World Bank—can have a domino effect on relations with all the other agencies. Whether or not such linkage is appropriate, it certainly appears necessary to ensure that only a really major breakdown in any one channel or relationship should be allowed to trigger a cessation of disbursements through other channels (or the holding up of a Paris Club rescheduling). It is arguable that if the injunctions of the Interim and Development Committees regarding cross-conditionality were implemented fully, no such domino effect would be allowed at all. Each institution would have to go through its own decisionmaking process on the basis of an independent and objective evaluation of the facts on their merits.

THE REGIONAL DEVELOPMENT BANKS

According to Dr. Eduardo Lizano, the Inter-American Development Bank has not yet participated in cross-conditionality, although as he puts it, "the forces and pressures for changing this situation are well known." Problems of cross-conditionality are likely to be even more difficult for the regional development banks than for the World Bank and IMF, because the overlapping of their responsibilities with those of the World Bank is much greater than the corresponding functional overlap between the Bretton Woods institutions themselves. There have already been cases in which regional development banks have been accused of undercutting the World Bank in certain countries by maintaining lending programs at times when the World Bank was seeking changes in the policies of the governments concerned as a condition for further lending. Additional pressures for uniformity might well lead to a considerable reduction in the freedom of action of the regional development banks, which might tend to become, in effect, regional arms of the World Bank. On the other hand, the same considerations, referred to above, that indicate the desirability of maintaining the independent roles and functions of the Bank and Fund point to the need for ensuring corresponding independence for the regional development banks, subject only to a requirement for the fullest possible consultation and cooperation with other agencies operating in the same fields, particularly the World Bank.

9

The International Monetary System and Development

The Future of the International Monetary System[*]

Precarious as the present state of the international monetary system may be (or nonsystem, as some would describe it) it is as well to keep in mind the fact that there are even greater economic perils facing the international community. These are due to the conflicts and tensions between the major powers on questions of macro-management of the world economy, the large current trade imbalances and the protectionism to which they give rise, and above all the failure of the international community to develop a rational long-run strategy for dealing with the world debt crisis, as a result of which much of the Third World has been in a state of persistent economic depression for most of the present decade and no end of the problem is in sight. We cannot enter into these matters because our agenda concerns the system, not the behavior of the members of the system. But one has to be careful not to blame the system for the policy errors of its members. No doubt the system should be designed in such a way as to make it easier for members to follow harmonious policies aiming at full employment, but no system can overcome a fear of the consequences of full employment.

It is the fear of full employment, or of high levels of employment, that is at the root of many of the current problems of the world economy. Propositions of doubtful validity relating rates of inflation to levels of employment are invoked to justify policies that discourage growth and development in the industrial countries and that create a world economic environment in which it is impossible for the great majority of developing countries to adjust to their present problems under conditions of adequate growth. It is unlikely that the problems of the international monetary system can be solved except in the context of an expanding

*Originally published, in an earlier version, in Omar F. Hamouda, Robin Rowley, Bernard M. Wolf, ed., *The Future of the International Monetary System* (Aldershot, England: Edward Elgar, 1989).

world economy that would create sufficient economic room to accommodate the adjustments that are facing industrial and developing countries
alike without imposing intolerable burdens on any of them.

Any inquiry into the future of the international monetary system has
to start with some set of assumptions about the kind of world in which
it will be expected to function. The Bretton Woods system was based
on the assumption that various forms of malfunctioning of the world
economy can be corrected by governments if they take the right kinds of
steps. There was a considerable variety of opinion as to what those steps
should consist of, but there was a general presumption that solutions
were in the hands of governments.

This general presumption has come under fire in the 1970s and 1980s
and the view has gained ground that it is the market that knows best,
not the governments, and that the best thing governments can do is to
allow themselves to be guided by the market and to create conditions
under which the market will be able to operate with as little interference as possible. Side by side with deregulation of the private sector,
as many activities of the public sector as possible should, on this view,
be turned over to private enterprise. These policies appear to command
wide public support in most of the industrial countries.

THE EXCHANGE RATE SYSTEM

But the international monetary system has provided little if any comfort for those espousing these views. It is generally agreed that floating
exchange rates have not brought with them the advantages that were
expected. According to the IMF the short-term (monthly or quarterly)
variability of nominal exchange rates for the seven major currencies was
about six times greater under floating rates than during the last decade
of adjustable par values.[1] Exchange speculation has been destabilizing,
not stabilizing as had been predicted. Even more serious is the fact
that exchange rate misalignment has also been at least as great if not
greater than during the Bretton Woods period. For example, in the second quarter of 1985 the real effective exchange rate of the U.S. dollar
was over 50 percent above the level implied by purchasing power parity.[2]
As the Group of Twenty-Four has pointed out, much of the medium-
term movement in real exchange rates reflects not the changing pattern
of competitiveness but rather inconsistencies in the fiscal and monetary
policies pursued by the major industrial countries.[3]

Even those most staunchly opposed to government interference with
the market place have found themselves compelled to advocate such

interference to correct what they regard as market errors or imperfections. Thus U.S. Treasury Secretary James Baker told the IMF on September 30, 1987, "We have agreed that we should be concerned about the predictability and stability of exchange rates"; and statements by several ministers of the Group of Ten, including Secretary Baker, to the effect that the decline of the dollar had gone far enough implied agreement that in the absence of such statements and the tacit threat of coordinated exchange intervention by central banks, the markets would be likely to force the dollar down below long-run equilibrium levels.

As a result of the failures of the floating exchange rate system a good deal of attention has been given to the possibility of setting up a target zone system that would seek to avoid the destabilizing uncertainties of floating rates without reintroducing the rigidities of a par value system. The Group of Twenty-Four has given tentative support to this proposal, urging that it be carefully studied. The proposal also has support within the Group of Ten, but the majority of Group of Ten members oppose it on several grounds, including the difficulties likely to be experienced in achieving consensus on the determination of the zones, and the danger of focusing attention on exchange rates rather than on the root cause of misalignment—namely the divergence of macroeconomic policies.

There is a good deal of substance in the latter point—perhaps more than the Group of Ten majority itself would allow. The issue is not simply the choice between fixed and floating rate systems or between these two systems and some hybrid that tries to combine the perceived virtues of both. The issue is whether the heavy emphasis placed by the international community and the IMF on the importance of adjustment through exchange rate changes is justified by the experience gained. Already in 1977 Professor Kaldor had reached the conclusion that "Unless the next few years bring some large and dramatic changes, the experiment of securing a more balanced relationship in the trade between industrial countries through exchange rate variations must be adjudged a failure."[4] He based this conclusion partly on the fact that, despite a 40 percent reduction in the effective exchange rate of sterling since 1972, imports had claimed a growing share of Britain's domestic absorption of manufactures while Britain's share in world exports of manufactures had continued to decline. Similarly a 31 percent gain in the cost competitiveness of the United States over a similar period had failed to stem the growth of import penetration or the decline of the U.S. share in world export markets for nonmilitary goods. Kaldor, it should be recalled, spoke as one who had repeatedly and forcefully advocated the devaluation of sterling ever since 1957, both as a private citizen and as a senior adviser to the U.K. Treasury.

More recent experience strongly confirms Kaldor's conclusion. The exchange rate of the U.S. dollar has declined more than 50 percent from its peak against the mark and the yen and yet the balances of payments of the Federal Republic of Germany, Japan, and the United States have been remarkably sluggish in their response. Not only are the relevant elasticities inherently low, and the time lags inherently lengthy, but the two surplus countries have, by various means, been able to slow down shifts in trade balances, for example by accepting reductions in export profit margins. At the same time it is reported that many U.S. exporters are preferring to see their profit margins raised rather than undertake the additional effort of expanding the volume of sales at more competitive prices.

Many experts are of the opinion that the decline of the dollar did not have the results expected of it because of the overriding influence of the U.S. budget deficit on the trade deficit. This belief relies on the accounting identity whereby gross private savings are equal to the sum of gross private investment, export surplus, and budget deficit. The conclusion is drawn that at any given level of private investment and private savings there is a necessary relationship between the external balance and the budget deficit.

First, however, it may be noted that Kaldor had reached his conclusion about the ineffectiveness of exchange rate changes long before the period of U.S. budget deficits and trade deficits from 1983 onward. Secondly, a mere accounting identity cannot reveal the nature of the complex interplay between the determinants of gross private savings or the direction of causality. Nor can private savings and private investment be assumed to be invariant with respect to the budget deficit and trade deficit. Indeed, at less than full employment the level of private savings is likely to be passive, responding to the movements in income generated by aggregate demand. Moreover, the larger the economy and the smaller the ratio of exports and imports to national income the less likely it is that one will find a strong relationship between the external balance and the macroeconomy. In the case of the United States, of the forty-three years from 1946 to 1988, twenty-nine were years in which there were budget deficits according to the national income definition. Only in six of these twenty-nine years—from 1983 to 1988—were budget deficits accompanied by external deficits on goods and services. Finally, the secular loss of market share both at home and abroad by U.S. manufacturing industry over a period of decades is not simply a question of price but results from long-run structural factors. It is not plausible to attribute all this to the budget deficit.

My conclusion is that the elimination of the U.S. budget deficit is neither a necessary nor a sufficient condition for the correction of the deficit in the U.S. balance of payments. It is, of course, possible that a reduction in the U.S. budget deficit, by depressing employment and income, would have led to a sufficient reduction in U.S. imports to improve the external balance. But even this is quite uncertain because of the impact of a fall in U.S. imports on the world level of activity and hence on the world demand for U.S. exports. It is, moreover, supposed to be one of the advantages of the floating rate system that it would increase the degree of freedom of major countries to follow domestic macro-policies of their own choosing. If countries cannot protect themselves against rising unemployment even through drastic depreciation of their currencies, what is the point of exchange rate flexibility?

We therefore seem to be at the opposite pole from that at which Keynes found himself. For Keynes it was essential to ensure that the United Kingdom would be free to devalue under the Bretton Woods system because that was the only way in which, as he thought, the United Kingdom could be sure of maintaining full employment in the event of a U.S. recession. Now, however, we see that even the United States cannot assure itself the level of employment that it wants by varying the exchange rate of the dollar, and the same consideration applies a fortiori to smaller countries.

The fact is that in the 1970s and 1980s alike even drastic changes in the exchange rates of the major industrial countries have not affected their balances of payments as quickly or as decisively as expected. The countries that are in surplus today are the same countries that were in surplus in the 1970s and, indeed, in the 1960s.

Thus the effectiveness of market forces and of the price mechanism in changing the current account balance at given levels of income has been greatly overestimated, with the result that too much has been expected of the exchange rate system. Owing to the inefficiency of markets, the range of exchange rates compatible with any given current account balance in the short and medium term appears to be quite wide, so that the actual level of the rate tends to be determined by factors unrelated to long run equilibrium. Indeed, since the system is continually in flux, the long-run equilibrium itself presents a moving and elusive target.

Alexandre Lamfalussy raises the question whether the downturn of the dollar in 1985 occurred because the market finally realized that the current account imbalances were becoming unsustainable or because the authorities intervened to help bring it about.[5] His answer is that we shall never know, though it is arguable, he says, that without intervention the decline would have been delayed. If he is right on the latter point, as seems likely, market forces were much weaker and concerted intervention much more effective in changing the trend of exchange rates than was generally anticipated. And if purchasing power parity is any guide (which, however, seems less and less plausible) the dollar's decline has gone much too far because on that basis the dollar should, according to McKinnon, be worth about 200 yen instead of the current 125 to 135.[6]

It also seems to follow from Lamfalussy's point that so long as the major governments are in broad agreement on the level and pattern of exchange rates they have no reason to fear being overwhelmed by disruptive capital movements. The mere fact that intercountry capital movements are far larger than the flows across the exchanges resulting from current transactions does not necessarily mean that the former will always determine the direction of exchange rate changes. The market does not, in general, have at its disposal information that would provide a firm anchor for medium-term or long-term exchange rate expectations, so that the direction of the market at any particular time depends on predominantly short-term and speculative influences that could readily be overcome by evidence of strongly concerted interventions by the major industrial country authorities.

Capital controls, could, of course, be employed to reinforce any chosen configuration of exchange rates. It is noteworthy that for all the globalization of capital markets that has taken place, it is recognized that the viability of the European Monetary System (EMS) has depended significantly on the capital controls maintained by the weaker members of the system.[7] Apart from direct capital controls, it is also possible to regulate capital flows by various tax devices. A tax on international financial transactions as proposed by Tobin[8] would, as pointed out by Keynes in connection with a similar proposal at the domestic level, mitigate "the predominance of speculation over enterprise."[9]

The foregoing considerations, particularly the stickiness of current account balances in the face of exchange rate changes, imply that a return to an adjustable peg system is feasible so long as the macroeconomic policies of the major countries are not too far out of line with one another. On the other hand, if there are major divergences in the policies of these countries, no other system, whether based on target zones, on objective indicators for macroeconomic policies, or on strengthened surveillance within the existing system would constitute any significant improvement over the present exchange rate arrangements.

One crucial shortcoming of the latter approaches is that they involve major uncertainty as to the degree of commitment of governments to more stable exchange rates. Particularly in the case of the soft version of the target zone proposal, the lack of firm official commitments to prevent exchange rates from moving beyond the zonal limits would be a clear incentive to exchange markets to test the limits repeatedly in the expectation that sooner or later the governments would give way. And since the markets have little or no basis on which to determine medium-term or long-term trends in exchange rates, the problems of volatility and misalignment would persist. A more stable exchange rate system probably cannot be achieved without a clear and widely publicized commitment by the major industrial countries to a particular pattern of exchange rates and to the measures of concerted intervention required to defend that pattern.

As noted earlier, there is no longer any dispute about the need for more stable exchange rates. The importance of reducing or eliminating the enormous risks to long-term investment that result from steep unforeseen changes in exchange rates is in itself a sufficient reason for giving high priority to greater stability. And since there is probably not much to choose between a target zone system and an adjustable peg from the standpoint of the degree of policy harmonization required for the success of each, it may be worth going the extra distance toward the adjustable peg instead of selecting a halfway house that may turn out to be neither the one thing nor the other.[10]

TOWARD A WORLD CENTRAL BANK?

It is sometimes suggested that the establishment of a world central bank would go a long way toward providing remedies for the ills of the international monetary system. While it is recognized that this would take many years to accomplish, the setting of the objective together with step-by-step approaches toward its realization are viewed as a helpful direction in which to proceed.

The basic difficulty, however, is that just as a national central bank is an instrument of a politically unified national government so also would a world central bank depend on a high degree of international political unification—that is to say on some kind of world central government. The monetary policies of a world central bank could never be relied upon to affect all countries equally, and acceptance of such policies by those countries experiencing less favorable consequences than others would depend on a degree of international solidarity that is not to be found in a world of separate sovereign states.

Thus the view that the establishment of a world central bank would make for a better international monetary system solves the problem by assuming it away. The problem is to find a solution, not for a politically unified world but for a world of independent sovereign states having diverse and often conflicting interests and objectives.

If the IMF had any aspirations toward becoming a world central bank in due course, they must have received a rude shock at the time of the Jamaica Agreement in 1976. The IMF historian has described this development as follows: "Jamaica signaled a turning point in the Fund's history in yet another way. The Fund's regulatory functions and its role as custodian of international monetary arrangements were de-emphasized. Increased attention was to be devoted to the role of the Fund as a provider of financial assistance, especially to its developing members." [11]

In proposing a realistic approach to the possible evolution of the IMF toward a world central bank, Richard Cooper was certainly well aware of the de facto curtailing of Fund responsibilities in the Jamaica Agreement.[12] Taking a time horizon of twenty years he postulated a world of sovereign states with autonomous national monetary policies and national currencies floating against one another, but a world with an increased perception of economic interdependence and the need for coordination of various aspects of economic policy. This perception would lead to "heavy management of exchange rates and acceptance of the implied restraints on the exercise of full monetary autonomy."

Cooper's key behavioral assumption was that world reserves can influence world economic activity, at least for a time. A more generous level of world reserves would, he suggested, result in less restrictive economic policy by member countries, and vice versa.

He proceeded to trace the possible evolution of the IMF toward the standing of a world central bank as a lender of last resort, as a source of international liquidity, as a contributor to global economic stabilization and to the management of exchange rates, and as the provider of an "intermediating arrangement for making key economic decisions" through a strengthened Interim Committee.

These were quite modest objectives when they were first suggested by Cooper in 1983, but the trend of the present decade has, for the most part, been in a quite different direction. The major shareholders of the IMF, so far from encouraging evolution along the above lines, have continued the trend begun in the Jamaica Agreement by cutting back even the existing functions of the IMF still further.

As a realist, Richard Cooper recognized that any prohibition on increments to foreign currency reserves was "highly improbable" but he did count on the IMF to contribute to the growth of international reserves, particularly *net* reserves. The Group of Ten, however, now questions the need for SDRS on the grounds that any creditworthy country can borrow whatever reserves it needs and—by implication—that any country that is not creditworthy had better put its house in order so as to allow it to join the ranks of those able to borrow reserves when necessary.

Similarly, in regard to stabilizing the world economy, Cooper saw a possibility that the IMF could adjust the volume of SDR creation and the conditionality required of borrowers in a countercyclical manner and enlarge the CFF "with little or no conditionality" so as to be able to cope with the effects of severe recessions, if necessary by lending SDRS through the facility. Here again the trend of Fund practice has been exactly the opposite. No SDRS have been issued since 1981, access to Fund resources has been reduced, and the conditionality of Fund lending has been progressively tightened without regard to prevailing world economic conditions. Worst of all, the whole character of CFF has been so altered that it no longer lends itself to use as a countercyclical instrument: CFF is now little more, in effect, than a fifth credit tranche carrying upper credit tranche conditionality.[13]

Thus most of the proposals for a gradual evolution of IMF responsibilities that seemed modest and realistic when Professor Cooper put them forward in 1983 now appear unrealistically radical in the context of 1988. It would take major reversals of the policies of such countries as the Federal Republic of Germany, Japan, and the United States to put the IMF back into a position from which advances along the lines of Cooper's ideas could be contemplated.

It may be useful to examine the background of these matters in greater depth. The fact that the IMF has been converted into an agency that deals mainly with the balance-of-payments problems of developing countries is well known. What is, perhaps, less clearly recognized is the progressive shift in the direction of Fund activities even within this field, so as to limit IMF assistance as much as possible to high conditionality programs, to the detriment of other programs that ought to have been expanded rather than contracted. Moreover, a major step toward the collective management of international liquidity has been sharply reversed.

THE ROLE OF THE SDR

As mentioned above, the major Group of Ten countries see no future for the SDR, but it should be noted that the group is sharply divided on this subject. The majority of the members of the Group of Ten recognize that severe strains in liquidity conditions have built up in the system—strains that are reflected in the decline of reserves in relation to imports and foreign debt, the lopsided distribution of reserves, and the rise of barter trade.[14]

The major industrial countries, however, take the position that international liquidity has come to embrace not only monetary authorities' actual holdings of reserve assets, but also credit arrangements that permit the acquisition of reserves from private and official sources. Thus, it is contended, countries may obtain reserves from financial markets provided that they maintain their creditworthiness. It is, however, admitted by the Group of Ten that the terms on which reserves are supplied by the market are affected by the financial policies of reserve-currency countries. Some members of the Group, moreover, consider that arrangements for the provision of liquidity have not been optimal, or conducive to gradual adjustment toward noninflationary growth. They also point out that sudden and marked shifts in the terms and conditions on which international liquidity is made available, late recognition of and abrupt response to changes in creditworthiness, and the very limited access that certain groups of countries have to market borrowing are factors that cannot be ignored. The position of the major countries is not very persuasive on this matter. The overwhelming majority of developing countries have never been in a position where they could rely on access to private or official sources for acquiring reserves. Such access, therefore, simply has not entered into any assessment of their need for reserves. A number of developing countries did reach the position during the 1970s where they could borrow from financial markets to supplement reserves. Such building up of reserves was considered essential in strengthening their credit standing and hence their borrowing capabilities. But this kind of ready access to the financial markets disappeared with the onset of the debt crisis, thereby disrupting their reserve planning at the very time that they could least afford such disruption.

A significant indicator of the shortage of reserves in non-oil developing countries and of the importance that they have attached to strengthening their position in this respect is the fact that from the end of 1982 to the end of 1984 they increased their reserves by more than $25 billion, despite the fact that this meant an even sharper curtailment of imports of goods of which they were greatly in need. These facts, incidentally, are relevant to the argument frequently advanced to the effect that developing countries would immediately spend any SDRs allocated to them. There is, of course, no reason why they should not do so if circumstances so require, but the evidence cited above shows that developing countries are well aware of the benefits as well as costs of holding reserves. If, therefore, reserve needs were not satisfied through allocations of SDRs, the burden of further attempts to strengthen reserves would have to fall on additional compression of imports.

The refusal of the major industrial countries to agree to issue SDRs is, therefore, not only a violation of the Articles of Agreement which require all member countries to cooperate with the Fund in making the SDR "the principal reserve asset in the international monetary system" (Article XXII). It also creates a serious imbalance between those countries that are able to borrow reserves and those that are compelled to earn their reserve holdings through additional curtailment of imports at a time when the Fund and the World Bank are in full agreement that the most important constraint on the heavily indebted developing countries is a shortage of imported goods. Nothing that these countries can do in the immediate future could restore their ability to borrow from private markets.

Moreover, if, as is implied in the reasoning of the major Group of Ten countries, the level of reserves held by creditworthy countries is demand-determined and if such countries can borrow whatever reserves they need whenever they need them, the question at once arises why the holdings of non-gold reserves by the industrial countries have been rising rapidly and continuously during the present decade.

Stated fears of SDR-induced inflation lack credibility. Even if developing countries were to spend their entire allocations of SDRs on imports from developed countries, the demand pressure generated by such means would be minimal. Fund staff estimates show that if all SDRs received by developing countries were fully transferred to developed countries and reflected on to their monetary base, a total allocation of, say, SDR 10 billion to all countries would increase the monetary base of developed countries by less than 2 percent. It is noteworthy that this is smaller than the spread between the upper and lower limits of money-supply targets in many developed countries. It should also be recalled that in 1981 the Fund staff put forward options for SDR allocations ranging from SDR 4 billion to SDR 19 billion a year, taking the position that none of these magnitudes would be sufficient to generate inflationary pressure of demand. Since 1981 inflationary pressures have subsided, so that there would be even less danger of excessive demand under present conditions.

The Group of Ten states that developments in the international monetary system have lessened official interest in an internationally issued and administered reserve asset. They suggest that "The expansion of international financial markets has provided a flexible and efficient source of reserves for many countries, and [that] the emerging multicurrency reserve system has reduced dependence on a single currency in international settlements and reserve holdings." They go on to say that "The Deputies recognize that these developments have affected the rationale for the SDR, including the objective of placing the SDR at the center of the system as the main reserve asset."[15]

In arguing that the availability of borrowing facilities supersedes the need for SDRs, however, the Group of Ten are forgetting their own report of July 7, 1966, which reads in part as follows: "In the past the need for international liquidity has been met by improving credit facilities as well as by additions to reserves. In the future, credit facilities can no doubt continue to play a constructive role, but their use can be only a partial and temporary substitute for reserves which are at the full disposition of the country holding them."[16]

Moreover, regardless of what the Group of Ten Deputies now say about the adequacy of credit facilities in supplying reserve needs, it is clear that the governments of the countries they represent are as mindful as ever of the superiority of reserves that "are at the full disposition of the country holding them." Notwithstanding the fact that dollars have not been officially convertible into gold since 1971 and despite the volatility of the market price of gold, the central banks of the industrial countries have kept gold as a major reserve asset. In fact gold, valued at market prices, amounted to over 45 percent of the total value of the reserves of industrial countries at the end of 1986, only slightly less than the 47 percent recorded at the end of 1970, just before the dollar's link to gold was broken.

The same considerations that prompt the Group of Ten industrialized countries to maintain within their reserves an asset, namely gold, that is at their "full disposition" apply also to developing countries. Consequently, it is of the highest importance for these countries to be able to benefit from SDR allocations, the SDR being, in some respects, a substitute for gold that is free of the costs and risks associated with gold. If the Group were to maintain the position that no new allocations of SDRs should take place either now or in the foreseeable future, this would be tantamount to asserting that unless developing countries are prepared to use their own resources to buy gold, they are not entitled to the benefits of acquiring reserve assets that would be at their full disposition, and not subject to the goodwill of any one country.

To sum up, the best way of meeting the liquidity requirements of developing countries is through adequate annual allocations of SDRs. The Group of Twenty-Four points out that the allocation of SDRs to developing countries would not only meet the unfulfilled absorptive capacity of developing countries but also reduce the pressures on the industrial countries to accommodate an improvement in the current account balances of developing countries. In other words, allocations of SDRs to developing countries would yield benefits not only to these countries but to the international community as a whole, since they would reduce the need for developed countries to accept import surpluses of goods from the developing countries in payment of their debt service.

COUNTERCYCLICAL FUNCTIONS OF THE IMF?

At a meeting of the UN Sub-Commission on Employment and Economic Stability held in 1949 the U.K. member, Sir Roy Harrod, expressed regret that in their replies to a questionnaire addressed to them by the UN Secretary-General almost all governments had stated that if faced with unemployment and balance-of-payments difficulties as a result of declining exports, they would resort to import restrictions. This, said Harrod, implied disregard of the ideas of international cooperation developed at Bretton Woods. If necessary, international arrangements should be strengthened so that governments would gain confidence in their effectiveness and not feel compelled to resort to import restrictions. For example, the resources of the IMF should be increased and its tasks broadened through the addition of central banking functions. Michal Kalecki, representing the Secretary-General, commented that the IMF reply to the questionnaire indicated that that institution did not have the resources required to resist a major economic downturn, and the IMF representative at the meeting concurred with Kalecki's view.

Subsequently the resource base of the IMF was greatly expanded (though less than in proportion to world trade), but the idea that the IMF had a countercyclical role to play in the world economy never made much headway until the establishment of CFF in 1963. Even then, the rationale for CFF was not directly addressed to countering worldwide recession but was virtually limited to compensatory lending to countries experiencing shortfalls in export earnings for reasons beyond their control. Such shortfalls were, of course, a likely accompaniment to a setback in business activity in some or all of the developed countries, and supporting commodity markets was, after all, one of the methods available for dealing with such setbacks. But CFF was not intended as a means of sustaining the level of demand in industrial countries.

The first facilities oriented directly toward countercyclical activity by the IMF were the oil facilities of 1973–74, which were intended to prevent the increase in oil prices of that period from triggering a worldwide recession. The conditions laid down for drawings on the oil facilities were totally different from any that the Fund has ever required before or since. In fact, the conditions came close to the semiautomaticity of drawings envisaged by Keynes and many others during the negotiations that preceded the Bretton Woods Conference. The IMF historian notes that there was "virtually no conditionality attached to the 1974 oil facility."[17] Countries drawing on the facility were expected to sustain appropriate levels of economic activity and employment, while minimizing inflation, and not to impose new, or intensify existing, restrictions on trade and payments.

It is of considerable interest to recall the reasoning that was used to explain this strategy—embodying an approach that would probably not command a consensus in the IMF of today. In a note presented to the Committee of Twenty in January 1974, the Managing Director stated that in the short run the group of oil importing countries would have to accept the deterioration of the current account in its balance of payments, since attempts to eliminate the additional current deficit caused by higher oil prices through deflationary demand policies, import restrictions, and general resort to exchange rate depreciation would serve only to shift the payments problem from one oil importing country to another and to damage world trade and economic activity.[18]

The adoption of this countercyclical program was due in large measure to the insight and determination of the Managing Director, Johannes Witteveen, who carried the day against the strong opposition of the then U.S. Treasury Secretary George Shultz and, to a lesser extent, of the Federal Republic of Germany. Sir Joseph Gold, in explaining the conditions under the oil facilities, pointed out that there was, at that time, no fixed relationship between the resources made available by the Fund unconditionally or on the basis of mild conditionality and the resources for which stronger conditionality was applied. In the case of the oil facilities, he said, the Fund wished "to deter hasty adjustment by such measures as competitive devaluation or restrictions that members would have been tempted to adopt in order to deal with balance-of-payments difficulties caused by the increased costs of imports of oil."[19]

The opposing forces were, however, too strong for Witteveen to be able to carry his program forward on the scale he considered necessary. At the 1974 annual meetings he called for increased official recycling of funds from oil exporters to oil importers and for a substantial increase in recycling through the Fund. His position was supported by developing countries as well as by a number of developed countries. The U.K. Chancellor of the Exchequer, Denis Healey, argued for the investment of a significant proportion of oil revenues in international organizations in exchange for some type of asset issued by the Fund. France and Italy also favored increased recycling by the Fund. The United States, however, considered that the recycling function should be undertaken by commercial banks to the greatest extent possible, continued to favor collective action by the industrial countries in resistance to OPEC policies, and proposed a "financial safety net" for the industrial countries. Agreement was ultimately reached on a relatively small second oil facility, so that the great bulk of the recycling was carried out by the commercial banks, as advocated by the United States.

This proved to be a most unfortunate decision, since it led to the excessive buildup of commercial bank debt, with the debtor countries absorbing the entire interest rate risk, that has brought the development of many countries in the Third World to a halt in the 1980s and perhaps beyond.

Since 1980 the low conditionality options referred to by Sir Joseph Gold appear to have been closed off. Particularly noteworthy is the 1983 decision of the Fund's Executive Board with regard to CFF, which appears to have changed the character of the facility on a permanent basis, removing, in one go, by far the largest single source of low conditional IMF resources. In so doing, the board acted in a manner entirely inconsistent with the Fund's own traditional doctrine that cases in which balance-of-payments deficits are temporary and self-reversing should be handled by financing and not by adjustment. As a Fund pamphlet has pointed out: "Deficits stemming from adverse transitory (external or internal) factors typically call for temporary resort to financing. Mechanisms have been devised in the Fund and elsewhere to cope with situations of this sort—the Fund's compensatory financing and buffer stock facilities and the European Community's STABEX Fund are examples of such mechanisms.[20]

In April 1988 the IMF adopted in principle a contingency mechanism in combination with CFF to make it possible to "maintain the momentum of adjustment in the face of a wider range of adverse external shocks."[21] The wider range of shocks, it is understood, may include increases in interest rates on funds borrowed from abroad. While this decision represents an important new departure and a modest enhancement of the range of IMF capabilities to respond to the balance-of-payments needs of its members (severely limited, however, by an increase in access to resources quite inadequate to the scale of demands likely to arise) it does not alter the fact noted earlier that the original character of CFF has been so changed as to prevent its use as a countercyclical instrument with—in Professor Cooper's words—"little or no conditionality." This can be seen from the statement by the Interim Committee that "Use of the contingency element would be attached to a Fund-supported adjustment program."[22] It is indeed a curious example of IMF logic that under this formula country A would be required to adopt strict measures of adjustment simply because country B, the source of a past variable interest rate loan to A, decides for domestic reasons having nothing to do with A to raise interest rates—even temporarily. Indeed, B's need to raise interest rates could conceivably be the result of mismanagement of aggregate domestic demand. The fact that A was not responsible would in no way relieve it of the need for strong measures of adjustment in return for a contingency drawing, while B would be under no compulsion to adjust unless it was forced to seek IMF assistance—something that is not very likely if B happens to be an industrial country.

In order to be able to deal effectively with the many different kinds of balance-of-payments problems that may arise, the Fund needs to be able to deploy an array of resources ranging from unconditional to highly conditional, depending on circumstances. Moreover, the Fund's resources need to be adequate for all these purposes, which means that the ratio of Fund quotas to world imports needs to be restored to the level envisaged at Bretton Woods—equivalent to something of the order of 16 percent of world imports, compared with the present ratio, which is less than 6 percent.

A COMMODITY LINK

Another useful element in providing countercyclical protection for the international monetary system would be to establish a policy link with commodity markets. On September 30, 1987, U.S. Treasury Secretary Baker startled his audience at the annual meetings of the World Bank and Fund by saying that "the United States is prepared to consider utilizing as an additional indicator in the coordination process, the relationship among our currencies and a basket of commodities, including gold. This would be simply an analytical tool helpful as an early-warning signal of potential price trends." Rudiger Dornbusch has ridiculed this proposal as a mere political gesture toward those who favor the gold standard.

But the proposal could be interpreted differently, and there are perfectly sound arguments in its favor. Professors Kaldor, Hart, and Tinbergen submitted a paper to the first conference of UNCTAD in 1964 in which they set out the case for an International Commodity Reserve Currency. The key point of the paper was that the most effective development of the international monetary system would lie not along the lines of a further extension of the key currency system, nor in the creation of a world paper currency, nor in the revaluation of gold, but in the monetization of real assets other than or in addition to gold. They proposed that the IMF should create its own currency which should be convertible both into gold and into a bundle of the thirty or so principal commodities in world trade. This would make it possible to create a world currency reserve which would expand in line with the production and use of primary products: as the authors pointed out, it is the supply of primary products that is the ultimate constraint on world economic growth. By the same token, such a scheme would provide an effective instrument for stabilizing the terms of trade between primary products and manufactures.

Kaldor recognized that there were certain practical difficulties in the scheme and that it would be highly complicated in operation. Consequently, in an article in the *Lloyds Bank Review* of July 1983, he advocated instead the scheme recommended by Keynes during World War II for worldwide price stabilization by means of buffer stocks for as many commodities as possible.[23] Kaldor argued that a buffer stock scheme linked to the use of SDRS would provide the world with a basic money unit that would be stable in terms of primary commodities. The existence of an international reserve currency that was stable in terms of commodities would, he felt, exert a strong dampening effect on wage-induced inflation.

It was a critical element in Professor Kaldor's approach to the subject that a commodity reserve currency, or a commodity stabilization scheme financed by SDRS, would lead to the stabilization not only of commodity markets but of the world economy as a whole. It would, moreover, secure the highest sustainable rate of economic growth for the world as a whole—that is, the highest rate of world industrial expansion that the growth of supplies of primary products would permit.[24] This would occur because if primary products were in excess supply there would be an increase in investment in stocks of these commodities that would generate a corresponding increase in the rate of growth of demand for industrial products; the converse would hold true in case of a shortage of primary products. In his view, moreover, it was not labor or capital that was the ultimate constraint on growth but the supply of primary products, and stabilization of the commodity markets would encourage the maximum expansion of commodity output.

Kaldor had been skeptical all along about the viability of an international paper currency without commodity backing. This was not because he himself saw any theoretical necessity for commodity backing. But he foresaw, quite correctly, that the world's bankers would never feel really comfortable with an unbacked paper currency at the international level, and that they would prefer to hold one or more of the key currencies such as the dollar. On this he proved to be absolutely right: as noted earlier, the Group of Ten has now openly raised the question whether the SDR has any future at all as an international reserve currency.

It is a long way even from Kaldor's modified scheme to Secretary Baker's proposal for a commodity price indicator. The two ideas do, however, have something important in common. They both acknowledge the merits of stabilizing commodity prices and recognize that sharp movements upward or downward in the general level of commodity prices are indicators of potential economic trouble ahead. Kaldor would rely on a mechanism linked to a commodity-based SDR to provide the impulses needed for stabilization. Secretary Baker, by implication, would see a shift in commodity prices as a signal, along with other signals, for increasing or decreasing the world level of effective demand. There is an important place for ideas along these lines in a reform of the international monetary system.

SURVEILLANCE

Considerable attention has been devoted in recent years to the development of IMF surveillance over the macroeconomic policies of its members. Both the Group of Ten and the Group of Twenty-Four dealt at length with this subject in separate reports published in 1985.

The Group of Ten was quite candid in its report in recognizing that during the period of floating exchange rates "surveillance has not been as effective as desirable in influencing national policies and in promoting underlying economic and financial conditions conducive to exchange rate stability. . . . [Some] countries appear to have been able on occasion to sustain policy courses not fully compatible with the goals of international adjustment and financial stability."[25] They therefore presented proposals for strengthening surveillance both bilateral and multilateral. They pointed out that effective surveillance implies the assessment of all policies affecting trade, capital movements, external adjustment, and the effective functioning of the international monetary system. They suggested that strengthened surveillance requires "enhanced dialogue and persuasion through peer pressure, rather than mechanically imposed external constraints."[26] Some members of the Group of Ten, however, consider that an element of constraint would also be required as well as greater publicity for policy conclusions reached as part of the process of consultation between the Fund and each of its members (under Article IV).

While the Group of Ten appears to have accepted the fact that surveillance of the major countries is more significant for the international community as a whole than surveillance of the developing countries, paragraph 41 of their report notes the existence of other institutions "of more limited membership" having a role in the surveillance process, notably the OECD. While the paragraph acknowledges that the central role of the IMF in surveillance should be preserved, the reference to OECD and other bodies conveys implicitly that in the view of the Group the Fund's role vis-à-vis the industrial countries is not, and should not be, necessarily the decisive one.

The Group of Ten also agrees that multilateral surveillance "should concentrate on countries which have a large impact on the world economy."[27] Moreover, "The specific content of multilateral surveillance should be the examination of the external repercussions of national policies and their interaction in the determination of the global environment."[28] The IMF should have the task of preparing documents analyzing these external repercussions of national policies of Group of Ten countries and the Group ministers and governors and Working Party No. 3 of the OECD should use the IMF documentation in assessing the appropriateness of the policies of members. Problems in the trade field should be taken up by GATT in cooperation with the IMF.

There is a good deal of common ground between the Group of Ten and Group of Twenty-Four reports, but the latter report goes further in certain important respects. In the first place, the Group of Twenty-Four considers that "Surveillance, to be effective, should be explicitly recognized as surveillance of the international adjustment process. . . . The design of such an international adjustment process, based on co-ordinated national economic policies, must aim at sustained growth of output, employment, and trade of all countries and ensure adequate real resource transfers to developing countries."[29] This clearly goes considerably beyond anything that the Group of Ten has thus far contemplated, let alone accepted.

In the second place, multilateral surveillance and bilateral (Article IV) consultations should form two stages of the surveillance process, rather than two parallel operations. The first stage should involve multilateral discussions and negotiations to be conducted on a regular basis within the framework of the IMF about a mutually consistent set of objectives, and a set of policies to collectively achieve these objectives. The aim might be to search for a set of outcomes or "objective indicators" or "targets" that appear to be sustainable in the medium term and desirable to all parties. This, says the Group of Twenty-Four, "should be quite feasible when the multilateral surveillance exercise is limited to a few major industrial countries, such as the key currency countries." The second stage would involve a comparison between the actual outcomes and the recommended targets or indicators, and a discussion of what measures would be appropriate when the two differ. The Group of Twenty-Four considers that this stage might be conducted most efficiently on a bilateral basis as part of Article IV consultations.[30] Multilateral surveillance should also take place in the IMF Board, which should examine "the international repercussions and interactions of national policies of the major industrial countries" and should recommend "a set of policies and the likely outcomes or performance indicators."[31]

Despite the foregoing Group of Ten and Group of Twenty-Four reports, and although it would appear quite natural in an increasingly interdependent world that machinery should be developed for confronting the macroeconomic policies of at least the major economic powers with one another, there is a certain vagueness and confusion at this stage about the content and boundaries of the subject, as well as about where responsibility lies.

One source of vagueness is the fact that the Fund's mandate, under Article IV. 3(b) is to "exercise firm surveillance over the exchange rate policies of members"—a responsibility that is in theory concerned largely with avoiding exchange rate manipulation. But the Fund management has taken a far broader view of its authority, a position supported by the Group of Twenty-Four, and the opening sections of its annual reports and studies of the world economic outlook deal with overall trends and macroeconomic policies. This approach has not been challenged by any of the Fund members, but the fact that it has not been formally endorsed possibly leaves some loopholes.

A second source of uncertainty is the extent of Fund responsibility in this field, especially vis-à-vis regional groupings. In April 1986 the IMF's Interim Committee indicated tentative agreement to the use of objective indicators in improving multilateral surveillance. But in the following month the seven Summit countries went further, asking their finance ministers to "review their individual economic objectives and forecasts collectively at least once a year . . . with a particular view to examining their mutual compatibility."[32]

Mention was made earlier of the trend since the Jamaica Agreement whereby Fund responsibilities and resources have been progressively cut back under the pressure of the industrial countries. Is it likely in such conditions that the major countries would be aiming at an intensification of Fund surveillance of the policies of its members? Perhaps so, but in that case there is at least some inconsistency between the erosion of Fund authority in the one area and its enhancement in the other.

The mere fact that policies of the major economic powers are confronted in more than one intergovernmental forum does not raise any difficulty so long as there is one ultimate authority to which the other fora channel their conclusions and so long as conflicts do not arise between any one forum and another. Since the IMF has a relatively large number of members it makes sense that problems arising among the major countries are discussed in any forum they choose, and this has been recognized by the Group of Twenty-Four, as noted above.

The question is one of substance, not form. Is the Group of Seven simply preparing the ground for the wider airing of surveillance issues in the IMF or are they reaching decisions that can be reported to the IMF but are not subject to change in that body? It has been reported by participants in both fora that, on the one hand, discussions of surveillance issues in the smaller groups have been less extensive and profound than in the Fund but that, on the other hand, the major industrial countries regard the Fund responsibility as being more in the nature of consultation than of supervision.

Peter Kenen raises an important question regarding the Group of Twenty-Four's integration of multilateral surveillance and bilateral (Article IV) consultations with major industrial countries. As he points out, the Summit countries assigned the whole process to their own officials, though the Fund's Managing Director was to continue to participate in their discussions.[33]

Kenen sides with the latter approach for analytical as well as political reasons. As he says, differences between outcomes and targets may not be due exclusively to one country's policies and should therefore be pursued in a multilateral framework. But if that multilateral framework is predominantly the Group of Seven, the Fund's role in surveillance becomes a distinctly secondary one, and the chances are that, as in many other matters, the developing countries will simply be presented with faits accomplis.

The problems for the present and future are clear. First and foremost there is the question how to persuade the major industrial countries that insistence on national economic sovereignty and associated prerogatives will, if pressed too far, be disastrous for all. Secondly, as noted at the outset of this paper, the problems of the international monetary system can be solved only in the context of an expanding world economy. Finally, there is the problem of how to reconcile the oligarchic propensities of the Summit countries with the insistence of the developing countries that they are now a sufficiently important factor in the world economy to have their views not merely recorded but taken effectively into account. None of these problems is new—the system has been wrestling with them for many years without much indication of significant progress.

CONDITIONALITY AND THE DESIGN OF FUND-SUPPORTED PROGRAMS

There has been widespread criticism of the design of Fund-supported programs and the conditionality that goes with them. It is often suggested that developing countries are opposed to IMF conditionality in principle, but this is quite wrong. The opposition is to the form and character of the conditions applied, not to the principle per se.

What can and should be questioned is the view now predominating among the major industrial countries that virtually all balance-of-payments lending should be at high conditionality—a view that is completely inconsistent with IMF experience and the Articles of Agreement. The Articles require the Fund to establish "adequate safeguards" for the "temporary" use of its resources (Article V. (3)(a)) but they also make it clear that maladjustments in balances of payments should be corrected "without resorting to measures destructive of national or international prosperity." (Article I(v)). The case for countercyclical Fund policies (as in the oil facilities of 1973–74) has already been stated above, necessitating an array of resources from unconditional to highly conditional, depending on circumstances.

Dissatisfaction with Fund-supported programs is not limited to developing countries. The address of U.S. Treasury Secretary Baker to the annual meetings of the IMF and World Bank in October 1985 stressed the importance of ensuring that adjustment under Fund-supported programs would be combined with growth. In so doing Secretary Baker was saying implicitly that the programs of austerity and economic contraction characteristic of the IMF in the past were no longer acceptable either to the developing countries or to the industrial countries.

The principal criticism of these programs by developing countries is that:

Irrespective of the causes of balance of payments difficulties, the Fund generally has insisted on heavy reliance on demand management policies for correcting maladjustments in external payments. Thus, developing countries have been required to curtail demand as a means of adjusting to changes in the external environment—such as the decline in growth of world trade, changes in energy prices, the declines in the availability of finance, soaring interest rates, and exchange rate variations, among others—even though these factors were already constricting their growth.[34]

The policies of expenditure reduction prescribed by the Fund have led to substantial losses of output and sharp curtailment of investment even in export industries. These losses have often been aggravated by import compression, while expenditure switching policies involving devaluation have added considerably to inflationary pressures. Moreover, a number of studies have shown that Fund programs almost invariably require much more severe constraints on the level of demand than would be necessary to attain their balance-of-payments objectives, with the result that noncompliance has been widespread, as have continuous breakdowns and revisions of the programs.

If the adjustment with growth objectives of the Baker Plan are to be attained, Fund-supported programs will have to be designed quite differently. Where the availability of finance for balance-of-payments support is very limited—as it usually is—and no effort is made to raise additional funds it is almost inevitable that the programs emerging from the Fund's financial exercises will be sharply deflationary, imposing declines in both output and investment. If the Fund is to take the growth objective seriously, it will have to assess the external capital requirements of growth-oriented adjustment programs and then participate actively in mobilizing the financial support needed over and above what the Fund itself can provide. At times of pressure on Fund resources, the Fund should be entitled to borrow from governments or even from capital markets. Adjustment programs that go beyond demand compression and seek to effect the structural changes needed for developing new export capabilities and efficient substitutes for imports inevitably call for a stepping up of investment which, in most developing countries, has a high direct or indirect import content in the form of capital goods, intermediates, raw materials, and other essential supplies.

The content of conditionality raises a whole spectrum of difficult problems, ranging from analytical to political. Since the external and internal transactions of any economy are closely interrelated there cannot be any question but that policies adopted to deal with domestic economic problems usually have direct or indirect implications for the balance of payments. It is this consideration that is held to justify involvement of the IMF in the domestic policies of its members.

At the same time, it would be absurd to suppose that the World Bank and the IMF, large and competently staffed as these institutions are, have the capability to direct the affairs of the developing countries from Washington. Moreover, in a democratic society those who run the economy are expected to be answerable to political constituencies, and the World Bank and IMF have no one but their member governments to report to.

There is, therefore, a strong case for limiting conditionality to the balance of payments. The World Bank and the IMF have a legitimate stake in balance-of-payments adjustment, and even if that implies examination of domestic policy variables, there is no need for such variables to form part of their conditions for lending. The proof of the pudding is in the eating, and the concern of the IMF is with improvement in the balance of payments. Moreover, limiting conditionality to the balance of payments does not mean any dilution of performance requirements. On the contrary, balance-of-payments conditionality can be every bit as tough as conditionality addressed to monetary targets—if not more so. With the failure of money demand functions to perform in a predictable manner, one never really knows what one will get by way of effects on the balance of payments when the economy achieves or fails to achieve a particular monetary target. With a balance-of-payments target, the Fund and its member countries would know exactly where the borrower stands—when additional measures are needed and when they can be relaxed.

It is also important for contingency mechanisms to be built firmly into Fund-supported programs, so that conditionality provisions can be reviewed in the event that there are any changes in the external conditions affecting a country's adjustment for reasons beyond its control. In particular, the failure of a program to generate the rate of growth that had been anticipated should automatically trigger a reconsideration of the entire program and, if necessary, the provision of supplementary resources.

One aspect of conditionality that went largely unnoticed until UNICEF drew attention to it is the effect of adjustment programs (whether national or international) on vulnerable groups within the population, particularly children. UNICEF reported rising levels of malnutrition and increases in morbidity in many parts of the world beginning in the early 1980s. Adjustment programs, said UNICEF, were transmitting and usually multiplying the impact on the poor and the vulnerable. UNICEF advocated a policy of "adjustment with a human face" that would undertake a conscious commitment to the protection of basic human welfare as part and parcel of adjustment programs, sustaining, in particular, the minimum nutrition levels of children and other specially vulnerable groups.[35] The IMF and World Bank have publicly expressed their full support of the objectives of the UNICEF drive, but it is too early to tell whether this support is being translated into the requisite modifications of the lending programs of these institutions.

THE DEBT OVERHANG

Views may differ as to the extent to which the world debt crisis is due to systemic factors as against the improvidence of individual countries and governments. There are, however, several points that should be noncontroversial. In the first place, as noted earlier, it was a unanimous decision of the entire Fund membership that countries should accept the deficits resulting from the first oil shock and avoid attempts at deficit reduction that would merely have the effect of shifting the burden elsewhere. This was a major factor in the building up of debt at the time.

Secondly, the policy of recycling petrodollar surpluses through the commercial banks rather than through the multilateral financial institutions, as Witteveen and others had proposed, was disastrous. Apart from the fact that the multilaterals would probably have exercised better control of their lending programs than the commercial banks did, they would not have transferred the entire interest rate risk to the borrowers.

Finally, the IMF is now deeply involved in the world debt problem in a capacity that is often difficult to reconcile with the need for the Fund to be regarded by all its members as an objective and independent entity able to take an impartial view of the relations between debtors and creditors.

Apart from these considerations, the sheer magnitude of the debt problem, the fact that it has led to a widespread and long-lasting economic depression in the Third World, as well as a perverse net transfer of resources from low-income to high-income countries; that it is blocking the normal channels of trade and thereby adding fuel to the fires of protectionism in the industrial countries; and above all that the total volume of debt is still rising—all these factors cannot fail to be a source of anxiety for all those concerned with the future security of the international monetary system.

It is not possible, within the limits of the present paper, to do justice to the analysis of this subject. What is clear is that by one means or another the debt overhang must be greatly reduced if it is not to constitute a persistent threat to the system. It is also clear that that reduction cannot come about through repayment of the entire debt either now or in the future unless the industrial countries are prepared to step up their rates of growth and import demand to the levels that prevailed during the Bretton Woods period—something that is quite feasible but is beyond reach for political reasons in the foreseeable future.

This being the case, there is no alternative to a program of massive debt relief for official and market borrowers alike. Thus far, proposals for such relief have failed to win support in the quarters that have the power of decision in this field. One reason is that the conventional wisdom maintains that the commercial banks will resume voluntary lending to debtor countries as soon as the latter reestablish their creditworthiness, and that debt relief should be ruled out because it would result in the indefinite postponement of the return to creditworthiness. The trouble with this approach is that after six years of the conventional wisdom and of draconic stabilization programs requiring not only reductions in per capita consumption but above all in investment, the debtors are even further from the promised land of creditworthiness than they were when they started. And the reason for this is precisely the debt overhang itself and the failure of the international community to create the environment of world economic expansion that would have permitted the debtors to grow out of the debt problem.

Moreover, as Richard Portes and Barry Eichengreen have pointed out, the proposition that debt relief would block the debtors' access to international capital markets for an indefinite period is contradicted by the historical evidence, which shows that countries obtaining debt relief have not suffered subsequent loss of access to capital markets to any greater extent than the countries that met their commitments in full.[36] On the contrary, under the right conditions debt relief tends to increase creditworthiness, not reduce it.

It is also clear that a situation in which the debtor countries are compelled to run trade surpluses with the creditor countries is, in the long run, unacceptable not only to the debtors but to the creditor countries as well, all of which would like to be running trade surpluses. It is, in fact, in the hard-headed interests of the creditor countries to make it possible for the debtor countries to regain their former importance as markets for the exports of industrial countries. As noted earlier, one of the great merits of substantial issues of SDRs to developing countries is that this would reduce the need for the developed countries to accommodate large import surpluses from the debtor countries in payment of debt service.

PROBLEMS OF UNIVERSALITY

Recent changes in the economic policies of the USSR obviously raise the question of Soviet participation in the international monetary and trading systems and of membership in the IMF and GATT. Many of the obstacles to such participation and membership may be eased as the new policies gather momentum: indeed, some of the socialist countries have already overcome these obstacles. The USSR participated actively in the Bretton Woods Conference and would have been entitled to claim membership both in the IMF and in the World Bank. One of the most important obstacles that stood in the way, however, was the unwillingness of the USSR to supply some of the information required under the Articles of Agreement, such as the level of its gold and foreign exchange reserves. The USSR's new readiness to provide the military information needed under the Agreement on Intermediate-Range Nuclear Forces, and to permit inspection in that context, suggests that the unwillingness to release economic information may likewise be modified. Despite its participation at Bretton Woods, the USSR would have to make application to become a member of the IMF and World Bank, and would have to go through the normal procedures to be accepted as such by the Boards of Governors.

A liberalization of Soviet international economic policies would probably not have much effect on the functioning of the international monetary system. Although it is not entirely clear how the level of the ruble exchange rate was originally determined, it appears that the rate is pegged to a basket of Western currencies in a fairly conventional way. Throughout the international monetary crises of the past twenty years the USSR has not created any difficulties for the system, and is even less likely to do so in view of improved East-West relations in the political and military fields. The USSR favors a major role for gold in the system, but very few members of the IMF support the idea of a return to the gold standard. However, a role for commodities (including gold) in the macromanagement of the world economy has been suggested by Secretary Baker, as noted earlier.

Certain questions would arise if the USSR sought membership in the IMF. It is unlikely that the USSR would, in joining the Fund, expect to avail itself of the Fund's conditional credit facilities. It would no doubt be as reluctant to do this as the major OECD countries are, and for the same reason—namely, unwillingness to subject itself to the requirements of conditionality. The USSR has hitherto been regarded by private capital markets as creditworthy and would, in the absence of some major catastrophe, be able to utilize the borrowing facilities available in those markets in the event of a need for balance-of-payments support. Under conditions of détente it might also be able to borrow from other governments on favorable terms. There is no reason to think that the USSR would have any difficulty with the SDR arrangements of the Fund, or that it would itself cause difficulties for those arrangements.

One possible difficulty might be that under Article VIII of the Articles of Agreement no member of the Fund may impose restrictions on the making of payments and transfers for current international transactions. However, many new members, including Poland, have availed themselves of the transitional arrangements in Article XIV whereby a member "may, notwithstanding the provisions of any other articles of this Agreement, maintain and adapt to changing circumstances the restrictions on payments and transfers for current international transactions that were in effect on the date on which it became a member." The USSR could also, presumably, claim Article XIV status, although it would be expected to make some effort to move to Article VIII status in due course. In principle, the Fund may, under Article XIV, Section 3, require a member to move from Article XIV to Article VIII status, but this is a provision that has never been invoked, and there is no reason to think that it would be invoked in the case of the USSR.

More significant in the long run, probably, is the problem of accommodating a country as important as the USSR in the procedures and decisionmaking process of the Fund. Under the system of weighted voting in the Bretton Woods institutions, formal challenges to the dominance of the major powers have been rare, and even though the developing countries could, in principle, muster a collective veto on many of the Fund's decisions requiring qualified majorities, in practice issues are never allowed to reach that stage. Instead, negotiations continue until the requisite degree of consensus is achieved. Occasionally, however, a proposal favored by the industrial countries has had to be dropped for lack of support by the developing countries.

A successful application by the USSR would, of course, result in the assignment of a quota to that country. That quota would not be large enough to give the USSR a veto on any Fund decision: at Bretton Woods the USSR was given a quota somewhat smaller than that of the United Kingdom. The USSR would, however, almost certainly seek to join the United States, United Kingdom, Federal Republic of Germany, France, Japan, Saudi Arabia, and China in having the right to appoint an Executive Director to the Executive Board and might well make its willingness to join conditional on the granting of this request.

Inevitably, the present members of the IMF would be concerned as to the manner in which the admission of the USSR to membership would affect the political balance in the Fund. They would have to reckon with the probability that the USSR would have its own distinctive point of view on matters coming up for decision. Even though it would not have a separate veto of its own, it might be able from time to time to mobilize sufficient support from other members to make the achievement of consensus a complex and difficult process.

The impact of the USSR on decisionmaking in the Fund is, however, ultimately a question of political accommodation that could probably be solved in the long run if the improvement in East-West relations in other fields goes far enough.

DEMOCRATIZING THE DECISIONMAKING PROCESS

Professor Cooper's idea of strengthening the Interim Committee could be a step in the direction of democratizing the decisionmaking process in the international monetary system. As long ago as 1973, at the annual meetings of the Fund and World Bank, U.S. Treasury Secretary George Shultz advanced the view that "The logic is strong that for the Fund to act effectively, member governments should have available a forum of workable size within the organization at which responsible national officials can speak and negotiate with both flexibility and authority." [37]

Subsequently the Committee of Twenty recommended the establishment of a "permanent and representative Council, with one member appointed from each Fund constituency" and with the participation of the Managing Director. The Council, which was to meet regularly three or four times a year as required, "will have the necessary decision-making powers to supervise the management and adaptation of the monetary system, to oversee the continuing operation of the adjustment process, and to deal with sudden disturbances which might threaten the system." [38]

Pending the amendment of the Articles of Agreement that was required to set up the new Council, the Board of Governors, in September 1974, established an Interim Committee structured along the lines of the Committee of Twenty. Until the requisite amendment was adopted, the new committee could have only advisory powers even though it invariably met—and continues to meet—at ministerial level. Decisions remained in the hands of the Executive Board except where the endorsement of the Governors themselves was required under the Articles.

It is, however, the Interim Committee that has survived and the Permanent Council that has been shelved. Margaret de Vries explains this by suggesting that "some long-time Executive Directors were concerned about a possible loss of power by the Executive Board" and that some of the Executive Directors elected by developing country members "regarded themselves as more experienced than their finance ministers who tended to be in office only for short periods."

A more important consideration for developing countries may have been that they were skeptical of the capacity of the IMF, with its weighted voting, to be evenhanded in its treatment of Fund members. They were prepared to accept a strong high-level Council in the Fund if that body were prepared to lean at least as heavily on the key currency countries as on the weaker members. If, however, this were not to be the case, the developing countries could only lose from a strengthening of Fund machinery.

Hence, the continuation in being of the Interim Committee might, they thought, be the best compromise. The Interim Committee, with its consensus procedure, would give developing countries a role in the political decisionmaking process in the Fund without creating the danger of high-level political pressures upon the less powerful countries.

Whether decisionmaking in the Fund would have become more democratic if the Permanent Council had been established is debatable. It is arguable that members of the Executive Board, as officials of the Fund separated from their home countries, tend to be more susceptible to institutional influences than officials coming to periodic meetings from capitals would be. This was one of the considerations that had weighed heavily with Keynes in opposing the U.S. view of the board as a body of officials earning high salaries and resident at IMF headquarters. Keynes had proposed that the board should not be in permanent session but should provide opportunities for senior officials of central banks and Treasuries to meet together at intervals in "a truly international body for consultation and cooperation on monetary and financial problems."[39] It was the U.S. view of the board that prevailed at the Savannah Conference, prompting the comment from Keynes that "the strength of the new institutions [i.e., of the World Bank as well as of the Fund] has been impaired both for effective action and for unwise interference alike."[40]

On the other hand, it is not very likely that the Group of Seven countries would have been more inclined toward a sharing of their decisionmaking powers with other Fund members simply because of the creation of a Permanent Council. Such a sharing of power could come about only if it were perceived that there were compelling reasons to do so, such as an overriding need to secure the cooperation of members outside the

314 International Development Policies

small group. The weakness of the developing countries, especially since 1982, has militated against any such development.

The result is that far from there being any pressure for the establishment of the Permanent Council recommended by the Committee of Twenty, even the opportunities provided by the existence of the Interim Committee have not been fully utilized. The Committee normally meets only twice a year for one day each time. This is entirely insufficient to allow for serious discussion or negotiation of any major policy issue in depth. Thus the fact that the participants are ministers of finance and governors of central banks does not mean that major policy issues are given thorough high-level examination. The Committee does make significant recommendations to the Executive Board for action but mainly on the basis of the board's own submissions. The Group of Twenty-Four would like the degree of the developed country voting dominance in the Interim Committee and Executive Board alike to be somewhat reduced but they do not aim at unweighted voting. This, however, is only the formal side of the question. The more important issue for the 1990s is to persuade the Group of Seven to engage in a meaningful and continuing dialogue on the salient problems arising in the international monetary and financial system. In other words, granted that predominant influence on the decisionmaking process will remain, as it does now, in the hands of the Group of Seven, it would not be unreasonable to expect a growing willingness of the group to be prepared to consult nonmembers in advance so that all interests could be taken adequately into account. That would require a great deal more than the perfunctory exchanges of views that take place at the one-day meetings, twice a year, of the Interim Committee.

RELATIONS BETWEEN THE BRETTON WOODS INSTITUTIONS AND THE UNITED NATIONS

One of the major sources of controversy between North and South in the United Nations in recent years has been the difference in perceptions of the relationship that should prevail between the United Nations and the Bretton Woods institutions. The OECD countries take the position that the IMF and World Bank are independent institutions with their own responsibilities and governing bodies and that the United Nations is not only not entitled to interfere in the exercise of those responsibilities in any way, but that it is not even competent to discuss the activities of the multilateral financial agencies.

This point of view no doubt reflects in part the difference in the distribution of voting power between the New York and Washington institutions. While the South has an overwhelming majority of the votes in the United Nations, it is the North that holds the majority of the voting power in the IMF and World Bank. Allowing the United Nations to discuss IMF and World Bank matters might, it is feared, undermine the preponderant influence of the major industrial countries in the field of international finance. Since it is the latter countries that supply most of the resources of the Fund and Bank, it is considered only reasonable that their views should determine the purposes for which those resources will be used.

The developing countries, on the other hand, point to the coordinating functions of the United Nations laid down in the UN Charter. Under Article 63 the Economic and Social Council "may coordinate the activities of the specialized agencies through consultations with and recommendations to such agencies and through recommendations to the General Assembly and to the Members of the United Nations." Moreover, under Article 64 the Economic and Social Council (ECOSOC) may not only take steps to obtain "regular reports" from the specialized agencies, but may also "obtain reports on the steps taken to give effect to its own recommendations and to recommendations on matters falling within its competence made by the General Assembly."

The North-South controversy over relations with the Bretton Woods institutions is, however, of relatively recent vintage. It is true that IMF and World Bank representatives to the United Nations have always been careful, whenever the occasion arose, to draw the attention of UN bodies to the agreements between the United Nations and the Bretton Woods institutions whereby each undertook to respect the authority of the other party to the agreement and accepted the fact that each institution was responsible to its own governing body of Member States and to no other.

This in no way prevented the United Nations from discussing broad questions of policy arising in the Bretton Woods institutions and, occasionally, making recommendations to them. Nor did the IMF or World Bank ever seek to prevent such discussions from taking place or such recommendations from being made.

In the early 1950s a UN proposal for the establishment of a fund for grant aid and low-interest, long-term loans to developing countries—known as SUNFED (Special United Nations Fund for Economic Development)—was a major factor leading to the decision to establish the International Development Association (IDA), and this has been recognized in documents of the World Bank. Similarly, the IMF official history recorded the role played by the United Nations in the creation of the CFF in the Fund: in May 1962 the UN Commission on International Commodity Trade invited the IMF to report on the question whether and in what way the Fund might undertake a responsibility for compensatory financing of export fluctuations, and such a facility was established by the Fund in the following year.

Many other examples of collaboration could be cited, including the UN Emergency Operation of 1974–75, established under a resolution of the General Assembly to mobilize financial assistance for the countries "most seriously affected" by the first oil crisis. Both the IMF and the World Bank placed certain members of their respective staffs at the disposal of the Secretary-General of the United Nations to cooperate in the Emergency Operation.

What stands in the way of a resumption of such collaboration is the intensity of the North-South conflict and the loss of mutual confidence. Yet there is no doubt that the United Nations could play a valuable role in airing certain issues, notably those that arise in seeking to achieve consistent international policies in the fields of trade, debt, international finance, and the macro-management of the world economy—policies in respect of which the responsibilities of international institutions are divided. It is well known that serious policy inconsistencies appear continually in these areas. Among them are the following:

- the inconsistency between the efforts of debtors to meet their debt service obligations and the protectionist policies of some of the creditor countries;
- the inconsistency between the Baker Plan's objective for IMF programs of "adjustment with growth" and the sluggish growth of the world economy as a whole;
- the inconsistency between the development objectives of the international community and the perverse net transfer of resources from debtor to creditor countries;
- the inconsistency between the recognition by the Fund and Bank of the urgent need of developing countries for additional import capacity and the failure of the same two institutions to supply financial resources commensurate with the generally accepted scale of the problem.

There is at present no international agency that is dealing systematically with these matters. UNCTAD has for some years been engaged in useful studies and dialogue on the inconsistency problems illustrated above, but its capacity for action is subject to the same limitations as those applying to other UN bodies on subjects related to the responsibilities of the Bretton Woods institutions. The Bank and Fund promote certain trade policies in their borrowing members and the Fund also takes broader account of the interaction between international trade and finance. But all this does not add up to effective action to ensure international policy consistency. Moreover, the Fund and Bank cannot escape the fact that their interests as creditor institutions tend to hamper them in devising international strategies and programs for dealing with the debt problem. This is perhaps the most important reason why six years after the onset of the debt crisis, the Third World economic depression persists, and no long-run international strategy for growing out of the depression has emerged. Indeed, no such strategy has even been discussed in public by the governments most affected as debtors or creditors, together with the private institutions that are also heavily involved.

For this reason alone, a rebuilding of confidence between North and South has become urgent so that the United Nations can resume its role as a forum in which ideas and experience can be exchanged on a broad front, without undue institutional limitations, and in which efforts at mutual persuasion can be undertaken in an atmosphere of willingness on all sides to reexamine entrenched positions.

The Case for the Link*

If all goes well, an important step forward is about to be taken in the evolution of international monetary cooperation. For the first time an attempt is to be made to regulate the supply of international reserves through a deliberate collective decision. If the new approach is successful, the total supply of world reserves will henceforward be adjusted to world requirements for reserves and not to such haphazard factors as the current flow of newly mined gold into official coffers or the deficits in the balances of payments of the reserve currency countries.

The creation of a new form of international liquidity is obviously not an end in itself, but one means among others of establishing a better framework for international economic cooperation within which countries may pursue rational economic policies, particularly policies for promoting higher living standards.

A key element in any improvement in the international environment

*Paper presented at a Hearing before a Subcommittee of the Joint Economic Committee of the U.S. Congress and included in a Congressional document entitled, "Linking Reserve Creation and Development Assistance" (May 28, 1969), pp. 5–15.

must necessarily be an increase in the flow of assistance to the less developed countries. It is now generally accepted at the national level that the community as a whole has a responsibility toward every one of its members, and that active measures are required to provide all members of society with minimum standards of social security and even, perhaps, of income.

Although it is not yet generally accepted that similar considerations apply on a worldwide basis, and that the logical next step after the welfare state is the welfare world, most people in the industrial countries would now recognize the need to provide assistance to the less developed parts of the world as well as the importance of seeking to narrow the growing gulf between incomes in the richer countries and in the poorer countries.

At the second United Nations Conference on Trade and Development held in New Delhi in 1968, the industrial countries accepted a commitment to provide assistance to the less developed countries equivalent to 1 percent of their gross national product. It proved impossible, however, to agree on a date for the achievement of this target largely because certain countries under balance-of-payments pressure did not feel able to commit themselves to an early expansion of foreign aid. The result is that the current flow of resources to the less developed countries averages only seven-tenths of 1 percent of the gross national product of the developed countries as a whole; and in the case of the United States the latest available figure is two-thirds of 1 percent of the gross national product. Nevertheless, we have it on the authority of the World Bank that "the developing countries could now absorb productively new external resources at least equal to what would correspond to the 1 percent of gross national product of the developed countries as a group."[41] In other words, the current flow of resources to the less developed countries is considerably below the amount that they could utilize effectively for increasing productive capacity and growth potential.

If the creation of a new type of international reserve takes place side by side with action to secure a better adjustment in international transactions, and if countries are thereby encouraged to liberalize their trade and aid policies, we might expect the flow of aid to increase without the need for providing a specific link between liquidity creation and the flow of assistance. It is not at all clear, however, that action will indeed be taken to remove the various obstacles to aid that have arisen during the past few years. Concern over the balance of payments and over the war in Vietnam have led to a questioning of the fundamental validity of aid programs as such; and many have sought to rationalize their doubts by pointing to cases in which aid has been wasted or misused. It is, therefore, no accident that we are now going through a period of profound disillusionment with aid programs, in the course of which much of the perspective has been lost, and impatience for quick results has caused people to forget that centuries of economic backwardness cannot be overcome within the span of a single decade.

Given the current mood of pessimism regarding aid prospects, it cannot be taken for granted by any means that an improvement in balance-of-payments positions, and a reversal of the factors which led originally to the curtailment of aid programs will necessarily be accompanied by a revival in such programs. Restrictions on aid once applied tend to perpetuate themselves and it is therefore only through a deliberate effort that an increase in the flow of resources to the less developed countries will be achieved. It is for this reason that the possibility of a deliberate link between reserve creation and development assistance is worthy of consideration.

The principal advantage of such a link is that it makes it possible to step up the flow of assistance to developing countries without involving individual developed countries in any risk of losing reserves. The fact that potential loss of reserves has become a major factor affecting the volume, terms, and conditions of aid programs is clear from the progressive increases that have taken place in the tying of bilateral aid as well as from the efforts made to introduce elements of tying into the operations of the IDA in connection with the current replenishment. The link would relieve governments of the anxiety that resources supplied to less developed countries might result in a weakening of their reserve positions.

A number of governments, while not necessarily concerned about their balance of payments or reserve positions, have found it difficult at a time of generally high taxes to propose increases in taxes for the purpose of expanding foreign assistance. On the other hand, at a given level of government revenue, it may be equally difficult to reorder social priorities in such a way as to make more room within the budget for an enlarged program of foreign aid. Since governments have accepted the 1 percent assistance target, it is to be presumed that they would welcome a way out of this impasse, and the advantage of the link is that it may enable them to respond to the need for more aid without having to raise taxes for this purpose.[42]

But the link might well also make a significant contribution to an improved international monetary system. It is a characteristic feature of the present situation that all developed countries would like to maintain surpluses in their balances of payments. Yet the only way in which all these countries could simultaneously succeed in achieving such surpluses would arise if, as a group, they maintained a sufficiently large export surplus with the less developed countries.

As matters now stand, the sum total of the surpluses on trade in goods and services that the industrial countries would like to maintain is considerably larger than the aggregate surplus with the less developed countries which they are currently prepared to finance through the flow of public and private capital. This means that insofar as any particular developed country succeeds in its objective with respect to its own external surplus, it does so only by frustrating the corresponding objectives of other developed countries. This conflict in turn tends to generate growing competition for available reserves as well as a serious danger of competitive protectionism and exchange depreciation.

The problem is, therefore, to find a means whereby the industrial countries as a group could finance an adequate surplus with the less developed countries as a group. The conditions for a satisfactory equilibrium in this respect are first that the aggregate surplus with the less developed world as a whole should be large enough in relation to the sum of the individual surpluses that each developed country would consider desirable in its own particular circumstances; and that the method of financing the surplus should be such as to contribute to an improvement in the international monetary situation and not to a deterioration. From this standpoint, if the developed countries give away the surpluses in the form of grants, this does not yield any benefit to the balances of payments of those donor countries that are currently in deficit. If they provide the resources in the form of loans, they acquire long-term claims on the developing countries, but these too are not generally regarded as providing a source of strength for the balance of payments, at any rate in the short run.

There would, therefore, be great advantages in an arrangement whereby export surpluses with less developed countries would be made to yield usable assets in the form of internationally accepted reserves. If it were possible for developed countries to earn additional reserves by enlarging their export balances with developing countries, they would probably be inclined to take a quite different view of such surpluses from the view which they take at the present time. In that case, they would see the same advantage in transferring real resources to less developed countries in exchange for additional reserves as in the traditional exchange of real resources for additional gold.

The question may be asked why the industrial countries should saddle themselves with the burden of having to earn the new reserves through transfers of real resources to the less developed countries: under the new arrangements for SDRS as they stand, they can obtain additional reserves without any cost at all.

This point is well grounded: there is no compulsion at all on the industrial countries to adopt a link between liquidity creation and development assistance. If they did accept the idea of such a link, it would be an entirely voluntary act of economic statesmanship. Indeed, it might even be suggested that once the industrial countries find that they are able to acquire SDRS costlessly, they will no longer be as concerned about running balance-of-payments surpluses as they are now.

It may, however, be doubted whether countries would in fact lose their proclivity for balance-of-payments surpluses, even if they were able to add to reserves by other means. For one thing, the employment-creating effect of such surpluses should not be overlooked. But even aside from that, it is doubtful whether a country could for long command confidence in the stability of its currency if it were adding to its reserves solely by virtue of the periodic receipt of SDRS, and was otherwise in balance-of-payments deficit. Rightly or wrongly, the currency of a country in such a position would probably be regarded as vulnerable and hence would be subject to speculative attack.

But even if this were not so, it would remain an important advantage of the link that it provides a unique method of tying together and reconciling a number of objectives which might otherwise tend to conflict. Since the industrial countries do, at the present time, all prefer to run balance-of-payments surpluses, the advantageous way of dealing with the potential inconsistency of these aims is not to find methods of doing away with the surpluses or making them unnecessary; but rather to channel the surplus resources thereby generated to the countries that stand in need of them. And insofar as the current flow of public and private capital to the less developed countries is inadequate to finance surpluses in the amounts desired by the industrial countries, individually and collectively, the creation of opportunities to earn reserves would make it possible to finance the remainder.

Various objections have been raised against the idea of the link. The Ossola Study Group set up by the major industrial countries reported that most of its members believed that the provision of capital to developing countries is quite distinct from the creation of reserves and should be achieved by other techniques. Yet it is difficult to see why the fact that a particular measure may achieve two different types of results at the same time should be regarded as invalidating it. A high tax on tobacco tends to restrain a harmful form of consumption at the same time as it adds to government revenue; and the fact that two objectives are thereby achieved rather than one is not generally regarded as an argument against such a tax.

However, the Ossola Study Group advanced a more serious objection when it expressed the fear that if the creation of new reserve assets were mixed up with the provision of development finance, there would be a danger that the requirements of the latter would begin to take priority over those of the former. This, it was felt, would introduce an inflexibility into whatever new monetary arrangements were introduced, and would thus impair the monetary quality of the new asset. The Ossola Group conceded that if the amount of reserve creation associated with development finance were kept at a modest fraction of the total creation of reserves the difficulties might not be insuperable. But the Group felt that it would be difficult to resist demands from developing countries, and even internal pressures in the industrial countries themselves, to give aid in this form.[43]

It is a perfectly valid point that liquidity creation should respond to world liquidity needs and not to aid requirements. As the UNCTAD expert group on international monetary issues put it:

We are quite clear that the amount of any new reserve creation should be determined by the monetary requirements of the world economy and not by the need for development finance. But once the need for additional reserves has been demonstrated and the amount of the addition determined on the basis of monetary requirements, the introduction of a link with development finance is entirely proper and desirable.[44]

It should also be borne in mind that under the arrangements for the creation of SDRs in the IMF, an 85 percent majority of the voting power of participants is required. It will be apparent that a majority as large as this is likely to err on the side of excessive caution rather than of excessive adventurousness: for it would take only a small minority of the industrial countries to block a proposal for adding to reserves at any particular time. Under these conditions the danger foreseen by the Ossola Study Group does not seem to be a serious one.

A third objection to the link was voiced by the Deputies of the Group of Ten when, in their report of July 1966, they stated that "We are agreed that deliberate reserve creation is not intended to effect permanent transfers of real resources from some countries to others."[45]

It is odd that this particular objection has been raised, because the traditional gold standard took precisely this form. In other words, under the gold standard, countries wishing to add to their reserves transferred real resources to the countries where the gold was mined, in the form of an export balance of goods and services. Similarly, countries wishing to acquire dollars or sterling may do so by transferring real resources to the United States or the United Kingdom, respectively. Thus the Deputies were, in effect, proposing an entirely new approach to reserve creation. It is difficult to understand why they should have felt it appropriate for industrial countries to earn gold by transferring real resources to the countries where the gold was mined, but inappropriate for them to earn the new reserve asset by transferring real resources to the less developed countries.

A fourth objection has been put forward by Professor Harry Johnson, who has suggested, by way of analogy, that the establishment of the Federal Reserve System would have been indefinitely postponed if the new central bank had been required to invest most of its assets in loans to poor people.[46] The implication is that the establishment of the system of SDRs might be prejudiced if SDRs were used for investment in the less-developed countries.

It is not entirely clear what Professor Johnson had in mind in making this comment. But in any case it would be wrong to suppose that what is involved here is an effort to misuse SDRs by making potentially unsound loans to less developed countries. The suggestion is rather that SDRs should be directly or indirectly used to provide additional resources for the World Bank group. And the financial standing of the World Bank is hardly comparable with that of "poor people."

The fact is that World Bank obligations have the highest standing in the financial community—a standing which is as strong as that of the joint and several guarantees by the major financial powers of the world on which it is based. Even if it were not the case (which it is) that there has never been a default on a World Bank loan to a less developed country, the fact that the Bank is supported by guarantees of the big powers means that its credit standing is, in effect, virtually as high as that of the big powers themselves. Thus the use of SDRs to augment the resources of the World Bank could not be regarded as prejudicing the new reserve asset in any way.

Two other objections to the link are frequently encountered. On the one hand, it has been suggested that it would not be worth complicating and encumbering the already difficult process of international monetary reform for the sake of an addition to the flow of aid which would in any case be relatively small. On the other hand, it is also argued that the utilization of new money to increase the flow of resources to the less developed countries would add to the danger of inflation.

It will be obvious that these two suggestions cannot both be valid. Either the flow of real resources engendered by the link would be small, in which case their inflationary effect would also be small; or if the inflationary effect is appreciable, then the flow of resources must also be appreciable.

However, it seems that the danger of inflation is in any case rather exaggerated. Even if the link resulted in the provision of additional resources to developing countries in an annual amount of as much as $5 billion—a much higher figure than is likely—this would add less than one-third of 1 percent to the demand for output in the OECD countries, which amounted to about $1,700 billion in 1968. This could hardly generate an inflationary problem of major concern to the developed countries.

Finally, it has been suggested that if the industrial countries are not prepared to expand their aid by direct means—that is, by direct contributions to bilateral and multilateral aid programs—they are not likely to be willing to do the same thing indirectly—that is, through the link. Alternatively, insofar as they do agree to the link, they may simply make offsetting cuts in other aid programs.

There is, of course, no magic about the link. Like other forms of assistance, it would be effective only insofar as it brought about a transfer of real resources from the industrial countries. To put the matter in another way, the real burden of aid is the same whether the transfer takes place by conventional methods or through such methods as the link.

On the other hand, it would be wrong to suppose that institutional obstacles play no part in preventing an expansion of aid programs. For example, as noted earlier, governments may be unwilling to raise taxes for the purpose of expanding aid programs, but may have much less difficulty in contemplating an increase in aid through a device such as the link, even though they know that the total real burden on the community may be the same.

The possibility that introduction of the link would tempt governments to reduce other forms of aid cannot be entirely dismissed. Indeed, problems of this type arise whenever new channels for aid are being considered. Thus, for example, it is always possible to argue that there is no point in replenishing the resources of IDA because the amount involved will be cut out of bilateral aid programs. Or, again, one can maintain that whatever resources are provided to the regional development banks, such as the Inter-American Development Bank, are only at the expense of the funds that would otherwise be available for the World Bank.

It is, however, unlikely that the opening up of new channels of aid adds nothing at all to the total flow. The net increase in the total level of aid resulting from the link may turn out to be less than the direct allocations of SDRS (or their equivalent in national currencies) to IDA would lead one to suppose. But there would probably be some net increase, and my own impression is that the net increase would be considerable.

We come finally to the question of the most suitable form for the link. Hitherto, in this essay, the discussion has taken place in terms of what might be called an "organic" link—that is to say, a link in which SDRS are themselves used, directly or indirectly, for the channeling of resources to the less developed countries. This would happen if, for example, SDRS were allocated to the World Bank and corresponding loans (either in SDRS or in national currencies) were made to less developed countries.

It would be possible to envisage a number of possible variants of the "organic" link, and consideration could be given to the technical advantages and disadvantages of each variant. However, one major consideration is that the amendment to the Articles of Agreement of the Fund currently in process of ratification by the Fund's member governments in effect rules out the holding of SDRS by multilateral institutions engaged in development assistance.[47] It hardly seems likely that governments which have brought themselves to the point of ratifying a major new departure in the Articles of Agreement of the Fund would, in the immediate future, act to reverse themselves on a salient feature of the new amendment.

There is, therefore, a strong case for considering an alternative link proposal originally put forward independently by Professor Triffin and by Dr. Patel, Economic Adviser to the Minister of Finance of India, and one of the members of the UNCTAD expert group referred to above. The essence of the proposal is that every act of international liquidity creation should be accompanied by voluntary contributions to IDA by all the Part I member countries of IDA—the size of the voluntary contribution being a certain uniform proportion of the share of every Part I country in international liquidity creation.[48]

Most of the objections to the link in its "organic" form do not apply to this alternative version. From a legal standpoint, there is nothing in the amendment of the Articles of Agreement of the IMF that would preclude such an arrangement. And from the standpoint of economic and banking policy, the alternative version of the link would provide for a clear separation between liquidity creation and development assistance, as recommended by the critics of the "organic" link.

What is involved, essentially, is the acceptance of parallel and simultaneous commitments to increase aid by developed countries benefiting

from allocations of sDRs. Since one of the objectives of new reserve creation is presumably to encourage more liberal trade and aid policies,
the assumption of such parallel obligations would be in the spirit of the
reform, while maintaining the separate and independent character of
the two processes—liquidity creation and the provision of development
finance.

The advantages of the link in the Triffin/Patel version may be summa-
rized as follows:

- It has the advantages of the "organic" link in permitting industrial
  countries to increase the flow of real resources to less developed countries, (a) without incurring any loss in reserves, and (b) probably without having to raise taxes.
- It meets some of the principal objections of the Deputies of the Group
  of Ten by establishing a clear separation between reserve creation and
  development assistance, and by avoiding a direct use of sDRs for a
  permanent transfer of real resources.
- It also avoids the danger that aid requirements might determine the
  amount of additional sDRs created by providing for assistance only as
  a parallel and voluntary process, which would itself always be subject
  to review.
- It assists in channeling the export surpluses universally desired by
  industrial countries toward the countries most in need of additional
  resources.
- It directs the increased flow of assistance to a multilateral institution,
  namely the International Development Association.

In the longer run, and once experience has been gained in the operation of a voluntary link, it might prove to be more generally acceptable
to governments than it is at the present time to build the link process
integrally into the system of liquidity creation itself. In that case it would
become possible to negotiate a further amendment to the Articles of
Agreement of the Fund to provide for such an arrangement.

The Link Reconsidered*

The primary objective of sDR creation is to add to world reserves in accordance with the monetary requirements of the world economy—what

*Paper submitted to the Canadian Parliamentary Task Force on North-South Relations,
September 18, 1980.

Article XVIII of the IMF Articles of Agreement refers to as the "long-term global need." The attainment of that primary purpose does not depend on any particular pattern of distribution of newly created SDRs. In order to achieve the purely monetary objectives of SDR creation, all that is necessary is that the level and rate of expansion of world reserves, including SDRs, should be consistent with the balanced growth of the world economy, free of inflationary or deflationary tendencies. A variety of SDR distribution patterns would, in principle, be compatible with the above aims, and the international community is therefore free to choose that particular pattern which, while consistent with the monetary requirements of the world economy, would at the same time facilitate the attainment of other objectives. The creation of SDRs is a collective act par excellence of the international community, generating savings of real resources by comparison with available alternatives—savings that may be regarded as accruing to the IMF membership as a whole. The method of distribution of the benefits of such savings is a matter for the membership to determine, and it is appropriate that such distribution should serve a worldwide objective that is second to none—namely the objective of development. Thus the case for the link is that the international community would, through the link, be employing internationally generated savings to attain collectively agreed goals, notably the achievement of the internationally accepted goals of development.

Despite the strength of the case, the Committee of Twenty, as is well known, was unable to reach agreement on the establishment of the link. There were a number of considerations that stood in the way of adoption of the link at that time, of which there were, perhaps, three that were paramount. The first was that it was considered improper for liquidity creation to be used to effect a transfer of real resources on a long-term basis for development purposes. Monetary reserves were for holding on a contingency basis and not for a permanent transfer of resources between countries. A second consideration was that it was feared that adoption of the link would lead to irresistible pressure for excessive SDR creation, with inevitable inflationary implications. A third counterargument was that the use of SDR allocations for aid purposes would be offset by reductions in aid through other channels, so that there would be no additionality.

In reevaluating these arguments in the context of the situation facing us today, there is one new factor that would appear to change the entire balance of the questions at issue. That new factor is the emergence of large current account imbalances that present a serious threat to international economic and financial stability. Present expectations are that the combined current account deficit of non-oil developing countries will amount to no less than $68 billion in 1980, increase further to $78 billion in 1981, and remain considerably larger in the next several years than they had been before 1979. At the same time there are growing indications that private capital markets may be unable or unwilling to continue providing balance-of-payments support to certain of the developing countries on the scale of previous years. Moreover, there are many countries, particularly the poorer ones, that do not qualify for balance-of-payments support from private institutions under conventional criteria of creditworthiness.

Thus the case for an SDR link is greatly strengthened by the fact that such a link could pay an invaluable role in the recycling process and would therefore make a major contribution to the stability of the international monetary system.

In the absence of some such means of adding substantially to the reserves of developing countries, the only alternative available to them would be to cut back their economies and development programs to the point at which their imports were forced into balance with their exports at a low level. Such a major retrenchment might be considered unavoidable and even desirable if deficits were primarily the result of overexpansion in these countries. But the reason for the deficits does not lie predominantly with domestically generated inflation, even though elements of such a condition may be present in some cases. Generally speaking, the principal cause of the new deficits is a deterioration in terms of trade that results from increases in the prices of imported goods, notably oil and manufactures, coupled with a slackening in export earnings due to business recession and growing restrictions on imports in the industrial countries. In the light of their share in total world imports of oil, it might have been expected that the industrial countries would incur the lion's share of the deficits that are the counterpart of the surpluses of the oil exporting countries. In fact, however, the industrial countries have been shifting an increasing proportion of these counterpart deficits on to the shoulders of the weaker non-oil developing countries. Even in 1980 the industrial countries' expected combined deficit of $52 billion is considerably less than one-half of the oil exporting countries' projected surplus of $115 billion. In 1981 this share is expected to decline sharply (to $17 billion as against an oil exporting countries' surplus of $95 billion).

How, then, is one to view the case for and against the link in the light of these developments? We have already referred to the manner in which the case for the link is strengthened in the situation confronting the world in the 1980s. There is general agreement that an efficient system of recycling is indispensable if the international monetary system is to cope successfully with the unprecedented strains caused by the current level of payments imbalances. The link could make a vital contribution to such recycling, a contribution that would be particularly important for the countries that are mainly or wholly dependent on official sources for balance-of-payments support—namely the weakest and poorest countries.

How does the new situation affect the arguments against the link? The first argument, it will be recalled, rejected the combination of liquidity creation and development assistance. But this argument loses much of its force if the objective of the SDR link is to facilitate the recycling process, for here the goal of the link moves much closer to the goal of liquidity creation. In the case of developing countries having access to private capital markets, the link would strengthen their capacity to borrow. And for the poorer countries SDRS provided through the link would fulfill the same function that balance-of-payments borrowing from the private market has performed in the industrial and more advanced developing countries.

The second counterargument, to the effect that the link would create pressure for excessive international liquidity creation, also takes on a new aspect. The extraordinary liquidity explosion of the last ten years through the expansion of reserve currency creation shows that the threat of SDR creation was greatly exaggerated. In fact the share of SDRs in reserves excluding gold declined from about 10 percent at the beginning of 1972 to only 4 percent at the present time, and this rapid decline is expected to continue. If the share were calculated as a proportion of reserves including gold at market prices, the decline would be even more drastic.

These developments have been accompanied by a major deterioration in the reserve position of non-oil developing countries. The total gross reserves (excluding gold holdings, which are small) of non-oil developing countries declined from the equivalent of 32 percent of merchandise imports before 1973 to 24 percent at the end of 1979; the decline in net reserves must have been considerably steeper. This was in spite of an increase in the need for reserves owing to the much greater variability of imports and exports for reasons beyond the control of the developing countries.

Article XVIII, Section 1(a), of the Fund's Articles of Agreement provides that "In all its decisions with respect to the allocation and cancellation of special drawing rights the Fund shall seek to meet the long-term global need, as and when it arises, to supplement existing reserve assets in such manner as will promote the attainment of its purposes and will avoid economic stagnation and deflation as well as excess demand and inflation in the world."

Even before the collapse of the Bretton Woods system there was some doubt as to the meaning to be assigned to the idea of a "long-term global need" for reserves. At various times during the past century the world has operated with very different ratios of reserves to imports, and it would be difficult to say which of these ratios corresponded to a long-term global need for reserves and which did not.

But, however this question might have been answered during the period of the gold standard or of the gold exchange standard, the advent of the system of generalized floating has changed the whole framework of the problem. Under the new dispensation developed countries can usually add to their foreign exchange holdings at will. This they can do either by borrowing reserve currencies, or by purchasing them, accepting any consequential decline in the exchange rate.

Thus the meaning of a "global long-term need" for reserves becomes quite uncertain under conditions in which the level of reserves is not only a function of the balance-of-payments positions of the reserve currency countries, but can be manipulated by the industrial countries generally in accordance with their respective demands for reserves. The one thing that is certain is that, as noted earlier, the share of SDRs in total reserves excluding gold has been and is declining sharply. This situation is not only inequitable as between developed and developing countries, but runs counter to Article VIII, Section 7, and Article XXII of the Articles of Agreement, which set forth the objective of making the SDR "the principal reserve asset in the international monetary system."

The third counterargument to the link was that it would not add to the total flow of real resources to developing countries. This was always, at best, a metaphysical argument, impossible to prove or disprove. The argument that the total flow of real resources to developing countries would not be increased has been used in efforts to defeat virtually every new proposal that has ever been made to this end, including the proposals to establish the World Bank, the International Development Association, and each one of the regional development banks. It is, of course, theoretically possible that none of these institutions has added to the flow of resources to developing countries, but is there anybody today who seriously doubts that they have done just that?

That still does not suffice to prove that the link would ensure additionality. The belief that it would do so derives from the view that collective pressure for additional aid within a framework of multilateral decisionmaking is more likely to be successful in the aggregate than the pressures exerted upon individual governments in a purely national context. There is also the consideration that once a multilateral decision in principle is taken to give developing countries a favored position in the allocation of SDRS, the implementation of that decision through successive SDR allocations by collective agreement is less likely to be undermined by political pressures in any one country, however large or powerful.

Finally, whatever risks there may be as regards additionality, those principally concerned, namely the potential developing country recipients, are prepared to accept them and take the consequences.

To sum up, the basic validity of the original case for the link has been greatly strengthened by developments of the past decade, including the collapse of the system of fixed exchange rates, the explosion of international liquidity through reserve currency creation and the enormous increase in the price of gold, and the advent of a situation of unprecedented imbalance which presents a dangerous threat to the stability of the international monetary system. SDR allocations distributed in a manner that would favor developing countries could make a vital contribution to the recycling process, and hence to world economic stability and recovery.

Notes

1 INTRODUCTION

1. *Partners in Development*, Report of the Commission on International Development, Lester B. Pearson, chairman (New York: Praeger, 1969), p. 9.
2. *North-South: A Programme for Survival*, Report of the Independent Commission on International Development Issues, Willy Brandt, chairman (Cambridge, Mass.: MIT Press, 1980), pp. 20–21.
3. An interesting example of this will be found in chapter 6 in the essay on the debt problem, "Strategies and Solutions." See n. 40 concerning a 1985 recommendation for "outright debt relief" by a Subcommittee of the Committee on Banking, Finance, and Urban Affairs of the House of Representatives. Many other such instances could be cited.
4. See chapter 2 below.
5. In an article published in 1980 Chung and Lee showed that there was no statistically significant difference between production techniques chosen by foreign and local firms in Korea. The methodology employed was later challenged by Howard Pack, who conceded, however, that "the major result of Chung and Lee about the absence of significant differences in factor choice between domestic and foreign firms is likely to be correct." (*Economic Development and Cultural Change*, October 1980, pp. 135–40, and April 1984, pp. 625–28.)
6. Donald Moggridge, ed., *The Collected Writings of John Maynard Keynes*, 25 (Royal Economic Society, 1980): 27, 29.
7. *IMF Survey* (February 9, 1981), p. 35.
8. Ibid.
9. Edward S. Mason and Robert E. Asher, *The World Bank Since Bretton Woods* (Washington, D.C.: Brookings Institution, 1973), p. 443.
10. "Structural Adjustment Policies, Report to the Group of Twenty-Four," by Sidney Dell, Carlos Diaz-Alejandro, Ricardo Ffrench-Davis, Toma Gudac, and Cristián Ossa, in *The International Monetary System and Its Reform*, ed. S. Dell, 2 (Amsterdam: North Holland, 1987): 541–56.
11. It is, however, argued in chapter 9 that the proposal for a link between liquidity creation and development finance would not be detrimental to the main functions of the Fund.
12. The 0.7 percent target relates to official flows only, whereas the 1 percent target includes also net flows of private capital.

2 THE INTERNATIONAL ECONOMIC ENVIRONMENT

1. See, for example, IMF, *World Economic Outlook* (Washington, D.C.: IMF, April 1982), p. 9.

2. *Business Week* (July 19, 1982), pp. 118–22.

3. From an address to a meeting of businessmen at Hamburg, Federal Republic of Germany, on March 5, 1982, on the occasion of the *Ostasiatisches Liebesmahl*.

4. Alexandre Kafka, an Executive Director of IMF, has suggested that a more appropriate characterization would be "beggar-my-poorest-neighbor" policies.

5. Concern was sometimes expressed at the relatively small spreads over the London Interbank Offered Rate (LIBOR) at which loans were made during this period, appearing to imply low profitability for the lending banks concerned. As pointed out in a study by the Group of Thirty, however, large banks are able to borrow at rates below LIBOR, so that the margins between their borrowing and lending rates significantly exceed reported spreads over LIBOR. See Group of Thirty, *The Outlook for International Bank Lending* (New York: Group of Thirty, 1981), pp. 23, 24.

6. Group of Thirty, *Risks in International Bank Lending* (New York: Group of Thirty, 1982), p. 7.

7. IMF, *Annual Report, 1982* (Washington, D.C., 1982), p. 1.

8. Bank of England, *Quarterly Bulletin* 22, no. 3 (September 1982): 328.

9. Ibid.

10. Bank for International Settlements, *Fifty-Second Annual Report* (Basle, Switzerland, June 14, 1982), p. 35.

11. Sir John Hicks, "What Is Wrong with Monetarism," *Lloyds Bank Review* 118 (October 1975).

12. The *New York Times* (May 31, 1982).

13. By "inflation" Viner meant an increase in the total amount of spendable funds. He was, however, also in favor of raising prices as a means of restoring business profit margins.

14. See Annual Message to Congress on the State of the Union, January 7, 1954, in *Public Papers of the Presidents: Dwight D. Eisenhower, 1954* (Washington, D.C.: U.S. Government Printing Office, 1960).

15. IMF, *World Economic Outlook* (April 1982), pp. 11, 12.

16. OECD, *Economic Outlook* 31 (Paris, July 1982): 31.

17. IMF, *World Economic Outlook* (April 1982), p. 11.

18. See "Restoring Fiscal Discipline: A Vital Element of a Policy for Economic Recovery," an address delivered by the Managing Director of IMF to the American Enterprise Institute, Washington, D.C., March 16, 1982; reproduced in *IMF Survey* 11, no. 6 (March 22, 1982): 81–87.

19. IMF, *World Economic Outlook* (April 1982), p. 54.

20. An OECD study, cited in the Report to the Brandt Commission (*North-South: A Programme for Survival* [Cambridge, Mass.: MIT Press, 1980], p. 67), suggested that the effect of the increased import demand of the oil-importing, developing countries was to add about 900,000 to the employed labor force of the industrial countries every year from 1973 to 1977.

21. IMF, *Annual Report, 1974* (Washington, D.C., 1974), Appendix II, Decision No. 4134-(74/4).

22. For an elaboration of this point, see Sidney Dell, *On Being Grandmotherly: The Evolution*

of IMF Conditionality, Essays in International Finance Series, no. 144 (Princeton, N.J.: Princeton University International Section, Department of Economics, October 1981). Reprinted in chapter 8 of this volume.

3 DEVELOPMENT OBJECTIVES

1. *Employment, Growth and Basic Needs: A One-World Problem* (Geneva: International Labor Office, 1976), p. 31.
2. Ibid., p. 32. This is the definition of basic needs adopted by the World Employment Conference, which is virtually the same as that proposed by the ILO staff.
3. Ibid., p. 43.
4. Ibid.
5. See Mário Henrique Simonsen, *Brasil 2001* (Rio de Janeiro, 1969), p. 285. Mr. Simonsen later became Minister of Finance of Brazil.
6. General Assembly Resolution 2626(XXV).
7. Ibid., paras. 12, 18. Para. 71 calls for particular efforts "to expand low-cost housing through both public and private programs and on a self-help basis, including through cooperatives, utilizing as much as possible local raw materials and labor-intensive techniques." Para. 68 calls for national targets for the provision of potable water.
8. UN Committee for Development Planning, "Report of the 6th Session" (5/15 January 1970), Document E/4776, para. 14. The other members of the Committee were Gamani Corea, Nazih Deif, A. N. Efimov, Paul Kaya, J. A. Lacarte, J. H. Mensah, Saburo Okita, Josef Pajestka, M. L. Qureshi, K. N. Raj, Jean Ripert, Germanico Salgado, Jakov Sirotkovic, Zdenek Vergner.
9. Ibid., paras. 28–29.
10. Ibid., para. 41.
11. Ibid., para. 15.
12. ILO, *Employment, Growth and Basic Needs*, p. 7.
13. *Dietary Goals for the United States*, Report prepared by the staff of the Select Committee on Nutrition and Human Needs, U.S. Senate (Washington, D.C.: U.S. Government Printing Office, February 1977), p. 20, and Appendix C.
14. Thomas T. Poleman, "World Food: Myth and Reality," *World Development* 5, nos. 5–7 (May–July 1977): 385–86. It also appears that there may have been widespread underestimation of calorie intake in the developing world owing to inadequate sampling of food items consumed. For example, a study of Kerala has shown that this factor has been responsible for a 30 percent underestimation of food consumption in that state. See United Nations, *Poverty, Unemployment and Development Policy: A Case Study of Selected Issues with Reference to Kerala*, UN Publication Sales No. E.75.IV.11, pp. 1, 22–24, 34–35.
15. This would be true even after making a generous allowance for the increase in per capita consumption from 1963 to 1974, when the proportion of malnutrition was estimated at 25 percent.
16. *Employment, Growth and Basic Needs*, p. 68.
17. Ibid., p. 8.
18. Ibid., pp. 32–33.
19. Ibid., p. 43.
20. Ibid., p. 43. In other words the 6 percent growth target is insufficient.
21. Raúl Prebisch, "Change and Development: Latin America's Great Task," Report

submitted to the Inter-American Development Bank, Washington, D.C., July 1970, mimeo, chapter 4, passim.

22. "Report of the 24th Pugwash Symposium" (Dar es Salaam: June 2–6, 1975) as published in *World Development* 5, no. 3 (March 1977): 257. The participants in the symposium were R. Andriambolona, O. Bassir, W. K. Chagula, Bernard T. Feld, L. K. H. Goma, M. Goldsmith, K. N. Hirji, M. M. Semakula Kiwanuka, I. M. Kaduma, I. Mann, P. Mwombela, D. Nkunika, M. S. Ntamila, C. H. G. Oldman, S. J. Patel, A. Parthasarathi, J. F. Rweyemamu, F. Sagasti, A. R. Sidky, and I. Sachs. The report was prepared by the Rapporteur of the Symposium, A. Parthasarathi.

23. Ibid.

24. Wassily Leontief, *The Future of the World Economy* (New York: Oxford University Press, 1977).

25. "Report of the 24th Pugwash Symposium," p. 257.

26. Ponna Wignaraja, "From the Village to the Global Order," *Development Dialogue*, 1 (Uppsala: Dag Hammarskjöld Foundation, 1977).

27. Jon Sigurdson, "Rural Industrialization in China," *World Development* 3, nos. 7–8 (July–August 1975).

28. Nicholas Kaldor, "The Role of Modern Technology in Raising the Economic Standards of the Less Developed Countries," paper presented to the International Conference on Technological Change and Human Development (April 1969).

29. One of the most disruptive features of urban life—traffic congestion—would not be difficult to remedy if there existed the political will to do so. Such is the power of the automobile industry that road transport (particularly the personally owned automobile) does not have to bear anything approaching the social costs of the congestion and pollution that it causes. Rectification of this anomalous situation by drastic restrictions or heavy taxation of personal use of automobiles in central cities, combined with adequate provision of public transport, would greatly increase the viability and amenity of urban living.

30. The ILO's Report to the World Employment Conference limits itself to saying that any transitional shortages of basic goods can be met by changing the composition of imports or increasing their volume, by food aid, or by a temporary rationing system. (*Employment, Growth and Basic Needs*, pp. 67–68). The problem is, however, of a much more than transitional character.

31. Ibid., p. 67.

32. Professor Michael Lipton refers to "the dark neo-Stalinist night in which almost all 'development experts' have lurched around since 1945, muttering half-coherent praises of instant industrialization." See Lipton, "The New Economics of Growth: A Review," *World Development* 5, no. 3 (March 1977): 267.

33. Paul Streeten, "Industrialization in a Unified Development Strategy," *World Development* 3, no. 1 (January 1975): 1–2.

34. Nicholas Kaldor, *Strategic Factors in Economic Development* (Ithaca, N.Y.: State School of Industrial and Labor Relations, Cornell University, 1967), p. 17.

35. *A Basic Human Needs Strategy of Development: Staff Report on the World Employment Conference* (Washington, D.C.: U.S. Government Printing Office, September 1976), p. 11.

36. Frances Stewart, *Technology and Underdevelopment* (London: Macmillan, 1977), p. 78.

37. See Suzanne Paine, "Balanced Development: Maoist Conception and Chinese Practice," *World Development* 4, no. 4 (April 1976).

38. The latter proposition is, of course, valid even where the distribution of income in recipient countries improves.

39. *A Basic Human Needs Strategy of Development*, p. 1.

40. U.K. Ministry of Overseas Development, *The Changing Emphasis in British Aid Policies: More Help for the Poorest* (H.M. Stationery Office, Cmnd. 6270, October 1975), p. 2.

41. Ibid., chapter 3, paras. 3–4.

42. The *OECD Observer* (November 1977), p. 20.

43. Robert McNamara, *Address to the Board of Governors* (World Bank, September 26, 1977), Annex III.

44. According to Hollis Chenery et al., *Redistribution with Growth* (New York: Oxford University Press, 1974), table 1.2, 72.9 percent of the population of Tanzania was living below the poverty line of $75 per capita income (in 1971 prices) in 1969. The corresponding percentages for some other countries were as follows: Dahomey 90.1; Chad 77.5; Burma 71.0; Madagascar 69.9; India 66.9; Sri Lanka 63.5; Sierra Leone 61.5; and Niger 59.9.

45. Uma Lele, *The Design of Rural Development* (Baltimore: published for the World Bank by Johns Hopkins University Press, 1975), p. 176.

46. Ibid.

47. Ibid., p. 69. "Intensity" is roughly measured by the ratio of extension workers to farmers.

48. U.K. Ministry of Overseas Development, *The Changing Emphasis in British Aid Policies*, chapter 3, paras. 4–5.

4 INTERNATIONAL TRADE POLICIES FOR DEVELOPMENT

1. William R. Cline, *Reciprocity: A New Approach to World Trade Policy* (Washington, D.C.: Institute for International Economics, September 1982).

2. Gary R. Saxonhouse, "The Micro- and Macroeconomics of Foreign Sales to Japan," in William R. Cline, ed., *Trade Policy in the 1980s* (Cambridge, Mass.: MIT Press, 1983).

3. Robert Z. Lawrence, "Imports in Japan: Closed Minds or Markets?" *Brookings Papers on Economic Activity* 2 (Washington, D.C.: Brookings Institution, 1987): 517–54.

4. Jagdish Bhagwati, *Protectionism* (Cambridge, Mass.: MIT Press, 1988), p. 70.

5. Henry R. Nau, "Bargaining in the New Round: The NICs and the United States," mimeo., July 18–20, 1986.

6. Commonwealth Secretariat, "The Uruguay Round of Multilateral Trade Negotiations: Commonwealth Interests and Opportunities," November 1986.

7. Karl P. Sauvant, "Services TDF and the Code," *The CTC Reporter* 22 (Autumn 1986).

8. Joel Davidow, "Antitrust and Transfer of Technology Rules: Recent Developments," *The CTC Reporter* 19 (Spring 1985).

9. Ibid.

10. Harald B. Malmgren, "Negotiating International Rules for Services," *World Economy* 8, no. 1 (Trade Policy Research Centre, London, March 1985).

11. Rachel McCulloch, "International Competition in Services," Working Paper No. 2235, National Bureau of Economic Research (May 1987).

5 FOREIGN INVESTMENT

1. Mutual Security Act of 1955, *Hearings before the Committee on Foreign Relations*, U.S. Senate, May 5–23, 1955, pp. 300–301.
2. Albert O. Hirschman, *How to Divest in Latin America and Why*, Essays in International Finance Series no. 76 (Princeton, N.J.: Princeton University International Section, Department of Economics, November 1969).
3. General Assembly Resolution 2626(XXV), October 24, 1970, para. 50.
4. *Summary of the Hearings Before the Group of Eminent Persons to Study the Impact of Multinational Corporations on Development and on International Relations*, UN Publication Sales No. E.74.II.A.9, p. 22.
5. *Report of the Group of Eminent Persons to Study the Impact of Multinational Corporations on Development and on International Relations*, UN Publication Sales No. E.74.II.A.5, p. 26.
6. Anthony Sampson, *The Sovereign State of ITT* (New York: Stein and Day, 1973), pp. 274, 286.
7. Seymour J. Rubin, "The Multinational Enterprise at Bay," *American Journal of International Law* 68 (1974): 479, 480.
8. Ibid. p. 480.
9. Ibid. The memorandum was released by the subcommittee in March 1974.
10. Bank for International Settlements Press Review, October 12, 1984.
11. The difference between loan and equity capital referred to by Secretary Baker is conceptually clear, but the data used in policy discussion tend to be highly misleading. Under standard definitions direct investment flows include substantial funds borrowed by local subsidiaries from parent companies abroad, so that the true equity component of such flows is much smaller than is commonly supposed. It is quite possible that as business conditions in debtor countries have deteriorated, the transnationals have increased the nonequity share of direct investment flows so as to assure themselves of a satisfactory return flow of income on such loans at a time of shrinking profits and hence profit remittances. These considerations do not, of course, gainsay the proposition that larger flows of equity capital would be desirable—they are merely a warning that even if a rise in foreign direct investment were to occur, that would not necessarily betoken a corresponding increase in the flow of equity capital.
12. Data in this and the following paragraph are from the IMF's *World Economic Outlook* (Washington, D.C., October 1989), which does not show any breakdown of net debtor developing countries—a category that excludes Iran, Kuwait, Libyan Arab Jamahiriya, Oman, Qatar, Saudi Arabia, Taiwan, and the United Arab Emirates.
13. Estimated by the IMF at $17.3 billion for 1988. As of October 1989 the forecast of net direct investment in net debtor developing countries in 1989 was $15.5 billion and in 1990 $17.9 billion.
14. See, for example, William R. Cline's *International Debt and the Stability of the World Economy* (Washington, D.C.: Institute for International Economics, September 1983), p. 71.
15. UN Centre on Transnational Corporations, *Transnational Corporations in World Development: Third Survey*, UN Publication Sales No. E.83.II.A.14, para. 88.
16. *Report of the Group of Eminent Persons*, p. 26.
17. Sanjaya Lall and Paul Streeten, *Foreign Investment, Transnationals and Developing Countries* (London: Macmillan, 1977).

18. Ibid., p. 178.

19. Ibid., p. 182.

20. U.S. Internal Revenue Service, "Multinational Companies (MNCS): Tax Avoidance and/ or Evasion Schemes and Available Methods to Curb Abuse," 18th Technical Conference of the Centro Interamericano de Administradores Tributarios, March 1977, mimeo, pp. 2, 22.

21. U.S. Comptroller General, "Report to the Chairman, House Committee on Ways and Means: IRS Could Better Protect US Tax Interests in Determining the Income of Multinational Corporations" (Washington, D.C., 1981), p.(i).

22. Revenue Canada, "Taxation, Tax Evasion and Tax Avoidance Schemes Jointly or Separately Used by Transnational Companies and Methods that May Eventually be Available to Eliminate or Decrease Them," 18th Technical Conference of the Centro Interamericano de Administradores Tributarios, March 1977, mimeo, p. 6.

23. 103 S. Ct.2933(1983).

24. *New York Times Magazine* (December 13, 1987), p. 67.

25. In a unanimous decision the U.S. Supreme Court ruled that foreign companies cannot challenge in federal court the validity of state taxes on their U.S. subsidiaries. See *Financial Times* (January 11, 1990).

26. Statement of U.S. Government Policy on International Investment, accompanying a Statement by the President of the United States, the White House, September 9, 1983.

27. *Financial Times* (February 5, 1986).

28. As reported in the *New York Times Magazine* (December 13, 1987), p. 64.

6   THE INTERNATIONAL DEBT CRISIS

1. *New York Times* (April 1, 1984).

2. *Selected Decisions of the International Monetary Fund and Selected Documents*, 10th issue (Washington, D.C.: IMF, April 30, 1983), p. 117. The ten participating countries were Belgium, Canada, the Federal Republic of Germany, France, Italy, Japan, the Netherlands, Sweden, the United Kingdom, and the United States. Switzerland joined the GAB in 1964.

3. Ibid., p. 142.

4. This essay was written in 1985. No recourse to GAB had been made up to the beginning of 1990.

5. Michel Camdessus, "Governmental Creditors and the Role of the Paris Club," in David Suratgar, ed., *Default and Rescheduling* (London: Euromoney Publications, 1984). The Paris Club is a group of creditor countries of the OECD, whose composition varies from case to case, and which meets with individual debtor countries seeking a rescheduling of debts owed to the public sector.

6. Remarks before the annual spring meeting of the Institute of International Finance, Washington, D.C., May 10, 1985.

7. Mário Henrique Simonsen, "The Developing Country Debt Problem," in Gordon W. Smith and John T. Cuddington, eds., *International Debt and the Developing Countries* (Washington, D.C.: World Bank, 1985), pp. 117–18.

8. IMF, *World Economic Outlook* (Washington, D.C.: IMF, May 1980), p. 9.

9. World Bank, *World Development Report 1982* (Washington, D.C.: World Bank, 1982), p. 27.

10. Carlos Diaz-Alejandro, "Latin American Debt: I Don't Think We Are in Kansas Any More," *Brookings Papers on Economic Activity* 2 (Washington, D.C.: Brookings Institution, 1984).

11. IMF, *Annual Report, 1983* (Washington, D.C.: IMF, 1983), p. 34. Table 10 in the IMF report shows a rise of $66.4 billion in the total current account deficit of non-oil developing countries from 1978 to 1981.

12. It has been widely observed that international debtors in the nineteenth and twentieth centuries up to World War II appear to have been much less concerned about the potential dangers of default than their counterparts of the 1970s and 1980s are—and they frequently did default, some of them repeatedly. The apparent contrast in attitudes appears to be due, at least in part, to the fact that before the war international debtors were dealing mainly with bondholders who, being scattered, found it difficult to exert concerted pressure against default, whereas today they have to contend with organized groups of banks which are readily able to mobilize their forces and obtain the backing of their home governments.

13. Opinion withdrawn on rehearing but available on *Lexis* 733 F.2d 23, April 23, 1984.

14. 757 F.2d 516 (2d Circuit, 1985). The court further rejected the contention that the act of state doctrine was applicable in the circumstances of this case, on the grounds that "the situs of the debt was in the United States, not in Costa Rica." Consequently, this was not "a taking of property within its own territory by [Costa Rica]."

15. "External Debt of Developing Countries," mimeo (Paris: OECD, 1981), p. 4.

16. Jacques de Larosière, "Resolving the World's Debt Problems: Adjustment, Financing, and Trade" (July 21, 1983), in *External Debt in Perspective*, articles reprinted from *Finance and Development* (September 1983).

17. For each debtor country seeking a rescheduling operation, the banks are represented by an advisory committee of lead banks, which take responsibility for establishing concerted positions and entering into negotiations accordingly with responsible officials of the debtor country. In the case of Mexico, the advisory committee consisted initially of fourteen banks with three cochairmen from Citibank, the Bank of America, and the Swiss Bank Corporation. Leadership was effectively in the hands of William Rhodes, the cochairman from Citibank.

18. See Joseph Kraft, *The Mexican Rescue* (New York: Group of Thirty, 1984), p. 49.

19. Data reported by Richard Dale and Richard P. Mattione in *Managing Global Debt* (Washington, D.C.: Brookings Institution 1983), p. 14, show that claims on Argentina, Brazil, and Mexico alone by the nine largest U.S. banks were equivalent to 112.5 percent of the banks' capital in June 1982 as against 81.1 percent for the next fifteen largest U.S. banks and 43.9 percent for all other reporting U.S. banks.

20. *Washington Post* (May 14, 1985).

21. Kraft (*The Mexican Rescue*, p. 51) reports that with respect to the $5 billion of new money, the agreement called for repayment over six years with a three-year grace period at a fee of 2.125 percent above the U.S. prime rate, or 2.25 percent over LIBOR. The upfront negotiating fee was 1.25 percent. As to the $20 billion of rescheduled money, the agreement extended the moratorium granted for 180 days beginning on August 23 through the end of 1984. Repayment was to be made over eight years with a grace period of four years. The fee was 1 percent, and the spread was 1.875 percent over LIBOR or 1.75 percent over the U.S. prime rate.

22. Ibid.

23. For comments along these lines see authorities cited by the *Wall Street Journal* (October 10, 1984).

24. World Bank, *Toward Sustained Development of Sub-Saharan Africa* (Washington, D.C.: World Bank, 1984).

25. Ibid., p. 13.

26. The following discussion draws heavily on Christine A. Bogdanowicz-Bindert, *Small Debtors, Big Problems: The Quiet Crisis* (Washington, D.C.: Overseas Development Council, 1985).

27. "Signatory Countries of the Cartagena Consensus, Joint Statement to the Interim Committee and the Development Committee, 12 April 1985," mimeo. Argentina, Bolivia, Brazil, Chile, Colombia, Dominican Republic, Ecuador, Mexico, Peru, Uruguay, and Venezuela had met in Cartagena on June 21–22, 1984. The Cartagena Consensus created a consultative mechanism of the participating countries for promoting a dialogue with the governments of the industrial countries and made a number of proposals for dealing with the debt crisis through cooperation between creditor and debtor nations.

28. G. K. Helleiner, "Balance of Payments Experience and Growth Prospects of Developing Countries: A Synthesis," *The International Monetary System and Its Reform*, ed. S. Dell, 3:961 et seq.

29. Rudiger Dornbusch and Stanley Fischer, "The World Debt Problem," *The International Monetary System and Its Reform*, ed. S. Dell, 3:907 et seq.

30. The chairman of the U.S. Federal Reserve Board has stated that "there is simply no realistic prospect—and no political support—for these organizations [the IMF and World Bank] to undertake a substantially larger amount of the financing needs of the heavily indebted countries. Indeed, the IMF, as a short- and medium-term lender, will before too long need to begin looking toward net repayments by some of the largest borrowers": *Washington Post* (May 14, 1985).

31. The former president of the Paris Club considers that one of the most important improvements required in current rescheduling procedures is provision for rescheduling interest payments when these threaten the success of otherwise sound stabilization programs (Michel Camdessus, "Governmental Creditors and the Role of the Paris Club," in D. Suratgar, ed., *Default and Rescheduling* [London: Euromoney Publications, 1984] p. 129). The chairman of the U.S. Federal Reserve Board is reported as having advocated a limit on the amount of interest to be charged to debtor countries, and the president of the Federal Reserve Bank of New York spoke in favor of such a limit or cap at congressional hearings in April 1984 (*New York Times*, May 7, 1984, p. D1). If such a cap on interest were to take the form of a maximum percentage of export earnings, or of some other ratio of this kind, substantial changes would be required in the U.S. regulatory and reporting framework, as noted earlier. It is, however, unlikely that Federal Reserve officials had this type of cap in mind.

32. Robert Solomon, "The United States as a Debtor in the 19th Century," *Brookings Discussion Papers in International Economics* (Washington, D.C.: Brookings Institution, May 1985), p. 19.

33. Barry Eichengreen and Richard Portes, "Debt and Default in the 1930s," *European Economic Review* 30 (Amsterdam: North Holland, 1986): 599–600.

34. United Nations, *Financing Africa's Recovery* (UN Department of Public Information, February 1988).

35. Joshua Greene, "The External Debt Problem of Sub-Saharan Africa," in IMF, *Staff Papers* (December 1989).

36. For a review of the main issues raised by these proposals see Paul Krugman, "Prospects for International Debt Reform," Report to the Group of Twenty-Four, UNCTAD Document UNCTAD/MFD/TA/34 (January 1986).

37. C. Fred Bergsten, William R. Cline, and John Williamson, *Bank Lending to Developing Countries: The Policy Alternatives* (Washington, D.C.: Institute for International Economics, April 1985), Options 22, 23. The summary in the text is quoted from John Williamson, "On the Question of Debt Relief," in an appendix to *Statement of the Roundtable on Money and Finance (Fourth Session)* North-South Roundtable (New York, December 1985), p. 25.

38. In November 1985 Robert M. Lorenz, senior Vice President of Security Pacific Bank (the seventh largest U.S. bank and the 10th largest bank creditor of the major Latin American debtors) proposed that U.S. banks should write off $30 billion of the debt owed by Latin American countries instead of continually rescheduling loans that would never be repaid. He said that the write-off could be phased over a period of 10–12 years.

39. Margaret Garritsen de Vries, *The International Monetary Fund 1972–78*, 1 (Washington, D.C.: IMF, 1985): 334, 341.

40. "Dealing with Debt, Rekindling Development: The U.S. Stake in the Performance of the World's Development Banks," a Report of the Subcommittee on International Development Institutions and Finance of the Committee on Banking, Finance, and Urban Affairs, House of Representatives 99th Congress, First Session, October 1985, pp. 36–37.

41. *Financial Times* (March 17, 1989), p. 6.

42. Harold Lever and Christopher Huhne, *Debt and Danger* (London: Penguin, 1985), chapter 9.

43. Ibid.

44. Ibid., pp. 139–40.

45. Paul Davidson, *Journal of Post-Keynesian Economics* 10 (1987/88): 323–38.

46. Ibid.

47. Testimony before the Committee on Foreign Relations, U.S. Senate, January 17, 1983. *Business Week* (February 28, 1983).

48. Eichengreen and Portes, "Debt and Default in the 1930s."

7   THE ADJUSTMENT PROCESS

1. Association of Banks in Malaysia Annual Lecture Series, Second Tun Ismail Ali Lecture, Kuala Lumpur, March 15, 1982, mimeo.

2. *Economic Report of the President* (Washington, D.C.: U.S. Government Printing Office, January 1973), p. 125.

3. Manuel Guitián, "Fund Conditionality and the International Adjustment Process," *Finance and Development* (June 1981).

4. In 1974 the IMF, referring to the structural surpluses generated by the rise in oil prices, had warned that "attempts to eliminate [the counterpart deficits] through deflationary demand policies, import restrictions and general resort to exchange rate depreciation would serve only to shift the payments problem from one oil-importing country to another and to damage world trade and economic activity." (See IMF, *Annual Report*,

1974, [Washington, D.C.: IMF, 1974], p. 26.) This warning was not, however, fully heeded, at any rate as far as the effects of deflationary demand policies and import restrictions were concerned.

5. For a more detailed analysis of this and other matters referred to in the present essay see Sidney Dell and Roger Lawrence, *The Balance of Payments Adjustment Process in Developing Countries* (Oxford: Pergamon, 1980).

6. World Bank, *World Development Report, 1978* (Washington, D.C.: World Bank, August 1978), pp. 15, 18.

7. Ibid.

8. IMF, *Fund History, 1966–71*, 1 (Washington, D.C.: IMF, 1976): 364–68. (Referred to subsequently as *Fund History, 1966–71*.)

9. *Fund History, 1966–71*, 1:368.

10. Carl P. Blackwell, "Reflections on the Monetary Approach to the Balance of Payments," *IMF Survey* (February 20, and March 6, 1978).

11. It is noteworthy that in the course of an address on May 8, 1978, the Managing Director of the IMF expressed the view that the problem of disequilibrium had been "exacerbated in some parts of the world by an increase in the number of governments whose position was insufficiently strong to enable them to undertake difficult adjustment measures." See *IMF Survey* (May 22, 1978), p. 147.

8 STABILIZATION, CONDITIONALITY, AND CROSS-CONDITIONALITY

1. It may be noted that the purposes of the IMF, as stated in Article I, did not, even after the amendments adopted in 1969 and 1978, include the elimination or reduction of inflation. Inflation is relevant to the IMF purposes to the extent that it contributes to balance-of-payments disequilibrium.

2. Article 55 of the UN Charter calls for the promotion of "higher standards of living, full employment, and conditions of economic and social progress and development."

3. Executive Board decisions 4134-(74/4) of January 23, 1974 and 4241-(74/67) of 13 June 1974 as recorded in IMF, *Annual Report, 1974*, pp. 108, 122–23. I am indebted to Alexandre Kafka, Executive Director of the IMF, for this point.

4. Alternative scenarios through the mid-1980s explored in the Fund's *World Economic Outlook*, published in June 1981, assumed that the real price of oil would either remain steady or continue to increase so that the current account surplus of oil-exporting countries would either decline from $96 billion in 1981 to some $50 billion by 1985, or remain approximately unchanged. No consideration was given to the possibility that the real price of oil might decline.

5. Executive Board Decision No. 6224-(79/135) provides in part that requests for drawings on the compensatory financing facility will be met when the Fund is satisfied that "the shortfall is of a short-term character and is largely attributable to circumstances beyond the control of the member."

6. *IMF Survey* (June 18, 1981). The use of the word "short-term" appears unnecessarily restrictive. It is implicit in the wording of Article I (v) cited earlier that the balance-of-payments difficulties for which Fund financing is appropriate may be characterized as "temporary" (i.e., likely to be reversed in due course) rather than as merely "short-term."

7. *IMF Survey* (February 9, 1981), p. 35.

8. Even if the fall in domestic consumption is unavoidable, the perception of the general

public may be that a government that devalues is responsible for the decline in living standards.

9. Brailovsky defines the real exchange rate as the weighted average of the ratio between domestic and foreign prices, both converted to a common currency, the weights corresponding to the area composition of trade.

10. Sir David Waley and Redvers Opie, who were also involved in the negotiations with the Americans, appear to have taken a more realistic view of the U.S. position, recognizing that credit would be obtained only "so long as the Fund thinks we are behaving reasonably" (see Horsefield, 1969, 1:73). Keynes may have been unduly impressed by the division of opinion among the U.S. negotiators regarding the imposition of conditions on drawing rights: negotiators both for the State Department and for the Federal Reserve System expressed the opinion, in the presence of British negotiators, that "no great country would submit" to the kind of scrutiny that the U.S. Treasury was envisaging (see Moggridge, 1980, 25:344–46).

11. U.S. National Archives and Records Service, Records relating to the Bretton Woods Conference, General Records of the Treasury Department, Record Group 56 (referred to subsequently as NARS), Box 1, File A-9.

12. A quite different Alternative A was put before the Bretton Woods Conference, involving much less significant deviations from the text of the Joint Statement than those discussed at Atlantic City. The new Alternative A was presented jointly by the United States and the United Kingdom and included the key words "entitled" and "represents" (see U.S. Department of State, 1948, 1:28–30).

13. The Executive Director from France, Jean de Largentaye, dissented from the Board's decision.

14. Keynes wrote on July 21, 1944, "We and we alone of the other delegations have spent 90 percent of our time [at Bretton Woods] trying to help [the Americans] and not make trouble for them" (Moggridge, 1980, 26:106).

15. Telegram from Balfour to Foreign Office, May 28, 1946, U.K. Public Record Office (subsequently referred to as PRO), Treasury File 236/1162.

16. It is remarkable that for nearly four years—from January 1944 to at least September 1947—the U.K. government seems to have believed that it was winning a battle that it was, in fact, in the process of losing. It is even more remarkable how deep a misunderstanding can persist in international discussions, even those between countries speaking the same language. By October 1948, however, George Bolton was drawing the IMF Board's attention to the "increasing number of interpretations reading into the Fund Agreement limitations which were not in the text. Because of such limitations the Fund was now of no use to its European members; it carried obligations but no benefits" (see Horsefield, 1969, 1:243).

17. It is ironic that in 1974–79 the Fund again reached a position in which it was often unable to "assist member countries in the kind of difficulties which the Articles had envisaged"—this time because of *too much* conditionality rather than too little.

18. In a letter to the author, Sir George Bolton, U.K. Executive Director from 1946 to 1952, writes that after the collapse of sterling convertibility in 1947, the activities of the Fund appeared to be a "stonewalling operation designed to protect the American reserves from being too heavily drawn upon as a result of Fund operations."

19. The following account of developments in 1967–68 is based on De Vries, 1976, pp. 338–47.

20. Quotas were to amount to "(say) 75 percent" of the average annual sum of each

country's exports and imports during the three prewar years. According to a contemporary estimate by Joan Robinson (1943), quotas were to total $36 billion if all countries joined, and $26 billion if only "United and Associated Nations and their dependencies" became members. The latter figure was used by Sir Frederick Phillips, of the U.K. Treasury, at a meeting of nineteen country representatives held in the U.S. Treasury on June 15, 1943. World imports amounted to about $60 billion in 1948 and were no doubt smaller in previous years.

21. Keynes also argued that the downward pressure on the economy of a debtor country resulting from a given loss of reserves is proportionally much greater than the corresponding expansionary impact on the rest of the world, simply because the debtor country is small compared with the world at large. But this line of argument seems to assume that deficits are necessarily more highly concentrated on particular countries than the counterpart surpluses. It is not clear why this should be so.

22. For a fuller treatment of this subject see Dell and Lawrence (1980, chapter 3).

23. As noted below, however, the Guidelines require the Fund only to "pay due regard" to domestic social and political objectives, as well as to the economic priorities and circumstances of members, including the causes of their balance-of-payments problems. Gold (1979b, pp. 22–25) points out that the phrase "the Fund will pay due regard" does not have mandatory force. Under Article I of the Agreement the Fund is required to adopt "adequate safeguards" when making its general resources available, and this requirement is considered to take priority over anything stated in the Guidelines. One difficulty here, of course, is that the phrase "adequate safeguards" is far from precise, and it can only be a question of judgment as to when safeguards are "adequate" and when they are not.

24. Net bank lending to non-oil developing countries in 1974–78 is believed to have exceeded $100 billion, equivalent to over $170 billion in 1980 (third quarter) prices.

25. For details see Dell and Lawrence (1980, chapters 1, 2).

26. The Group of Seventy-Seven, the parent body of the Group of Twenty-Four, is the political organ of the Third World. It has retained the name "Group of Seventy-Seven" for historical reasons, though its current membership exceeds 120.

27. The 600 percent limit does not take into account drawings under the compensatory and buffer stock financing facilities, or outstanding drawings under the oil facilities. New guidelines on the scale of Fund assistance to member countries following the completion of quota increases under the Seventh General Review provided, generally, for members to have an annual access to Fund resources of up to 150 percent of their new quotas, or up to 450 percent over a three-year period. For a complete review of the financial facilities of the Fund see *IMF Survey*, Supplement on the Fund (May 1981), pp. 6–10.

28. While, presumably, nobody would question the need for internal and external monetary stability, there is no explicit mandate to the IMF to act as "the guardian" in this matter. The purposes of the IMF are set out in six paragraphs of Article I of the Agreement, and while an argument could, perhaps, be sustained that monetary stability is a precondition for the attainment of some of these purposes, the term "monetary stability" is not even mentioned, let alone established as a primary objective of the IMF in its own right.

29. Horsefield (1969), 1:534.

30. Horsefield (1969), 2:421.

31. Goreux (1980), 34:37.

32. Ibid., 34:2.

33. Ibid., 34:25.

34. Ibid.

35. *Selected Decisions of the International Monetary Fund and Selected Documents*, Supplement to 10th Issue (Washington D.C.: IMF, March 31, 1984), p. 16.

36. Ibid, pp. 16–17.

37. Guitián (1981), 38:2. Emphasis supplied.

38. Dell and Lawrence (1980), p. 137.

39. Guitián (1981), 38:4.

40. *Towards a New Bretton Woods*, Report by a Commonwealth Study Group (G. K. Helleiner, chairman) (London: Commonwealth Secretariat, 1983), pp. 52–54.

41. The author gratefully acknowledges the opportunities given to him of consulting with members of the staffs of the IMF and the World Bank on the matters discussed in this essay.

42. Gold (1979b), p. 1.

43. The author gratefully acknowledges valuable suggestions regarding this paragraph, as well as other parts of this paper, from Sir Joseph Gold, who should not, however, be held responsible for the use made of those suggestions.

44. The term "arrangement" here refers to an IMF stand-by arrangement.

45. Under Article V, Section 5, Article VI, Section 1, or Article XXVI, Section 2(a), of the IMF Articles of Agreement.

46. *IMF Survey* (October 28, 1985), p. 309, para. 9(b).

47. *IMF Survey* (April 29, 1985), p. 186, para. 61.

48. *IMF Survey* (March 31, 1986), pp. 97, 108–9.

49. Ibid., p. 109.

50. Group of Twenty-Four (1986), p. 16, para. f.

51. *IMF Survey* (March 17, 1986), p. 92, para. 25.

52. It is, however, not clear whether the allegation of interference with domestic politics is the result of cross-conditionality per se or of simple conditionality. Dr. Lizano's paper contains a diagram indicating the establishment of direct relations between Paris Club countries and commercial banks on the one hand, and domestic employers' associations on the other; and between Paris Club countries and the domestic legislature—particularly the political parties represented in the legislature. Such relations could, of course, be the result of any kind of policy-based lending, with or without cross-conditionality. Dr. Lizano draws attention also, however, to the development of closer relations between the external agencies themselves—including not only the Paris Club countries and the commercial banks but the IMF, the World Bank, and the Inter-American Development Bank. What is implied, apparently, is that the various external agencies interact much more and are more effectively mobilized vis-à-vis domestic entities outside the government in situations where there is cross-conditionality. This is, again, not necessarily a result of cross-conditionality itself, but rather of the larger dimensions of, and linkages between, the external agencies involved.

53. Senate of Canada (1986), p. 8:16.

54. The Fund also has certain global responsibilities in relation to the functioning of the international monetary system, but these have no bearing on the subject matter of the present essay.

55. For a discussion of the background of this apparent anomaly see Dell (1984), pp. 165–67.
56. Gold (1981–82), pp. 513–14.
57. This paragraph is based in part on a section of Gold (1981–82), p. 508.
58. Ibid., p. 512.
59. This expectation was soon followed by a decision by the World Bank, acting on the initiative of the U.S. government, to issue in 1946 an interpretation of its own mandate as including "long-term stabilization loans." This mandate was never fully carried out, implementation being limited to modest amounts of program lending to a relatively few countries, as noted earlier.
60. American Bankers Association (1945), p. 20. The principal "desirable functions" of the Fund were considered by the ABA to be the creation of a forum for "international consultations and agreement on monetary policies," including the collection of information on monetary and economic matters and "the provision of stabilization credits."
61. De Vries (1985), p. 955.

8   REFERENCES TO STABILIZATION, CONDITIONALITY, AND CROSS-CONDITIONALITY

American Bankers Association, *Practical International Financial Organization Through Amendments to Bretton Woods Proposals* (February 1, 1945).

Bank of England, *Quarterly Bulletin* 18, no. 1 (March 1978).

Brailovsky, Vladimiro, with the assistance of Juan Carlos Moreno, "Exchange Rate Policies, Manufactured Exports and the Rate of Inflation" (Mexico: Institute for Industrial Planning, 1981), mimeo.

Committee of Twenty (Committee on Reform of the International Monetary System and Related Issues), *International Monetary Reform: Documents of the Committee of Twenty* (Washington, D.C.: IMF, 1974).

Crockett, Andrew D., and Saleh M. Nsouli, "Exchange Rate Policies for Developing Countries," *Journal of Development Studies* 13 (January 1977).

Dale, William B., "The Financing and Adjustment of Payments Imbalances," in *IMF Conditionality*, ed. John Williamson (Washington, D.C.: Institute for International Economics, 1983).

De Larosière, Jacques, Address to the 1981 Annual Meetings of the Fund and Bank, *IMF Survey* (October 12, 1981).

Dell, Sidney, *On Being Grandmotherly: The Evolution of IMF Conditionality* (Princeton, N.J.: International Finance Section, Princeton University, 1981). Reprinted in chapter 8 of this volume.

———, "A Note on Stabilization and the World Bank," *World Development* 12, no. 2 (1984).

Dell, Sidney, and Roger Lawrence, *The Balance of Payments Adjustment Process in Developing Countries* (New York: Pergamon, 1980).

De Vries, Margaret Garritsen, *The International Monetary Fund, 1966–1971*, vol. 1 (Washington, D.C.: IMF, 1976).

———, *The International Monetary Fund 1972–78*, vol. 2 (Washington, D.C.: IMF, 1985).

Diaz-Alejandro, Carlos F., "Southern Cone Stabilization Plans," in *Economic Stabilization in Developing Countries*, William R. Cline and Sidney Weintraub, eds. (Washington, D.C.: Brookings Institution, 1981).

Economic Report of the President (Washington, D.C.: U.S. Government Printing Office, 1973).

Fleming, J. Marcus, and Lorette Boissonneault, "Money Supply and Imports," *The Monetary Approach to the Balance of Payments* (Washington, D.C.: IMF, 1977).

Gold, Joseph, *Legal and Institutional Aspects of the International Monetary System* (Washington, D.C.: IMF, 1979a).

——, *Conditionality*, IMF Pamphlet Series No. 31 (Washington, D.C.: IMF, 1979b).

——, "The Relationship Between the International Monetary Fund and the World Bank," *Creighton Law Review*, vol. 15, no. 1 (1981–82).

Goreux, Louis M., *Compensatory Financing Facility*, IMF Pamphlet Series No. 34 (Washington, D.C.: IMF, 1980).

Group of Twenty-Four, Communiqué of the Ministers Issued September 22, 1978, *IMF Survey* (October 2, 1978), pp. 306–7.

——, Communiqué of the Ministers Issued March 6, 1979, *IMF Survey* (March 19, 1979a), pp. 86–87.

——, Outline for a Program of Action on Monetary Reform Endorsed by the Group of Seventy-Seven on September 29, 1979, *IMF Survey* (October 15, 1979b), pp. 319–23.

——, *Background of the Annotated Agenda and Press Communiqué*, 33d Meeting of Ministers (Buenos Aires, March 1986).

Guitián, Manuel, *Fund Conditionality*, IMF Pamphlet Series No. 38 (Washington, D.C.: IMF, March 31, 1981).

Hicks, Sir John, "What is Wrong with Monetarism," *Lloyds Bank Review* (October 1975).

——, "The Little that Is Right with Monetarism," *Lloyds Bank Review* (July 1976).

Horsefield, J. Keith, *The International Monetary Fund 1945–1965*, vol. 1 (Washington, D.C.: IMF, 1969).

Horsefield, J. Keith, ed. *The International Monetary Fund 1945–1965*, vols. 2, 3 (Washington, D.C.: IMF, 1969).

IMF, *Annual Report, 1974* (Washington, D.C., 1974).

——, *Annual Report, 1979* (Washington, D.C., 1979).

——, *World Economic Outlook* (Washington, D.C., 1980a).

——, *Annual Report, 1980* (Washington, D.C., 1980b).

——, *Annual Report, 1981* (Washington, D.C., 1981).

IMF Survey (various issues).

Kaldor, Nicholas, *Essays on Economic Policy*, vol. 1, chapters II.6 and II.7 (London: Duckworth, 1964).

——, *Further Essays on Applied Economics*, chapters I.l, II.8 (London: Duckworth, 1978).

——, *Memorandum of Evidence on Monetary Policy to the Select Committee of the Treasury and Civil Service* (London: H.M. Stationery Office, 1981).

——, "The Role of Devaluation in the Adjustment of Balance of Payments Deficits," in *The International Monetary System and Its Reform*, ed. S. Dell (Amsterdam: North Holland, 1987), 2:557 et seq.

Khan, Mohsin, and Malcolm D. Knight, "Stabilization Programs in Developing Countries: A Formal Framework," *International Monetary Fund Staff Papers*, vol. 28, no. 1 (March 1981).

Killick, Tony, "IMF Stabilisation Programmes," in *The Quest for Economic Stabilisation: The IMF and the Third World* (London: Heinemann Educational Books, in association with the Overseas Development Institute, 1984).

Legarda, Benito, et al., 'Measures to Strengthen the SDR," in *The International Monetary System and Its Reform*, ed. S Dell (Amsterdam: North Holland, 1987), 2:342 et seq.

Moggridge, Donald, ed., *The Collected Writings of John Maynard Keynes*, vols. 25, 26 (Royal Economic Society, published in the United States and Canada by Cambridge University Press, elsewhere by Macmillan, 1980).

Nyerere, Julius, "No to IMF Meddling," *Development Dialogue* 2 (1980): 7–9.

Park, Yung Chul, "The Variability of Velocity: An International Comparison," *IMF Staff Papers* (November 1970).

Robinson, Joan, "The International Currency Proposals," *Economic Journal* (June–September 1943).

Senate of Canada, *Proceedings of the Standing Committee on Foreign Affairs*, no. 8, seventh proceedings on Canada's participation in the international financial system and institutions (April 15, 1986).

U.S. Congress, *Bretton Woods Agreements Act, Hearings on H. R. 3314*, Senate Committee on Banking and Currency, 79th Cong., 1st sess., June 1945.

U.S. Department of State, *Proceedings and Documents of the United Nations Monetary and Financial Conference*, vol. 2 (Washington, D.C., 1948).

Wallich, Henry, "Federal Reserve Policy and the Economic Outlook," address to the Chesapeake Chapter of Robert Morris Associates (December 3, 1980), mimeo.

Williamson, John, *The Failure of World Monetary Reform, 1971–74* (London: Nelson, 1977).

——, "On Judging the Success of IMF Policy Advice," in *IMF Conditionality*, ed. John Williamson (Washington, D.C.: Institute for International Economics, 1983).

——, "The Economics of IMF Conditionality," in *For Good or Evil: Economic Theory and North-South Negotiations*, ed. G. K. Helleiner (Oslo: University of Oslo Press 1984).

9 THE INTERNATIONAL MONETARY SYSTEM AND DEVELOPMENT

1. IMF, *Exchange Rate Volatility and World Trade*, a study by the Research Department, Occasional Paper No. 28 (Washington, D.C.: IMF, July 1984).

2. Andrew Crockett and Morris Goldstein, *Strengthening the International Monetary System: Exchange Rates, Surveillance and Objective Indicators*, Occasional Paper No. 50 (Washington, D.C.: IMF, February 1987), p. 4.

3. Group of Twenty-Four, "The Functioning and Improvement of the International Monetary System," *IMF Survey*, Supplement (September 1985), para. 62.

4. Nicholas Kaldor, *Further Essays on Applied Economics* (London: Duckworth, 1978), p. xxi.

5. Alexandre Lamfalussy, "Current-Account Imbalances in the Industrial World: Why They Matter," in *International Monetary Cooperation: Essays in Honor of Henry C. Wallich* (Princeton, N.J.: Princeton University Press, December 1987), p. 36.

6. Ronald I. McKinnon and Kenichi Ohno, "Purchasing Power Parity as a Monetary Standard," Memorandum No. 276, Center for Research in Economic Growth, Stanford University (January 1988).

7. Crockett and Goldstein, *Strengthening the International Monetary System*, p. 15.

8. James Tobin, "A Proposal for International Monetary Reform," *The Eastern Economic Journal* 3, nos. 3–4 (July–October 1978): 155, 158–59.

9. John Maynard Keynes, *The General Theory of Employment, Interest and Money* (London: Macmillan, 1936), pp. 159–60.

10. Yilmaz Akyuz and Sidney Dell, "Issues in International Monetary Reform," in *International Monetary and Financial Issues for the Developing Countries* (UNCTAD, 1987), UN Publication Sales No.: E.87.II.D.3, pp. 39–44.

11. Margaret Garritsen de Vries, *The International Monetary Fund, 1972–78*, vol. 1 (Washington, D.C.: IMF, 1985), chapter 37.

12. Richard N. Cooper, "The Evolution of the International Monetary System Toward a World Central Bank," in *The International Monetary System, Essays in World Economics* (Cambridge, Mass.: MIT Press, 1987).

13. Sidney Dell, "The Fifth Credit Tranche," pp. 257–64 of this volume.

14. Group of Ten, "The Functioning of the International Monetary System," *IMF Survey*, Supplement (July 1985), para. 74.

15. Ibid. paras. 71–72.

16. Group of Ten, "Communiqué of Ministers and Governors and Report of Deputies" (July 1966), para. 7(d).

17. De Vries, *The International Monetary Fund, 1972–78*, 1:322.

18. IMF, *Annual Report, 1974*, p. 26.

19. Joseph Gold, *Conditionality*, IMF Pamphlet Series No. 31 (Washington, D.C.: IMF, 1979), p. 3.

20. Manuel Guitián, *Fund Conditionality*, IMF Pamphlet Series No. 38 (Washington, D.C.: IMF, 1981), p. 4.

21. IMF, *IMF Survey* (April 18, 1988), para. 7.

22. Ibid.

23. Nicholas Kaldor, "The Role of Commodity Prices in Economic Recovery," *Lloyds Bank Review* (July 1983).

24. Ibid., p. 29.

25. Group of Ten, "The Functioning of the International Monetary System," para. 36.

26. Ibid., para. 38.

27. Ibid., para. 49.

28. Ibid., para. 50.

29. Group of Twenty-Four, "The Functioning and Improvement of the International Monetary System, para. 77.

30. Ibid., para. 78.

31. Ibid., para. 79.

32. IMF, *IMF Survey* (May 19, 1986), p. 145.

33. Peter Kenen, "What Role for IMF Surveillance?" *World Development* 15 no. 12 (December 1987): 1447.

34. Group of Twenty-Four, "The Role of the IMF in Adjustment with Growth," *IMF Survey*, Supplement (August 10, 1987), para. 21.

35. A. C. Cornia, R. Jolly, and F. Stewart, eds., *Adjustment with a Human Face: Protecting the Vulnerable and Promoting the Growth* (New York: Oxford University Press, 1987).

36. Richard Portes and Barry Eichengreen, chapter in Richard Portes and Alexander Swoboda, eds., *Threats to International Financial Stability* (New York: Cambridge University Press, 1987).

37. George P. Shultz, "Statement by the Governor of the Fund and World Bank for the United States," *Summary Proceedings of the Annual Meeting of the Board of Governors, 1973* (Washington, D.C.: IMF, 1973).

38. Committee of Twenty, *International Monetary Reform: Documents of the Committee of Twenty* (Washington, D.C.: IMF, 1974), p. 18.

39. Donald Moggridge, ed., *The Collected Writings of John Maynard Keynes*, 26 (New York: Macmillan, 1980; London: Cambridge University Press, 1980): 221.

40. Ibid., p. 227.

41. United Nations, "Comments by Member States and Organizations Concerning International Development Strategy for the Nineteen Seventies," Document E/AC.56/L.1, p. 13.

42. This would not, of course, relieve the countries concerned of the need to make larger transfers of real resources.

43. Group of Ten, "Report of the Study Group on the Creation of Reserve Assets" (May 31, 1965), para. 138.

44. UNCTAD, *International Monetary Issues and the Developing Countries*, Report of the Group of Experts (New York, 1965), UN Publication Sales No. 66.II.D.2, para. 103.

45. Group of Ten, "Report to Ministers and Governors by the Group of Deputies" (July 7, 1966), para. 40.

46. Harry Johnson, review of Triffin's *Our International Monetary System* in *Book World* (August 11, 1968).

47. Article XXIII, Section 3, entitled "Other Holders," provides that the Fund by an 85 percent majority of the total voting power may prescribe as holders, nonmembers, members that are nonparticipants, and institutions that perform functions of a central bank for more than one member.

48. For the text of Dr. Patel's proposal see UN Document TD/B/115/Add. 2, August 14 1967.

Index

THE AUTHOR

Sidney Dell is at present a Senior Fellow in the United Nations
Institute for Training and Research (UNITAR). He was trained in
economics at Oxford and has spent more than four decades as an
economist at the United Nations. He is the author of *The United
Nations and International Business* (Durham, N.C.: Duke University
Press, 1990).

Library of Congress Cataloging-in-Publication Data
Dell, Sidney Samuel.
International development policy : perspectives for industrial
countries / Sidney Dell.
Includes index.
ISBN 0-8223-1079-1 (cloth).—ISBN 0-8223-1097-X (pbk.)
1. Economic development.   2. International trade.
3. International economic relations.   I. Title.
HD82.D378   1991
337—dc20   90-38618   CIP